PEOPLE, MARKETS, GOODS:
ECONOMIES AND SOCIETIES IN HISTORY
Volume 7

Slavery Hinterland

T0374693

PEOPLE, MARKETS, GOODS:
ECONOMIES AND SOCIETIES IN HISTORY

ISSN: 2051-7467

Series editors
Barry Doyle – University of Huddersfield
Nigel Goose – University of Hertfordshire
Steve Hindle – The Huntington Library
Jane Humphries – University of Oxford
Kevin O'Rourke – University of Oxford
Willem M. Jongman – University of Groningen

The interactions of economy and society, people and goods, transactions and actions are at the root of most human behaviours. Economic and social historians are participants in the same conversation about how markets have developed historically and how they have been constituted by economic actors and agencies in various social, institutional and geographical contexts. New debates now underpin much research in economic and social, cultural, demographic, urban and political history. Their themes have enduring resonance – financial stability and instability, the costs of health and welfare, the implications of poverty and riches, flows of trade and the centrality of communications. This new paperback series aims to attract historians interested in economics and economists with an interest in history by publishing high quality, cutting edge academic research in the broad field of economic and social history from the late medieval/ early modern period to the present day. It encourages the interaction of qualitative and quantitative methods through both excellent monographs and collections offering path-breaking overviews of key research concerns. Taking as its benchmark international relevance and excellence it is open to scholars and subjects of any geographical areas from the case study to the multi-nation comparison.

PREVIOUSLY PUBLISHED TITLES IN THE SERIES ARE
LISTED AT THE END OF THE VOLUME

Slavery Hinterland

Transatlantic Slavery and Continental Europe, 1680–1850

Edited by

Felix Brahm and Eve Rosenhaft

THE BOYDELL PRESS

First published 2016
The Boydell Press, Woodbridge

ISBN 978-1-78327-112-2

The Boydell Press is an imprint of Boydell & Brewer Ltd
PO Box 9, Woodbridge, Suffolk IP12 3DF, UK
and of Boydell & Brewer Inc.
668 Mt Hope Avenue, Rochester, NY 14620–2731, USA
website: www.boydellandbrewer.com

A catalogue record for this book is available
from the British Library

The publisher has no responsibility for the continued existence or accuracy of URLs for
external or third-party internet websites referred to in this book, and does not guarantee
that any content on such websites is, or will remain, accurate or appropriate.

This publication is printed on acid-free paper

Typeset by BBR, Sheffield

Contents

Illustrations

Contributors

Felix Brahm is Research Fellow in Colonial History at the German Historical Institute London. **Publications**: 'Armed with an Umbrella. Alexander Mackay and the Emerging Criticism of the East African Arms Trade', *Sources and Methods for African History and Culture. Essays in Honour of Adam Jones*, ed. G. Castryck, S. Strickrodt and K. Werthmann (Leipzig, 2016), pp. 291–304; 'Translokale Beziehungen und ihre Repräsentation. Sansibar-Stadt im 19. und 20. Jahrhundert', *Historische Anthropologie* 21:1 (2013), 67–84; 'The Overseas World – and Hamburg: On the Postwar Recreation of Locality in a German Port City', *Localities* 3 (2013), 103–23; '"Techniques éprouvées au cours des siècles": African Students at the Former School for Colonial Administrators in Paris, 1951–1967', *Comparativ* 21/1 (2011), 76–88; *Wissenschaft und Dekolonisation. Paradigmenwechsel und institutioneller Wandel in der akademischen Beschäftigung mit Afrika in Deutschland und Frankreich, 1930–1970* (Stuttgart, 2010); 'Handel und Sklaverei am "Tor zu Ostafrika". Hamburger Kaufleute auf Sansibar, 1844–1890', *Hamburg – Sansibar. Sansibar – Hamburg. Hamburgs Verbindungen zu Ostafrika seit Mitte des 19. Jahrhunderts*, ed. R. Bake (Hamburg, 2009), pp. 45–67.

Peter Haenger teaches history at a Basel secondary school and works as an independent historian. **Publications**: (on slavery and the slave trade): *Baumwolle, Sklaven und Kredite. Die Basler Welthandelsfirma Christoph Burckhardt & Cie. in revolutionärer Zeit (1789–1815)* (with Niklaus Stettler und Robert Labhardt) (Basel, 2004); *Slaves and Slaveholders on the Gold Coast: Towards an Understanding of Social Bondage in West Africa* (Basel, 2000); *Sklaverei und Sklavenemanzipation an der Goldküste: Ein Beitrag zum Verständnis von sozialen Abhängigkeitsbeziehungen in Westafrika* (Basel, 1997).

Catherine Hall is Professor of Modern British Social and Cultural History, University College London, and Director of ESRC/AHRC projects *Legacies of British Slave-ownership* and *Structure and significance of British Caribbean slave-ownership 1763–1833*. **Publications**: *Macaulay and Son. Architects of Imperial Britain* (New Haven, 2012); *Civilising Subjects. Metropole and*

Colony in the English Imagination 1830–1867 (Cambridge, 2002); 'Britain, Jamaica, and Empire in the Era of Emancipation', *Art and Emancipation in Jamaica. Isaac Mendes Belisario and his Worlds*, Tim Barringer, Gillian Forrester and Barbaro Martinez-Ruiz (New Haven, 2007), pp. 9–26; Introduction to Special Feature, 'Remembering 1807: Histories of the Slave Trade, Slavery and Abolition', *History Workshop Journal* 64 (Autumn 2007).

Daniel P. Hopkins is Emeritus Professor of Geography, University of Missouri, Kansas City. **Publications**: *Peter Thonning and Denmark's Guinea Commission: A Study in Nineteenth-Century African Colonial Geography* (Leiden, 2013); 'The Application of GIS to the Reconstruction of the Slave-Plantation Economy of St. Croix, Danish West Indies' (with Philip Morgan and Justin Roberts), *Historical Geography* 39 (2011), 85–104; 'Peter Thonning, the Guinea Commission, and Denmark's Postabolition African Colonial Policy, 1803–50', *The William and Mary Quarterly* 66 (2009), 781–808; 'Books and the geography of Denmark's colonial undertaking in West Africa, 1790–1850', *Geographies of the Book*, ed. Charles Withers and Miles Ogborn (Farnham, 2010), pp. 221–46.

Craig Koslofsky is Professor of History and Germanic Languages and Literatures, University of Illinois, Urbana-Champaign, and is currently writing a history of skin in the early modern world. **Publications**: 'Knowing Skin in Early Modern Europe, c. 1450–1750', *History Compass* 12:10 (2014), 794–806; *Evening's Empire: A History of the Night in Early Modern Europe* (Cambridge and New York, 2011); *The Reformation of the Dead: Death and Ritual in Early Modern Germany, 1450–1700* (London and New York, 2000).

Sarah Lentz is Assistant Lecturer in Early Modern History, University of Bremen. She is completing a dissertation on the spread of anti-slavery sentiment in the German territories and the involvement of Germans in the Atlantic abolitionist movement from the late eighteenth to the mid nineteenth century. **Publications**: '"[E]ine viel wichtigere Persönlichkeit [...] als der Präsident selbst". David Parish und die Finanzierung der US-Regierung im Krieg von 1812', *Die hanseatisch-amerikanischen Beziehungen seit 1790*, ed. Claudia Schnurmann and Heiko Herold (forthcoming 2016); 'David Parish, Alexander Baring and the US-American Government Loan of 1813. The Role of Nationality and Patriotism in Transatlantic Financial Networks in Times of War', *The London Journal for Canadian Studies* (forthcoming 2016).

Rebekka von Mallinckrodt is Professor of Early Modern History, University of Bremen, and Principal Investigator of the ERC Consolidator Grant Project *The Holy Roman Empire of the German Nation and its Slaves* (2015–20). **Publications**: *Sports and Physical Exercise in Early Modern Culture. New*

Perspectives on the History of Sports and Motion (forthcoming London, 2016) (with Angela Schattner); *Les mondes coloniaux à Paris au XVIIIe siècle. Circulation et enchevêtrement des savoirs* (Paris, 2010) (with Anja Bandau and Marcel Dorigny); *Bewegtes Leben – Körpertechniken in der Frühen Neuzeit, Katalog zur Ausstellung in der Herzog August Bibliothek Wolfenbüttel* (Wiesbaden, 2008); *Struktur und kollektiver Eigensinn. Kölner Laienbruderschaften im Zeitalter der Konfessionalisierung* (Göttingen, 2005); *Interkultureller Transfer und nationaler Eigensinn. Europäische und anglo-amerikanische Positionen der Kulturwissenschaften* (Göttingen, 2004) (with Rebekka Habermas).

Anne Sophie Overkamp is Assistant Lecturer in Early Modern History, University of Bayreuth. **Publications**: 'Stadtbürgerliche Fürsorge, christlicher Gemeinsinn und nützliches Erwerben: Die Armenfürsorge in Elberfeld und Barmen im ersten Viertel des 19. Jahrhunderts', *Sinngebung für Wirtschaft und Gemeinschaft. Konfessionelle und nichtreligiöse Gemeinsinnsmodelle im 19. und 20. Jahrhundert*, ed. Winfried Müller and Swen Steinberg (Bielefeld, 2014); 'Of Tape and Ties: Abraham Frowein from Elberfeld and Atlantic Trade', *Europeans Engaging the Atlantic: Knowledge and Trade, 1500–1800*, ed. Susanne Lachenicht (Frankfurt a.M., 2014); 'Vermehrung der Kenntnisse, Verfeinerung der Sitten – die Elberfelder Lesegesellschaft (1775–1818)', *Geschichte im Wuppertal* 19 (2010), 43–53.

Alexandra Robinson is Lecturer in Continuing Education, University of Liverpool, and a public historian. She has a research consultancy and carries out education work with the International Slavery Museum Liverpool, the Sandwell (West Midlands) Slavery Archive, and the project *Behind the Golden Gates – Warrington and the Slave Trade*. She has curated the historical inter-pretation of Fairview Plantation Great House, St Kitts, West Indies, and in 2013–14 the exhibitions '*And learn to respect human rights*' *Celebrating Edward Rushton's Legacy, 1814–2014* at the International Slavery Museum and the Museum of Liverpool, and *Rebellious Poetics* at the Victoria Gallery & Museum, Liverpool. **Publications**: 'Transatlantic Interchange in the Age of Revolution: The Caribbean Residence of James Stephen and British Abolitionism, 1783–1807' and 'Transforming Sites of Human Wrongs into Centres for Human Rights: The Birth of the Campaigning Museum', both in Franca Dellarosa (ed.), *Slavery: Histories, Fictions, Memory 1760–2007* (Naples, 2012).

Eve Rosenhaft is Professor of German Historical Studies, University of Liverpool. **Publications**: *Black Germany: The Making and Unmaking of a Diaspora Community 1884–1960* (monograph, with R. J. M. Aitken) (Cambridge, 2013); *Africa in Europe. Studies in Transnational Practice in the Long Twentieth*

Century (co-edited with R. J. M. Aitken) (Liverpool, 2013); *Civilians and War in Europe 1618–1815* (Liverpool, 2012); 'How to Tame Chance: Evolving Languages of Risk, Trust and Expertise in 18th-century German Proto-Insurances', *The Appeal of Insurance*, ed. Geoffrey W. Clark, Gregory Anderson, Christian Thomann and J.-Matthias Graf von der Schulenburg (Toronto, 2010), pp. 16–42; 'Women and financial knowledge in eighteenth-century Germany', *Women and Their Money. Essays on Women and Finance 1700–1950*, ed. Anne Laurence, Josephine Maltby and Janette Rutterford (London, 2008), pp. 59–72; 'Herz oder Kopf. Erfahrungsbildung beim Kaufen von Aktien und Witwenrenten im norddeutschen Bildungsbürgertum des späten 18. Jahrhunderts', *Historische Anthropologie* 14 (2006), 349–69.

Anka Steffen is a Ph.D. candidate and Researcher on the project 'The Globalized Periphery: Atlantic Commerce, Socioeconomic and Cultural Change in Central Europe (1680–1850)', Europa University Viadrina, Frankfurt an der Oder.

Klaus Weber is Professor of Comparative European Economic and Social History, Europa University Viadrina, Frankfurt an der Oder. **Publications**: *Deutsche Kaufleute im Atlantikhandel 1680–1830: Unternehmen und Familien in Hamburg, Cádiz und Bordeaux* (Munich, 2004); *Schwarzes Amerika. Eine Geschichte der Sklaverei* (with Jochen Meissner and Ulrich Mücke) (Munich, 2008); 'From Westphalia to the Caribbean: Networks of German Textile Merchants in the Eighteenth Century' (with Margrit Schulte Beerbühl), *Cosmopolitan Networks in Commerce and Society 1660–1914*, ed. Andreas Gestrich and Margrit Schulte Beerbühl (London, 2011), pp. 53–98; *Überseehandel und Handelsmetropolen: Europa und Asien, 17.–20. Jahrhundert* (co-edited with Frank Hatje) (Hamburg, 2008).

Roberto Zaugg is a Fellow of the Swiss National Science Foundation at the University of Lausanne. **Publications**: *Stranieri di antico regime. Mercanti, giudici e consoli nella Napoli del Settecento* (Rome, 2011); *Union in Separation. Diasporic Groups and Identities in the Eastern Mediterranean (1100–1800)* (co-edited with G. Christ, F. J. Morche, W. Kaiser, S. Burkhardt and A. D. Beihammer) (Rome, 2015); *Joseph Furttenbach, Lebenslauff 1652–1664* (co-edited with K. von Greyerz and K. Siebenhüner) (Cologne, 2013); *Maritime Frauds between Norms and Institutions (17th–19th c.) / Frodi marittime tra norme e istituzioni (secc. XVII–XIX)* (co-edited with B. Salvemini), special issue of *Quaderni Storici* 48/143 (2013); 'Zwischen Europäisierung und Afrikanisierung. Zur visuellen Konstruktion der Kapverden auf kolonialen Postkarten', *Fotogeschichte* 30/118 (2010), 17–28.

Acknowledgements

This volume grew out of a conference ('The Slave Business and its Material and Moral Hinterlands in Continental Europe', April 2012) hosted by the University of Liverpool and the International Slavery Museum; the conference was generously funded by the German Research Foundation (Deutsche Forschungsgemeinschaft), the German History Society and the Economic History Society (which also cofinanced this publication). We are grateful both to our sponsors and to colleagues who attended the conference but were unable to contribute to the volume. Other friends, colleagues and students too numerous to thank each by name have discussed various aspects of the topic with us or otherwise supported this project. A *grand merci* also goes to the two anonymous peer reviewers for their efforts and helpful comments on both the rationale and the manuscript. In the closing stages of the production process, we are particularly grateful that Catherine D'Alton agreed to map the flows of people, goods and ideas explored in this book, and that Katharina Kamphausen supported this complex undertaking. Unfortunately, for various reasons, the map did not go to press. The team at Boydell & Brewer has been professional and supportive at every point in the process.

Introduction

Towards a Comprehensive European History of Slavery and Abolition

FELIX BRAHM AND EVE ROSENHAFT

Genealogies

On an uncertain date in the early 1780s, a medical student at the University of Göttingen drew a sketch in the autograph book of one of his fellow students (Fig. 0.1). The sketch represents an enslaved black woman and her child standing next to a barrel and a box marked 'Caffe', and bears the caption 'Ce qui sert à vos plaisirs est mouillé de nos larmes'.

The model for the sketch is certainly the best-known illustration in the 1773 work of Jacques-Henri Bernardin de Saint-Pierre, *Voyage à l'Isle de France* (Fig. 0.2). Bernardin's work was an account of his visit to the slave island of Mauritius and was recognised in its own day as a key abolitionist text – not least because of the very pointed messages purveyed by Jean-Michel Moreau's engravings.[1] A comparison of the two images suggests that the sketch was drawn from memory, and as such it tells us something both about the circulation of slavery and anti-slavery discourses in continental Europe in the late eighteenth century. It also reveals the extent to which visions of the slave Atlantic took root in the consciousness of Europeans of whom we might presume that they were at best observers of, and not party to, the traffic in human lives and the exploitation of human bodies that the pictures critique.

As the serendipity that sometimes drives academic research would have it, it was only in the course of compiling this volume that we identified the author of the sketch, who signs himself C. Heyne, as the brother of Therese Huber. Sarah Lentz's account of Huber's career (chapter 8) makes clear that this fact locates Carl Heyne and his sketch at an early stage in the development

---

1   Vladimir Kapor, 'Reading the image, reviewing the text – on the reception of Bernardin de Saint-Pierre's *Voyage à l'Ile de France* (1773)', *Word & Image* 28 (2012), 302–16.

Figure 0.1. *Stammbuch* of Johann Carl Tutenberg, Entry by C. Heyne c.1781

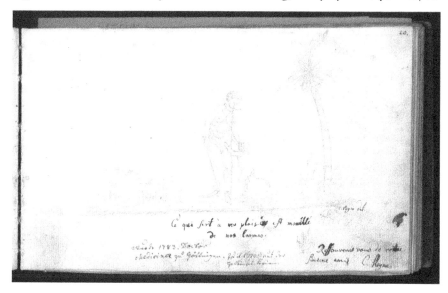

Figure 0.2. Jean-Michel Moreau le
jeune: 'Ce qui sert à vos plaisirs est
mouillé de nos larmes'. Illustration
from [Jacques-Henri Bernardin
de Saint-Pierre], *Voyage à l'Isle de
France* ... (Amsterdam, 1773)

of a personal network of abolitionist propagandists which not only crossed borders but reached into territories distant from the Atlantic coast.

At the same time, the context in which the sketch was produced throws up more poignant questions about material and moral (or what we might call objective and subjective) engagement in slavery on the part of contemporaries who were not engaged directly in the slave trade or the operation of plantations, and who might live hundreds of miles from any slaving port. At about the same time as Carl Heyne was drawing his anti-slavery image, Friedrich Münter was arriving in Göttingen to study classics and theology. The correspondence between Friedrich and his father, Balthasar, survives, a central theme of which is the family finances. Balthasar Münter, the well-to-do chief pastor in Copenhagen's German-speaking church, offers a running commentary on the state of mind engendered by the ups and downs of the trade in Danish trading company shares on which he has recently embarked. As Daniel Hopkins makes clear in his study of Julius von Rohr, another German in Danish service (chapter 6), the purpose of those trading companies was to gain and maintain a foothold for Denmark in the Atlantic slave trade, and (should there be any doubt) a letter of 1786 makes clear that it was an objective of which Balthasar Münter was aware. By contrast with Carl Heyne, though, Münter makes no place in his imagination for the objects of his investment. Rather, in picturing his profits (and losses) in material form, he fixes on what they can buy in his own world: early retirement and an estate on which to enjoy it.[2] Looking outward from the moment of a hypothetical encounter between two students in Göttingen (Friedrich Münter almost certainly studied with Carl Heyne's father, a professor of classics), this volume aims to display new research and to provoke new thinking about the ways in which people and places in continental European states which were not *directly* involved in transatlantic slavery were implicated in its origins, development and consequences. The territories considered include the German-speaking lands, Italy and Denmark, whose slaving history was short and until recently forgotten, and we characterise these as hinterlands of the slave economy.

Hinterlands

In geographical and social terms, Balthasar Münter, a member of the Copenhagen elite, was of course at no distance at all from the Atlantic trade. Seeing him as a German, though (he was born in Gotha, a very long

---

2 Eve Rosenhaft, 'Herz oder Kopf. Erfahrungsbildung beim Kaufen von Aktien und Witwenrenten im Norddeutschen Bildungsbürgertum des späten 18. Jahrhunderts', *Historische Anthropologie* 14 (2006), 349–69; Christian Degn, *Die Schimmelmanns im atlantischen Dreieckshandel. Gewinn und Gewissen* (Neumünster, 1974), p. 212.

way from any seacoast), and from the perspective of Göttingen, allows us
to think of him as a model hinterlander in two respects. His home territory
is geographically remote, and he is involved in the slave trade but also at a
remove: even as an investor, his purchase of company shares distances him
from the materiality of the trade in a way that buying a share in a journey
or insuring a ship does not. His letters throw up the third dimension, that
of moral distance. It is in this complex sense of the interplay of distance
and involvement that we deploy the notion of 'hinterland' in our title and
throughout the volume.

'Hinterland' begins as a spatial term, though, and like many spatial terms
it has a problematic history; using it calls for acknowledgement of that
history. Its genealogy is closely connected to the history of spatial planning
and imagining in the nineteenth and twentieth centuries. It was frequently
employed in human geography, political economy and geopolitics, and usage
peaked in the 'Scramble for Africa' in the last decades of the nineteenth
century.

Apart from regional names (such as the Hinterland in Upper Hesse),
we encounter the term for the first time in the 1840s. The 1849 issue of the
Deutsches Zollvereinsblatt, addressing the closed borders with Russia, stated:
'Prussia has no hinterland' – meaning that the Province of Prussia had no
access to land beyond its borders and therefore could not function as an intermediary trader. Emphasising its untapped potential, the article pleaded for
the industrialisation of the province and particularly of its textile industry.[3]
Here we find the term hinterland applied in a sense close to our own: to
identify an inland area that is economically or politically related to a port city
or a coastal area and connected via different transport routes (roads, rivers or
canals). This usage was directly related to contemporary thinking about the
the involvement in *Weltverkehr* (world traffic/world trade) or the *Weltstellung*
(position in the world) of particular European countries and regions which
were geographically or developmentally distant from economic centres.[4]

Not long afterwards, hinterland received another meaning. It became an
area 'lying behind' a civilisational centre or outpost, a meaning freighted with
a sense of backwardness. For example, in the *Ergänzungsblätter* of Meyer's
Encyclopaedia of 1870, we read of Russia as 'located behind a Europe which

3   'Preussen hat kein Hinterland' (in spaced letters). *Deutsches Zollvereinsblatt*, Mittheilungen,
7/2 (1849), 19, referring to an article by Prof. Dr Schubert in the *Zeitschrift des Vereins für
deutsche Statistik*.
4   See e.g. [Josef von Hormayr and Arnold Duckwitz], *Fragmente über Deutschlands und
insonderheit Bayerns Welthandel und über die Wichtigkeit des einzigen, ganz deutschen
Stromes, der Weser* (Munich, 1840), p. 37; 'Die preußischen Ostprovinzen und ihre Weltstellung',
*Die Gegenwart. Eine enzyklopädische Darstellung der neuesten Zeitgeschichte für alle Stände.
Erster Band* (Leipzig, 1848), p. 122; 'Belgien und die Belgier', *Das Ausland. Ein Tagblatt für
Kunde des geistigen und sittlichen Lebens der Völker* 108 (1847), p. 430.

is western and divided into many parts, a gigantic hinterland, barely half cultivated, of raw natural strength'.[5] Apart from the geographical banality that Russia lies 'behind' Western Europe (as seen from there) and the assertion of a different grade of cultivation, it is impossible to say whether the term hinterland is already being used here to express a vision of domination or exploitation.[6]

However, during the last two decades of the nineteenth century, the latter semantic content took shape in the context of high imperialism, particularly during the course of the 'Scramble for Africa', and further progressed into twentieth-century geopolitics. When getting their first foothold in African coastal areas, Europeans usually employed 'hinterland' to denote the area behind the coastal line, an area 'not yet' under full control, 'not yet' colonised. The Germans even introduced the term into colonial diplomacy to encompass and to claim a reputedly 'natural' sphere of interest behind the coastal area, one oriented towards both physical and human geographical criteria.[7] Hinterland thus became a key term in colonial politics and colonial literature – and it was during this time that it was assimilated into both English and French vocabulary.[8] The term was also introduced into military language to denote an area behind the front (on one's own side).

In current scholarship, hinterland is still an established term in geography for a catchment area around or behind a nodal point (usually a transport node). In history, the term is seldom used, not least because of its problematic background. Reflecting on areas lying apart from identified centres, historians engaging in global and universal history prefer terms such as periphery, fringes, margins or borderlands. But as Angelika Epple has pointed out, the term periphery ('periphery within') is not a suitable equivalent to hinterland, because the centre–periphery dichotomy does not necessarily apply for a hinterland; the latter may take an active part in global relations and – as she demonstrates for the case of Solingen – may be a profiteer from the colonial

---

5 *Ergänzungsblätter zur Kenntnis der Gegenwart* 5/5 (1870), p. 279.

6 Angelika Epple notes that Friedrich List was named as having coined the term in the sense of a potential area of colonisation, but that the attempt to verify this remained unsuccessful. Angelika Epple, 'Globale Machtverhältnisse, lokale Verflechtungen. Die Berliner Kongokonferenz, Solingen und das Hinterland des kolonialen Waffenhandels', *Ränder der Moderne – Neue Perspektiven auf die Europäische Geschichte (1800–1930)*, ed. C. Dejung and M. Lengwiler (Cologne, 2016), pp. 65–91, with reference to Klaus Thörner, *'Der ganze Südosten ist unser Hinterland'. Deutsche Südosteuropapläne von 1840 bis 1945* (Freiburg, 2008).

7 See 'Hinterland', *Deutsches Kolonial-Lexikon*, ed. H. Schnee, 3 vols (Leipzig, 1920), vol. 2, p. 68.

8 See publications such as: J. C. Ernest Parkes, *Elementary Handbook of Geography of the Colony of Sierra Leone and Its Hinterland* (Freetown, 1894); Abel Delafosse, *La Situation dans l'Hinterland du Dahomé* (Paris, 1895); Frederic Walter Fuller, *Egypt and the Hinterland: With a Frontispiece and a Map of Egypt and the Sudan* (London, 1901); Paul Patté, *Hinterland Moï* (Paris, 1906).

system.[9] This is exactly what makes the term interesting in our context. It appears particularly suitable in light of our starting point: the observation that there actually *were* interrelations with the transatlantic slave business of regions lying beyond the port cities and capitals, usually connected through these nodal points with the Atlantic world. But the term leaves open the quality of these relations, the active or passive role the hinterland played, and the effects these relations had on the respective area. It also allows us to avoid the suggestion implicit in the term 'periphery' that areas in continental Europe were subordinate in importance to the Atlantic world.[10] Last but not least, the term hinterland allows for productive engagement with the current historiography of slavery and abolition, which focuses on the Atlantic, by signalling that the states and regions that were neighbours to the great Atlantic trading economies were certainly *beyond* their coastlines, but not necessarily *behind* them.

Historiographies

The history of transatlantic slavery is one of the most active and fruitful fields of international historical research. However, it is only recently that historians have started to look beyond the familiar Atlantic axis. Whereas *Western* Europe has always been part of the history of transatlantic slavery – all the more so when it comes to abolition – historical research has long ignored other European regions. Shifting the focus beyond Europe's principal slave-trading nations and cities, this volume focuses on territories that were not directly involved (or were relatively minor participants) in the traffic in Africans, but were – as will be shown – linked in various ways with the transatlantic slave business, the plantation economies that it fed, and the consequences of its abolition.

With this new regional focus, this volume reconsiders key aspects of the relationship between slavery (outside Europe) and the dynamics of (European) societies. The authors tackle both 'material' and 'moral' implications, and the correlation of both. This investigative horizon was first called up by Eric Williams: As early as 1944, Williams assumed that investment capital for industrialisation in the eighteenth century originated from the profits of slave labour in the Caribbean and that British abolitionism arose – or became salient – only at the moment when profits were declining and it was possible

9   See Epple, 'Globale Machtverhältnisse'.
10 Cf. Susanne Lachenicht: 'Europeans Engaging the Atlantic: Knowledge and Trade, c.1500–1800. An Introduction', *Europeans Engaging the Atlantic: Knowledge and Trade, 1500–1800*, ed. S. Lachenicht (Frankfurt a.M., 2014), pp. 7–21.

to view slavery as an out-of-date mode of production.[11] A considerable amount of research has been devoted to unravelling these issues, particularly in the Anglo-American context. After a generation of studies exploring the macroeconomic links between slavery and capitalist development, Joseph Inikori restated the core thesis for the twenty-first century.[12]

While the argument for the global contribution of the slave business to economic modernisation remains controversial, the general approach has also borne fruit in detailed work on the extent to which particular cities and communities had a stake in or were shaped – culturally as well as in terms of local industries and economies – by the slave trade and its profits. After the important work done in the 1990s on the Atlantic ports in Britain and France,[13] more research since has shone a light on the slavery sources for the growth and glamour of the imperial capital cities.[14] Beginning from and elaborating the proposition, as one contemporary said of Liverpool, that 'almost every man ... is a merchant and almost every order of people is interested in a Guinea cargo',[15] attention has also turned to the ways in which individuals in the metropoles were implicated as small investors in a business that was constantly on the lookout for investment because it was capital-intensive and highly profitable, but also risky,[16] as holders of financial instruments secured against slave enterprises, as well as being absentee slave-owners. Much of the evidence for this lies in the records of claims for compensation following

11 Eric Williams, *Capitalism and Slavery* (Chapel Hill, 1944). See also: Barbara L. Solow and Stanley L. Engerman, *British Capitalism & Caribbean Slavery. The Legacy of Eric Williams* (Cambridge, 1987).

12 Joseph E. Inikori, *Africans and the Industrial Revolution in England. A Study in International Trade and Economic Development* (Cambridge, 2002); J. E. Inikori, S. D. Behrendt, M. Berg, W. G. Clarence-Smith, H. den Heijer, P. Hudson, J. Singleton and N. Zahedieh, 'Roundtable: Reviews of Joseph Inikori's *Africans and the Industrial Revolution: A Study in International Trade and Economic Development*, with a response by Joseph Inikori', *International Journal of Maritime History* 15 (2003), 279–361. See also Nicholas Draper, 'The City of London and slavery: evidence from the first dock companies, 1795–1800', *Economic History Review* 61 (2008), 432–66.

13 Madge Dresser, *Slavery Obscured: The Social History of the Slave Trade in an English Provincial Port* (London, 2001); David Richardson, Suzanne Schwarz and Anthony Tibbles, eds, *Liverpool and Transatlantic Slavery* (Liverpool, 2007); Jean-Michel Deveau, *La Traite rochelaise* (Paris, 1990); Éric Saugera, *Bordeaux, port négrier. Chronologie, économie, idéologie, XVIIe–XIXe siècles* (Paris, 1995); Olivier Pétré-Grenouilleau, *L'Argent de la traite* (Paris, 1996) and *Nantes au temps de la traite des Noirs* (Paris, 1998) (on Nantes); Alain Roman, *Saint-Malo au temps des négriers* (Paris, 2001).

14 Nuala Zahedieh, *The Capital and the Colonies: London and the Atlantic Economy, 1660–1700* (Cambridge, 2010); Allan Potofsky, 'Paris-on-the-Atlantic from the Old Regime to the Revolution', *French History* 25 (2011), 89–107.

15 James Wallace, *A General and Descriptive History of the Ancient and Present State of the Town of Liverpool* (Liverpool, 1795), p. 229.

16 Herbert S. Klein, *The Atlantic Slave Trade* (Cambridge, 1999).

abolition. In the principal slaving nations, following *that* money has exposed new paths through which slavery contributed to fuelling metropolitan growth; it has also called into question post-abolition moral triumphalism.[17] And a richly suggestive literature on the implication of the transatlantic slave trade in the emergence of modernity in financial practices has clustered around the 1783 insurance suit precipitated by the murder of over 130 African captives on the *Zong*.[18]

The question of conscience has not been set aside, however. In the Atlantic frame, that is in the Anglophone and Francophone contexts, research on the moral and cultural implications of the slave business has gone beyond Williams' approach of interrogating the relationship between moral and economic dynamics in the growth of abolitionism.[19] Cultural historians have linked the emergence of a readiness to take responsibility for the slave business and its overthrow with new if ambivalent constructions of the public and private personality, and the forms of cultural production which reflect them.[20] Studies of abolitionism and the language of emancipation have considered the ways in which slavery-related discourses coloured and were driven by (re-)visions of empire or national liberation,[21] and other movements

---

17   Nicholas Draper, *The Price of Emancipation. Slave-Ownership, Compensation and British Society at the End of Slavery* (Cambridge, 2010); Potofsky, 'Paris-on-the-Atlantic'. For initial research on Amsterdam slave-owners based on compensation files see http://www.ghhpw. com/slave-owners-in-amsterdam.php (accessed 14 June 2015) and Dienke Hondius, 'Mapping Urban Histories of Slavery', *WerkstattGeschichte* 66–67 (2015), 135–48. The economics of Dutch involvement in the slave trade and plantation economy, though an intrinsic part of the history of a premier maritime nation, has similarly only recently attracted scholarly attention: see Piet C. Emmer, *The Dutch Slave Trade, 1500–1850*, transl. C. Emery (New York, 2006); Johannes Postma, *The Dutch in the Atlantic Slave Trade, 1600–1850* (Cambridge, 1990); Kwame Nimako and Glenn Willemsen, *The Dutch Atlantic. Slavery, Abolition and Emancipation* (London, 2011); K. J. Fatah-Black and M. van Rossum, 'Wat is winst? De economische impact van de Nederlandse trans-Atlantische slavenhandel', *Tijdschrift voor Sociale en Economische Geschiedenis* 9 (2012), 3–29.
18   Ian Baucom, *Specters of the Atlantic. Finance Capital, Slavery, and the Philosophy of History* (Durham, NC, 2007); Anita Rupprecht, 'Excessive Memories: Slavery, Insurance and Resistance', *History Workshop Journal* 64 (2007), 6–28; Geoffrey Clark, 'The Slave's Appeal: Insurance and the Rise of Commercial Property', *The Appeal of Insurance*, ed. G. W. Clark, G. Anderson, C. Thomann and J.-M. Graf von der Schulenburg (Toronto, 2010), pp. 52–74; James Walvin, *The Zong: A Massacre, the Law and the End of Slavery* (New Haven, 2011).
19   See in particular Roger Anstey, *The Atlantic Slave Trade and British Abolition, 1760–1810* (London, 1975); Seymour Drescher, *Econocide. British Slavery in the Era of Abolition* (Pittsburgh, 1977); J. R. Oldfield, *Popular Politics and British Anti-Slavery. The Mobilisation of Public Opinion against the Slave Trade, 1787–1807* (London, 1998).
20   Baucom, *Specters of the Atlantic*; Amit Rai, *Rule of Sympathy. Sentiment, Race and Power 1750–1850* (New York, 2002).
21   David Brion Davis, *The Problem of Slavery in the Age of Revolution* (Ithaca, 1975); David Gaspar and David Geggus, eds, *A Turbulent Time. The French Revolution and the Greater Caribbean* (Bloomington, 1997); Christopher Leslie Brown, *Moral Capital: Foundations of*

for reform, notably the women's movement.[22] But this is one area in which big questions remain open: If we extend our vision of the mental world of a slaving Europe beyond political and humanitarian sentiment, to take in imagination and knowledge and the way in which they inform action, then even at the mundane level of economic choices there is more that is worth knowing about the implication of individual economic actors in one of the earliest globalised businesses. What kinds of social, intellectual and information networks are salient to understanding the long-term impacts of the slave trade (for example, in mobilising labour or investment in the hinterlands, or in the development and communication of technologies and scientific knowledge) as well as individual and public responses to it? What can the case of slavery tell us about when and how people with a measurable material interest, but who are not already embedded in long-standing maritime-mercantile networks, come to see themselves as participants in a global business? And what can it tell us about how and when (if at all) awareness of one's material stake in an aspect of global trade prompts awareness of ethical implication and/ or moral-political engagement? Here the question of how and when (if ever) those who benefited from the slave economy (indirectly, at second hand, or as subaltern agents) reflected on the nature of the business, calls for exploration and analysis in its own right as a laboratory for a history of ethical investment, and bearing in mind that the politics of boycott was pioneered by abolitionist women.

Our knowledge about the rise of abolitionist sentiment in European countries other than Britain and France is still very sketchy or non-existent. It was not until 2005 that the first study was published with analysis on how the moral problem of slavery and slave trade was treated in Portugal.[23] On the German-speaking countries, research is just beginning.[24] Significantly, it was a shift in economic history studies towards a similar concern with particular economic actors that led historians of continental Europe (our 'hinterlands') to begin to address these questions. It made it possible to trace an Atlantic trade network, including the slave trade, which was to a significant extent

British Abolitionism (Chapel Hill, 2006); Srividhya Swaminathan, *Debating the Slave Trade: Rhetoric of British National identity, 1759–1815* (Farnham, 2009).

22 Clare Midgley, *Women against Slavery: The British Campaigns, 1780–1870* (London, 1992); Pamela Scully and Diana Paton, eds, *Gender and Slave Emancipation in the Atlantic World* (Durham, NC, 2005); Kathryn K. Sklar and James B. Stewart, eds, *Women's Rights and Transatlantic Antislavery in the Era of Emancipation* (New Haven, 2007).

23 João Pedro Marques, *The Sounds of Silence: Nineteenth-Century Portugal and the Abolition of the Slave Trade* (New York, 2005).

24 Andreas Gestrich, 'The Abolition Act and the Development of Abolitionist Movements in 19th Century Europe', *Humanitarian Intervention and Changing Labor Relations. The Long-Term Consequences of the Abolition of the Slave Trade*, ed. M. van der Linden (Leiden, 2011), pp. 245–62.

transnational and reached far into the European mainland. Thus, Klaus
Weber and Margrit Schulte Beerbühl demonstrated systematically the extent
to which German merchants were actively integrated into the Atlantic trade
system – through family networks and via port cities like London, Hamburg,
Cadiz and Bordeaux.[25] It has also become clear that European continental
hinterlands served both as suppliers of investment, labour and trade goods
for the slave trade and of materials for the Atlantic plantation economies, and
also as processors and consumers of slave-produced commodities. Studies
of how involvement in trade networks either centred on or dynamised by
the slave economy contributed in turn to key economic developments in the
hinterlands remain scarce, however.[26] Some important early research findings
are hidden in local and regional historiography, and some of this work has
given a new airing to the findings of earlier scholars which were previously
neglected as marginal to the main story.[27] However, local and regional historiography had often been unconcerned with the ways in which the respective
regions were implicated in transnational processes and global history,[28] or in
the slave trade in particular. It was only about a decade ago that the scholarly
community learned with some surprise about the significant extent to which
the early modern economy of a country like Switzerland was interwoven with

25   Klaus Weber, *Deutsche Kaufleute im Atlantikhandel 1680–1830: Unternehmen und
Familien in Hamburg, Cádiz und Bordeaux* (Munich, 2004); Margrit Schulte Beerbühl, *Deutsche
Kaufleute in London. Welthandel und Einbürgerung (1660–1818)* (Munich, 2007).
26   Jochen Meissner, Ulrich Mücke and Klaus Weber, *Schwarzes Amerika. Eine Geschichte
der Sklaverei* (Munich, 2008); Klaus Weber, 'Deutschland, der atlantische Sklavenhandel
und die Plantagenwirtschaft der Neuen Welt (15. bis 19. Jahrhundert)', *Journal of Modern
European History* 7/1 (2009), 37–67; Klaus Weber, 'The Atlantic Coast of German Trade:
German Rural Industry and Trade in the Atlantic, 1680–1840', *Itinerario. European Journal of
Overseas History* 26 (2002), 99–119; Michael Zeuske, *Handbuch Geschichte der Sklaverei. Eine
Globalgeschichte von den Anfängen bis zur Gegenwart* (Berlin, 2013).
27   E.g. Hermann Kellenbenz, 'Deutsche Plantagenbesitzer und Kaufleute in Surinam vom
Ende des 18. bis zur Mitte des 19. Jahrhunderts', *Jahrbuch für Geschichte von Staat, Wirtschaft
und Gesellschaft Lateinamerikas* 3 (1966), 141–63; Adam Jones, 'Brandenburg-Prussia and
the Atlantic slave trade', *De la traite à l'esclavage*, ed. S. Daget, 2 vols (Nantes, 1988), vol. 1,
pp. 283–98; Nils Brübach, '"Seefahrt und Handel sind die fürnembsten Säulen eines Etats".
Brandenburg-Preussen und der transatlantische Sklavenhandel im 17. und 18. Jahrhundert',
Amerikaner wider Willen. Beiträge zur Sklaverei in Lateinamerika, ed. R. Zoller (Frankfurt
a.M., 1994), pp. 11–42; Mark Häberlein and Michaela Schmölz-Häberlein, *Die Erben der Welser.
Der Karibikhandel der Augsburger Firma Obwexer im Zeitalter der Revolutionen* (Augsburg,
1995); Astrid Petersson, *Zuckersiedergewerbe und Zuckerhandel in Hamburg im Zeitraum von
1814 bis 1834: Entwicklung und Struktur zweier wichtiger Hamburger Wirtschaftszweige des
vorindustriellen Zeitalters* (Stuttgart, 1998).
28   On this problem see Angelika Epple, '"Global" und "Area History". Plädoyer für eine
weltgeschichtliche Perspektivierung des Lokalen', *Area Studies und die Welt. Weltregionen und
neue Globalisierung*, ed. B. Schäbler (Vienna, 2007), pp. 90–116.

the slave trade.[29] Similarly, research in particular industrial sectors has thrown up significant links with slavery in the context of Atlantic trade; notable here are the textile industry,[30] iron and iron goods,[31] sugar refining[32] and also niche areas such as glass bead production.[33]

The Volume

The essays in this volume build out from, supplement and in some places interrogate previous research on slavery's European hinterlands. The accounts they offer range in time from the first, short-lived attempt at establishing a German slave-trading operation in the 1680s to the involvement of textile manufacturers in transatlantic trade in the first quarter of the nineteenth century. In some respects they invite us to look at what we know about developments in the Atlantic slave economy and its European metropolises in a new light.

They reinforce our understanding of the flows of goods that linked the Atlantic trade with the cities and towns of the interior. Anka Steffen and Klaus

---

29 Thomas David, Bouda Etemad and Janick Marina Schaufelbuehl, *Schwarze Geschäfte. Die Beteiligung von Schweizern an Sklaverei und Sklavenhandel im 18. und 19. Jahrhundert* (Zurich, 2005); Niklaus Stettler, Peter Haenger and Robert Labhardt, *Baumwolle, Sklaven und Kredite. Die Basler Welthandelsfirma Christoph Burckhardt & Cie. in revolutionärer Zeit (1789–1815)* (Basel, 2004). This issue was anticipated by the pioneering work of Hans Werner Debrunner, 'Basel und der Sklavenhandel – Fragmente eines wenig bekannten Kapitels der Basler Geschichte', *Basler Stadtbuch 1993* (Basel, 1994), pp. 95–101.

30 Klaus Weber, '"Krauts" und "true born Osnabrughs": Ländliche Leinenweberei, früher Welthandel und Kaufmannsmigration im atlantischen Raum vom 17. bis zum 19. Jahrhundert', *IMIS Beiträge* 29 (2006), 37–69; Margrit Schulte Beerbühl and Klaus Weber, 'From Westphalia to the Caribbean. Networks of German Textile Merchants in the Eighteenth Century', *Cosmopolitan Networks in Commerce and Society 1660–1914*, ed. A. Gestrich and M. Schulte Beerbühl (London, 2011), pp. 53–98. On the linen industry in Europe see Brenda Collins and Philip Ollerenshaw, eds, *The European Linen Industry in Historical Perspective* (Oxford, 2003). On the global cotton trade see Giorgio Riello, *Cotton. The Fabric that Made the Modern World* (Cambridge, 2013); Sven Beckert, *King Cotton. Eine Geschichte des globalen Kapitalismus* (Munich, 2014).

31 Peter W. Klein, 'The Trip Family in the 17th Century. A Study of the Behaviour of the Entrepreneur on the Dutch Staple Market', *Acta Historiae Neerlandica* 1 (1966), 187–211; Chris Evans and Göran Rydén, *Baltic Iron in the Atlantic World in the Eighteenth Century* (Boston, MA, 2000).

32 On the complex Atlantic history of sugar see Sidney W. Mintz, *Sweetness and Power: The Place of Sugar in Modern History* (New York, 1985); Stuart B. Schwartz, ed., *Tropical Babylons. Sugar and the Making of the Atlantic World, 1450–1680* (Chapel Hill, 2004).

33 Ulf Vierke, *Die Spur der Glasperlen. Akteure, Strukturen und Wandel im europäisch-ostafrikanischen Handel mit Glasperlen*, Bayreuth African Studies Online 4 (June 2006), https://epub.uni-bayreuth.de/887/1/vierke1.pdf (accessed 29 March 2016); Karin Pallaver, 'From Venice to East Africa: History, Uses and Meanings of Glass Beads', *Luxury in Global Perspective: Commodities and Practices, c.1600–2000*, ed. K. Hofmeester and B. S. Grewe (forthcoming).

Weber demonstrate how closely the Silesian textile industry was interwoven
with the Atlantic trade, and with the slave trade in particular. Anne Sophie
Overkamp builds on her research into the long-standing practice of merchant-
manufacturers in the Wupper Valley as suppliers to the plantation economy,
examining their efforts to maintain Atlantic trade relations during the
turbulent decades around 1800. Peter Haenger anatomises the involvement
in the Atlantic slave trade of the Burckhardts, a merchant family from Basel,
and Alexandra Robinson uncovers the Italian hinterland of the Earle family
of Liverpool, for whom entry into the bead trade meant opening up a new
eastern frontier in their slave-trading activities.

Our contributors also show us flows of people in a new light. Drawing on a
recently discovered manuscript journal, Craig Koslofsky and Roberto Zaugg
examine on a micro level how a German 'hinterlander' from Franconia, the
ship's surgeon Johann Peter Oettinger, became involved in the Atlantic slave
business – physically as well as economically – and reflect on the hinterland
as a source of maritime labour for the trade. Another European specialist
with a 'migration background' from continental Europe studied here is the
natural historian and botanist Julius von Rohr. Daniel Hopkins traces the
itinerary of the German/Danish scientist, who, among other projects, was
sent by the Danish Crown to investigate the cotton cultivation in various
Caribbean colonies, motivated by the idea of supporting the Danish textile
industry. Interestingly, it is largely through the eyes of the scholars with whom
he interacted on his global travels that we gain insight into his own views
of slavery, relayed within the conversations that also exchanged scientific
knowledge. We also learn to see the flow of people as two-way: Rebekka
von Mallinckrodt shows us Europe as a destination and indeed a market for
enslaved Africans, even if only on a small scale. A substantial body of scholarship has shown that slavery was not unfamiliar in Europe, particularly in the
Mediterranean.[34] But in early modern times, slavery was increasingly pictured
as something external to Europe, and especially to the continental states.[35]
By closely examining the networks of trafficked African servants reaching

34 Robert C. Davis, *Christian Slaves, Muslim Masters: White Slavery in the Mediterranean,
the Barbary Coast, and Italy, 1500–1800* (Basingstoke, 2003); Wolfgang Kaiser and Guillaume
Calafat, 'The Economy of Ransoming in the Early Modern Mediterranean', *Religion and
Trade: Cross-Cultural Exchanges in World History, 1000–1900*, ed. F. Trivellato, L. Halevi and
C. Antunes (Oxford, 2014), pp. 108–31; Wolfgang Kaiser and Guillaume Calafat, 'Violence,
Protection and Commerce: Corsairing and *ars piratica* in the Early Modern Mediterranean',
Persistent Piracy. Maritime Violence and State Formation in Global Historical Perspective,
ed. S. Eklöf Amirell and L. Müller (Basingstoke, 2014), pp. 69–92; Klaus Weber, ed., *Europas
Sklaven*, special number of *WerkstattGeschichte* 66–67 (2015).
35 Sue Peabody, *'There Are No Slaves in France': The Political Culture of Race and Slavery in
the Ancien Régime* (New York, 1996); Jürgen Osterhammel, *Sklaverei und die Zivilisation des
Westens* (Munich, 2000).

Europe, Rebekka von Mallinckrodt argues persuasively that it is accurate to use the term slavery in connection with German-speaking territories in the early modern period. She thereby heralds a new research agenda, which calls for bringing slavery studies into dialogue with the (still new, though better established) study of the black presence in Europe. If these flows of people, goods, capital and indeed ideas were to be traced on a map, the resulting network would reveal itself to be something less recognisable and far more complex than the transoceanic triangle that has hitherto been an icon for the slave trade.

Black Presence, Black Agency

This volume aims to explore not only impersonal 'impacts' and 'flows', but also, and more especially, questions of individual agency, responsibility and conscience. In that context, our eye is first and foremost – to use the language of Holocaust studies – on the perpetrators, accomplices and bystanders, on those who had the power to act and the power to effect change within European society. And these were in the main and, more importantly, by definition, people whose agency derived from the fact that they were racialised as white in a world increasingly divided by race. One of the consequences of the slave trade though, was that it brought people of African descent into Europe in increasing numbers and saw them in roles whose variety we are just beginning to understand. Some of the essays in this volume show us Africans and people of African descent in interaction with white actors, as agents of their own lives and of historical change. The case study at the centre of Rebekka von Mallinckrodt's chapter arose from the effort of 'a Moor purchased in Copenhagen' to sue for his freedom in Prussia in 1780, and she makes reference to other, less anonymous black bondsmen, such as *Hofmohren* ('court Moors') like Angelo Soliman and Anton Wilhelm Amo. Their rise to respectability, even to academic careers and their status as prodigies marks the extent (and the limits) of the normality of a black presence in continental Europe at the height of the transatlantic slave trade. Julius von Rohr's enslaved research assistants also appear as African(-American) actors here, and we think we know their names, Julius and Marcus.

Some black agents intervene from off-stage, so to speak: There are the Haitian revolutionaries who rewrite not only the history of Atlantic slavery and its abolition, but also the trading conditions within which European merchant-manufacturers like the Frowein brothers – as studied by Anne Sophie Overkamp – had to operate. Not least significant among the African actors who feature here are the members of the slave-trading African elites, exemplified by the anonymous purchasers of trade goods and William Earle's correspondent, Duke Abashy. Their notorious particularities of taste and their eye for quality in commodities like Venetian beads should leave us wondering whether the flows that reached at a minimum from the Americas to the eastern Mediterranean by way of the west coast of Africa involved two-way transfers not only of people and goods but also of taste (as we know resulted from trade with East Asia).

Knowledge Economies, Science and Race

Knowledge and imagery of all kinds certainly circulated, and Johann Peter Oettinger appears in this volume as an early consumer and conveyor of travellers' tales or popular knowledge about the wider world, including exotic peoples and racialised 'others'. Julius von Rohr represents here a more familiar and enduring truism: the involvement of Enlightenment science, and especially of botany, in the global panoptic project of European expansion.[36] Indeed, we have learned to see the emergence of modern notions of 'race' in the context of Enlightenment anthropology as associated with the transatlantic slave trade. Paradoxically, the roots of the discursive power of 'race' are commonly identified in the work of German philosophers, Kant and Hegel, whose knowledge of transatlantic slavery can hardly be denied (or must at least be presumed), but who were not in any known sense directly involved.[37] Another German, Kant's contemporary Johann Friedrich Blumenbach, often features as the father of scientific racism, because of his taxonomy of the races of mankind based on the study of skulls.[38] In Central Europe, African bodies were the object not only of travellers' curiosity but also of more scholarly scientific interest, and Africans in service at German courts were sometimes anatomised after their death.[39] At one and the same time Anton Wilhelm Amo, as well as Marcus and Julius, were each in their own way, subjects of

36 See, for example: James McClellan III, *Colonialism and Science. Saint Domingue in the Old Regime* (Baltimore, 1993); Roy MacLeod, ed., *Nature and Empire: Science and the Colonial Enterprise*, special number of *Osiris* 15 (2000); James Delbourgo and Nicholas Dew, eds, *Science and Empire in the Atlantic World* (New York, 2008); Peter Boomgaard, ed., *Empire and Science in the Making: Dutch Colonial Scholarship in Comparative Global Perspective, 1760–1830* (New York, 2013).

37 For critical approaches see Andrew Valls, ed., *Race and Racism in Modern Philosophy* (Ithaca, 2005); Sarah Eigen and Mark Larrimore, eds, *The German Invention of Race* (Albany, 2006). On Hegel, the *locus classicus* is still Susan Buck-Morss, 'Hegel and Haiti' published in 2000 in the journal *Critical Inquiry*, and then reprinted and expanded in *Hegel, Haiti and Universal History* (Pittsburgh, 2009).

38 John H. Zammito, 'Policing Polygeneticism in Germany, 1775: (Kames,) Kant, and Blumenbach', *The German Invention of Race*, ed. S. Eigen and M. Larrimore (Albany, 2006), pp. 35–54.

39 Sünne Juterczenka, '"Chamber Moors" and Court Physicians. On the Convergence of Aesthetic Assumptions and Racial Anthropology at Eighteenth-Century Courts in Germany',

science. In the current state of research it would be difficult to provide a third German option to the comparison between France and Britain that Seymour Drescher attempted in 1992 regarding the extent of racist thinking and the penetration of scientific racism before and after abolition.[40] But it tells us something about the intellectual openness that Germany's distance from the slave trade permitted – or at any rate the particular synergies that the German economic and political scene favoured or allowed – that Johann Friedrich Blumenbach argued in favour of the mental capacity of Africans and that his niece, Therese Huber (the subject of chapter 8), was an active propagandist for abolition.

Moral and Political Economies: Freedom and Unfreedom

What is clear from the present essays is that the nexus between race and unfreedom associated with the slave trade, as with anti-slavery discourses in the Anglophone and Francophone Atlantic, is not meaningful in all cases. Thus, it is striking that William Earle deals with Duke Abashy on ostensibly equal terms as a businessman, and when it comes to Abashy's sons, kidnapped by a slaver, Earle characterises them as 'free men' a priori. Whatever Earle was thinking, the words he used signal a discursive context quite distinct from that of the slaver for whom Africanness spelled enslavability. In Central Europe, distinct taxonomies and the practices that underlay them become visible in the encounter with slavery discourses. The situation of the 'court moors' sketched by Rebekka von Mallinckrodt reminds us that the forms of experience available to black people, as to white people, in most of continental Europe in the eighteenth century were significantly shaped by both a court culture and an estate-based order that were already obsolete in Britain and decaying in France, in which freedom was a particular and not a general principle, and privilege was the gift of arbitrary power.[41]

Beyond this though, the territories of the Holy Roman Empire had their own system of unfree labour on the land, ranging from personal labour obligations in a demesne system to *Leibeigenschaft* or serfdom; this was

---

Entangled Knowledge. Scientific Discourses and Cultural Difference, ed. K. Hock and G. Mackenthun (Münster, 2012), pp. 165–82.

40 Seymour Drescher, 'The Ending of the Slave Trade and the Evolution of European Scientific Racism', *The Atlantic Slave Trade. Effects on Economies, Societies, and Peoples in Africa, the Americas, and Europe*, ed. J. E. Inikori and S. L. Engerman (Durham, NC, 1992), pp. 361–96.

41 Anne Kuhlmann, 'Ambiguous Duty. Black Servants at German Ancien Régime Courts', *Germany and the Black Diaspora: Points of Contact, 1250–1914*, ed. M. Honeck, M. Klimke and A. Kuhlmann (New York, 2013), pp. 57–73.

most fully developed in the eastern regions of Prussia.[42] In this volume, *Leibeigenschaft* appears as an object of political speculation: Rebekka von Mallinckrodt proposes that Frederick the Great and his advisers hesitated to intervene in a relationship of chattel slavery for fear of making concessions to enlightened demands for the abolition of serfdom. In Sarah Lentz's chapter, the observed reality of serfdom features as a point of reference for Therese Huber's reflections on the moral consequences of unfreedom. And Anka Steffen and Klaus Weber explore this kind of unfree labour as an economic reality that played a role in manufacturing as well as in agriculture, which meant that linens produced in Germany for export as trade goods or for use on plantations already combined free and unfree labour in their weave. And their careful exploration of the everyday lives of Silesian weavers reveals a startling dynamic in which the low price of unfree labour simultaneously forestalled modernisation in the hinterland and helped to keep costs low in the Atlantic slave economy.[43]

A consequence of the wars precipitated by the French Revolution was the legal abolition of personal service obligations in agriculture (celebrated as the 'emancipation of the peasants') in Prussia in 1807, but as these authors make clear the actual liberation of the unfree peasants took a considerable time. Moreover, the post-Napoleonic restoration in the German states was particularly unfriendly to arguments for liberty or even reform. The Carlsbad Decrees of 1819 ushered in more than a decade of political repression in which political associations were banned and public discussion of anything that carried with it the faintest whiff of the legacy of the French Revolution was subject to a tight and sometimes brutal regime of censorship and police surveillance.[44] The significance of this is apparent in Sarah Lentz's study of Therese Huber: the constraints under which she operated in her work as a jobbing journalist also shaped (and limited) the ways in which she could be active in the cause of abolition. This suggests that looking beyond revolutionary and colonial conflicts to take into account the condition of Europe under the post-Napoleonic settlement may add a new dimension to our understanding of Atlantic slavery and its abolition.

---

42   Heide Wunder, 'Agriculture and Agrarian Society', *Germany. A New Social and Economic History. Vol. II 1630–1800*, ed. S. Ogilvie (London, 1996), pp. 63–99; William W. Hagen, *Ordinary Prussians. Brandenburg Junkers and Villagers, 1500–1840* (Cambridge, 2002).

43   The multiple interactions between discourses of feudal unfreedom and Atlantic slavery invite further research, and on both sides of the Atlantic. In antebellum Charleston, the Gothic style of architecture was reserved for buildings associated with the management of slaves: Maurie D. McInnis, *The Politics of Taste in Antebellum Charleston* (Chapel Hill, 2005), pp. 195–239.

44   See most recently George S. Williamson, '"Thought Is in Itself a Dangerous Operation": The Campaign against "Revolutionary Machinations" in Germany, 1819–1928', *German Studies Review* 38 (2015), 285–306.

Sentimental Economies: Gender

Therese Huber stands out among the individuals pictured here as the one who explicitly uses the languages both of slavery and of *Leibeigenschaft* in a critical voice. She also applies them to herself, characterising herself as a serf in relation to her publisher and her work as slavery. Here she stands not only for the presence of abolitionist ideas in Germany, but also for the importance of personal and familial networks in sustaining progressive politics of all kinds in the wake of the French Revolution and the reaction that followed. Like slave trading, and indeed like early modern science, abolitionism was often a family business and, similar to merchant networks, abolitionist networks could cross borders without losing their character as nexuses of family and friendship ties, and bearers of intimacy. Within the modern model of the bourgeois family that emerged as transatlantic slavery was reaching its climax, the maintenance of affective ties was delegated to women, while they were notionally excluded from public activity. That exclusion from the public sphere was nowhere near comprehensive, as women's activism in the cause of abolition reminds us. But Therese Huber's private and public writings, produced in a political context that was peculiarly unwelcoming to public debate of any kind, show very clearly the labour involved in negotiating the gap between what a woman might feel or think and what she might say. Indeed, her letters in particular show her shaping a personality within that space, and that is the work of gender.

Significantly, in an age in which the 'man of feeling' was a model for modern masculinity, we find men engaged in the same work of self-construction grappling with the dissociation between the codified call of sentiment and the demands of the market. The two editions of the memoirs of Oettinger – the original in which the travelling barber displays a fascination with black (women's) bodies but an indifference to their abuse, and the nineteenth-century reworking which supplies expressions of revulsion at the horrors of the slave trade – show us two models of masculinity under construction. For men as well as women, the apogee of the slave trade which came between the two Oettinger texts coincided with the articulation of a new model of gender: elite men of the late eighteenth century were educated in principles of philanthropy and learned the values of the heart from authors like Rousseau, Goethe and Sterne. The inhuman trade in men and women posed a challenge to those values of the kind that should have made it a key locus for the negotiation of a masculine identity that effectively combined the capacity to love and the capacity to act in the world of the market. That such a negotiation took place is apparent in some cases. Ernst Schimmelmann, the plantation owner and director of Denmark's slave-trading Guinea Company who features in Daniel Hopkins' chapter, wrote (significantly) to his fiancée in 1782:

If only, instead of bringing disorder and ruin to one part of the world to multiply avarice, mendacity and betrayal, we could join together and work for the dawn of happier days. ... But it's obviously impossible nowadays to serve men in any way other than providing them with gold. ... But crimes against others do not go unpunished: After years and centuries there follows vengeance. Our slaves in America are already producing goods of a luxury which is ruining us Europeans.[45]

Schimmelmann's reflection on the moral cost of slave-produced goods resonates with the observation of Bernardin de Saint-Pierre with which this chapter opened, though in a different key.

Other men, perhaps most men, who were directly engaged in the slave trade responded to the challenge by consciously or unconsciously enforcing the dissociation between the two spheres; this is what Peter Haenger suggests of the slave-trader Christophe Bourcard (represented by his portraitist – Fig. 3.2 – in sentimental mode). Similarly, when Alexandra Robinson's subject, William Earle, wrote to his fiancée about slaving, it was his own discomforts in 'this overbusy, noisy trade' of which he complained. Of course, that dissociation called for rationalisation in terms that reduced the claim of enslaved Africans to be regarded as fellow men. It is difficult to resist the proposition that this dissonance was what called for and drove the elaboration of racial discourses, but as noted above, in the Europe of the eighteenth century social taxonomies could be much more complex than is allowed for by the simple binary of 'race'. The words of Schimmelmann and Earle signal other contemporary concerns entangled with the formation of bourgeois masculine identity: luxury consumption, work–life balance. We might then prefer to see that racial binary as under construction in dialogue with binary gender categories as middle-class individuality sought a way out of early modern structures.[46] And if we look forward into the nineteenth century we find new dynamics in the interactions between notions of race, humanitarian sympathy and visions of slavery.

45 Degn, *Die Schimmelmanns*, p. 194.
46 On masculinity, sentiment and slavery, see Catherine Hall, 'Competing Masculinities: Thomas Carlyle, John Stuart Mill and the Case of Governor Eyre', in C. Hall, *White, Male and Middle Class. Explorations in Feminism and History* (Cambridge, 1992), pp. 255–95. On sentiment and attitudes to slavery more generally, see Markman Ellis, *The Politics of Sensibility: Race, Gender and Commerce in the Sentimental Novel* (Cambridge, 1996); Rai, *Rule of Sympathy*; George Boulukos, 'Capitalism and Slavery: Once More, with Feeling', *Affect and Abolition in the Anglo-Atlantic, 1770–1830*, ed. S. Ahern (Farnham, 2013), pp. 23–43.

Differential Chronologies:
Abolition, Anti-slavery and Colonialism

Resituating transatlantic slavery – remapping it, so to speak – calls not only for attention to the geographical 'margins' or 'hinterlands' of the trade, but also for new chronologies. Just as they were affected by the transatlantic trade, European hinterlands 'fed' slave enterprises, with goods, knowledge and personnel, and these processes imply temporal as well as geographical relations. Scholarship on transatlantic slavery is increasingly turning its attention to the ambivalent consequences of abolition and post-abolition arrangements in both slave and metropolitan economies, including studies of indentured replacement labour and schemes for the removal of former slave populations to Africa.[47] One consequence of studies that have emphasised such ambivalence in the slave-trading states has been to extend the time frame for both material and moral enquiry. For those European states that ended slavery in their empires before 1850, in each national-imperial context, the moment of legal 'abolition' was in fact the beginning of a protracted process of sorting out legal and financial issues, and in that sense we have learned to see abolition as more (or less) than the end to an inhuman institution. Increasingly, historians are arguing that the abolition of the slave trade served to prolong the life of slavery as an institution and was even intended by some of its advocates to do so.[48] In the newest work, it is often attention to post-abolition developments that has thrown new light both on the slave trade and slave-ownership, as well as on their enduring consequences in Europe and the world, combined with ambivalence in the relationship between anti-slavery and colonialism,[49] and between abolitionism and racism.[50]

The time frame set in our title, from the late seventeenth to the mid

47   See, for example: Frederick Cooper, Thomas C. Holt and Rebecca Scott, *Beyond Slavery. Explorations of Race, Labor, and Citizenship in Post-Emancipation Societies* (Chapel Hill, 2000); Draper, The *Price of Emancipation*; Marcel van der Linden, ed., *Humanitarian Intervention and Changing Labor Relations: The Long-Term Implications of the Abolition of the Slave Trade* (Leiden and Boston, MA, 2011); Kate Marsh, '"Rights of the Individual", Indentured Labour and Indian Workers: The French Antilles and the Rhetoric of Slavery Post 1848', *Slavery & Abolition* 33 (2012), 221–31; Céline Flory, *De l'esclavage à la liberté forcée. Histoire des travailleurs engagés africains dans la Caraïbe française au XIXe siècle* (Paris, 2015).
48   Nicholas Draper, 'The British State and Slavery: George Baillie, Merchant of London and St Vincent, and the Exchequer Loans of the 1790s' (2015), www.ehs.org.uk/dotAsset/de55e1a1-c7f6-450b-9a1a-831601ae46d9.docX (accessed 29 March 2016).
49   Albert Wirz, 'Abolitionisten als Wegbereiter des Kolonialismus. Zur Tradition und Widersprüchlichkeit sozialreformerischen Handelns in Afrika', *Hundert Jahre Einmischung in Afrika: 1884–1984*, ed. E.-M. Bruchhaus (Hamburg, 1986), pp. 23–43; Suzanne Miers and Martin Klein, eds, *Slavery and Colonial Rule in Africa* (Ilford, 1998).
50   Catherine Hall, *Civilising Subjects: Metropole and Colony in the English Imagination, 1830–1867* (Cambridge, 2002); Cooper, Holt and Scott, *Beyond Slavery*.

nineteenth centuries, acknowledges this extended development. Anne Sophie Overkamp underlines that it was post-revolutionary Haiti after all that served as a new gateway into the South American and Caribbean market for the Elberfeld merchant house of Abraham & Brothers Frowein. She thus shows how in dynamic interaction with the world war that brought the 'age of revolutions' to its end and itself called for the rearrangement of the European state system, abolition ushered in a new phase in the triangular relationship of America–Europe–Africa, heralding new forms of agency and new sources of conflict as well as new opportunities for profit and exploitation.

It is particularly important to extend the chronological frame if we want to capture the moral and material mobilisation of the hinterlands around slavery and its implications. Involvement in post-abolition political projects was certainly more widespread in Europe than direct engagement with the slave trade, as a consensus on the immorality of the slave trade (once achieved) informed both missionary activity and European colonialism in the nineteenth century. In this volume Daniel Hopkins demonstrates in the Danish case how within a slaving economy the project of abolition met the idea of colonisation in West Africa, while Peter Haenger links the work of the Basel Mission in the nineteenth century to the city's slave-trading history. However, active engagement in the slave business was not a precondition for the intensified missionary work and new colonial projects in Africa, which notably created new or expanded spaces for the activity of women and black people. In the musings of Therese Huber, as in the reflections of the Basel Missionaries, the connection between anti-slavery sentiment and a 'civilising mission' broadly conceived is explicit. More generally, it was in those projects that Germans in particular first mobilised on a large scale around questions of slavery.

Although European states adopted anti-slavery legislation at the Congress of Vienna 1814/15 and thereafter,[51] in continental Europe the question of slavery remained an elite discourse. But from the 1860s onward, anti-slavery gained ground in continental Europe, and in the 1880s, a phenomenal burst of anti-slavery sentiment and engagement can be observed in several continental European countries.[52] While there is still much research to be done, it is clear that this anti-slavery movement was sustained by both Catholic and Protestant groups, it was focused on slavery and slave trade within the African

51   See Helmut Berding, 'Die Ächtung des Sklavenhandels auf dem Wiener Kongreß 1814/15', *Historische Zeitschrift* 219/2 (1974), 265–89; William Mulligan and Maurice Bric, eds, *A Global History of Anti-Slavery Politics in the Nineteenth Century* (Basingstoke, 2013).

52   Arno Sonderegger, 'Antisklaverei und Afrika: Zur Geschichte einer Bewegung im langen 19. Jahrhundert', *Internationalismus und die Transformation weltweiter Ungleichheit: Grenzüberschreitende Reformpolitik im 19. und 20. Jahrhundert*, ed. K. Fischer and S. Zimmermann (Vienna, 2008), pp. 85–105.

continent, and it became closely linked to European colonial politics.[53] Reports
from missionaries and explorers in Africa had been reaching Europe with
increasing frequency since the 1850s; the travel reports of David Livingstone,
probably the most influential critic of the slave trade within Africa, were
published in several European countries. European knowledge about Africa
increased and what people learned about Africa was that it was the continent
where slavery persisted. At the same time, the plight of slaves in the American
South was drawing attention, not least through the circulation of anti-slavery
bestsellers like *Uncle Tom's Cabin* by Harriet Beecher Stowe. But in Africa
the fight against slavery appeared simpler and could be associated with the
struggle against civilisational backwardness and unbelief. In 1868, the French
Archbishop of Algiers, Charles Martial Lavigerie, founded the Société des
Missionnaires d'Afrique, known as the 'Pères blancs' or White Fathers,
explicitly devoted to the fight against slavery in Africa. Lavigerie initiated a
Catholic anti-slavery movement that reached a European hinterland particularly in Italy and Germany.[54] In the 1880s, Protestant missionary societies
also became engaged in anti-slavery and the topic was debated intensively in
missionary publications.

This was the point when the 'problem' of slavery in Africa became closely
connected with the 'Scramble for Africa'. Although anti-slavery in late-
nineteenth-century Europe should not be misunderstood as pure legitimi-
sation strategy, it is evident that the fight against the slave trade and slavery
in Africa became the best justification for colonial intervention, particularly
in East and Central Africa. Bismarck, for example, used the fight against
slavery in the Parliament to earn the support of the Catholic Centre Party
for colonial engagement in East Africa.[55] The international blockade of the
East African coast in 1888/9 (a concerted action of Germany, Great Britain,
Italy and Portugal), was officially proclaimed a measure against the illegit-
imate overseas slave trade, although the main purpose of the action was to
block the importation of arms. Becoming a part of the 'civilising mission',

53 Suzanne Miers was the first to point out the close interrelation between abolitionism
and colonialism in Europe: see Suzanne Miers, 'The Brussels Conference of 1889–1890: The
place of the slave trade in the policies of Great Britain and Germany', *Britain and Germany
in Africa. Imperial Rivalry and Colonial Rule*, ed. P. Gifford and W. R. Louis (New Haven,
1967), pp. 83–118; Suzanne Miers, *Britain and the Ending of the Slave Trade* (London, 1975).
In addition, see Miers and Klein, *Slavery and Colonial Rule in Africa*; see also Cooper, Holt
and Scott, *Beyond Slavery*; Olivier Pétré-Grenouilleau, ed., *From Slave Trade to Empire.
Europe and the colonisation of Black Africa 1780s–1880s* (London, 2004); Richard Huzzey,
Freedom Burning: Anti-Slavery and Empire in Victorian Britain (Ithaca, 2012); Daniel Laqua,
'The Tensions of Internationalism: Transnational Anti-Slavery in the 1880s and 1890s', *The
International History Review* 33 (2011), 705–26.
54 François Renault, *Lavigerie, l'esclavage africain et l'Europe, 1868–1892*, vol. 2: *Campagne
antiesclavagiste* (Paris, 1971).
55 Meissner, Mücke and Weber, *Schwarzes Amerika*, p. 238.

Figure o.3. Newspaper advertisement for the German Anti-slavery lottery,
1891

the lofty goal of fighting slavery also provided an opportunity for diplomacy
between the competing European powers. It formed a common concern of
the Congo Conference of 1884/5 and was central for the 1889/90 conference
in Brussels.[56] And it should be noted too, that anti-slavery politics could
(and still can today in memory politics) combine with anti-Arab and anti-
Muslim notions: for example, during the rebellion on the East African coast
against the early German colonial regime, the German government branded
its military measures as a crusade against slave-trading Arabs.[57]

Slavery in Africa was instrumentalised by European colonial politics
– yet as a cause it also moved ordinary people in Europe and gave rise to
large-scale humanitarian fundraising. In 1891 the German Anti-slavery
Committee (Deutsches Antisklaverei-Komitee) in Koblenz (in the Prussian
Rhine Province) initiated an Anti-slavery lottery (Fig. o.3). Promoted through

56 Miers, *Britain and the Ending of the Slave Trade*; see also Stig Förster, Wolfgang J.
Mommsen and Ronald Robinson, eds, *Bismarck, Europe, and Africa. The Berlin Africa
Conference 1884–85 and the Onset of Partition* (London, 1988).
57 Klaus J. Bade, 'Antisklavereibewegung in Deutschland und Kolonialkrieg in Deutsch-
Ostafrika 1888–1890. Bismarck und Friedrich Fabri', *Geschichte und Gesellschaft* 3 (1977),
31–58.

church organisations and newspapers, the lottery raised the immense sum of almost 2 million Reichsmark.[58] The Committee financed a number of expeditions and even ordered ships to be carried overland to Lake Victoria, in order to counter the slave trade there.

This second outpouring of anti-slavery sentiment and the 'civilising' projects that accompanied it brought hinterlanders to the fore. While we are accustomed to seeing Germans in particular as late arrivals to European expansion, nineteenth-century colonial and missionary projects staked a claim to leadership in a new project of modernity. If we understand the Atlantic slave economy as a key driver in the formation of classical European modernity though, the questions addressed by the chapters that follow and the complex asymmetries of material interest and moral engagement they pursue are by no means peculiar to the hinterlands under investigation here. In drawing territories like Germany, Italy and Denmark into the net of slaving modernity, we invite further reflection on the *internal* hinterlands of the Atlantic slaving metropolises.

---

58   Jan-Georg Deutsch, *Emancipation without Abolition in German East Africa, c.1884–1914* (Oxford, 2006), pp. 104f.

1

Ship's Surgeon Johann Peter Oettinger:
A Hinterlander in the Atlantic Slave Trade, 1682–96

CRAIG KOSLOFSKY AND ROBERTO ZAUGG

The life and travels of the barber-surgeon Johann Peter Oettinger (1666–1746) connect a Central European hinterland, the region of Franconia in south-western Germany, with the Atlantic slave trade by way of the Dutch West India Company (WIC) and the Brandenburg African Company (BAC). The small town of Künzelsau, where Oettinger died a respected barber-surgeon in 1746, lies only about ten miles from the tiny village of Orendelsall where he was born, son of a Lutheran pastor, in 1666. But as a young man Oettinger travelled across the Holy Roman Empire and the Dutch Republic, and then on to the West Indies and Africa in the course of making that ten-mile journey. Oettinger recorded his travels in a vivid manuscript journal, written from 1682 to 1696, but until now his account was known only through a partial and heavily manipulated retelling, published in 1885–86 by Paul Oettinger (1848–1934), a Prussian officer and descendant of Johann Peter.[1] Paul Oettinger based his shortened and heavily rewritten 'edition' on a clear and apparently accurate 1779 copy of the original manuscript. This copy, by Johann Peter's grandson, Georg Anton Oettinger (1745–after 1831), was handed down within the Oettinger family until 1982, when it was donated, together with

---

1   In this literary undertaking, Paul Oettinger was supported by Vice Admiral Ludwig von Henk (1820–94), a member of the German Colonial Society (Deutsche Kolonialgesellschaft) and a future MP of the German Conservative Party (Deutschkonservative Partei). Their text was first serialised in the popular magazine *Schorers Familienblatt. Eine illustrierte Zeitschrift* 6 (1885), pp. 134–7, 150–1, 180–3, 262–4, 398–9 and 412–15, and then as a separate book: Paul Oettinger, *Unter kurbrandenburgischer Flagge. Deutsche-Kolonialerfahrungen vor zweihundert Jahren. Nach dem Tagebuch des Chirurgen Johann Peter Oettinger* (Berlin, 1886). This 'edition' has been partially translated and annotated by Adam Jones, ed., *Brandenburg Sources for West African History 1680–1700* (Stuttgart, 1985), pp. 180–98. On Johann Peter Oettinger see also Hartmut Nöldeke, *Die Fregatte 'Friedrich Wilhelm zu Pferde' und ihr Schiffs-Chirurg* (Herford, 1990).

other family papers, to the Geheimes Staatsarchiv Preußischer Kulturbesitz in Berlin. There it remained unnoticed by scholars until discovered by the authors during their initial researches in 2010–11. The discovery of this eighteenth-century manuscript copy of the original journal, titled 'Reisebeschreibung und Lebenslauf von Johann Peter Oettinger' (Travel Account and Biography of Johann Peter Oettinger)[2] allows us, for the first time, to truly examine the barber-surgeon's travels in Europe and in the Atlantic world.

Although Johann Peter Oettinger travelled much farther than most other journeymen-surgeons, his travel account belongs to a common genre, the journeyman's diary, which served to document the itineraries of a craftsman's travels and the masters with whom he had worked.[3] Oettinger's travels can be divided into seven segments: a journey through the Holy Roman Empire and the Dutch Republic (1682–88), his first transatlantic voyage on a Dutch vessel to the Caribbean and Suriname (1688–90), a second journey in the Dutch Republic and to East Frisia (1690–92), a second Atlantic voyage with a Brandenburg vessel to West Africa and the Caribbean (1692–93), an arduous journey from western France to East Frisia (1693–94), a third journey in the northern territories of the Holy Roman Empire (1694–96), and finally the return trip to his home town Künzelsau (1696). Among its many themes, this rich account allows us to examine three significant axes that connected the hinterlands of Central Europe with the Atlantic slave trade: migration, micro-investment and the construction of race. Before we examine these themes, a brief introduction to the Brandenburg African Company is necessary, as Oettinger's travels in the service of this enterprise generated the longest section of his account, which in turn emerges as one of the major narrative sources for the history of the company.

The Brandenburg African Company: A Hinterland State Enters the Transatlantic Slave Trade

Chartered in 1682 and officially dissolved in 1717, the Brandenburg African Company (BAC) – which in September 1692 was renamed the 'Brandenburg African-American Company' (BAAC) – undertook the first sustained engagement with Africa and the Atlantic slave trade by a German state.[4] The BAC holds a

---

2   Geheimes Staatsarchiv Preußischer Kulturbesitz (GStA PK, Berlin), VI. HA, Familienarchiv Oettinger, 12, 'Reisebeschreibung und Lebenslauf von Johann Peter Oettinger'.
3   Sigrid Wadauer, *Die Tour der Gesellen. Mobilität und Biographie vom 18. bis zum 20. Jahrhundert* (Frankfurt a.M., 2005).
4   On the BAC/BAAC see Richard Schück, *Brandenburg-Preussens Kolonial-Politik unter dem Grossen Kurfürsten und seinen Nachfolgern (1647–1721)*, 2 vols (Leipzig, 1888); Hermann Kellenbenz, 'Die Brandenburger auf St. Thomas', *Jahrbuch für Geschichte von Staat, Wirtschaft*

unique place in the history of connections between German-speaking hinterlands and the early modern slave trade, so it merits closer examination here.

The BAC was created by Elector Frederick William I (r. 1640–88) on the
initiative of the Dutch émigré merchant, ship-owner, and privateer Benjamin
Raule (1634–1707), first director of the company and first 'Director-General'
of the nascent Brandenburg-Prussian navy. In 1682, the Elector of Brandenburg
ruled a patchwork of overwhelmingly agrarian territories spread across
Central Europe, still depopulated by the effects of the Thirty Years' War.
Frederick William I looked to mercantilist policies to enrich his hinterland
territories through global trade and the model for prosperity through trade
was the Dutch Republic, to which he had close ties of religion and marriage.
With the founding of the BAC in 1682, Frederick William used Dutch capital
and maritime expertise to carve out a place in the Atlantic slave trade.

With access only to the eastern Baltic, Brandenburg-Prussia was a typical
hinterland country and possessed none of the geopolitical prerequisites for the
triangle trade. But the pull of the Atlantic economy was powerful. To enter
this world, the Brandenburgers patched together a new network of Atlantic
harbours and trade sites. After a voyage in 1680–81 from the Baltic port of
Pillau to the Gold Coast in the south-west of modern-day Ghana, they signed
an agreement (1683) with the port city of Emden, giving them access to the
North Sea. Starting in 1683 they built trading posts on the Gold Coast: the

---

und Gesellschaft Lateinamerikas 2 (1965), 196–217; Adam Jones, 'Brandenburg-Prussia
and the Atlantic Slave Trade', *De la traite à l'esclavage*, ed. S. Daget, 2 vols (Paris, 1988),
vol. 1, pp. 283–98; Nils Brübach, '"Seefahrt und Handel sind die fürnembsten Säulen eines Etats".
Brandenburg-Preussen und der transatlantische Sklavenhandel im 17. und 18. Jahrhundert',
Amerikaner wider Willen. Beiträge zur Sklaverei in Lateinamerika, ed. R. Zoller (Frankfurt
a.M., 1994), pp. 11–42; Jürgen G. Nagel, 'Die Brandenburgisch-Africanische Compagnie. Ein
Handelsunternehmen', *Scripta Mercaturae* 30 (1994), 44–94; Till Philip Koltermann, 'Zur branden-
burgischen Kolonialgeschichte. Die Insel Arguin vor der Küste Mauretaniens', *Brandenburgische
Entwicklungspolitische Hefte* 28 (1999), 8–31; Ulrich van der Heyden, *Rote Adler an Afrikas
Küste. Die brandenburgisch-preußische Kolonie Großfriedrichsburg in Westafrika*, 2nd edn
(Berlin, 2001); Andrea Weindl, *Die Kurbrandenburger im "atlantischen System", 1650–1720*,
Arbeitspapiere zur Lateinamerikaforschung II/3 (2001), http://lateinamerika.phil-fak.uni-koeln.
de/fileadmin/sites/aspla/bilder/arbeitspapiere/weindl.pdf (accessed 12 February 2015); Sven Klosa,
*Die Brandenburgische-Africanische Compagnie in Emden. Eine Handelscompagnie des ausge-
henden 17. Jahrhunderts zwischen Protektionismus und unternehmerischer Freiheit* (Frankfurt
a.M., 2011); Malte Stamm, 'Das Koloniale Experiment. Der Sklavenhandel Brandenburg-Preussens
im transatlantischen Raum 1680–1718' (unpublished dissertation, University of Düsseldorf, 2011),
http://d-nb.info/1036727564/34 (accessed 10 May 2014). Previous to the BAC, the only – brief and
unsuccessful – attempt of a German state to enter the triangular trade had been made by the Duchy
of Courland: see Otto Heinz Mattiesen, *Die Kolonial- und Überseepolitik der kurländischen
Herzöge im 17. und 18. Jahrhundert* (Stuttgart, 1940); Edgar Anderson, 'The Couronians and
the West Indies. The First Settlements', *Caribbean Quarterly* 5/4 (1959), 264–71; Karin Jekabson-
Lemanis, 'Balts in the Caribbean. The Duchy of Courland's Attempts to Colonize Tobago Island,
1638 to 1654', *Caribbean Quarterly* 46/2 (2010), 25–44.

major fort of Grossfriedrichsburg in Pokesu (Princess Town), as well as the Dorotheenschanze in Akwida and the Sophie Louise-Schanze in Tacrama.[5] In December 1685 Brandenburg-Prussia negotiated a thirty-year treaty with Denmark, allowing the BAC to sell enslaved Africans on the Danish island of St Thomas in the Caribbean. In 1687 they became treaty partners with the Emirs of Trarza, who allowed them to use the existing island-fort of Arguin (just off the coast of modern-day Mauritania) as a trading post and supply station.[6] Its attempts to acquire its own Caribbean islands and to establish territorial colonies failed, but Brandenburg-Prussia developed an essential network of Atlantic bases, each secured by agreements with local authorities.[7]

From the start, the slave trade was conceived as an important aspect of the BAC, though trade for gold and ivory was also meant to play a significant role in the company's commercial strategy. Alternative commodities continued to be sought on the African coasts for the whole period, especially in Mauritania, where gum arabic and ostrich feathers always constituted the core business. But by 1685 it was clear that the greatest profits could only be made with human cargo. As Frederick William I explained in September of that year: 'His Electoral Highness intends, because the African Company cannot develop without the trade of slaves to America, that one should establish the slave trade on the island of St. Thomas.'[8] With a harbour in the Caribbean guaranteed by the treaty with Denmark, the BAC could now fully engage in transatlantic trade. In 1687 Director Raule reported to Frederick William I that the first BAC slave ship had arrived at St Thomas, and that 'the slave trade … is becoming the foundation of our company.'[9]

As Malte Stamm has shown, most of these captured Africans were re-exported from St Thomas to French possessions (especially St Croix) and to minor British islands.[10] A significant (although not always traceable) share of the BAC's captives were, however, sold directly to English and French planters, whose demand overrode the mercantile monopolies of the chartered companies, or to Dutch merchants on Curaçao and St Eustachius, from whence they were brought – illegally or through the *asiento de negros* system – to the Spanish mainland. In 1693 Robert Morrison, an English agent in Holland, described the BAC testily as 'an Emden company trading under the Elector of Brandenburg's patent to Guinea'. He complained:

---

5   The BAC also tried to establish itself in Takoradi but after a few years it lost this base to the WIC.
6   An English translation of these agreements can be found in Jones, *Brandenburg Sources*.
7   Stamm, *Das Koloniale Experiment*, pp. 237ff.
8   GStA PK, I. HA, Repositur 65, Marine und Afrikanische Kompaniesachen, Nr. 40 (formerly Nr. 11), fol. 324v. On Brandenburg-Prussia's base on St Thomas see also Waldemar Westergaard, *The Danish West Indies under Company Rule (1671–1754)* (New York, 1917), pp. 71–94.
9   Schück, *Brandenburg-Preussens Kolonial-Politik*, vol. 2, p. 303.
10 Stamm, *Das Koloniale Experiment*, chapter 5, sections 2, 6 and 7.

Though they [the BAC] pretend they send their ships to an island called St. Thomas in the West Indies, belonging to the Danes, which does not produce forty hogsheads of sugar a year, it is evident from their papers that the [return] cargoes were purchased at St. Croix, Martinique and other French islands.

In light of the incessant conflict in the Caribbean, he noted that 'this company, under pretence of trading to St. Thomas, supplies all the French islands with provisions and necessaries of war'.[11]

English and French planters' demand for slaves always exceeded the supply provided by their national chartered companies, and the BAC sought to profit from this gap. Between 1682 and 1715, ships sailing under the flag of Brandenburg-Prussia disembarked and sold at least 19,240 captive Africans.[12] Overall Brandenburg-Prussia's share of the slave trade remained well below that of the Dutch, whose ships delivered 87,391 African captives to the Americas during the same period.[13] However, if we focus on the Caribbean between 1690 and 1700, when the Brandenburg slave trade was at its height, the BAC/BAAC share is much higher. In these years, the Company disembarked 15,293 captives in the Caribbean on thirty-six voyages, whereas the vessels flying the Dutch flag delivered about 21,806 to the same region on fifty-two voyages. For about a decade, then, the BAC/BAAC was a growing force in the triangular trade and real competition for the Dutch in the most important slave import market of the New World.

Inevitably, this success drew the attention of their European rivals. Pressure from the Dutch in Africa and the general growth of the British slave trade in the Caribbean were a constant challenge to the Company. The most important factor of the BAAC's decline – though certainly not the only one – were the attacks on its fleet by the French.[14] The BAC/BAAC fleet, which never had more than sixteen ships at any one time, lost fifteen vessels between 1693 and 1702.[15] Oettinger's return voyage to Europe in 1693, for example, ended when his ship, the *Friedrich Wilhelm zu Pferde*, was seized and burned by the French

---

11   Extract of a letter from Robert Morrison, agent to the Transport Commissioners in Holland (10/20 April 1693), in W. J. Hardy and E. Bateson, eds, *Calendar of State Papers. Domestic series, of the reign of William and Mary ... 1693* (London, 1903), p. 95.

12   An estimated 23,583 captives were embarked from the shores of Africa; 18.4 per cent of them died on board. The data concerning slave voyages by vessels flying the flag of Brandenburg-Prussia are taken from Stamm, *Das Koloniale Experiment*, pp. 398–401.

13   For slave voyages by Dutch ships see the *Trans-Atlantic Slave Trade Database* (http://www.slavevoyages.org).

14   Eleven ships were captured or confiscated by the French, six by the English, five by the Dutch, one by the Danes and one by an English pirate. Most of them were never returned to the BAC/BAAC. Moreover, a dozen vessels suffered shipwreck and one was probably destroyed during a slave revolt. Stamm, *Das Koloniale Experiment*, pp. 398–400.

15   Nagel, 'Die Brandenburgisch-Africanische Compagnie', p. 90.

in November of that year. After 1700 the fortunes of the BAC/BAAC declined rapidly. In 1717 the Company's fortresses on the Gold Coast were sold to the Dutch, and the Brandenburg African-American Company was dismissed as a 'chimera' by King Frederick William I (1713–40), who was much more interested in Prussia's military position in continental Europe than by overseas trade.

On the Gold Coast, however, the BAC was no chimera. In the 1690s its main trading post, the 'handsome and reasonably large' fort of Grossfriedrichsburg, was comparable to the Dutch headquarters at Elmina in size and strength.[16] From their first voyage to the Gold Coast in 1680–81, the Brandenburgers signed treaties with local rulers, traded for gold, ivory, and slaves, and attacked and defended trading posts along the coast. In 1692 the BAC joined with the English Royal African Company (RAC) and the Dutch WIC to send a common embassy to Denkyira, an inland kingdom that had become a major source of gold and slaves.[17] And further east, the Brandenburgers were in contact with the King of Hueda, in present-day Benin, to whose court in Savi Oettinger was admitted in early 1693.[18]

The manifold activities of the BAC/BAAC generated entrepreneurs' proposals, business records, travel accounts, and official reports – an interwoven set of texts in Dutch and German linking Berlin, its Baltic ports, and Emden with Arguin, the Gold Coast, and the Caribbean.[19] The company tapped into an existing network of connections and opened new migratory channels between the hinterlands of Central Europe and the Atlantic world.

Maritime Labour and its Migratory Hinterlands

While there has been some recent work on merchants from continental regions investing their capital in slaving voyages,[20] the participation of poor migrant workers from various hinterlands in the slave trade has been repeatedly noted

16   William Bosman, *A New and Accurate Description of the Coast of Guinea* (London, 1705), p. 7.
17   Kwame Yeboa Daaku, *Trade and Politics on the Gold Coast 1600 to 1720. A Study of the African Reaction to European Trade* (Oxford, 1970), p. 159.
18   'Reisebeschreibung und Lebenslauf', pp. 73–88. On the history of Hueda see Robin Law, '"The Common People Were Divided". Monarchy, Aristocracy and Political Factionalism in the Kingdom of Whydah, 1671–1727', *The International Journal of African Historical Studies* 23/2 (1990), 201–29; and J. Cameron Monroe, *The Precolonial State in West Africa. Building Power in Dahomey* (Cambridge, 2014), pp. 47–52.
19   On the importance of written communication in the making of merchant companies see Miles Ogborn, *Indian Ink. Script and Print in the Making of the English East India Company* (Chicago, 2007), pp. 1–26, and the literature cited there.
20   For a general overview on investment by individual German merchants and the importance of cloth and manufactured goods from the Holy Roman Empire in the slave trade, see Klaus

but scarcely analysed. The nationally and racially mixed crews on Atlantic merchant ships are frequently described as a motley bunch of desperados or, with more empathy, as a cosmopolitan proletariat.[21] Thanks to works like that of Patricia Fumerton and Emma Christopher we now know more about the social life of sailors on English and British ships in the seventeenth and eighteenth centuries, but still there is much work to do for slaving vessels from other countries and periods.[22] It would be especially helpful to know more about the lives of ordinary crew members *before* they were recruited to serve on the slave ships. More background on their migratory paths would allow us to go beyond the cliché of a ship's company thrown together by chance and assess the depth of the connections between the Atlantic and more remote areas. The extensive presence of German-speaking sailors, craftsman and surgeons in the Dutch East India Company (Vereenigde Oostindische Compagnie, VOC) has been reconstructed in detail.[23] German-speaking labourers were so numerous in the ranks of the VOC that in the seventeenth and eighteenth centuries they had a specific role in settling the Cape Colony in South Africa.[24] There is no systematic study on the place of migrants from the Holy Roman Empire in the WIC, but their involvement seems similar. And like the German hinterland merchants who migrated to Atlantic ports in the eighteenth century,[25] many of these maritime workers

Weber, 'Deutschland, der atlantische Sklavenhandel und die Plantagenwirtschaft der Neuen Welt (15. bis 19. Jahrhundert)', *Journal of Modern European History* 7/1 (2009), 37–67; for a special focus on Prussia and Saxony, see Michael Zeuske and Jörg Ludwig, 'Amerikanische Kolonialwaren und Wirtschaftspolitik in Preussen und Sachsen. Prolegomena (17./18. und frühes 19. Jahrhundert)', *Jahrbuch für Geschichte Lateinamerikas* 32 (1995), 257–301; and on Switzerland see Niklaus Stettler, Peter Haenger and Robert Labhardt, *Baumwolle, Sklaven und Kredite. Die Basler Welthandelsfirma Christoph Burckhardt & Cie. in revolutionärer Zeit (1789–1815)* (Basel, 2004), as well as Thomas David, Bouda Etemad and Janick Marina Schaufelbuehl, *Schwarze Geschäfte. Die Beteiligung von Schweizern an Sklaverei und Sklavenhandel im 18. und 19. Jahrhundert* (Zurich, 2005).

21   The latter perspective is adopted especially by Peter Linebaugh and Markus Rediker, *The Many-Headed Hydra. Sailors, Slaves, Commoners, and the Hidden History of the Revolutionary Atlantic* (Boston, MA, 2000).

22   Emma Christopher, *Slave Ship Sailors and their Captive Cargoes 1730–1807* (Cambridge, 2006), and Patricia Fumerton, *Unsettled. The Culture of Mobility and the Working Poor in Early Modern England* (Chicago, 2006), chapter 6. For a comparative overview see Paul van Royen, Jaap Bruijn and Jan Lucassen, eds, *'Those Emblems of Hell'? European Sailors and the Maritime Labour Market, 1570–1870* (St John's, Nfld, 1997).

23   Roelof van Gelder, *Das ostindische Abenteuer. Deutsche in Diensten der Vereinigten Ostindischen Kompanie der Niederlande (VOC), 1600–1800* (Hamburg, 2003), and Iris Bruijn, *Ship's Surgeons of the Dutch East India Company. Commerce and the Progress of Medicine in the Eighteenth Century* (Leiden, 2009).

24   Gerrit Schutte, 'Company and Colonists at the Cape, 1652–1795', *The Shaping of South African Society, 1652–1820*, ed. R. Elphick and H. Giliomee (Cape Town, 1979), pp. 283–323.

25   Klaus Weber, *Deutsche Kaufleute im Atlantikhandel 1680–1830. Unternehmen und Familien in Hamburg, Cádiz und Bordeaux* (Munich, 2004).

came not from coastal areas, but from regions farther inland. In the account of his BAC/BAAC voyage Oettinger mentions several fellow hinterlanders including soldiers from Eisfeld, Dresden, and Strasbourg.[26] As a 1688 muster roll shows, only a minority of the employees of the Company serving on the Gold Coast were actually subjects of the Prince-Elector of Brandenburg-Prussia itself. Most came from other territories of the Holy Roman Empire and from the Dutch Republic. Men from Scotland, Courland, Hungary, and Poland-Lithuania also found work at the BAC trading posts in West Africa.[27]

How can we explain this migratory phenomenon? We might be tempted to use a traditional push-and-pull model: no doubt the boom of Atlantic seafaring and the wage differentials between the rich Dutch Republic and the poorer German states played an important role.[28] But to presume that these German-speaking labourers were automatically and directly attracted from their home towns to the labour-hungry ports of Rotterdam, Amsterdam, or Emden would be mistaken. As Oettinger's journal shows, their stories are far more complex.

When Johann Peter Oettinger first left his home village of Künzelsau in 1681, he was fifteen years old and he sought neither to work in the Dutch Republic nor to discover the wide world of the Atlantic. He simply moved to the neighbouring town of Schwäbisch Hall to do an apprenticeship as a barber-surgeon.[29] About eighteen months later he completed this educational migration and returned to Künzelsau. But he did not stay long: as with all craftsmen, after his apprenticeship he was obliged to travel as a journeyman. So he left Künzelsau again. During the first two years of his journey he stayed in Heidelberg, Pforzheim, Philippsburg and Worms, working in each town for several months for an established barber-surgeon.[30] This first segment of his

26 'Reisebeschreibung und Lebenslauf', pp. 53, 63 and 107.
27 Jones, *Brandenburg Sources*, pp. 145f. For a detailed discussion of the heterogeneous make-up of the BAC/BAAC garrisons on the Gold Coast – which in later years also included employees born in the Americas, in West Africa and even in India – see Roberto Zaugg, 'Grossfriedrichsburg, the First German Colony in Africa? Brandenburg-Prussia, Atlantic Entanglements and National Memory', *Shadows of Empire in West Africa. New Perspectives on European Fortifications*, ed. J. K. Osei-Tutu and V. E. Smith (forthcoming).
28 For a push-and-pull analysis of seasonal migrations in the North Sea area, see Jan Lucassen, *Migrant Labour in Europe 1600–1900. The Drift to the North Sea* (London, 1987). More specifically on migrant labourers in the Dutch maritime sector, see Jelle van Lottum, *Across the North Sea. The Impact of the Dutch Republic on International Labour Migration, c.1550–1850* (Amsterdam, 2007).
29 On barber-surgeons in Schwäbisch Hall, see Andreas Maisch, '"Confusion" und "Contusion". Barbiere in der Stadt', *Auf Leben und Tod. Menschen und Medizin in Schwäbisch Hall vom Mittelalter bis 1950*, ed. H. Krause and A. Maisch (Schwäbisch Hall, 2011), pp. 85–122; for a more general study of this professional sector see Sabine Sander, *Handwerkschirurgen. Sozialgeschichte einer verdrängten Berufsgruppe* (Göttingen, 1989).
30 'Reisebeschreibung und Lebenslauf', pp. 1–4.

craftsman's migration, regional in scope, was likely based on social networks which he had already established before leaving home.

In 1685 Oettinger decided to travel north-east from Worms to Kassel, then east to Jena to visit a brother studying theology there. However, in none of the cities along this route did he find steady work, so his stays were all brief. He then tried his luck in the south, in Nuremberg, but found no suitable employment there either. After months without work, Oettinger went back to the south-western territories of the Holy Roman Empire where his connections were better; he then worked for more than a year in Mainz and in the small town of Bingen before heading down the Rhine to Düsseldorf. In Düsseldorf – or more likely in Aachen – he seems to have learned about opportunities in the Dutch Republic and decided to try his luck there. In Amsterdam he worked for a year in the practice of Nicolaus Ravenstein, a surgeon from Hamburg. Only when his employment contract with Ravenstein ended did he decide to take the WIC surgeons' examination, accept an offer from this mercantile enterprise, and leave for his first transatlantic voyage to the Caribbean and Suriname.[31]

This connection between craft migration and maritime work, seen in the lives of other barber-surgeons,[32] is apparent in his second voyage as well. After returning from the West Indies, Oettinger could have continued in the service of the WIC. But he did not. Instead he moved to Harderwijk, where he worked for two years in the practice of an established barber-surgeon. We can presume that he grew better and better integrated in a regional network of social relations and information about job opportunities. When he left Harderwijk, he did not head back to south-west Germany, but instead travelled to Hallum and then to Emden in East Frisia, where in 1692 he was engaged by the BAC to sail to West Africa and St Thomas as a surgeon on board the *Friedrich Wilhelm zu Pferde*.

31   On the WIC, see Johannes Postma, *The Dutch in the Atlantic Slave Trade, 1600–1815* (Cambridge, 1990); Henk J. den Heijer, *Goud, ivoor en slaven. Scheepvaart en handel van de Tweede Westindische Compagnie op Afrika, 1674–1740* (Zutphen, 1997); Pieter C. Emmer, *The Dutch Slave Trade 1500–1850* (New York, 2006).

32   See, for example, the travel accounts of Andreas Josua Ultzheimer (from Swabia, born 1578) and of Samuel Brun (from Basel, 1590–1668), who in the early seventeenth century visited Africa as a ship's surgeon on Dutch vessels, or the autobiography of Oettinger's contemporary Johann Dietz (1665–1738), who worked as a military surgeon in the armies of the Elector of Brandenburg and as a ship's surgeon aboard a whaling vessel: Samuel Brun, *Schiffarten, welche er in etliche newe Länder und Insulen zu fünff underschiedlichen malen mit Gottes hülff gethan* (Basel, 1624); Andreas Josua Ultzheimer, *Warhaffte Beschreibung ettlicher Reisen in Europa, Africa und America 1596–1610. Die abenteurlichen Weltreisen eines schwäbischen Wundarztes*, ed. S. Werg (Stuttgart, 1971); Johann Dietz, *Mein Lebenslauf*, ed. F. Kemp (Munich, 1966). The travelogues of Ultzheimer and Brun have been partially translated and critically annotated by Adam Jones, ed., *German Sources for West African History 1599–1699* (Wiesbaden, 1983), pp. 18–96.

The third continental migration of Oettinger was hardly voluntary. It began in Brest, where the crew of the Brandenburg ship was disembarked after capture by a French fleet in November 1693. In the winter of 1693–94 Oettinger walked (!) from Brittany to Emden in order to collect his pay from the BAAC at their headquarters. Once arrived in Emden, however, he did not seek to return to his family (although he had not seen them for twelve years). Instead, he sought new opportunities. He first travelled south, but his new East Frisian connections drew him back to Aurich. There he worked in the practice of a barber's widow with whom he seemed to settle down. It was only the steady pressure of his family which made him leave this woman and travel back to his home village, Künzelsau.[33]

As Oettinger's travels show, the presence of hinterland workers in the Atlantic slave trade depended on multipolar geographical mobility. Many hinterlanders worked in the Atlantic economy, but we suspect that few left home with Atlantic ports in mind. The direction of their mobility was constantly reoriented by the networks and information they accessed during their travels. At each stage, migrants had to decide whether to stay or move on. And if they decided to leave, they needed information, resources and connections to choose another goal.

In the end, Oettinger's migration led him back to his home village. But he had many opportunities to stay elsewhere along his route. In West Africa, he was offered an employment as chief surgeon in the Brandenburg fort of Grossfriedrichsburg,[34] and in Aurich he found a barber-surgeon's practice and perhaps also a potential wife. The routes Oettinger travelled look quite tangled and confused. But it is these connections that wove the fabric of the early modern Atlantic world together with its migratory hinterlands.

Personal Trade as Micro-Investment in the Slave Business

More research is needed to assess possible trade connections between Oettinger's home region, Franconia, and the Atlantic world. The Swabian region of neighbouring Württemberg was producing linen for export by the mid seventeenth century, and it is possible that WIC or BAC ships carried linen from Swabia or Franconia in their holds.[35] Oettinger's personal investment in the Atlantic trade is evident in his journal. When he returned to Amsterdam in January 1690 after his first trip to the West Indies, he noted

33 'Reisebeschreibung und Lebenslauf', pp. 147–8.
34 Ibid., p. 59. He was also asked to stay at St Thomas but declined the offer: 'They wanted me to stay on land as a surgeon, but I didn't care for the idea.' Ibid., p. 109.
35 Hans Medick, *Weben und Überleben in Laichingen 1650–1900. Lokalgeschichte als Allgemeine Geschichte* (Göttingen, 1997), pp. 83–91.

that upon arrival 'the noble West-Indian masters of the Company inspected our crates [*Kisten*] and released us from our oath'.[36] These crates remind us of the breadth of small-scale participation in Atlantic trade by the employees of the chartered companies.[37]

After his second West Indian voyage, Oettinger was returning to Emden aboard the *Friedrich Wilhelm zu Pferde* in November 1693 when the frigate was, as mentioned above, attacked by several French naval vessels.[38] The French plundered the cargo, took the crew prisoner and then burned the BAAC ship. Although Oettinger notes thankfully that 'no one was allowed to take anything from us once we were on their [the French] ship', he had only the clothes on his back.[39] He lamented that 'my crates of sugar, tobacco, cotton, medicines, and everything else was gone'.[40] Oettinger gives no specific account of the number or value of the crates, but had noted earlier in the journal that 'I was often on shore buying cotton and tobacco' while in St Thomas.[41] Clearly, he had hoped his investment in these commodities would bring a fine profit when he reached Emden.

This hinterlander's micro-investment reveals an often overlooked aspect of the Atlantic trade. Chartered companies allowed limited private trade by certain employees on board (the captain and a few others), but such dealings are largely invisible in company records. The personal trade of lesser employees such as the young Oettinger appears only in cases of conflict. Evidence is limited, but this micro-investment alongside the Atlantic slave trade seems to have been common. In 1681, for example, 'Doctor [Samuel] Stone' (a surgeon employed by the RAC on the Gold Coast) made and then retracted an allegation regarding private trade against RAC official James Nightingale.[42] Together Stone and Nightingale then accused another RAC official, Francis Frankland, of trading privately with the Portuguese and with English interlopers. Moreover, the two men claimed that RAC officer Arthur Wendover had purchased numerous textiles from a Dutch interloper ('46 fine

36 'Reisebeschreibung und Lebenslauf', p. 27.
37 See Van Gelder, *Ostindische Abenteuer*, pp. 180–3, and Bruijn, *Ship's Surgeons*, pp. 182–90, on the opportunities for private trade by German and other employees of the VOC.
38 The *Friedrich Wilhelm zu Pferde* had taken on a large cargo of cocoa beans at St Thomas and the decision to sell it to the Spanish by stopping at Cadiz on the return voyage to Emden led to the ship's disastrous encounter with the French. Oettinger and the crew protested the detour to Cadiz (see 'Reisebeschreibung und Lebenslauf', pp. 111–12). On the cargo of the *Friedrich Wilhelm zu Pferde*, see Kellenbenz, 'Die Brandenburger', p. 207.
39 And his gold, hidden in a bandage on his leg. 'Reisebeschreibung und Lebenslauf', pp. 115–16.
40 'Reisebeschreibung und Lebenslauf', p. 116.
41 'Reisebeschreibung und Lebenslauf', p. 110.
42 Robin Law, ed., *The Local Correspondence of the Royal African Company 1681–1699*, vol. 1: *The English in West Africa 1681–1683* (Oxford, 1997), docs 90 and 401.

sletias,[43] 5 sayes,[44] and 7 perpetuanoes')[45] for his own local trade. Similarly, the records of the BAC concerning the Zeeland interloper *Creutz*, seized by the BAC on the Gold Coast in 1686, show that when it was taken, the ship's second mate ('Unter Stürmann') and surgeon 'had made their own particular cargoes',[46] and the first mate had a private venture worth 70 Gulden on board.[47] In 1699 the governor of the RAC fortress in Anomabu, Gerrard Gore, complained to the RAC headquarters at Cape Coast Castle that the 'serjeant' and soldiers of the fortress 'have ever since they have been here had interlopeing goods, and sould at under prices in the towne ... cheaper than the Companys prices in the Castle'. One of the men, 'Daniel Vanchesterfleet souldier', had 'two roles [rolls] of tobacco and a cask of Barbadoes rumme' to trade. Gore reported that the sergeant told him that such private trade 'was none of my business, and that he and them might doe what they pleased, I was to mind the Company goods and nothing else'.[48] Small and smallest-scale private commerce seems common to even the lowest-ranking employees. One suspects that company officials tolerated private ventures because the officials were usually trading privately themselves and needed their subordinates to keep quiet about it. Further, the forthright resistance to Gore's attempts to suppress private trade at Anomabu suggests that these employees felt they had a right to trade on their own.

Access to private trade was sought by officials and subordinates alike. In 1714 RAC official William Brainie complained that 'the Compa[ny] think it very hard to allow even the first of their Servants to gain anything considerable on this Coast'. Brainie then compared his plight with the freedom of the crew of the interloper *Saint Thomas*, captained by Jacob Burgeson. Brainie noted that, in contrast, 'Capt. Burgisson's Sailers (as I have it from their own mouths) have in this one voyage gaind some £60 others 70 and others 100 or more pounds'.[49] In this case 'even' the lowest-ranking crew members took the opportunity to trade.

The implications of this micro-investment in the Guinea trade and in

43   Linen cloth, originally from Silesia but also made in England and the Netherlands.
44   Fine woollen cloth, made in England and the Netherlands.
45   Hard-wearing serge (wool) cloth made in England.
46   Interrogation of the former director and bookkeeper of Grossfriedrichsburg, Joost van Colster and Daniel Reindermann (Emden, 9 March 1686), GStA PK, I. HA, Repositur 65, Marine und Afrikanische Kompaniesachen, 42, 8r–22v. A partial translation of this document has been published by Jones, *Brandenburg Sources*, doc. 61.
47   Interrogation of the first mate of the Dutch interloper ship Dirck Blaues (Emden, 27 Febr. 1686), Stadtarchiv Emden, Protokoll XIV, 1, p. 46.
48   Robin Law, ed., *The Local Correspondence of the Royal African Company 1681–1699*, vol. 3: *The English in West Africa 1691–1699* (Oxford, 2006), doc. 930.
49   E. Donnan, ed., 'Accounts of Fort Commenda', *Documents Illustrative of the History of the Slave Trade to America*, vol. 2: *The Eighteenth Century* (Washington, 1931), doc. 79, p. 190.

the products of slave labour deserve further consideration. If this kind of personal trading on one's own account was a widespread and lasting feature of the Atlantic world, then common sailors, soldiers and barber-surgeons were more personally invested (financially and emotionally) in the Atlantic system than has previously been assumed.[50] This aspect of the slave business scarcely appears in the records of the chartered companies, but sources like Oettinger's diary provide a glimpse of its extent.

Race, Gender and Slavery

Johann Peter Oettinger saw much more of the world than his fellow hinter-landers. What did he learn on his travels from Künzelsau to Curaçao and from Emden to the Gold Coast and St Thomas? He learned that he could seek his fortune in the Atlantic world, a world of slavery and trade. Like the majority of his contemporaries, Oettinger did not understand his participation in the slave trade as a moral issue.[51] He witnessed the daily and manifold atrocities committed on a slave ship and in his role as a surgeon he participated actively in the practices which enabled them, such as the careful inspection of captive Africans for purchase.[52] We note that in his journal – which he certainly knew would be read by his family, if not more widely – he did not obscure the violence committed against enslaved persons, nor did he feel compelled to justify these acts and his personal participation in the trade. He describes the branding of newly purchased Africans (on the shoulder with letters 'CABC' for Churfürstliche Africanische Brandenburgische Compagnie), the Middle Passage, the torture of slaves, and slave labour without comment.

His abiding moral concern is not with the slave trade, but with property and theft. He notes carefully when something is stolen from him, or when the property of others is taken. Indeed, property and its possession are a key theme in his journal. His narrative tells the adventures of his property: the gold he hides from the French under a bandage on his leg, his lost crates of sugar and tobacco, the gold ring he receives from a grateful patient in Grossfriedrichsburg, and rings stolen and recovered just before he leaves Grossfriedrichsburg for the Slave Coast. He notes carefully that the

---

50   See Marcus Rediker, *The Slave Ship. A Human History* (New York, 2007), and Fumerton, *Unsettled*, p. 102.

51   To extend the metaphor of the hinterlands and borderlands, one could argue that Europeans like Oettinger, lacking any moral perspective on the trade, occupied a no man's land rather than a hinterland.

52   'Reisebeschreibung und Lebenslauf', p. 83. These enslaved Africans were themselves often hinterlanders, marched more or less long distances from sites of capture inland to the slave-trading posts on the coasts of West Africa.

possessions of those who died at sea were auctioned off, with the proceeds to be given to their heirs when the ship returned home.

How did Oettinger understand human beings as property? He first encountered gang slavery as he arrived in Curaçao on his voyage with the WIC in 1688: 'Arrived on the 25th of September at 5 or 6 in the evening; at Curaçao our ship was pulled on land or on the dock with a rope by some hundred naked Moors, men and women.'[53] Race and gender mark one another in Oettinger's descriptions of African bodies, just as they do in seventeenth-century images. The 23-year-old Oettinger tended to about three hundred men and women enslaved by the WIC on a three-month journey from Curaçao to Suriname in 1688–89.[54] During the voyage three African women gave birth. He described how 'they bind the [newborn] child on their back with an old linen cloth, throw their breast to him over the shoulder, and let him suckle. They look like a pair of young apes.'[55] In the early seventeenth century Theodor de Bry was one of the first to represent a recurring image in the depiction of African women: the claim that they could suckle their children over their shoulder (see Fig. 1.1).[56] As Jennifer Morgan has shown, this image powerfully dehumanised African women, and it had a broad reach, echoing across the Atlantic world.[57]

Oettinger's perception of childbirth among the enslaved Africans also prompted comparison with an animal:

53 'Reisebeschreibung und Lebenslauf', p. 17.
54 Cornelis Ch. Goslinga, *The Dutch in the Caribbean and in the Guianas 1680–1791* (Assen, 1985), p. 167, cites the WIC order to ship these slaves, classed as *magrones* (sick, weak, or injured slaves), to Suriname.
55 'Reisebeschreibung und Lebenslauf', p. 21.
56 See Elizabeth A. Sutton, *Early Modern Dutch Prints of Africa* (Aldershot, 2012), p. 143. On the representation of Africa and the Africans in the works published by the de Bry family, see Ernst van den Boogaart, 'De Bry's Africa', *Inszenierte Welten. Die west- und ostindischen Reisen der Verleger de Bry, 1590–1630 / Staging New Worlds. De Bry's Illustrated Travel Reports, 1590–1630*, ed. S. Burghartz (Basel, 2004), pp. 95–157, and Dorothee Schmidt, *Reisen ins Orientalische Indien. Wissen über fremde Welten um 1600* (Cologne, 2015). On representations of Africans in early modern German culture, see in the first instance Marília Dos Santos Lopes, *Afrika. Eine neue Welt in deutschen Schriften des 16. und 17. Jahrhunderts* (Stuttgart, 1992), and Peter Martin, *Schwarze Teufel, edle Mohren. Afrikaner in Geschichte und Bewußtsein der Deutschen* (Hamburg, 2001).
57 Jennifer L. Morgan, '"Some Could Suckle Over Their Shoulder". Male Travellers, Female Bodies, and the Gendering of Racial Ideology, 1500–1770', *The William and Mary Quarterly*, 54/1 (1997), 167–92. The Scottish traveller William Lithgow described the same practice by the women of northern Ireland after a visit there in 1620: 'The other as goodly sight I saw, was women travayling the way, or toyling at home, carry their Infants about their neckes, and laying the dugges over their shoulders, would give sucke to the Babes behinde their backes, without taking them in their armes.' William Lithgow, *The Totall Discourse of the Rare Adventures & Painefull Peregrinations of Long Nineteene Yeares Travayles from Scotland to the Most Famous Kingdomes in Europe, Asia and Affrica* (Glasgow, 1906), p. 378.

Figure 1.1. 'Von den Weibern und ihrer Kleidung daselbst', detail. Illustration from Johann Theodor and Johann Israel de Bry (eds), *Orientalische Indien*, vol. 6: [Pieter de Marees], *Wahrhafftige historische Beschreibung deß gewaltigen Goltreichen Königreich Guinea* (Frankfurt a.M., 1603)

> I was quite familiar with the three children born on the way because I was their midwife. The mother lies in no child-bed; instead she walks around and stretches out like a cat with its young.[58]

Oettinger's European contemporaries understood the pain of childbirth as a curse that marked all women descended from Eve. Women who bore children differently, seemingly without pain, might not possess the same humanity as Eve's Christian descendants.[59] This gendered and dehumanising perspective on African bodies was also part of Oettinger's education as he travelled from hinterland to metropole to colony.

At the end of the nineteenth century, when European colonialism in Africa was at its height and ideas of racial superiority had fully developed into a 'scientific' system, the question of slavery was, of course, considered in clearly different terms. In early modern times, one of the strongest factors in the consolidation of the idea of black inferiority was the emergence of slaveholder societies in the Americas based on the permanent reproduction of the 'colour line'.[60] By contrast, in the second half of the nineteenth century, when all European states had abolished both the slave trade and slavery, anti-slavery ideas were integrated into 'the catchall project known as the "civilising mission"'.[61] Thus, after maintaining intricate relations with slave-exporting African states for centuries and ultimately removing about twelve million enslaved Africans, slavery in Africa was now highlighted as one of the most evident signs of the Africans' 'barbarity'. Abolition became an ideological tool for the legitimation of the continent's conquest by European powers.

The literary retelling of Johann Peter Oettinger's journal, published in 1885–86 by his great-great-grandson Paul Oettinger, bears the signs of this contradiction. As noted above, the published text is far from being a faithful edition of the manuscript. Rather, the events and settings provided by the manuscript are transformed into a sort of historical novel. To enhance the pleasure of a popular readership, Paul Oettinger – who for decades worked as editor-in-chief of the *Deutsche Militärzeitung*, one of the many newspapers

---

58 'Reisebeschreibung und Lebenslauf', p. 21.
59 See Jenny Shaw, *Everyday Life in the Early English Caribbean: Irish, Africans, and the Construction of Difference* (Athens, GA, 2013), pp. 33–4, on claims that Irish, Native American and African women gave birth with little or no pain.
60 See most recently Cristina Malcolmson, *Studies of Skin Colour in the Early Royal Society. Boyle, Cavendish, Swift* (Farnham and Burlington, VT, 2013), and Andrew Curran, *The Anatomy of Blackness. Science and Slavery in an Age of Enlightenment* (Baltimore, 2011). The development is summarised in Robin Blackburn, *The Making of New World Slavery. From the Baroque to the Modern, 1492–1800* (London, 1998), pp. 307–50.
61 Adiele Eberechukwu Afigbo, *The Abolition of the Slave Trade in Southeastern Nigeria, 1885–1950* (Rochester, NY, 2006), p. 31. On the connection between anti-slavery and imperialism, see also Amalia Ribi Forclaz, *Humanitarian Imperialism. The Politics of Anti-Slavery Activism, 1880–1940* (Oxford, 2015).

published at that time for a military audience – transformed the rather dry
and often elliptic style of the barber-surgeon's annotations into exuberant
prose, evoking – in a quite stereotypic way – exotic landscapes and the harsh
but manly life of adventurous seafarers. To this end, various entirely invented
passages were added to the story, infusing it with the rhetoric of African
inferiority, enriched by common tropes taken from nineteenth-century
racist, pseudo-ethnographic discourse. Again, gender was a central to the
presentation of race.[62] On the one hand, African woman were depicted as
exploited by their men ('As in the case of most uncivilised people, women are
considered only as beasts of burden'); on the other, the African women are
imagined as thieving ('They have little concept of "mine and thine" and my
Negro women servant stole from me as well') and sexually voracious ('I found
the young Negresses not at all shy ... and I was more than a little astounded
by the coquettish arts of seduction used by these savages').[63] In other words,
Africa was represented as a world where neither male authority over women,
nor the material and carnal desires of women were disciplined by the norms
of civilisation. Again, it is important to note that these and similar passages
have no reference point at all in the original diary. They were entirely the work
of Paul Oettinger.

Paul Oettinger's agenda, however, was not only literary. He rewrote his
ancestor's diary with a clear political goal. The timing of his publication
makes this clear. After remaining inside the family for generations, the story
of Johann Peter Oettinger was for the first time presented to a broader public
in 1885 – the year of the Berlin Congo Conference and just a year after the
German Empire had entered the 'Scramble for Africa'. By publishing the
barber-surgeon's story under the title *Unter kurbrandenburgischer Flagge.
Deutsche-Kolonialerfahrungen vor zweihundert Jahren* (Under the Flag of
the Electorate of Brandenburg. German Colonial Experiences Two Hundred
Years Ago), Paul Oettinger joined the rapidly growing trend celebrating the
BAC as the precursor of modern German colonialism – a trend clearly aimed
at providing a historical basis for contemporary imperial politics.[64] The

62   On the link between gender and race in modern colonial culture, foundational works include
Malek Alloula, *The Colonial Harem* (Minneapolis, 1986); Anne McClintock, *Imperial Leather.
Race, Gender and Sexuality in the Colonial Context* (New York, 1995); Ann Laura Stoler, *Carnal
Knowledge and Imperial Power. Race and the Intimate in Colonial Rule* (Berkeley, 2002).

63   Oettinger, *Unter kurbrandenburgischer Flagge*, p. 45. This passage about the 'seductive
negresses' was further appropriated by Wilhelm Jensen, who integrated it into his own historical
novel on the BAC: *Brandenburg'scher Pavillon hoch! Eine Geschichte aus Kurbrandenburgs
Kolonialzeit* (Berlin, 1902); on this issue see Wolfgang Struck, *Die Eroberung der Phantasie.
Kolonialismus, Literatur und Film zwischen deutschem Kaiserreich und Weimarer Republik*
(Göttingen, 2010), p. 83.

64   Klaus-Jürgen Matz, 'Das Kolonialexperiment des Grossen Kurfürsten in der
Geschichtsschreibung des 19. und 20. Jahrhunderts', *'Ein sonderbares Licht in Teutschland'.*

Prince-Elector Frederick William, Benjamin Raule and other initiators of the
BAC were praised as heroes and integrated into German national history as
the first German colonisers of Africa. The appropriation of the BAC 'epos'
by the colonial culture of the *Kaiserreich* had to face, however, one major
problem: the basis of the company in the slave trade. In the seventeenth and
early eighteenth century it had been the 'foundation' of the company, but by
the end of the nineteenth century slavery was considered as an atrocity now
practised only by the 'inferior races' which European colonisers were called to
'civilise'. In the case of Paul Oettinger's literary manipulation of the barber-
surgeon's journal, the slave trade could not be obliterated, being the very
purpose of the voyage on the Brandenburg frigate that Johann Peter joined in
1692. Thus, to 'save' his ancestor and maintain him as a positive figure, Paul
Oettinger added another completely invented passage, in which Johann Peter
'writes' as a compassionate man, instinctively opposed to the cruelties of the
slave trade:

> what a chill of horror came over me, as I entered the places [on board
> the ship] in which the unlucky victims were kept, inhaling the horrid
> atmosphere in which they were forced to live ... and my heart convulsed
> when I was forced to watch as those who bore the shape of men were
> treated like animals.[65]

Paul Oettinger's text integrated the sufferings of the middle passage, which
had become (thanks to abolitionist literature) a central element in Western
discourse on slavery, into a new German colonial vision. Thus the account
of Johann Peter Oettinger offers us insights into the daily life in the Atlantic
world in the seventeenth century, but also allows us to follow the shifting
attitudes towards slavery in German culture, from the Old Regime to the late
nineteenth century.

*

The travel journal of Johann Peter Oettinger reveals a wealth of seldom-seen
connections between the Atlantic world and its seventeenth-century Germanic
hinterlands. It is a valuable source for the history of the BAC/BAAC, the most
significant attempt of a German state to participate in the slave trade. And
it is a significant document for the reconstruction of migratory, economic,
and cultural connections between this business and other German hinterland

---

Beiträge zur Geschichte des Grossen Kurfürsten von Brandenburg (1640–1688), ed. G. Heinrich
(Berlin, 1990), pp. 191–202; Adjaï Paulin Oloukpona-Yinnon, *Unter deutschen Palmen. Die
'Musterkolonie' Togo im Spiegel deutscher Kolonialliteratur (1884–1944)* (Frankfurt a.M.,
1998), pp. 69ff; Zaugg, 'Grossfriedrichsburg'.
65   Oettinger, *Unter kurbrandenburgischer Flagge*, p. 63.

areas.[66] These themes suggest that autobiographical texts and other sources of the history of everyday life are indispensable for our understanding of trans-continental contacts and exchanges. Study of the common people – individuals and families – who laboured to connect the early modern Atlantic to its various hinterlands can reveal far broader and more capillary connections than seen in the existing scholarship. Travel from the hinterlands to the Atlantic world meant an extraordinary new set of experiences, opportunities, and social interactions. The Oettinger journal reveals these connections, and their perception and representation by a young man working his way through – and investing in – the Atlantic economy.

66 Our research on Oettinger and his journal will produce two works. The first, a monograph by Roberto Zaugg, will contextualise and assess Oettinger's migration, his slave ship voyages and his cross-cultural contacts at the court of Savi in the West African kingdom of Hueda. This study will also examine how Oettinger's journal has been handed down by his descendants and manipulated during the late nineteenth century in the context of German colonialism. The second project will be an English edition of Oettinger's journal edited and introduced by Craig Koslofsky and Roberto Zaugg. This translation will make the journal more accessible for research and teaching.

2

'Citizens of the World': The Earle Family's Leghorn and Venetian Business, 1751–1808

ALEXANDRA ROBINSON

Studies of Liverpool slave-traders' account books have allowed us identify suppliers of trade goods and processors and refiners of slave-produced goods: they have demonstrated that the reach of the transatlantic slave trade went far beyond the local hinterland of port cities and that hinterland producers were in fact deeply embedded in transnational trade. The evidence offered by this study of the Earle Papers affords an opportunity to locate the activities of this slave-trading family beyond Liverpool and to identify the reach of that hinterland. Traditionally the slave trade has been seen as 'Atlantic' or 'colonial': this study of the Earles' Leghorn business makes a new case which supports the interpretation of the eighteenth century as a time of globalisation, in a world in which Liverpool and its slaving merchants are a driving force and, self-consciously, 'citizens of the world'. The trajectory of the Earle family's progress exemplifies the degree to which the slave trade was closely bound up with ancillary trades – that is, the production and procurement of trade goods and the refining and distribution of slave-produced goods – which penetrated not only the economy of the Atlantic basin but that of continental Europe and the proto-global economy altogether.

The main focus of this case study is the Leghorn business which was started up in 1751 – a key moment in Liverpool's rise and an indication of the self-confidence of the founding partners, Thomas Earle and Thomas Hodgson; Liverpool merchants had come of age. The decision of leading Liverpool slave-traders to establish merchant houses first in Livorno, and then in Genoa and Civitavecchia, may throw light not only on the continental European reach of the slave trade but also offers an example of the emergence of a new model of integration. The company was to become the leading British merchant house in Livorno. Equally, the founding of a subsequent company, in partnership with William Davenport, which would source beads from Venice used to buy men and women in Africa, is another example of an

Italian connection with the slave trade. A word about the sources: the Earle papers were collected in the late nineteenth century by T. Algernon Earle and donated to the Merseyside Maritime Museum in 1993. The records are of major significance for the history of Liverpool's slave trade; they include details of the outfitting of slave ships and the use of bills of exchange as well as ships' logs, one of which records a mutiny on board a slave ship.[1] As far as the scope of this case study is concerned, the collection, while invaluable, has its limitations and at best offers a glimpse of key moments in the operation of the Earle's concerns, best achieved for the 1760s via the letterbook of William Earle 23 January 1760 to 23 September 1761.[2] Unfortunately, there are no corresponding records for the Leghorn company at this juncture; here the records depend on the letters of Joseph Denham, Thomas Earle's one-time agent in Livorno (later in Genoa and Civitavecchia), but the majority of these were written in fact to Thomas Earle's wife.[3] Thomas Earle's side of the correspondence has not survived and would have been of greater value, prone as Denham was, even in his letters to Thomas Earle, to comment on the social and personal, rather than business matters. The same observation applies to the letters from Joseph Denham to his wife between 1762 and 1774, though perhaps with more justification.[4] The Partnership Papers of 1763 to 1836[5] reveal the range of the family's business interests and the degree to which vertical and horizontal integration were applied to the portfolio. The fuller record given by the letterbook for the Leghorn trade 1801–08[6] cannot be taken as representative, given the exceptional circumstances of the Napoleonic Wars, nor is it supported by documents relating to the Earles' wider portfolio, although the file entitled 'Correspondence of Thomas (junior), William (junior) and Willis Earle re Leghorn Business 1817', does make some contribution in that respect.[7] Merseyside Maritime Museum also holds the Business Papers of William Davenport & Co. for 1745 to 1797,[8] which are of great value since Davenport and William Earle, and later his sons, were regular partners in slaving voyages from the 1750s onward and partners in the Bead

1   Dawn Littler, 'The Earle Collection: Records of a Liverpool Family of Merchants and Shipowners', *Transactions of the Historic Society of Lancashire and Cheshire* 146 (1997), 93–106, here pp. 93–6.
2   National Museums Liverpool, Maritime Archive & Library (NMLMA), The Earle Papers (D/Earle): D/Earle/2/2 Letterbook of William Earle January 1760–September 1761.
3   NMLMA D/Earle/3/2, 1–32 Letters to Mr and Mrs Earle from Joseph Denham, Italy 1763–81.
4   NMLMA D/Earle/3/3, 1–16 Letters from Joseph Denham to his wife, 1762–1774.
5   NMLMA D/Earle/4/1–2 Partnership Papers 1763–1836.
6   NMLMA D/Earle/2/3 Letterbook regarding the Leghorn Trade.
7   NMLMA D/Earle/3/4/1–34 Correspondence of Thomas, William and Willis Earle re Leghorn 1817.
8   NMLMA D/DAV The Papers of William Davenport & Co., 1745–1797.

Company which was established in 1767, the records of which are included in the Davenport Papers.[9]

One of the difficulties encountered by historians of the slave trade is the lack of business records which would allow the study of Liverpool slave merchants' total portfolio. Some Liverpool slave-traders can be identified as almost exclusively involved in the slave trade – this accounts for some thirty merchants in the period from 1750;[10] the rest, though they may have at times made this their key activity, had other interests which sometimes took precedence. The lack of information about the slavers' other activities has made it difficult to identify the interrelationship between sectors and to estimate the extent to which the slave trade or the Atlantic trade as a whole penetrated the wider economy. David Richardson considers the trade with the American colonies as 'the most dynamic component of the external trade sector from 1660 onward',[11] and it was slave-produced goods which were central to that trade. Nicholas Draper, investigating the impact of slavery on the City of London, has traced the flow of profits from the trade into the banking, insurance, manufacturing and transport infrastructure of the developing British economy. He concludes that although slavery was not the dominant sector in the British economy 'it was more important than any other domestic or foreign sector in stimulating industrialization'.[12] The figures indicate that one-third of London's and two-fifths of Liverpool's and Bristol's economic activity were slave trade related.[13]

Previous studies of Liverpool slaving merchants have focused on their slaving activities, determining the scale and respective profitability of the slavers,[14] or the market structure, composition and organisation of the

9   NMLMA D/DAV/2/1–3 Bead Cash Book.

10   Brian W. Refford, 'The Bonds of Trade: Commerce and Community in the Liverpool Slave Trade, 1695–1775' (unpublished dissertation, Lehigh University, 2005).

11   David Richardson, 'The British Empire and the Atlantic Slave Trade, 1660–1807', *The Oxford History of the British Empire*, vol. 2: *The Eighteenth Century*, ed. P. J. Marshall (Oxford, 1998), pp. 440–54.

12   Nicholas Draper, 'The City of London and slavery: evidence from the first dock companies, 1795–1800', *Economic History Review* 61 (2008), 432–66.

13   According to Draper, what is most significant is the importance of the slave economy in terms of financial activity: it accounted for a significant proportion of the liquidity in London; in 1797 the narrow slave economy (not including plantation trades) accounted for almost 30 per cent of overseas paper, and over 10 per cent of total London liquidity. If we include the plantation trade the share would increase to 44 per cent of overseas bills and 21 per cent of the total. As he argues, 'The London-based financiers, whether merchant creditors or bankers, had thus become part of an integrated credit system which was dependent on slavery and the continuation of slavery was in turn driven by the logic of the credit system's needs.' Ibid., p. 451.

14   Roger Anstey, *The Atlantic Slave Trade and British Abolition 1760–1810* (London, 1975); David Richardson, 'Profits in the Liverpool Slave Trade: The Accounts of William Davenport, 1757–1784', *Liverpool, the African Slave Trade and Abolition*, ed. R. Anstey and P. E. H. Hair (Liverpool, 1976), pp. 60–90; Nicholas J. Radburn, 'William Davenport, the Slave Trade, and

slave-trading community.[15] The Earle papers offer a broader picture of the way in which the slave trade permeated business over three generations, and via the Earles' Italian house it allows a glimpse of the way in which the Atlantic trade was intertwined with the continent of Europe.

Liverpool: Capital of the Slave Trade

Outstripping London and Bristol in the 1740s, by the last quarter of the eighteenth century Liverpool became the world capital of the slave trade. Liverpool's merchants were responsible for 55 per cent of British slaving voyages between 1750 and 1780, and 75 per cent between 1780 and 1807.[16] By this time, Liverpool was the leading outport in the British Atlantic, 'perhaps the most important in the Atlantic trade'.[17] This rapid expansion can be attributed to a combination of factors, notably locational advantages including a hinterland that was both a producer and a market, and an infrastructure that supported growth. Liverpool ships had the relative safety of a northern passage which gave them access to the free port of the Isle of Man (till 1765) and Irish provisioning. A merchant oligarchy operated with remarkable cohesion undertaking the building of the first open, commercial, wet dock in Europe (1715) and investing in an emerging system of docks and canals. This made Liverpool the best-served port in Britain, crucially connected from the 1730s to Manchester and the nascent textile industry with access to coal from the Lancashire coalfield and salt from the Cheshire plain, and with iron and guns from the Midlands. However, it should be noted that London finance was vital to financing the Liverpool slave trade throughout the period.[18] Cotton cloth (originally re-exported from India until Manchester copies entered the frame), guns, gunpowder, glass beads, iron goods and salt were key slave trade goods specifically identified and itemised by African traders; access to the right goods was vital to the success of the slaving voyage. Equally Liverpool's capacity to process, refine and distribute slave-produced goods was a major advantage.

Merchant Enterprise in Eighteenth-Century Liverpool' (unpublished MA Thesis, Victoria University of Wellington, 2009).
15 Steve Behrendt, 'Human Capital and the British Slave Trade', *Liverpool and Transatlantic Slavery*, ed. D. Richardson, S. Schwarz and A. Tibbles (Liverpool, 2007) pp. 66–97; Sheryllynne Haggerty, *Merely For Money? Business Culture in the British Atlantic, 1750–1815* (Liverpool, 2012); Refford, 'The Bonds of Trade'.
16 Richardson, 'The British Empire and the Atlantic Slave Trade', p. 446.
17 Haggerty, *Merely For Money?*, p. 5.
18 Richardson, 'The British Empire and the Atlantic Slave Trade', p. 446.

A Family Concern

This study focuses on the Leghorn business in relation to the trading activities of the Earle family. In the first instance, this was made up of the three Earle brothers: the eldest brother Ralph (1715–90), but more especially Thomas (1719–81, known as Thomas of Leghorn; Fig. 2.1) and the youngest brother William (1721–88), since they were co-partners in almost all their concerns.[19] Thus we can see the connections between the slaving ventures and the distribution of Atlantic slave-produced goods, and get a feel for how they perceived the direction of their businesses, where they saw opportunities and how they responded to them. This involves looking at a third company, a classic case of vertical economic integration: created solely for the supply of beads and cowries to slave-traders, it was known as the William Davenport & Co. Bead Company or, in Venice, as the Liverpool Company. The Leghorn business was the springboard for this new departure in the sourcing of trade goods. It was a partnership of seven: the three Earle brothers, Thomas Earle's Leghorn partner Thomas Hodgson, an Earle brother-in-law John Copeland and two others who were regular Earle partners in slaving ventures, William Davenport and Peter Holme. Davenport was the banker and account keeper for the concern but Earle & Hodgson & Co. effected the greatest number of transactions.

Three generations of the Earle family were directly involved in the slave trade, making 374 investments in 176 voyages and were responsible for the forcible transportation of 126,318 Africans across the Atlantic.[20] John Earle senior (1674–1749), was co-owner of Liverpool's first recorded slaving voyage in 1699 and was responsible for half the Liverpool slaving voyages in the first twenty years of its involvement in the slave trade. Earle was one of a number of merchants who hailed from Warrington, eighteen miles from Liverpool.[21] Incoming merchants like Earle brought with them connections which helped shape the patterns of trade from Liverpool, drawing on Irish provisioners, the textile and gunpowder producers from Cumbria, the cotton and linen producers of South Lancashire, the salt refiners of Cheshire and the

19 NMLMA D/Earle/4/1–2 Partnership Papers 1763–1836.
20 Calculations made for the WYRES (Warrington Humanities Network, International Slavery Museum, Warrington Museum) project 2010, using the Trans-Atlantic Slave Trade Database (http://www.slavevoyages.org), cross-referenced with figures in Appendix 1 of David Pope, 'The Wealth and Aspirations of Liverpool's Slave Merchants', *Liverpool and Transatlantic Slavery*, ed. D. Richardson, S. Schwarz and A. Tibbles (Liverpool, 2007), pp. 164–226 (Appendix pp. 194–207); the figures refer to individual investments in voyages made by the members of the Earle family.
21 Warrington was the subject of the WYRES project cited in note 20. Researched in collaboration with students from six Warrington schools, it is the only project to date on Liverpool's immediate hinterland.

Figure 2.1. Thomas Earle of Leghorn. Oil, School of Baton, n.d.

copper manufacturers of Cheshire, North Wales and South Lancashire. But the activities of the Earle family in their various guises allow us look further afield to locate the hinterland implicated by the slave trade.

Describing themselves as 'wine' or 'iron merchants', or 'Levant' and 'Italian' merchants, the sons and grandsons of John Earle exploited to the full the trading opportunities afforded by the slave trade and the Atlantic trade. The 176 voyages were just one facet of their related enterprises, but, by the mid eighteenth century, the slave trade had become the key to virtually all their concerns. John Earle's ironmongery business was passed on to his third son, William Earle: ironmongery figures strongly in the bills of lading for barter goods in his slave ships but he also supplied other slave merchants with Guinea kettles, shackles and manacles in the main, and also the ironwork required to outfit the ships themselves. By the 1760s William and Thomas Earle were dealing in enslaved Africans and trade goods for their purchase, and were involved in the refining distribution and re-exportation of slave-produced goods to the continent of Europe. They and their close business partners, such as Hodgson, Davenport and Copeland were successfully integrating all their interests.

The market in slaves and in Atlantic slave-produced goods rose dramatically in the 1760s, and the available finance for investment was marked after the end of the Seven Years War in 1763. The acquisition by Britain of territories in the Caribbean (Dominica, Grenada, Saint-Vincent and the Grenadines, and Tobago) promoted a new phase in settlement, one which was even more acutely exploitative. That year Ralph Earle went into partnership with his brother's Leghorn partner, Thomas Hodgson, in a sugar refinery in the Haymarket, Liverpool. In 1766 all the Earle brothers of the second generation formed another syndicate, but an entirely novel one, to source beads and cowries at the lowest possible cost and to supply them to their own slave ships and to the Liverpool slave-trading community. Beads for the slave trade had been commonly freighted to the Isle of Man where they were warehoused duty free until collected by Liverpool slave-traders. In 1765 the Isle of Man's free port status had been terminated by the I.O.M. Purchase Act which brought it into the British customs system. Within three years the Liverpool Bead Company was supplying 48 per cent of the beads to English slave merchants – that is, of all beads re-exported from England.[22]

Syndicating the slave ventures was a feature of the slave trade and this company had transferred the principle to the sourcing of trade goods (iron and beads) and to the refining and distribution of slave-produced commodities. In this case the syndicate may have been confined to seven partners but the finance

22   Saul Guerrero, 'Venetian Glass Beads and the Slave Trade from Liverpool 1750–1800', *Beads. Journal of the Society of Bead Researchers* 22 (2010), 52–70, here p. 55.

came from the wider Liverpool merchant community.[23] The Bead Company was extremely profitable over a relatively short period from 1766 to 1780: it may be regarded as exceptional, or at least a new departure in business practice and an example of the extraordinarily fast response of this group of Liverpool traders to changing economic conditions, something to which we will return to later.

As far as the Earles' business was concerned, by 1767 they had covered almost all the bases. Applying both vertical and horizontal integration they had reduced risks and competition and strengthened the family concerns. Thomas Earle died in 1781 and his brother William retired in 1788, passing on his and his brother's companies to his sons, Thomas (1754–1822) and William (1760–1839). The result was a formidable company, T. & W. Earle & Co., which went into partnership with another successful slave-trader, Thomas Molyneux. Molyneux ran an iron company, so the Earles now had direct access to the iron bars which were particularly sought by traders on the Gold Coast. The shipping records show disbursements to Earle of Redcross Street and Earle & Molyneux, supplying the iron bars and ironmongery to their own and other slaving ventures.[24]

The Leghorn/Livorno Context

At this point it is useful to consider Livorno's historic connections with the slave trade and the history of British commercial connections there. Constructed between 1573 and 1617, Livorno had one of the first enclosed docks in the world with sophisticated warehousing and quarantining. The creation of a safe wet dock was not the only thing that Liverpool and Livorno had in common: in 1739 the Tuscan Secretary of State refers to the rapid rise of Livorno – arguing here it should remain free:[25]

> It is enough to be persuaded of this [if you reflect] that Livorno was only a swamp while thanks to the security promised and granted in the privileges of the Free Port, it has become in less than a century one of the most important cities in Italy and the only source of income for the state.[26]

23   The Bead Cash Book records repayment of funds to Liverpool slave-traders, as much as £1,000 per person, which had been used to finance the company start-up.
24   University of Liverpool Library, Special Collections and Archives (ULSCA), Liverpool Trade and Shipping 1782–1919, Dumbell Papers, MS 10. 48, e.g. supplying *The Golden Age*, Captain Joseph Fayrer, in 1784; ULSCA, Liverpool Plantation Papers (Schofield) DP179 D514/1/25 ii, Ledger of ships.
25   It acquired free port status in 1590.
26   Giulio Rucellai, 11 August 1739, cited by Francesca Bregoli, 'Jewish Scholarship, Science, and the Republic of Letters: Joseph Attias in 18th-Century Livorno', *ALEPH. Historical Studies in Science & Judaism* 7 (2007), 97–181, here p. 170.

This had been the Medici's strategy in the seventeenth century and it had paid off: the privileges extended to foreign traders meant that Livorno became the key port for the whole of Italy, acting as an entrepôt, redistributing cargoes in the Mediterranean and linking Europe with the colonial markets of the Americas. With the encouragement of the Medici this transit trade was carried out largely by foreign merchants. For Jewish merchants, who numbered approximately 15 per cent of the population in 1735, these privileges meant they lived freely in the town and not, as elsewhere in Italy, in a ghetto. There were some Tuscan exports – textiles, marble, coral and Leghorn hats. Of course the Italian contribution to the development of the Atlantic market was long-standing in terms of technology and capital: from the seamen and their skills in navigation to the Italian bankers who funded the empires of the Portuguese and Spanish in the sixteenth century.

There was, then, a well-established pattern of Atlantic imports into Livorno over the sixteenth and seventeenth centuries, supplied by the Portuguese in the first instance, but in the seventeenth century the Dutch and the British were plying slave-produced products such as sugar, coffee, spices, silver and dyewoods from the Americas, and ivory, gold, pepper and captive Africans from Africa. A sugar refinery was constructed in Livorno in 1622 and one in Genoa in 1630, but it was the North Atlantic which stole the initiative in the seventeenth century. Some would argue that at this stage the southern Mediterranean was relegated to the periphery of world trade, but the market remained attractive. Re-exports from the Americas were a major component of British trade in the port of Livorno and from there they were distributed to Genoa, Venice, Civitavecchia, and ports in the Levant and North Africa. The value of British exports (including re-exports) to Italy had been rising steadily, doubling in the first half of the eighteenth century, but in the ten years after the opening of Earle & Hodgson & Co. they more than doubled again (1756, £278,000; 1770, £746,000).[27] English merchants had been a considerable presence in Livorno since the beginning of the seventeenth century, referred to as the 'English Factory'; they had a cemetery there from 1623. By the last quarter of the eighteenth century English merchants in the virtually free port of Livorno (which they called Leghorn), which operated neutrality from the mid seventeenth century,[28] were supplying all of Italy and Sicily, and to a considerable extent the Levant, with British manufactures.[29]

27   Elizabeth Boody Schumpeter, *English Overseas Trade Statistics, 1697–1808* (Oxford, 1960), p. 17.
28   Livorno was declared neutral in 1646, sanctioned by the treaty of London 1718.
29   J. B. Williams, *British Commercial Policy and Trade Exports 1750–1850* (Oxford, 1972), p. 39.

Earle & Hodgson & Co.: Leghorn, Genoa and Civitavecchia

The market for Atlantic goods was well established when Thomas Earle opened his merchant house in 1751 with its headquarters in Leghorn and a branch at Genoa, then a further one in Civitavecchia in 1768. The business of the Leghorn house and its connections with the slave trade have largely gone unnoticed or were thought to have been restricted to the company's purchase of beads. The family biographer does give a clue to the Atlantic connection: the Leghorn business 'sent home to them all the produce of Italy ... Their chief trade seems to have been in coffee, oil, pimentos, hides and marble' – but his emphasis is on the marble: 'the fine white marble for sculpture and ornamental purposes, the first of which ever imported to Liverpool was sent by Mr Earle'.[30]

He omits the regular distribution or re-export of West Indies sugar, tobacco, cocoa and indigo, as well the supply of beads directly to slaving vessels. The business records reveal that the company was servicing slave-produced commodities and supplying trade goods for the slave trade, and apart from the Earle partners, there are references to other Liverpool slavers present at Leghorn, such as John Hardman and John Bolton whom Denham mentions in his correspondence. In connecting with the merchants of Livorno, Earle & Hodgson & Co. had gone global, trading with the slave-produced goods of the Atlantic, bringing in silk from Tuscany and Venice and the Levant, beads from Venice, cotton from the Levant, cowries from the Maldives and local coral from the coast around Livorno.

Entries in the 1801–08 letterbook show Earle & Hodgson & Co. dealing in Atlantic goods, despite the troubled international situation: On 16 December 1801, Earle & Hodgson & Co. write from Liverpool to advise Hodgson in Livorno that '2 ships are nearly ready to sail for Italy':

The Mercury for Genoa and Leghorn
    38 boxes Havana sugars, 3 casks and 72 bags of St Domingo coffee, 75 bags of ginger, 4 puncheons of Jamaica rum, fine flavoured, 10 hogsheads of Virginia tobacco.
    The Testimony, for Naples and Leghorn 30 chests of white and 20 of brown Havana sugar, 13 casks of very good coffee, 55 boxes and 1 tierce of Havana sugar for Messers Naylor also under your care for Naples if a better price there, ... suspect tobacco will do better there (Genoa).[31]

Earle also adds an order for Leghorn hats and fabric, and several orders for marble, all for slave-traders – Mr Parke of Highfield, Liverpool, and Mr Gregson, also of Liverpool.

30 T. Algernon Earle, 'Earle of Allerton Tower', *Transactions of the Historic Society of Lancashire and Cheshire* 42 (1890), 15–76, here pp. 41–2.
31 NMLMA D/Earle/2/3 Letterbook 1801–1808 regarding the Leghorn Trade.

Earle & Hodgson & Co. acted for other companies in the sale of slave-produced goods, but there is also evidence that they acted on their own behalf: via records of a number of ships held in the Dumbell Collection we can find that T. & W. Earle & Co. have consignments of slave-produced goods brought in to Liverpool on, for example, Leyland and Bullin ships.[32] The details of the business for that period are useful to a degree but not fully representative given the disruption caused by the Revolutionary Wars; even the brief period of peace, 1802–03, was hardly business as usual. Earlier in 1796, during the French Revolutionary Wars, the French seized Livorno and twenty British merchants were forced out of the port: in the case of Earle & Hodgson & Co., which was now Earle, Hodgson & Drake (the new partner being John Drake of Chester), they were fortunate to have their agent, Giuseppe Fantecchi, *in situ*, though business was drastically reduced.

The details of the company's business in the early years are less well evidenced in the extant papers and it may never be possible to deduce exactly what proportion of the Earles' business was dedicated to procuring trade goods for the African trade or servicing slave-produced goods. However, for the later period we can identify some of their suppliers either in or into Leghorn and, in the case of Venetian beads, estimate the effect of the market on that declining economy. Earle & Hodgson & Co. transactions can also be traced in the Bead Company records. And of course the Leghorn business should not be seen in isolation; Thomas and William Earle (senior) were copartners and their activities were complementary if not entirely enmeshed. Therefore, the modus operandi has been to explore the records of both companies – that is William Earle & Co. and Earle & Hodgson & Co., side by side. This is a necessary strategy given the gaps in the remaining records of Earle & Hodgson & Co.

William Earle was described variously as a 'ship's husband', a slave-trader or a Levant trader, ship-owner and ironmonger. Over his thirty-four-year career as a merchant he invested £98,000 in 117 slaving voyages and was the tenth largest Liverpool slave-trader of his generation (1740–90). Initially, as the third son, he was 'apprenticed to the sea', then rose to command slave ships and work in partnership with major slavers like William Davenport (the seventh largest slave-trader in Liverpool).[33] He inherited his father's ironmongery business in Redcross Street, Liverpool, which became his headquarters. His early years as a slave ship's captain were of inestimable value to the two companies, and in particular his knowledge of the nuances of the African end of the enterprise. In 1753 he invested in his first co-venture in the *Grampus* and in the following year, the *Mercury*, which we can see being fitted out for Livorno with Earles' ironmongery from his own company

32   ULSCA, Liverpool Trade and Shipping 1782–1919, Dumbell Papers, MS 10. 51.
33   Radburn, 'William Davenport', p. 108.

at Redcross Street.[34] The details of William Earle's trade are best evidenced in his letterbook for January 1760 to September 1761.[35] This window on William Earle's business is limited to only twenty months, but its 267 letters include correspondence with over sixty different contacts, ranging from fish traders from all over Britain and the Isle of Man, to Italian bead merchants, London bankers and West Indian slave factors. It is of enormous value when set alongside the Leghorn correspondence and the records of the William Davenport Bead Company.

William Earle records that the cargo loaded onto the *Mentor* for a voyage to Whydah (today Benin) in September 1761 includes '2000 [pieces of] silitias [linen], 20 tonnes of cowries and 40 boxes of pipes'[36] – that is, cane pipes which were cut and polished to create the famous *conterie* beads from Murano, Venice.[37] A letter from Liverpool of 20 February 1760 shows him dealing in Aleppo beads and a basket of Leghorn Nandoes (beads) via Peter Abraham Lucard,[38] and four more orders for the same in February and March; at the same time he is buying sugar from the Liverpool slave-traders Sparling and Bolden, and buying and selling Africans on his own account.[39]

In 1760, at the start of the letterbook, William Earle had already invested in twelve slaving voyages and in the twenty months covered by the letterbook he invested in seven voyages. The pattern of trade demonstrated in these intense twenty months, combined with what we know of his slaving ventures from the Trans-Atlantic Slave Trade Database,[40] reveal his understanding of the way the acquisition of cargo for purchasing Africans worked; this would be the key to the development and exploitation of the bead trade. Writing to one of his bead suppliers, Peter Abraham Lucard, he observed 'the want of them [beads] for assortment may ruin a voyage'.[41] Beads were an attractive component of the so-called barter basket: A. G. Hopkins referred to slave ships as 'floating

34   NMLMA D/DAV/2/1, entry for 28 October 1754.
35   NMLMA D/Earle/2/2 Letterbook of William Earle January 1760–September 1761. The majority of the letters are addressed to suppliers and bankers about the procurement of and payment for trade goods, and to agents about the sale of enslaved Africans.
36   NMLMA D/Earle/2/2 Letterbook of William Earle January 1760–September 1761, William Earle to William and James Manson, 22 September 1761. On linen textiles as trade goods, see chapter 4 in this volume.
37   See note 56 below for evidence that the unfinished canes were also being used as such or possibly finished in West Africa.
38   NMLMA D/Earle/2/2 Letterbook of William Earle January 1760–September 1761, William Earle to Peter Abraham Lucard, 20 February 1760.
39   For the parallel transactions see respectively NMLMA D/Earle/2/2 Letterbook of William Earle January 1760–September 1761, W. Earle to Sparling and Bolden, 9 April 1760 and 20 February 1760.
40   Trans-Atlantic Slave Trade Database (http://www.slavevoyages.org).
41   NMLMA D/Earle/2/2 Letterbook of William Earle January 1760–September 1761, W. Earle to Peter Abraham Lucard, 19 September 1760.

Figure 2.2. Venetian trade beads, seventeenth/eighteenth century

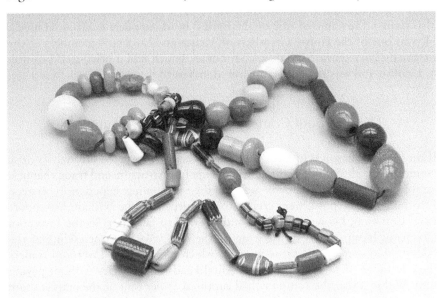

supermarkets', while S. B. Alpern declares 'glass beads were among the all-time bestsellers, with many billions landed in barrels, cases and casks from start to finish of the slave trade'.[42] But more than this, William Earle is alluding to two things that were key to the operations of that particular set of African traders: the fact that at the point of sale, where traders are in direct competition, success depends on the suitability of the cargo being recognised, and also that it must be recognised quickly. As he declared, 'dispatch is the life of everything'.[43] The deal had to be done sharply, and the fast turnaround was famously what gave the Liverpool traders the edge.

Beads were an established long-term item of trade to Africa and the mark-up on the beads tended to make them the most profitable trade goods, alongside gunpowder and arms. Using two account books for the voyages of *Earl of Liverpool* in 1797 and 1798, Saul Guerrero has compared the prime cost of the main barter cargoes with the barter value achieved in the bight of Bonny in West Africa: gunpowder and beads increased their value, while firearms retained their original value; textiles and iron and brassware, on

---

42 A. G. Hopkins, *An Economic History of West Africa* (London, 1973), p. 11; S. B. Alpern, 'What Africans Got for Their Slaves', *History in Africa* 22 (1995), 5–43, here p. 22.
43 NMLMA D/Earle/2/2 Letterbook of William Earle January 1760–September 1761, W. Earle to Isaac Dove, 22 April 1761.

the other hand, lost one-third, one-sixth and one-half of their value, respectively.[44] The account books of the *Earl of Liverpool* in the Dumbell papers also furnish the name of one of the Earles' bead suppliers – Mr A. Fonseca. He was one of the Fonseca brothers of Venice and Livorno – members of the originally Portuguese Sephardic community, which had a privileged position in Livorno and was strongly represented in Venice.[45]

The Liverpool Company and its Venetian Suppliers

If the Leghorn business of Earle & Hodgson & Co. prospered through its close connection with William Earle & Co., so the infrastructure and trade channels established by the former, as well as their freighting experience between Livorno and Liverpool, were crucial to the success of the William Davenport Bead Company, known in Venice (and referred to hereafter) as the Liverpool Company. It appears to spring from nowhere in 1766 after the ending of the Isle of Man's free port status in 1765, which had allowed Liverpool traders the advantage of re-exporting continental beads and cowries without paying duty. Within a year the company had captured 27 per cent of the market share of bead exports to Africa.[46] The correspondence of Earle & Hodgson & Co. is testimony to the importance of the company, with bead agents in London requesting to be involved with it, and the connections which Earle, Hodgson and Copeland had via the Leghorn business are the common denominator. The tendency has been to associate the Bead Company with Davenport since he kept the accounts and sold out to John Copeland in 1772 (although the articles of partnership are in the Earle, rather than the Davenport Collection, while the Bead Cash Book and Bead Account Book and Ledger are in the latter). Close examination of the accounts, however, shows how much of the business came from Earle & Hodgson & Co. directly, or via their contacts, especially in terms of sourcing. Irrespective of the relative contributions of the partners, on the face of it the Bead Company looks like an excellent piece of marketing on the part of Earle, Davenport *et al*. But there is another element to the equation which Guerrero has explored – that is the part played by Venetian agents in capturing direct trade with the Liverpool Company and the degree to which there was government intervention both there and in Britain.

By 1768 English bead re-exports relied heavily on the Bohemian supply and to a lesser degree on the Dutch. It is clear that the Venetian suppliers were actively seeking to win the Liverpool Company's orders. The Venetian

44   Guerrero, 'Venetian Glass Beads', pp. 59–60.
45   ULSCA, Liverpool Trade and Shipping 1782–1919, Dumbell Papers, MS 10. 50, 51, 52.
46   Guerrero, 'Venetian Glass Beads', p. 55.

Resident in London, Conte de Vignola, had been making overtures to the Liverpool Company since 1767 and these show up in the report of one of the Venetian *Inquisitori alle Arti* to the *Serenissimo Principe*, Paolo Querini, 6 September 1767: 'Many have been the approaches that ... our Resident has made to the British Court with the purpose of introducing a direct trade of glass beads ... to the British Nation.' He continues: 'Vignola ... proposes to his Excellency a trade with the Company of Liverpool ... of glass beads from Venice – a word that in English covers not only what we call in Venice the *contarie* [*sic*] but also the manufacture of *suppialume* [*perle a lume*].'[47]

The Venetian focus was on the quality of the goods; the Liverpool Company was motivated by cost, and they went with the Bohemian suppliers until, in 1768, problems with the Rhine river tolls held up deliveries. Venetian suppliers had already been successful earlier that year in getting a large consignment worth £988 for the Bead Company carried on the *Polly*, a Davenport ship; the whole cargo in this case was insured for £2,811.[48] De Vignola continued to press for more and negotiated a deal which involved lobbying the British government; he managed to secure Parliamentary approval to warehouse Venetian beads for re-export duty free for up to five years. Venetian quality still meant the cost was 5 per cent higher than for goods from Bohemian suppliers, but the Bead Company was aware of the importance of quality in the African trade. John Copeland, referring to a large purchase of Venetian beads via the London bead agent, Peter Thellusson, commented that he found them to be 'of a good kind' though 'rather small'.[49] Thomas Hodgson seemed to go along with this: 'the Venetian beads are not only well made but superior to [the beads] made in Bohemia'.[50] De Vignola also offered the Liverpool Company good terms of credit – eighteen months – which was not common for Venetian traders who usually dealt in cash.

The records do not continue in such detail after 1776, by which time Davenport had handed over to John Copeland following the failure of the company banker, Joseph Wimpey of London. David Richardson has estimated that the company sold beads to the value of £39,000 up to July 1770,[51] and the turnover of at least £10,000 a year continued until the market was disrupted by the crash of 1780–81, from which the bead market appeared not to recover; the price per pound of beads more than doubled after 1781 (from nine pence in 1768 to two shillings in 1782).[52] Clearly more work needs to be done here but the evidence from alternative sources such as the

47 Guerrero, 'Venetian Glass Beads', p. 52.
48 NMLMA D/DAV/2 Bead Cash Book.
49 NMLMA D/DAV/6/11. Letters to William Davenport re the Bead Business.
50 Guerrero, 'Venetian Glass Beads', p. 54.
51 Richardson, 'Profits in the Slave Trade', p. 63.
52 Guerrero, 'Venetian Glass Beads', p. 57.

Dumbell Papers and the contested claims from Willis Earle in 1817 show bead consumption continuing on the part of Liverpool slave-traders.[53] Guerrero suggests that the men who were the driving force behind the Bead Company, Davenport and Thomas Earle, were out of the picture after 1782 and this may well be the reason for a change in direction in the case of Earle & Hodgson & Co. which was subsumed into T. & W. Earle & Co. in 1788.[54]

How far the bead purchase via Earle & Hodgson & Co. in the first instance, and the later partnership of the Liverpool Company after 1766, affected the Venetian glass bead industry may only be indicated at this stage. At a time of relative Venetian decline, the glass sector had doubled in size during the second half of the century. Glass beads specifically rose from 7 per cent to 70 per cent of the total of Venetian glass exports from the end of the sixteenth century till the end of the eighteenth.[55] There is evidence that political intervention played some part in encouraging and preserving this export and that the historic strengths of superior Venetian technology and quality were not to be sacrificed despite competition, specifically from the French, the Bohemians and the English. The efforts of the Venetians to secure Liverpool patronage of their glass trade, and the concessions awarded to the Earles (the Venetians certainly knew what the beads were for), show that they had no moral scruples about it either. To what extent can we extrapolate from this to view Venice directly, and Leghorn to a lesser degree, as having a stake in the slave business?

There is evidence of early Venetian involvement in bead supply to Africa and it was long established in West Africa in particular. Although there was no indigenous glass production prior to the slave trade, an indigenous trade in beads pre-dated the first direct European contact and there is evidence of glass-working in West Africa using imported glass. In his *Description and Historical Account of the Kingdom of Guinea* (1602), Pieter de Marees gives the example of imported beads being modified in Elmina, Ghana, where he witnessed the polishing of imported beads and the firing of glass chips and powdered glass.[56] These beads were imported into West Africa, prior to the slave trade, via the trans-Sahara trade route, and the trade in them was a significant contributor to the emergence and prosperity of Ghana and Mali in the eighth and thirteenth centuries, and to the kingdoms of Benin and Akan

53   ULSCA, Liverpool Trade and Shipping 1782–1919, Dumbell Papers, MS 10. 50, 51, 52; NMLMA D/Earle/3/4/1–34, Correspondence of Thomas, William and Willis Earle re Leghorn 1817.
54   Guerrero, 'Venetian Glass Beads', p. 56.
55   Ibid., p. 53.
56   He describes Venetian pipe beads and short pieces of glass cane from Murano being worn as a string of beads round the knees, and that people come down to the coast from other states to buy them. He reports Ghanaians breaking the glass canes into four or five little pieces, and polishing them: Pieter de Marees, *Description and Historical Account of the Gold Kingdom of Guinea*, trans. Adam Jones and Albert van Dantzig (Oxford, 1987), pp. 34, 53, 80.

in the sixteenth century. Excavations of grave goods in the Kingdom of Kongo (Lower Congo) from the fifteenth to the nineteenth centuries associate burial of glass beads with high-status figures.[57] European export of glass beads as trade goods in the slave trade was not, therefore, a new trading pattern, but an example of the way slave trade goods integrated into existing networks. B. L. Anderson makes reference to an African bead specialist, Solomon D'Aguilar, who operated in Liverpool in the 1760s.[58] Evidence from archaeological sites indicate that Venetian and Dutch glass were the first sources for beads introduced by slave-traders, but by 1750 the Dutch glass industry had collapsed and de Marees comments as early as 1602 that the majority of European beads brought to Ghana were Venetian.

Venice in the mid seventeenth century was the most advanced industrial city in Europe with glass-making, naval construction, and textile, chemical and metallurgical production; it was the entrepôt for the whole Mediterranean.[59] Its secret processes were carefully though not successfully guarded, and the stamp of quality was closely protected. The survival of the glass industry during its so-called decline in the eighteenth century reveals that the Venetian economy was more layered than it might first appear. It has been estimated that glass items as a whole constituted the most important commodity shipped from Venice.[60] The old 'quality' glass products – large mirrors and 'cristallo' – suffered particularly from French and Bohemian competition and went into decline, but bead exports increased to fill the gap, making up 'about three quarters of the main glass export revenues' in the second half of the eighteenth century.[61] As early as 1728, the French philosopher Montesquieu observed that in the *Fondamenta dei Vetrai* (the road in Murano which housed the glass furnaces) eighteen of the furnaces were producing 'glass and glass beads [*verroteries*] for the negroes'.[62] In 1752 the French consul reported 2,500 people involved in glass bead-making in Murano; by 1780 it had risen to 6,064.[63]

Guerrero asks how the Venetian bead-makers managed to compete with

57   Christopher R. DeCorse, *An Archaeology of Elmina: Africans and Europeans on the Gold Coast from 1400 to 1900* (Washington, DC, 2001), p. 189.
58   B. L. Anderson, 'The Lancashire Bill System and its Liverpool Practitioners', *Trade and Transport: Essays in Economic History in Honour of T. S. Willan*, ed. W. H. Chaloner and B. M. Ratcliffe (Manchester, 1977), pp. 59–97, here p. 72.
59   Richard Rapp, 'The Unmaking of the Mediterranean Trade Hegemony: International Trade, Rivalry and the Commercial Revolution', *Journal of Economic History* 35 (1975), 499–525.
60   Francesca Trivellato, 'Murano Glass, Continuity and Transformation, 1400–1800', *At the Centre of the Old World: Trade and Manufacture in Venice and the Venetian Mainland*, ed. P. Lanaro (Toronto, 2006), pp. 143–77, here p. 163, citing Jean Georgelin.
61   Guerrero, 'Venetian Glass Beads', p. 63.
62   Charles-Louis de Secondat, Baron de La Brède et de Montesquieu, *Voyage en Italie*, *Voyages de Montesquieu*, ed. A. de Montesquieu, 2 vols (Bordeaux, 1894), vol. 1, pp. 19–276, here p. 32.
63   Trivellato, 'Murano Glass', p. 163.

other European producers when the rest of the glass sector was in decline. He suggests that the glass canes which were used to make the beads were actually mass-produced and exported to France, for example, to be finished there.[64] So Venetian beads, and canes for the making of beads, destined for the slave trade, were supplied Europe-wide. The export of the unfinished canes shows a sustained demand driven by the slave trade, and the export – whether it indicates that local (Italian) finishers could not satisfy the demand or simply that the French were able to make a good offer for the unfinished canes – shows that trade fuelling productive cross-border interchanges in continental Europe. In arguing that glass beads had become the mainstay of industrial Venice by the late eighteenth century, Francesca Trivellato makes explicit that the history of Venetian glass 'is thus no longer only the story of the precious objects conserved in museums all over the world, but also, indeed above all, the story of the *perline di vetro* (the glass beads), destined for the slave trade'.[65] She indicates the difficulty in dealing with the history of the fine objects which are eulogised in the accounts of Venice in its prime, their purpose to buy the liberty of millions of Africans. This is all the more invidious, she indicates, since her study also establishes that these beads were most likely fashioned by women.[66]

Private Conscience and the Slave Trader's Mindset

The wide range of documents in the Earle Collection, including travel journals for example, also furnish glimpses of the mindset of the slave-traders. William Earle senior, the ship's husband, reveals his antipathy towards the reality of this trade. In a letter to, his fiancée, he wrote in 1751:

> The Calabars are very difficult. I had my cloathes torn off my back since I arrived. … If they will let me get well out of the river I think to never lay it in their power to hurt me again. I carefully avoid any disputes with them. … I am so surfeited with their insolence this time I fear that tho' I had made no protestations to you not to go again, my own inclination would be the same and [to] retire[d] from this overbusy noisy trade.[67]

Ten years later William Earle had extricated himself from the role of ship's husband. In a much-cited letter of 1761, he offered reassurance to a Calabar trader, Duke Abashy, whose two sons had been 'erroneously' enslaved:

64   Guerrero, 'Venetian Glass Beads', p. 64.
65   Francesca Trivellato, *Fondamenta dei Vetrai: Lavoro, tecnologia e mercato a Venezia tra Sei e Settecento* (Rome, 2000), p. 183 and back cover.
66   Ibid., p. 4 and Parte Seconde, VII.
67   NMLMA D/Earle/3/1, W. Earle to Anne Winstanley, 30 August 1751.

We have not yet heard from the schooner being brought in to Frenchman's port as I told you before. I make no doubt of getting your boys back from Frenchman's as they are all free men and no slaves. ... You know very well I love all Calabar and do not want to wrong, nor ever did I wrong any man one copper. If your two boys be living I will get them for you

'[A]s they are all free men and no slaves': William Earle seems very clear himself about the difference between the slave and the free man, but what the criteria are and how he reconciles the anomalous nature of his thinking, remain unspoken.[68]

In 1808, while folding up Earle & Hodgson & Co., Thomas Earle junior wrote lamenting the state of affairs with the abolition of the slave trade and the resumption of the Napoleonic Wars; he talked of transferring into trade with Brazil. He wrote from London, 18 January 1808, to Signor Luigi in Lisbon: 'Many are looking towards the Brasil trade but as yet it wants arrangement.' It is most likely that Earle was thinking not of the illegal slave trade (in which a number of Liverpool merchants continued to operate following abolition) but the legal trade with Brazil which Liverpool pursued very successfully after 1807. In any case there is no evidence here of moral qualms on the score of the trade in human lives itself. Later on the same year he wrote to Mr John Cailler, a former agent with Earle & Hodgson & Co., in Lisbon: 'We are sorry to hear ... your present situation is become so destitute of employment – for you who are a *citizen of the world*, to remain inactive is very hard.'[69] It has been suggested that when William Davenport retired from the slave trade and indeed all trading activities in 1786, entering instead the market for financial securities, it may have been partly in response to the challenge posed by abolitionist critics of whose activities in Liverpool he must have been aware.[70] There is no indication that Thomas and William Earle viewed their trading activities with any regret. Rather, in their own eyes their trade rendered them pillars of society, now connected through marriage to the local grandee, the Earl of Derby, and they were truly 'citizens of the world'.

---

68 NMLMA D/Earle/2/2, W. Earle to Duke Abashy, 10 February 1761. Reprinted in Paul E. Lovejoy and David Richardson, 'Letters of the Old Calabar Slave Trade, 1760–1789', *Genius in Bondage: Literature of the Early Black Atlantic*, ed. V. Carretta and P. Gould (Lexington, KY, 2001), pp. 89–115, here p. 99.
69 NMLMA D/Earle/2/3 Letterbook 1801–1808 regarding the Leghorn Trade.
70 Radburn, 'William Davenport', p. 29.

3

Basel and the Slave Trade:
From Profiteers to Missionaries

PETER HAENGER

Translated by Eve Rosenhaft

More than ten years ago the participation of Swiss businesses in the trans-atlantic slave trade was the subject of a number of initiatives in the Swiss federal parliament (Nationalrat), as well as in some of the cantonal parliaments. The parliamentary interpellations were linked to the 2001 UN conference in Durban, South Africa, at which there was a debate on African demands that former slave-trading nations provide compensation. In September of that year Jean-Daniel Vigny, then the Swiss human rights representative at the UN, had observed that such demands presented no problem for Switzerland, since Switzerland had 'had nothing to do with slavery, slave trade or colonialism'. The parliamentarians who raised the question insisted that there was no way in which such a moral 'blank check for Switzerland' could be justified, given the energetic opportunism of Swiss merchant houses in the period of the trade.[1]

In answer to the parliamentary questions the Swiss federal government (Bundesrat) did not deny that 'various Swiss citizens' had been 'involved to a greater or lesser degree in the transatlantic slave trade' – a fact which the Bundesrat 'most deeply regrets'. But the government also insisted that Switzerland had 'never been a colonial power' and in that sense differed fundamentally from the colonial powers 'at the level of responsible action'.[2]

1   See for example the interpellation of Pia Hollenstein in the Nationalrat, 5 March 2003, http://www.parlament.ch/d/suche/seiten/geschaefte.aspx?gesch_id=20033014 (accessed 28 February 2016).
2   Most recently, Harald Fischer-Tiné pointed out in the *Neue Zürcher Zeitung* (18 November 2014) that 'the development of trade and industry in Switzerland during the nineteenth century' was characterised by the 'disproportionately large significance of overseas trade and in particular of the export of Swiss products to colonies (or former parts of colonial empires that

The participation of Swiss individuals in the slave trade was thus admitted, while at the same time a clear distinction was made between the responsibility of the state and public authorities on the one hand and that of private individuals and firms on the other. The Bundesrat was making clear that official Switzerland bore no guilt for the tragedy of the slave trade.

In addition, the Bundesrat recalled in its statement that Switzerland had helped to frame the declaration and the action plan that emerged from the World Conference against Racism in Durban. Both documents characterise slavery and the slave trade, apartheid and genocide as 'crimes against humanity'. Moreover, the Swiss government declared that 'injustices perpetrated [in Switzerland] in the era of colonialism and slavery [must] be critically acknowledged and processed'.[3]

A critical response to the past was indeed a long overdue, since Jean-Daniel Vigny's statement echoed the official Swiss version: How could a small country, far from the Atlantic coast and with no colonial history, have been involved in the slave trade?[4] In the light of the 2004 bicentenary of the establishment of the Haitian republic, which led to the UN declaring it the 'International Year of Commemoration of the Fight against Slavery and its Abolition',[5] a number of studies were produced focusing on the Swiss involvement in the trade. Among these were two general accounts, one by Thomas David, Bouda Etemad and Janick Marina Schaufelbuehl and one by Hans Fässler.[6] I wrote a third study together with Niklaus Stettler and Robert Labhardt. It examines the business activities of three generations of the Basel merchant family, the Burckhardts, in the period of revolutionary ferment between 1780 and 1815. The case study shows that Swiss merchants were firmly tied into international networks at the end of the eighteenth century and consequently took part in the slave trade though geographically removed from its centres. However, the maritime conflict between France and England between 1792 and 1815 led many of these businessmen to turn their attention to their nearer hinterlands,

had become independent)'. In view of the fact that asymmetrical imperial power relations are grounded mainly in economic dominance, Fischer-Tiné refers to a 'secondary imperialism' in the case of Switzerland.

3   Reply of the Bundesrat to the interpellation of Pia Hollenstein, 16 June 2003, http://www. parlament.ch/d/suche/seiten/geschaefte.aspx?gesch_id=20033014 (accessed 28 February 2016).

4   See the article by Konrad J. Kuhn and Beatrice Ziegler, 'Die Schweiz und die Sklaverei: zum Spannungsfeld zwischen Geschichtspolitik und Wissenschaft', *Traverse* 16 (2009), 116–30.

5   Although 2004 marked the Haitian bicentenary, the commemorative year was declared not on the island itself but in Cape Coast, Ghana. The Cape Coast fort was a centre of the transatlantic slave trade, in which enslaved men and women were held in cells awaiting their 'transshipment' to the Americas.

6   Thomas David, Bouda Etemad and Janick Marina Schaufelbuehl, *Schwarze Geschäfte. Die Beteiligung von Schweizern an Sklaverei und Sklavenhandel im 18. und 19. Jahrhundert* (Zurich, 2005); Hans Fässler, *Reise in Schwarz-Weiss: Schweizer Ortstermine in Sachen Sklaverei*, 2nd edn (Zurich, 2006).

becoming financiers of local industrialisation.[7] The following account draws on the results of our investigations and our German-language publications.

The Burckhardt Company Archives

Between 1789 and 1812 the firm Christoph Burckhardt & Cie., with its headquarters in the Segerhof in Basel, carried on a worldwide wholesale trade in textiles, cotton goods and dyestuffs, but also in colonial goods such as sugar, coffee and cocoa. Set up by Christoph Burckhardt-Merian (Fig. 3.1), the firm managed most of its trade in colonial goods through Bourcard Fils & Cie., a firm founded in Nantes in 1790 by the second son of the family, Christophe. But the firm Christoph Burckhardt & Sohn created by Christoph Burckhardt-Vischer, father of Burckhardt-Merian, was already engaged in the trade in textiles and colonial goods in the first half of the eighteenth century.

The business activities of the various Burckhardt companies constitute an important chapter in the history of Basel and of Switzerland. But for a long time economic historians showed little interest in the company archives of the three firms, known as the 'Segerhof archives', although they have survived in their entirety. One reason for this is the extremely opaque structure of the archive. Any researcher has to fight their way through tens of thousands of business letters, many of them formal and repetitive, and to attempt to decipher a form of bookkeeping that is very difficult to understand. Moreover, the first attempt to put the archives in order, undertaken by Carl Burckhardt-Sarasin (a great-grandnephew of Burckhardt-Merian), provided a second reason for researchers' neglect. It is clearly the result of a massive investment of time, but hardly offers a usable path through the jungle of files. Burckhardt-Sarasin's innumerable transcriptions and bland summaries of the sources, often strung together in confused and patchy ways, repeatedly frustrate scholarly analysis of Segerhof documents. Anybody working on the history of the Burckhardt family companies can hardly avoid speculating on the motives that guided his organising hand.

In 1948, once the Segerhof correspondence and bookkeeping records had

<hr/>

7   Niklaus Stettler, Peter Haenger and Robert Labhardt, *Baumwolle, Sklaven und Kredite. Die Basler Welthandelsfirma Christoph Burckhardt & Cie. in revolutionärer Zeit (1789–1815)* (Basel, 2004); Peter Haenger and Robert Labhardt, 'Basel und der Sklavenhandel. Das Beispiel der Burckhardtschen Handelshäuser zwischen 1780 und 1815', *Suisse–Afrique (18e–20e siècles): De la traite des Noirs à la fin du régime de l'apartheid*, ed. S. Bott, T. David, C. Lützelschwab and J. Marina Schaufelbuehl (Münster, 2005), pp. 25–42; Niklaus Stettler, 'Regionalisierung trotz Globalisierungsstrategie: Die Grosshandelsfirma Christoph Burckhardt & Cie. in Basel und ihre Tochtergesellschaft Bourcard Fils & Cie. in Nantes 1789–1813', *Globalisierung – Chancen und Risiken: Die Schweiz in der Weltwirtschaft 18.–20. Jahrhundert*, ed. H.-J. Gilomen, M. Müller and B. Veyrassat (Zurich, 2003), pp. 99–111.

Figure 3.1. Christoph Burckhardt-Merian (1740–1812). Oil, August Friedrich Oelenhainz, 1795

been donated to the Swiss Business Archives (*Wirtschaftsarchiv*) in Basel by the Burckhardt family, the then Director of the archives entrusted the organising and cataloguing of the files to Carl Burckhardt-Sarasin.[8] It was at this point that he discovered that his forebears had not been simply the solid merchants whom he would have been happy to memorialise to the glory of the family. Rather, the old Burckhardt firms had been involved in the trans-atlantic slave trade for decades and had had no compunctions about providing equipment for pirate ships and smuggling operations. Information that could besmirch the family's honour could of course not be made accessible. Fear of exposing the family and indeed the whole of the bourgeois elite to the attacks of their political opponents in the city began to be the driving force in Carl Burckhardt-Sarasin's historical work.

Thus, in one of his reports to the director of the Wirtschaftsarchiv, he wrote that he had to 'fulfill the urgent wish of the family' to protect 'every trace' of his ancestors' 'participation' in the slave trade from 'potential exploitation by unauthorised persons'.[9] With the agreement of the archive administration he proceeded to place all compromising files in sealed boxes. And in his historical writing Burckhardt-Sarasin devoted not a single word to the involvement of his forebears in the slave trade.

Year after year Burckhardt-Sarasin conscientiously ordered the letters from the Segerhof archive. He filed the whole set of incoming correspondence – about 100,000 business letters – in 350 boxes. He prepared abstracts of the contents of the letters and compiled them under keywords. Here too, 'consideration for the family' dictated that under the keyword 'slave trade' he reported only on those files that he had not put under seal. And in 1953, on his eightieth birthday, the University of Basel granted him an honorary doctorate in acknowledgement of his archival and historiographical achieve-ments. Only after Burckhardt-Sarasin's death in 1971 were the sealed boxes in the Segerhof archive opened and made available to researchers.[10]

---

8   Schweizerisches Wirtschaftsarchiv (SWA), PA 444.71, Carl Burckhardt-Sarasin, 'Aus der Geschichte der Grosshandelsfirmen und Indiennes Fabriques Christoph Burckhardt & Sohn in der Goldenen Müntz und dem Ernauerhof, Christoph Burckhardt & Cie. Im "Sägerhof" mit seiner Nanter Filiale' (unpublished MS, Basel, 1951).

9   SWA, HS 420, A, Carl Burckhardt-Sarasin, Arbeitsberichte, Rapport für das erste Quartal 1959.

10   The implication of his ancestors in the slave trade troubled Carl Burckhardt-Sarasin so much that he made some notes justifying the slave trade under the title 'The treatment of the slaves' and included them with the sealed files. In his notes he maintained that the kidnapping of African men and women by 'Arabian slave traders' was carried out with 'dreadful acts of cruelty', but after their purchase by European traders 'the slaves had generally been treated quite well'. He based his claims on the memoirs of the Prussian slave-trader Joachim Nettelbeck. According to Burckhardt-Sarasin, Nettelbeck had 'provided for good sanitary arrangements, good sleeping and recreational spaces and healthy, plentiful food on his ships'. 'Above all,' Burckhardt-Sarasin argued, still citing the Prussian slave-trader, Nettelbeck had provided 'for

But, even after the release of all the sealed files, scholarly interest in the
Segerhof archive remained limited. International slavery research neglected
the role of the 'hinterlands', and in Switzerland the slave trade was not a topic
anyway. It was only in 1983 that the Basel Africanist Hans W. Debrunner,
who was principally interested in the activity of Swiss in the colonial context,
published an article on Bourcard Fils & Cie. in Nantes and the slave ship
Intrépide. The English historian Patrick Crowhurst worked with material
from the Segerhof archive, but he was primarily interested in smuggling and
state-licensed piracy and less in the Burckhardts' slave business. Similarly,
Peter Fierz's dissertation on the family's shipping operations was essentially a
study in business history. Although Fierz undertook to assess the profit that the
Burckhardts gained from the slave trade and piracy, the results were inconclusive
because many of the final accounts from individual expeditions are missing.[11]

Late-Eighteenth-Century Basel and the
Burckhardts' Indiennes Business

Let us take a look at the city of Basel towards the end of the eighteenth
century. One of the first censuses carried out there showed that 15,040 people
were living in the city in 1779. This made Basel the second largest city in
the old Swiss Confederation; only Geneva had more inhabitants, probably
more than 20,000. In comparison with the European metropolises these were
modest figures; the population of Paris was more than half a million in 1800.[12]
   Of Basel's 15,040 inhabitants 6,856 were male and 8,184 female; they lived
in 3,569 households, in 2,120 houses. Although the city enjoyed a long period
of civil peace before the revolution of 1798, there were significant divisions and
inequalities. Only half of the residents, 7,607 men and women, were citizens of

physical exercise' by the captives in the form of 'gymnastics and performing their national
dances' – the latter in order 'to keep the slaves in good spirits': SWA, HS 420, N 4, Notizen von
Carl Burckhardt-Sarasin zur Sklavenschiffahrt.
11   Hans W. Debrunner, 'Basel und der Sklavenhandel – Fragmente eines wenig bekannten
Kapitels der Basler Geschichte', *Basler Stadtbuch 1993* (Basel, 1994), pp. 95–101; Patrick
Crowhurst, 'The Effect of War on the Swiss Cotton Trade: Christophe Burckhardt of Basle
1793–1810', *Textile History* 18/1 (1987), 17–32; Patrick Crowhurst, *The French War on Trade:
Privateering 1793–1815* (Aldershot, 1989); Peter Fierz, *Eine Basler Handelsfirma im ausgehenden 18. und zu Beginn des 19. Jahrhunderts: Christoph Burckhardt & Cie. und verwandte
Firmen* (Zurich, 1994).
12   Wilhelm Bickel, *Bevölkerungsgeschichte und Bevölkerungspolitik der Schweiz seit dem
Ausgang des Mittelalters* (Zurich, 1947), pp. 61–3; and Wilhelm Bickel, *Bevölkerungs-Ploetz,
Raum und Bevölkerung in der Weltgeschichte*, 4 vols (Würzburg, 1955), vol 2, pp. 12, 28. In
the eighteenth century the city of Basel had the lordship of rural areas surrounding the city
amounting to an area of about 380 square kilometres with about 23,000 'subjects'. Serfdom was
only abolished in 1795 under the influence of the French Revolution.

the city. Only male citizen guildsmen had the right to exercise a *Handelsschaft*, or free trade or business. They alone were *regimentsfähig*, qualified to hold political office, and they alone were able to buy land and houses without the express permission of the City Council. Residents of the city who didn't possess the Basel citizenship were called *Hintersassen* and were completely excluded from political life. They were prohibited from carrying out a trade or profession independently, and they had to pay an annual fee that was scaled according to social status and the amount of property they owned. The majority of *Hintersassen* scraped by as household servants or day labourers.[13]

In the Middle Ages, the guildsmen, with their monopoly of independent economic activity, had constituted the only significant economic force, but commercial practices were changing. Technological innovations like the ribbon loom made larger-scale production possible. Emerging systems of manufacture based on subcontracting and putting-out competed with artisanal production and eroded the foundations of the guild system. They could not be integrated organically into a social structure that depended on the jealously guarded privileges of particular occupational groups.

While the craft producers remained limited by their specialisation and small workshop production deploying a few journeymen, merchants had enjoyed a considerable expansion of their scope for activity since the seventeenth century. They invested in long-distance trade and in textile-printing works known as Indiennes factories. They lent money, handled bills of exchange or ran large transport businesses. The merchant could no longer be confined to any particular sphere of activity or occupational group; rather, he was a long-distance trader, factory owner, merchant-manufacturer, and banker all in one. In the eighteenth century that kind of all-round entrepreneur was called a *marchand-fabriquant-banquier*. The fact that the city was still ringed by its medieval walls stood in strange contrast to the global trade connections of Basel's merchants.

Political power had been becoming concentrated in the hands of ever fewer families since the seventeenth century. Some of these were old-established families like the Burckhardts, and some were the descendants of Huguenots like the Sarasins who had been forced to flee France after the revocation of the Edict of Nantes in 1685. The circle to which these families belonged was largely closed to outsiders. Marriages were carefully arranged so as to maintain social status and exclusivity. They used their power to press forward the erosion of the old guild system: while the guildsmen were able to prevent the establishment of large manufacturing establishments within the city walls,

---

13 Emil Schaub, *Aus dem Leben des Basler Kaufmanns im achtzehnten Jahrhundert, 94. Neujahrsblatt der GGG* (Basel, 1916); Claudia Opitz, 'Von der Aufklärung zur Kantonstrennung', *Basel. Geschichte einer städtischen Gesellschaft*, ed. G. Kreis and B. von Wartburg (Basel, 2000), pp. 150–85.

outside the walls the merchants maintained Indiennes factories drawing on an extensive pool of day labourers.

Wealthy Basel merchant families indulged in an opulent lifestyle, although the City Council regularly issued sumptuary regulations aimed at limiting luxurious indulgence. Elegant rococo residences, clothing with expensive silk and lace trimming, and luxuriously appointed coaches displayed their business success and refined taste. Hefty bills were run up for the orders of meat, wine and spices that were regularly delivered to merchant houses. And while ordinary people made do with local produce, wealthy Baslers enjoyed tea, coffee and chocolate from the far corners of the globe.

Between 1650 and 1720 fashion in clothing was dominated by the 'Indian wave'. Indiennes were cotton fabrics, printed using techniques originally developed in India and then adopted and adapted in Europe. The Indiennes produced by this method, also known as *Kattundruckerei* (cotton printing) or *Zeugdruck* ('print stuff', i.e. cloth), were brightly patterned and colourfast. They were very popular in the eighteenth century and used for a wide range of purposes: clothing, wallpaper and upholstery.

In Basel the rise of Indienne production was driven by the arrival of Huguenot refugees from France. A year after the revocation of the Edict of Nantes, the French government introduced a strict ban on the importation, production and use of printed fabrics. The purpose was to protect the domestic textile industry, based mainly on linen and woollen cloths, from foreign competition. As a result, Basel, Neuenburg, Bern, Zurich and Biel became the centres for Indienne production in Europe. The Huguenots brought with them knowledge about new production techniques which guaranteed greater efficiency in the printing of the cloth.[14]

In the following century Indienne production became one of the most important export businesses in Basel, alongside silk ribbon- and stocking-weaving. The *Basler Handlungs-Schema*, an early trade directory of 1789, lists no fewer than twenty-two ribbon factories, most producing for export, twelve stocking factories and six Indienne factories.[15] The key element of the Burckhardts' business activities was the trade in textiles, and especially in the coveted Indiennes. The firm's periodic inventories show that the Burckhardts held many fabrics and textiles as well as dyes for printing cotton in their warehouses. The actual production and printing of their textiles was carried

14   See André Holenstein, 'Globale Ökonomie in lokalen Kontexten. Die Bedeutung der Indiennes-Produktion für die Schweiz im 18. Jahrhundert', Tobias Kaestli, 'Indiennes-Fabrication in Biel von 1747 bis 1842' and Ariane Koller, 'Begehrte Konfliktstoffe. Eine kurze Geschichte der Indiennes', all in *Textilkunst im 18. und 19. Jahrhundert. Wirtschaftswachstum dank Sklavenhandel?*, ed. cooperaxion.org, http://www.cooperaxion.org/_wp/wp-content/uploads/2012/01/kurzref_publ_online_312.pdf (accessed 28 February 2016).
15   Staatsarchiv Basel-Stadt (StA BS), Basler Handlungs-Schema 1789.

out by the Rosenburger family, who had an Indienne factory and produced exclusively for the Burckhardts on a piecework basis. According to a surviving 'accord' between the Burckhardts and Peter Rosenburger, Rosenburger processed 7,272 lengths of Indienne, 4,614 patenas (more highly coloured prints) and 10,586 handkerchiefs, at a total cost of 50,836 Gulden.[16]

Other sources tell us that from 1785 onward the Burckhardts had shares in the textile printing and weaving business of Johann Jakob Zürcher in Cernay (Alsace). The reason for expanding into Alsatian territory was a ban on the import of foreign textile products that was introduced in France at that time. The Cernay production seems to have been quite significant; an inventory of 1790 shows more than ten thousand lengths of white and printed cotton cloth, whose total sale value was estimated at over 50,000 Taler.[17]

At the end of the eighteenth century there were probably three hundred printers and engravers employed in the six Basel Indienne factories, alongside an unknown number of auxiliary workers. It seems very likely that most of the skilled printers and engravers were not citizens of Basel, but *Aufenthalter* whose right to reside in the city depended on the their employers' goodwill and payment of a cash security. As a rule there were no written contracts, but only verbal agreements of employment.[18]

The labour market for Indienneurs, the skilled printers and engravers without whom the new textile production businesses could not survive, was regulated by the government. The City Council made both the flight of such workers and poaching of labour by employers punishable by law.[19] This combination of dependence on employers' goodwill and legal constraints on seeking better conditions kept wages low. The Indienneurs slaved for more than twelve hours a day in the factories, handling chemicals that damaged their health. In good times they probably earned enough to support themselves and their families. In large families though, survival depended on the work of the wife and children. And a period of price inflation could mean disaster for the family of an Indienneur.[20]

---

16   SWA, HS 420, G 1.2, Peter Rosenburger & Söhne, Basel, Cto. Crt. für Lohndruckerei und Appretur, 1755 bis 1799. Translator's note: The handkerchief (*mouchoir*) was a large square scarf or kerchief, a standard item of apparel for European men and women, and often worn on the head in Africa. Up to sixty handkerchiefs were printed onto a single length of fabric, to be cut into individual items by the retailer or purchaser (Information courtesy of John Styles, University of Hertfordshire).

17   Historisches Museum (Hist. Mus.), 1988.255, Inventar der Christoph Burckhardt & Sohn (hereafter CBS) im Haus zur Goldenen Müntz 1790.

18   Christian Simon, *'Wollt ihr euch der Sklaverei kein Ende machen?' Der Streik der Basler Indiennearbeiter im Jahre 1794* (Allschwil, 1983), pp. 11, 47.

19   Hist. Mus., 1901.188, Mandat des Basler Rathes vom 10. März 1753. Erlassen zu Gunsten der Indienne Fabrik des Emanuel Ryhiner.

20   Simon, *'Wollt ihr euch der Sklaverei kein Ende machen?'*, p. 43.

Getting into the Slave Trade

Indiennes were seen as the main barter goods in the triangular trade. 'No good deal on slaves without Indiennes' was a catchphrase in Nantes, France's principal slaving port. Printed cottons produced in Europe were very popular with African slave-traders and rulers. In 1759 the embargo on Indiennes was lifted in France, and from the 1760s onward citizens of Basel and Neuenburg ran Indienne factories in Nantes. Among these were also establishments run by Huguenot pioneers in the industry who had returned to France. Some 80–90 per cent of the Indiennes manufactured in Nantes were produced by manufacturers who had their origins in Switzerland.[21] And it was the business connections to these Swiss compatriots and co-religionists that made it possible for the Burckhardts to enter the slave trade.

In La Rochelle, for instance, the Basel brothers Emmanuel and Nicolas Weis fitted out ships for the transatlantic slave trade; in Nantes, the Baslers Georges Riedy and Benjamin Thurninger had their main office, with branches in Brest and Lorient. Between 1783 and the outbreak of the French Revolution Riedy & Thurninger fitted out ten slave ships and supplied Indiennes for the slave trade to the merchant house Thurninger frères & Cie. Riedy & Thurninger even had a branch on Saint-Domingue which organised the sale of captured Africans to the planters there.[22] Benoît Burcard, a distant relative of Christoph Burckhardt-Vischer, was a shareholder in the respected merchant house Pelloutier, Bourcard & Cie. in Nantes from the late 1770s onward. This firm, too, was active in the slave trade and ran the *négrier* (slave ship) *Comte de Tréville*.[23]

Since trading in enslaved people was an extremely risky business in the late eighteenth century and called for substantial amounts of capital, the costs of a voyage were usually spread across a number of investors. Between 1789 and 1793, the costs of equipping a slave ship in the port of Nantes was estimated to be at least 100,000 livres, but the costs could easily be four times that amount. One-half to two-thirds of the cost was made up by the cargo destined to be bartered for African captives.[24] On top of that, advance pay for the crew had to be provided, food purchased and insurance paid. In order to spread the costs and risks as widely as possible, ship-owners sent prospectuses about planned voyages to business partners, who could then purchase *Actions*, or shares in the

---

21   David, Etemad and Schaufelbuehl, *Schwarze Geschäfte*, pp. 25f, 56f.

22   Louis Dermigny, 'Négociants bâlois et genevois à Nantes et à Lorient au XVIIIe siècle', *Mélanges d'Histoire Économique et Sociale en hommage au Professeur Antony Babel*, 2 vols (Geneva, 1963), vol. 2, pp. 39–56; Edouard Delobette, *Ces Messieurs du Havre. Négociants, commissionnaires et armateurs de 1680 à 1830* (Caen, 2005), p. 225.

23   Markus A. Denzel, *Der Preiskurant des Handelshauses Pelloutier & Cie aus Nantes (1763–1793)* (Stuttgart, 1997), p. 436.

24   Olivier Pétré-Grenouilleau, *Nantes au temps de la traite des Noirs* (Paris, 1998), p. 69.

enterprise represented by paper certificates. Between 1761 and 1807, investors could hope for an average return of 9.5 per cent on their capital.[25]

In all, the three Burckhardt firms took part in twenty-one slaving journeys; if we presume an average of 350 captives per journey, the Burckhardts participated in the forcible transportation of 7,350 men and women from Africa to the Caribbean.[26] Historians have estimated a mean mortality of 15 per cent among those transported in the French slave trade.[27] If we accept these figures, roughly 1,100 people lost their lives in the slaving enterprises in which the Burckhardts were involved.

The sources on the three firms do not make it possible to calculate the profits made on individual slaving voyages. All that has survived are the periodic inventories of Christoph Burckhardt & Sohn, which provide information about assets remaining at the end of each year. Mention of slaving enterprises in the correspondence of the successor firm Christoph Burckhardt & Cie. barely helps to clarify the situation, since balance sheets for specific aspects of business that began before the outbreak of the French Revolution are incomplete or non-existent.

That said, there is clear evidence for the amounts invested in individual slave ships by the three firms. This usually amounted to about 10,000 to 15,000 livres per expedition. But it could be as much as 20,000 livres, as in the case of the slaver *Maréchal de Mouchy*, which set sail in 1783.[28] All in all, during the period in question the three firms invested some 400,000 livres in the transatlantic slave trade. In addition to this there were the warehouses that the Burckhardts maintained in the establishments of various French slavetraders. The family calculated their value at 30,000 livres in 1790.[29]

The existence of those warehouses points to the fact that the Burckhardts were not simply interested in direct profits from their shares in slaving expeditions. As owners of Indienne factories they had their eye on the West African markets, where there was a significant demand for light printed cotton fabrics. In the case of the slave ship *Conquérant*, in which the Burckhardts' share was just 10,000 livres, we know that the family gave 450 bolts of Indienne, coloured green-yellow and purple-yellow, to the Le Havre shipowners Mangon Laforest & Cie. as part of the cargo, on commission for sale in Angola. In addition, the holder of an *Action* was entitled to a share of cargoes returned from the Caribbean.[30]

25   Albert Wirz, *Sklaverei und kapitalistisches Weltsystem* (Frankfurt a.M, 1984), p. 34.
26   Ibid.
27   Ibid., p. 38.
28   SWA, HS 420, G 1.3,15, Extrait des Comptes d'Interets sur divers Navires, 1774–1787.
29   Hist. Mus., 1988, 255, Inventar der CBS im Haus zur Goldenen Müntz 1790.
30   SWA, HS 420, E 1, Briefkopierbücher der Bourcard Fils & Cie. (hereafter BFC), Vorgeschichte, 1789–1790.

The Establishment of a Firm in Nantes
and the *Intrépide* Fiasco

As was usual at the time, the second son of Christoph Burckhardt-Merian, Christophe (Fig. 3.2), had spent part of his training as a merchant abroad. On 11 February 1890 Christophe Bourcard – then in Nantes – wrote to his uncle Jean Battier in Basel: 'I asked my father in my last that I wanted to settle down here ... My growing business activities really make it necessary. I'll essentially stock India goods, especially for printing and the kind that are suitable for the slave trade.'[31] Christophe's letter shows that the firm Bourcard, Legrand & Cie., later renamed Bourcard Fils & Cie., was founded with the exclusive purpose of taking part in the Atlantic trade in cotton, slaves and colonial goods. Christophe had no intention of drawing a large number of investors into his new company. Rather, his plan was that only family members and trusted business partners of his father should be involved as investors with limited liability. On 30 April 1791 the firm in Nantes was already showing a balance of about 300,000 livres. The capital came mainly from Basel investors.[32]

In spite of the fact that the slave trade was still prospering in France around 1790, trading relations with Saint-Domingue, France's most important colony, were a growing worry for Nantes merchants. In 1790 they invested more than 10.5 million livres in slave voyages. Commodities bought in the Antilles in turn made up more than three-quarters of the value of goods traded locally in Nantes.[33] Dependent on the trade in slaves and colonial goods, the merchants of the city now had to fear the revolutionaries in the capital who were calling for the abolition of slavery in the name of human and civil rights.

The merchant communities in Atlantic port cities proceed to defame abolitionists as malign incendiaries aiming for the economic ruin of countless people in France. An alliance of merchants and colonial plantation owners put so much pressure on the National Assembly in Paris that it held back from the general emancipation of the slaves. In protest against the continuation of slavery and the slave trade, the slaves on Saint-Domingue revolted, leading to ten years of conflict which nearly put an end to trade between France and the colony.

In Nantes, Bourcard completely misread developments in the Caribbean. He was counting on a rapid improvement in the general situation, ignoring the many voices in revolutionary France that were denouncing slavery as incompatible with the ideas of civilisation and progress, and the most fundamental principles of humanity. He only considered the slave trade in terms of

31   Ibid.
32   SWA, HS 420, F 289.3, Bourcard, de Laure & Le Grand, Nantes, 1791, Inventaire générale.
33   Pétré-Grenouilleau, *Nantes au temps de la traite des Noirs*, p. 153.

Figure 3.2. Christophe Bourcard (1766–1815). Drawing, Anonymous artist, c.1780

profit. Thus his letter of 24 December 1791 ended with optimistic remarks about the state of the market:

> Cargoes and equipment for the slave trade are generally too expensive, but Blacks fetch high prices in St Domingue. In our experience, they can be sold in Port-au-Prince for 2200 to 2500; you even hear that the best looking ones fetch up to 3000, but those are the absolute elite of the slave cargo.[34]

This was the point at which Christophe Bourcard succeeded, after complicated negotiations with Nantes businessmen, in becoming the responsible owner of the slave ship *Intrépide*.[35] Bourcard invested more than 100,000 livres in the slave ship, abandoning the caution of his father and grandfather, who had restricted their commitments to the purchase of a limited value in shares in individual slaving expeditions.

The story of the slave ship *Intrépide* illustrates how far the slave trade had become a lottery by the end of the eighteenth century, and particularly in the wake of the French Revolution. She sailed from Nantes on 8 January 1792 with instructions to acquire four hundred Africans in Old Calabar on the West African coast, sell them in Saint-Domingue and return to France with colonial goods. The strength of British competitors in the Old Calabar slave markets meant that the ship had to wait offshore for a full year, rather than the usual four months. The length of the wait had disastrous consequences: epidemics of smallpox and diarrhoea broke out, and both African captives and crew members died. In April 1793 the *Intrépide* set off across the Atlantic. A form signed by the captain notes the purchase of 240 individuals in all.

Normally slave-traders reckoned with a mortality of 10–15 per cent among Africans in transit and framed their insurance policies accordingly. In the end, though, the *Intrépide* expedition suffered a mortality rate of over 70 per cent. As a result of the slave revolt in Saint-Domingue the *Intrépide* had to dock in Cayenne in French Guiana. But her arrival there came at an unfavourable moment, because the revolutionary government in Paris had banned the slave trade in July 1793. The result was the rapid fall of prices for slaves and the surviving African captives on the *Intrépide* had to be sold very cheaply. Bourcard Fils & Cie. lost about 125,000 livres on the *Intrépide* expedition; the project represented an enormous miscalculation for Christophe Bourcard.[36]

34   SWA, HS 420, F 289.5, BFC to Christoph Burckhardt & Cie. (hereafter CBC), 24 December 1791.
35   Ibid.
36   SWA, HS 420, N 2, Dokumente zum Sklavenschiff *Intrépide*, 1792–1802.

The Continuation of the Slave Trade in
the Face of Moral Objections

Bourcard Fils & Cie. in Nantes never recovered from the *Intrépide* fiasco. Until it was dissolved in 1815 the firm remained dependent on financial support from its parent company in Basel. In spite of their bad experience Bourcard and his business partners did not give up hope of succeeding in the slave trade. In February 1808 – just a year after the British government had declared the slave trade illegal under pressure from abolitionists and the public – the slave-trader Bazilic Leray wrote to Christophe Bourcard expressing his optimism about developments in international maritime trade. Soon, he argued, there would be a peace settlement, and then the hour would come again for ships' suppliers ready to take risks. It was therefore necessary to start planning future projects. It was completely clear to Leray that slaving expeditions to the coast of West Africa would offer the greatest business advantages and generate large profits, for the French and Spanish colonies needed enormous numbers of workers and the English competitors had been removed from the scene.[37]

Six years later, following Napoleon's exile to the Mediterranean island of Elba and the peace treaty between France and the European great powers, the hour had arrived. The victorious British attempted to persuade the French restoration government under Louis XVIII to adopt their policy of abolition, and the French promised in the treaty of 30 May 1814 to follow the British and do everything in their power to bring an end to the slave trade. But in view of the reduced state of the French Atlantic ports and their merchant communities they begged a transitional period of five years, during which it remained legal to fit out slave ships to meet the demand of the recovered West Indian colonies for labour.[38]

The resumption of the triangular trade also provoked interest in Basel. Frères Merian, for example, who had officially withdrawn from international trade in 1810, asked Bourcard Fils & Cie. in October 1814 for information about all movements in the slave trade and in the trade in colonial goods. They were particularly interested to know what measure of profits could be expected from such operations.[39] Christophe Bourcard did not fail to respond to the requests of Jean-Jacques and Christoph Merian and gave them reliable information about how and how well slave ships in Nantes were fitted out.[40]

37 SWA, HS 420, N 3.3, Leray to BFC, 13 February 1808.
38 Hugh Thomas, *The Slave Trade. The Story of the Atlantic Slave Trade: 1440–1870* (London and New York, 1997), p. 582.
39 SWA, HS 420, F 282, Frères Merian to BFC, 13 October 1814.
40 SWA, HS 420, E 47, Briefkopierbücher der BFC, 1812 bis 1818, pp. 124 and 177.

80 PETER HAENGER

In spite of their obvious interest the Merians made no moves to get involved in the restarted slaving business – at least not through Bourcard Fils & Cie.

In 1814, seven years after the British ban on trading in slaves, Bourcard invested in two of the slaving expeditions being organised by Nantes ship-owners. The *Petite Louise*, a 118-ton brig built in 1815 and carrying a crew of twenty-six, was fitted out by long-standing business partners of Bourcard, the merchant house Houdet & Neveu. Bourcard contributed 15,300 francs towards the total costs of 100,356 francs. Also in Nantes, Bourcard invested 5,000 francs in the voyage of the *Cultivateur*, a somewhat larger ship at 315 tons and with a crew of forty, which was being fitted out by the ship-owners Rossel & Boudet at the same time.[41] Captain Chaveau of the *Petite Louise* was commissioned to sail to Cap Lopez on the coast of Gabon, to purchase at least 150 Africans, both men and women. They were to be taken to one of the French colonies in the Caribbean. The *Cultivateur*, captained by Bazilic Leray, was to sail to Bonny at the mouth of the Niger and take 450 Blacks on board.

Just a few days before the two ships were due to sail, the Emperor Napoleon, returned from Elba, decreed an immediate ban on the slave trade on the advice of his enlightened minister Benjamin Constant. Napoleon, who twelve years earlier had angered many of his admirers all over Europe by reversing the ban on slavery introduced by the Jacobins in 1794, hoped to assuage his British opponents with this measure.[42] In spite of the new ban the *Cultivateur* left the port of Nantes on 1 April 1815. Two days later the *Petite Louise* also put to sea, in an area that was being patrolled for slave ships by the British Navy.[43]

Six months later the news reached Christophe Bourcard in Nantes that the *Cultivateur* had been captured by the British Navy in the Niger Delta and taken to the British military port of Plymouth. Charles Rossel, the *Cultivateur*'s owner, travelled to London, where he employed lawyers to help him get the ship released. And the British Admiralty Court decided in favour of the Frenchman; the presiding judge could see no legal grounds for the British Navy to disrupt the maritime trade of foreign states. The *Cultivateur* was thus able to leave Plymouth on 24 January 1816. The ship was then refitted and sent to Ambriz on the coast of Angola, where Captain Leray acquired 178 adult men, 90 women, 166 boys and 85 girls in trade for a large quantity of textiles and weapons.

41 SWA, HS 420, N 1, Alle Sklavenschiffe A–Z, 1782–1815, *La Petite Louise, Le Cultivateur*.
42 Thomas, *Slave Trade*, p. 586; Pétré-Grenouilleau, *Nantes au temps de la traite des Noirs*, p. 182.
43 In 1816, the *Petite Louise* successfully returned to Nantes. Captain Chaveau had bought Africans in Cap Lopez (present-day Gabon) whom he then sold in Cayenne (French Guiana). The documents in the Wirtschaftsarchiv contain no reference to possible profits made during this slaving journey.

Figure 3.3. Excerpt from the return account of the voyage of the *Cultivateur*, 1817

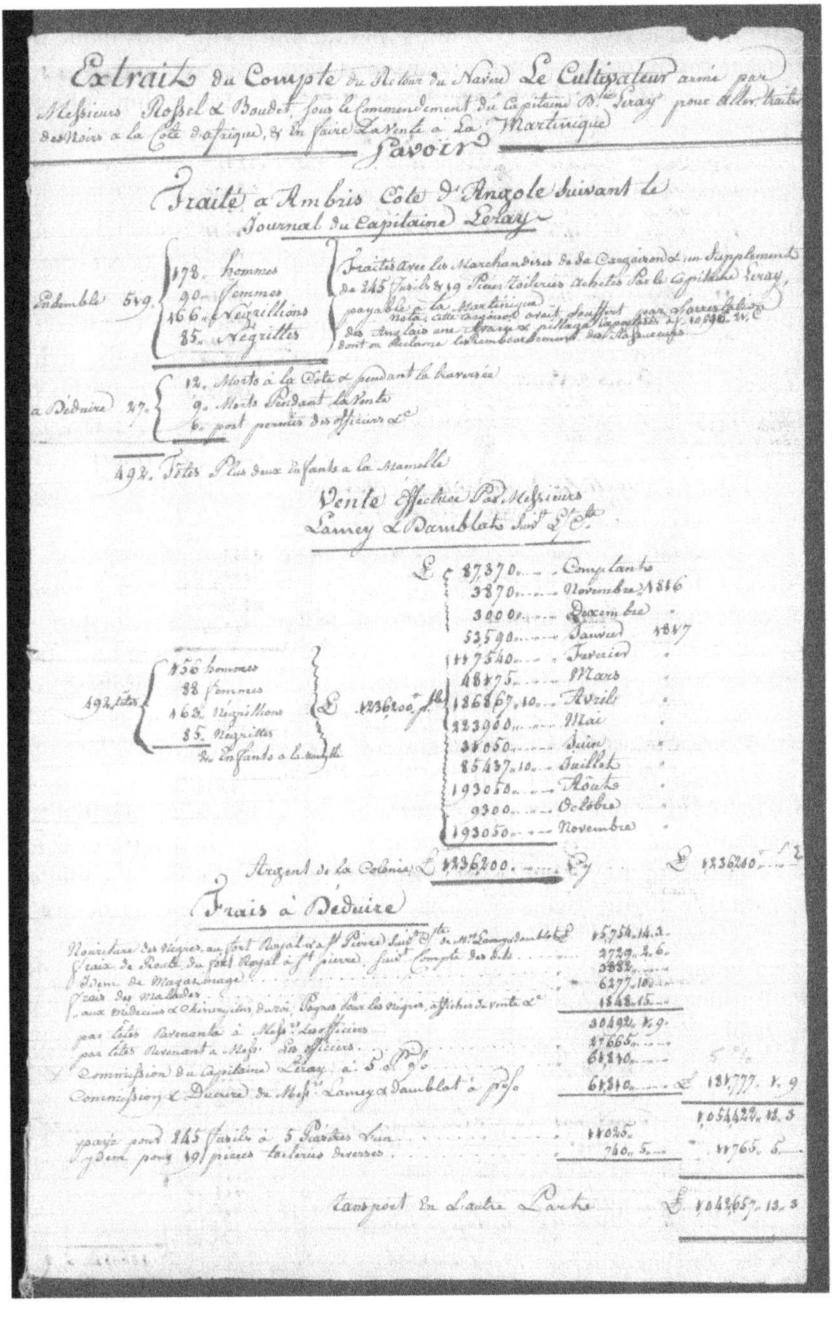

An 'Extrait du Compte du Retour du Navire *Le Cultivateur*', which can be seen in the Swiss Business Archives (Fig. 3.3), provides detailed information about the subsequent course of this slaving expedition. During the stay of the *Cultivateur* on the Angola coast and its onward journey to Martinique in the Caribbean, twelve enslaved men and women died. As was usual, when they arrived in Martinique six of the Africans were assigned to the ship's officers as *port permis* – to be sold on the officers' own account. Between November 1816 and November 1817 – during which period nine more died – 492 were auctioned in Martinique. The 156 men, 88 women, 163 boys and 85 girls (including two infants born during the voyage) brought the *Cultivateur*'s investors 1,236 million livres in colonial currency. This represented an interim profit of 83 per cent.[44]

Christophe Bourcard did not live to hear of the *Cultivateur*'s arrival in Martinique. With his business in ruins he committed suicide in October 1815. There are no final accounts for the voyages of the *Cultivateur* in the archives, but it is clear from the surviving documents that 16,236 francs in profits from the expedition were paid to his heirs in Basel.[45]

Moral Discourses

The insight that the slave trade was an anachronistic and inhuman business was not one that moved Christophe Bourcard, although it was well established in popular consciousness after the victory of the abolitionists in England. In his dealings with partners and employees, as revealed in his business correspondence, Bourcard appears as a man of feeling, but at no point in the course of his business career did he give any consideration to the fate of the enslaved African men and women.

In Basel itself abolitionist arguments were entirely familiar in enlightened and philanthropic circles. The enlightened thinker, philanthropist and town clerk Isaak Iselin, for example, condemned the slave trade as completely incompatible with the rights of man. In Basel as elsewhere, critics of the colonial system inspired by the Enlightenment did not tire of pointing out the connection between the consumption of sugar in Europe and slave labour in the Caribbean and America. The image of the lump of sugar wet with the tears of suffering slaves was popular; it can be found, for example, in the correspondence between Pierre Mouchon, pastor of the French congregation in Basel, and the revolutionary Basel politician Peter Ochs.[46] The Basel printer Johann Heinrich Decker also published the *Hinkender Basler Bote*, a popular

44   SWA, HS 420, N 1, Alle Sklavenschiffe A–Z, 1782–1815, *Le Cultivateur*.
45   Ibid.
46   Beat von Wartburg, *Musen & Menschenrechte. Peter Ochs und seine literarischen Werke* (Basel, 1997), p. 110.

almanac, which appeared in a parallel French edition in Alsace and Franche-Comté. In pursuit of Decker's project of popular enlightenment, the almanac brought news of the work of anti-slavery activists in France to a wider public.[47]

It is noteworthy that the representative of Basel's *grande bourgeoisie*, Christophe Bourcard, re-entered the slave trade just at the point when the Basel Mission was being set up in his home town. While the Burckhardts and their significant network of relatives and local business partners had profited from trading in captive Africans for many years, individuals from pietist-influenced circles of the city acted as founders and supporters of this missionary society. Its creation followed in the wake of a counter-revolutionary religious revival, and the Basel Mission began its activities in close association with the British Church Missionary Society (CMS), which in turn had strong personal and ideological links to the abolitionist movement in Britain. At the behest of the CMS the Basel Mission prepared young men from Switzerland and Württemberg for work in Sierra Leone. Later the Basel Mission worked independently in Liberia for a short time, and then on the Gold Coast, notably in Danish-controlled Osu and Akuapem. In his instructions to the first Basel missionaries to be sent out to Liberia, Mission Director Christian Gottlieb Blumhardt made it unmistakably clear that mission work in Africa was understood as restitution for the injustice done to Africans in the transatlantic slave trade.[48] Blumhardt probably did not know that Basel merchants had been involved in the trade.

In the 1840s the Basel Mission recruited emancipated slaves in Jamaica and arranged for them to settle in the small Gold Coast state of Akuapem, forming the nucleus of a founding Christian congregation. Later the leadership of the mission would confront the problem of slave-ownership in its own mission communities on the Gold Coast and institute a radical prohibition of slavery – in contrast to its British counterparts like the Methodist, Anglican or Scottish Presbyterian missions. But on the Gold Coast slavery was a much more complex institution that European anti-slavery discourse took account of. The starting point for European debates was a dichotomy between the slave and the free born, but the social reality of the Gold Coast was characterised by a broad spectrum of relations of dependency and clientelism, with varying forms and consequences. There, slavery represented a continuum of differing degrees of social unfreedom.[49]

47   David, Etemad and Schaufelbuehl, *Schwarze Geschäfte*, p. 127.
48   'Auszüge aus der Instruktion für unsere auf der nordamerikanischen Colonie Liberia in West-Afrika arbeitenden Missionarien. Vom Oktober 1827', *Evangelisches Missionsmagazin* 15 (1830), 451–82.
49   Peter Haenger, *Slaves and Slaveholders on the Gold Coast. Towards an Understanding of Social Bondage in West Africa*, ed. J. J. Shaffer and P. E. Lovejoy, transl. C. Handford (Basel, 2000).

Conclusion

The institutionalised Christian humanitarianism of the Basel Mission unques-
tionably represents an important chapter in the city's historical narrative. The
headquarters of the mission society, now known as Mission 21, occupies a
grand building which was the largest private building in the city when built in
1860 and today houses a hotel alongside the mission offices. And – how could
it be otherwise? – the so-called Mission House stands in the Missionsstraße
(Mission Street). Behind the facades of the respectable eighteenth-century
patrician houses, nobody ever expected to find traces of the slave trade.
But since the city is now, as it was then, an important hub for international
commerce, it can hardly be a surprise that the great Basel merchant houses
were implicated in the trade, because at that time anybody who engaged in
cross-border commodity trade – and especially if it involved printed textiles –
was as a rule *ipso facto* involved in the triangular trade, if only indirectly. And
so the participation of Basel merchants in the slave trade has now found its
own place in Basel's historical narrative.[50]

Swiss involvement in the transatlantic slave trade is a topic that is sensitive
and difficult to get a grip on. Because of the country's geographical position
as a hinterland, people simply assumed that there had been no Swiss
involvement in either slavery or the slave trade, and historical scholarship
accordingly paid the topic little attention for a long time. Until the publication of the works mentioned at the beginning of this chapter, articles on
the subject appeared only in specialist literature. Those publications are now
out of date and difficult to find, as they are scattered across journals which
are known only to a few specialists.[51] Carl Burckhardt-Sarasin's approach to
the documents in the Segerhof archive in the 1950s may be symptomatic: for a
long time, not only did people not want to know about Swiss involvement in
the slave trade, but some also had an interest in keeping the past hidden.

As far as the Burckhardt merchant houses are concerned, they stood in
an intermediary position between long-distance and domestic trade. In the
space of twenty years the Burckhardts extended their sphere of operation
from Central Europe and France to West Africa and the French Antilles, but
also to Russia and the Levant. Thanks to their Nantes branch Christoph
Burckhardt & Cie. was able to take part in the triangular trade and in cross-
border regional trade between the Swiss Confederation, Southern Germany
and Alsace. In their commercial operations the Burckhardts could rely on an
extensive network of regional and international business connections. With

---

50   In 2011 and 2012 the Basel Historical Museum offered a guided museum tour with the
title 'Dirty business in noble spaces' (https://zasb.unibas.ch/de/ueber-uns/zasb-2012/2012-06-22-
events/; Programmzeitung. Kultur im Raum Basel. Januar 2012, Nr. 269, 73).
51   David, Etemad and Schaufelbuehl, *Schwarze Geschäfte*, p. 11.

the establishment of Bourcard Fils & Cie. in Nantes, the Burckhardts intensified their involvement in the slave trade: the company was created for no other purpose than to take advantage of the opportunity presented by the slave trade. Bourcard Fils & Cie. provided Christoph Burckhardt & Cie. with the most important colonial goods, while the latter in its turn gained access to new markets for its Indienne products through Nantes.

The expansion of these business activities took place for the most part in the extended French economic sphere. Orientation towards Paris, however, made the Burckhardts' enterprises dependent on the opportunities and risks that arose from the French political situation at the time of the Revolution and the wars that followed. The war at sea with England led to the loss of the French colonial empire and the French fleet; overseas markets and sources of raw materials were lost. It was above all the cities on the French Atlantic coast that suffered under these blows. This explains the disaster that Bourcard Fils & Cie. suffered with the slave expedition of the *Intrépide* at the beginning of the 1790s. A new initiative in the slave trade in 1814/15 could do nothing to change the fact that the firm in Nantes had hardly any room for manoeuvre after the fiasco of the *Intrépide*.

For the Swiss cotton industry, by contrast, Napoleon's continental blockade against England opened up new opportunities. High costs meant that French manufactures were not in a position to take over the continental markets which were closed to the British by the blockade. Here Swiss producers and businesses moved in to fill the gap, earning substantial profits through both legal trading and the smuggling of English goods. Letters in the Segerhof archive show that Christoph Burckhardt & Cie., too, engaged in smuggling activities.[52]

In the Basel region the development of local industries accelerated, offering new investment opportunities for firms like Christoph Burckhardt & Cie. But until his death in 1812, Christoph Burckhardt senior remained a cautious businessman, who preferred investing calculable amounts in small enterprises to taking big risks with buying or starting up industrial enterprises deploying new technologies. The heirs of Christoph Burckhardt-Merian wound up the firm after his death and began to invest their capital individually in local industry.

---

52 SWA, HS 420, C 34, Briefkopierbücher der CBC, geordnet nach Jahreszahlen und Nachfolgefirmen, 1805 bis 1806, CBC to Meuron & Bovet, 11 January 1806, p. 337; HS 420, C 33, Briefkopierbücher der CBC, geordnet nach Jahreszahlen und Nachfolgefirmen, 1805–1806, CBC to Meuron & Bovet, 12 March 1806, p. 379.

4

Spinning and Weaving for the Slave Trade: Proto-Industry in Eighteenth-Century Silesia[1]

ANKA STEFFEN AND KLAUS WEBER

Textiles were the most important merchandise in the barter trade for Africans destined for slavery, serving both as a consumer good and as a currency. Throughout the four centuries of the transatlantic slave trade, fabrics of all sorts made up about 50 per cent of the value shipped to Africa. Leslie Clarkson states that cotton figures most prominently in the literature relevant to the history of textiles, as a commodity which Europeans have always desired and which has been prominent in early intercontinental trade (including in the barter trade for enslaved Africans), in the slave-based economy of the American South, and in the Industrial Revolution in Great Britain.[2] At the same time, she concludes that linen has been almost entirely overlooked by scholars – although the fabric was ubiquitous in Europe, for clothing, bedding, tablecloths, packaging, canvas, and more. Even a more recent essay collection on the European linen industry treats mainly the British, Irish and North American aspects, and hazards some glances into Sweden, Belgium and nineteenth-century Germany, when linen was already in irreversible decline; the omnipresent linen trade of seventeenth and eighteenth century northern France and Central Europe is completely ignored.[3] Its importance has been taken into account by a number of German scholars, but their

---

1 We are indebted to Chris Smith (London) and Eve Rosenhaft (Liverpool) for their reading and for ironing out our English. Any remaining errors are ours.
2 Leslie Clarkson, 'The Linen Industry in Early Modern Europe', *The Cambridge History of Western Textiles*, ed. D. Jenkins (Cambridge, 2003), pp. 472–93. See also Giorgio Riello and Prasannan Parthasarathi, eds, *The Spinning World. A Global History of Cotton Textiles, 1200–1850* (Oxford, 2009); Sven Beckert, *Empire of Cotton. A Global History* (New York, 2014).
3 Brenda Collins and Philip Ollerenshaw, eds, *The European Linen Industry in Historical Perspective* (Oxford, 2003).

studies on some particular textile regions, published in German, have not had the impact they deserved.[4]

It is true that homespun linen lacks the glamour of silk, the ornaments and the brilliant colours of calicoes and the dignity of woollen cloth, but in spite of all its inconspicuousness it was one of the products that closely linked the peoples around the Atlantic basin with those in Atlantic hinterlands, and it did so over centuries. A history of linen can very well illustrate how distant regions established trade relations and thus constituted a wider, previously non-existent, socio-economic fabric. This chapter will first introduce the overall importance of export-oriented linen production for certain regions of the Holy Roman Empire. It will then scrutinise the conditions which helped to make the landlocked province of Silesia one of the major suppliers of textiles on Atlantic markets, and the living conditions of the textile workers in the region. The formerly Austrian, then Prussian province of Silesia is of particular interest because there the institution of serfdom survived well into the nineteenth century, in contrast with Germany's more western textile regions, such as Westphalia, the Rhineland or Swabia. In Silesia and in some other Prussian provinces, serfs not only worked the land but were also employed in spinning and weaving. The chapter concludes by proposing that Silesia's linen trade not only supplied the Atlantic world with certain types of textiles but also helped to make the 'New World' plantation economy more profitable than it would otherwise have been, because under its regime of unfree labour, such fabrics were produced at particularly low cost.

The Central European Economy and the Atlantic World

Central European provinces like Lusatia, Silesia and Bohemia had already been integrated into the European textile economy during the sixteenth century, when the Fuggers and Nuremburg textile magnates transferred much of their rural linen production from Swabia and Franconia further east. These prominent entrepreneurs were capitalising on the lower wages to be paid there.[5] Many of these textile regions were devastated during the Thirty Years War, but had fully recovered by 1700.

---

4 Axel Flügel, *Kaufleute und Manufakturen in Bielefeld. Sozialer Wandel und wirtschaftliche Entwicklung im proto-industriellen Leinengewerbe von 1680 bis 1850* (Bielefeld, 1993); Hans-Werner Niemann, *Leinenhandel im Osnabrücker Land. Die Bramscher Kaufmannsfamilie Sanders 1780–1850* (Bramsche, 2004); Marcel Boldorf, *Europäische Leinenregionen im Wandel. Institutionelle Weichenstellungen in Schlesien und Irland (1750–1850)* (Cologne, 2006).
5 Arno Kunze, 'Die Verlagsbeziehungen des Nürnberger Handelskapitals zum sächsisch-böhmischen Leinwandproduktionsgebiete im 16. und 17. Jahrhundert' (unpublished dissertation, Halle, 1925); Gustav Aubin and Arno Kunze, *Leinenerzeugung und Leinenabsatz im*

Lusatia is situated on the upper length of the River Spree and thus well connected with the River Elbe. The Elbe also provided Bohemia with direct communication to the sea port of Hamburg. This Habsburg province produced not only linen, but also metal items and glassware. From the 1680s, traders from the remotest Bohemian mountain villages travelled as far as London, Amsterdam and Cadiz to distribute their merchandise. As in Westphalia and the Rhineland, a combination of different commodities created synergies for marketing. In Bohemia, new roads were built during the eighteenth century for the smooth transportation of fragile commodities to the riverboats on the Elbe.[6]

The old-established Westphalian linen trade had always been directed towards the ports of Amsterdam, Bremen and Hamburg, and towards British markets. They naturally benefited from the closer integration of the North Sea region into the Atlantic economy, in particular after the Thirty Years War. The merchants of larger Westphalian cities like Bielefeld, Osnabruck and Warendorf tightened their links with rural linen spinning and weaving, and established efficient institutions for quality control and marketing. A steady migration to Hanseatic and Dutch ports, and to London, secured a significant urban presence of Westphalian merchants and many of them actually made their way into the elite society of these cities. This strategy ensured a tight vertical integration of their family-based business.[7] The main transport route through Westphalia was the River Weser, with the Hanseatic city of Bremen on its estuary into the North Sea. The river's upper course also links Hessian linen regions with Bremen.

Among the regions mentioned, Silesia is the one most distant from the North Sea shores. Yet, its economic importance and its reliance on long-distance trade is illustrated with a Prussian achievement in civil engineering and a Prussian military adventure. The Prince-Elector Frederick William initiated the construction of a canal which linked the River Oder (flowing from Silesia into the Baltic Sea) with the River Spree (feeding the Havel, which in turn feeds the River Elbe), thus completing a navigable waterway of some 760 kilometres, from Silesia's capital Breslau (today Wrocław) into the port of Hamburg. Merchants using this direct route to the North Sea avoided the Danish sound toll, but had to pay newly established Prussian duties. The canal was opened in 1668, with thirteen watergates on its length of 28 kilometres.

östlichen Mitteldeutschland zur Zeit der Zunftkäufe: Ein Beitrag zur industriellen Kolonisation des deutschen Ostens (Stuttgart, 1940).

6 Milan Myška, 'Proto-Industrialisation in Bohemia, Moravia and Silesia', European Proto-Industrialisation, ed. S. Ogilvie and M. Cerman (Cambridge, 1996), pp. 188–207; Klaus Weber, Deutsche Kaufleute im Atlantikhandel 1680–1830: Unternehmen und Familien in Hamburg, Cádiz und Bordeaux (Munich, 2004), pp. 75–9, 133–43.

7 Weber, Deutsche Kaufleute im Atlantikhandel; Margit Schulte Beerbühl, Deutsche Kaufleute in London. Welthandel und Einbürgerung (1600–1818) (Munich, 2007).

From 1740 until 1763, Frederick William's great-grandson Frederick II (the Great) waged three costly wars for the conquest of Silesia, which had thus far been a province of the Habsburg Empire. After the change of ruler, the linen magnates in Silesia's wealthy trading towns readily adapted to Prussian rule and intensified their exports via Hamburg, while the older links with Upper Germany and Austria were neglected.

The orientation of Central Europe's rural industries towards the sea corresponded to the growth in the eighteenth century's maritime trade. The slow but steady pacification of the Atlantic basin and of the Caribbean, along with the suppression of piracy, contributed to a reduction of transaction costs, which encouraged more individual traders to enter into the business, including the slave trade.[8] German merchants too benefited from these changes. A significant number of them did so by establishing themselves in a seaport of a slave-trading nation and operating under its flag.[9] To what extent did this presence of a German commercial elite in major port cities of colonial empires have an impact on the Central European hinterlands? This question can only be answered by a quantitative assessment of the exportation of Central European products.

The taste of consumers in colonial markets is reflected by an 1806 report of British merchants to Parliament: 'The Spanish Traders are very strongly prejudiced in favour of German linens … When a Spanish trader comes into a store in a British [Caribbean] Island, the first article he asks for is German linens.'[10] Another report, dated 1744, reported that the seventy thousand enslaved people on Barbados were 'usually clothed with Foreign "Osnabrughs"'.[11] Such labelling demonstrates that the products from particular northern German regions had made themselves a name, as 'stout Weser flaxen', 'true born Osnabrughs', 'true born Tecklenburghs' (Tecklenburg is a county in the province of Westphalia), or 'Creguelas de Westphalia' and 'Rosas de Westphalia'.[12]

These fabrics were in demand not only in American colonies, but also in Africa, where the proportion of German manufactures among the barter

8   Pieter C. Emmer, *The Dutch in the Atlantic Economy, 1580–1880. Trade, Slavery and Emancipation* (Aldershot, 1998), pp. 12–32.
9   Klaus Weber, 'Deutschland, der atlantische Sklavenhandel und die Plantagenwirtschaft der Neuen Welt (15. bis 19. Jahrhundert)', *Journal of Modern European History* 7/1 (2009), 37–67; Klaus Weber, 'Mitteleuropa und der transatlantische Sklavenhandel: eine lange Geschichte', *WerkstattGeschichte* 66–67 (2015), 7–30.
10   Otto-Ernst Krawehl, *Hamburgs Schiffs- und Warenverkehr mit England und den englischen Kolonien 1840–1860* (Cologne, 1977), p. 441.
11   British Parliamentary Papers, *House of Commons, Sessional Papers of the Eighteenth Century*, 19 vols (Wilmington, 1975), vol. 19: *Reports & Papers 1742–1760*, pp. 18–19.
12   Edith Schmitz, *Leinengewerbe und Leinenhandel in Nordwestdeutschland (1650–1850)* (Cologne, 1967), pp. 33, 86, 92.

commodities used for the purchase of slaves was significant.[13] Even the assortments on board the early Portuguese slave ships were made up entirely of merchandise produced outside Portugal, mostly from more Central and Eastern European regions.[14] Bills of lading preserved from the 1660s show that hardly any East India ship would set sail from Britain for Africa without a substantial quantity of Silesian linen in its holds, labelled 'sletias'.[15] The slave ship *Amiral*, which left Bordeaux for the Guinea coast in 1744, had the bulk of its cargo made up of textiles, as most slavers would. Out of the total of 5,095 bales of cotton and linen on board, 1,440 derived from Nantes, there were far smaller batches from Rouen and Amsterdam, but as much as 2,720 from Hamburg.[16] The British ship *Mermaid* offers a similar picture: in 1732, before setting off for the Guinea coast, its captain had purchased textiles in Rotterdam, with a total value of £23,335. Half of them were 'sletias'. Much of the remainder, labelled 'bretannies' and 'cambrics', may also have been of German origin.[17] Counterfeits of the traditional linen from Cambrai and French Brittany were made in Germany, and much of it was distributed via Dutch harbours.

Such individual observations on overseas markets are confirmed by broader data from German regions of textile production. In his examination of the Prussian customs registers, Alfred Zimmermann emphasises the significantly Atlantic bias of the exports from Silesia. From the 1740s to the 1780s, more than three-quarters of its linen produce – the annual value was oscillating roughly between 3 and 6 million Reichsthaler – was destined for the markets of Western European sea powers. Some of it was even shipped directly to the Americas, but only a tiny fraction of the exports was sent east (to the Russia, Poland, Hungary and Ottoman regions).[18] Far smaller German territories also exported large quantities: in the late 1780s, the annual linen exports of the Westphalian County of Ravensberg were worth some 750,000 Thaler.[19] Similarly structured export markets have been observed in the case of metalwares from the Rhineland.[20]

---

13   Herbert S. Klein, *The Atlantic Slave Trade* (Cambridge, 1999), p. 114.

14   Alan F. C. Ryder, 'An Early Portuguese Trading Voyage to the Forcados River', *Journal of the Historical Society of Nigeria* 1/4 (1959), 294–321.

15   Margaret Makepeace, 'English Traders on the Guinea Coast, 1657–1668: An Analysis of the East India Company Archive', *History in Africa* 16 (1989), 237–84, here pp. 239, 255–68.

16   Éric Saugera, *Bordeaux port négrier. Chronologie, économie, idéologie, XVIIe–XIXe siècles* (Paris, 1995), pp. 246, 352.

17   Kazuo Kobayashi, 'British Atlantic Slave Trade and East India Textiles, 1650s–1808' (University Working Paper, Osaka, 2010).

18   Alfred Zimmermann, *Blüthe und Verfall des Leinengewerbes in Schlesien. Gewerbe- und Handelspolitik dreier Jahrhunderte* (Breslau, 1885), pp. 460–7.

19   Schmitz, *Leinengewerbe und Leinenhandel*, p. 81.

20   Wilfried Reininghaus, *Die Stadt Iserlohn und ihre Kaufleute* (Münster, 1995), p. 585.

This pattern has been confirmed by a case study on British foreign trade: In the first half of the eighteenth century about 15 per cent of all imports to Britain consisted of linen. As Karin Newman has pointed out, 70–80 per cent of all these linens came from Germany, and 90 per cent of this volume was re-exported across the Atlantic. This implies that around 1700, about two-thirds of all British linen exports were of German origin. Irish linen followed in second place, and English-woven produce only ranked third.[21] If the annual average of the bales of German-made linen channelled through Britain during these years had been unrolled and pieced together, it would have produced a length of 11,000 kilometres – large enough to span the Atlantic from Britain to New England and on to Jamaica.

The French and Spanish contexts provide similar examples. The accounts of the important French trading house of *Fornier frères*, established in Cadiz, reveal that out of the total of its textile purchases between 1768 and 1786, amounting to a value of 12 million Reales, almost two-thirds were made in Germany. The major place of purchase was Hamburg, followed by Silesia.[22] This pattern illustrates the decline of French linen industry. In 1793 alone, Catalan industries imported nearly 1.1 million metres of linen from Hamburg.[23] All these examples illustrate the extent to which the book *The European Linen Industry*, cited above, is missing the wider picture.

The huge volume of rural textile production for export markets also had an impact on population growth and social structure in Central Europe. German labour-intensive proto-industries typically emerged in regions where poor soil and climate obliged the rural population (including women and children) to earn additional income for the purchase of food they could not produce themselves. The poor wages which cottagers would accept attracted textile producers to transfer manufacturing to such provinces. The general tendency was a move from more western and urban to more eastern and rural areas. With ever-increasing volumes of German manufactures being exported, such hitherto poor regions became permanent importers of food, allowing for an escape from the Malthusian trap. How narrow this escape was can now be tested through a closer consideration of the case of Silesia, focusing on the mountainous region surrounding Hirschberg (today Jelenia Góra). This small but commercially very powerful town, situated in the foothills of the Giant Mountains, was the province's most prominent centre for the processing and sale of linen.

21   Karin Newman, 'Anglo-Hamburg Trade in the Late Seventeenth and Early Eighteenth Centuries' (unpublished dissertation, London, 1979), p. 202.
22   Robert Chamboredon, 'Une société de commerce languedocienne à Cadix: Simon et Arnail Fornier et Cie (Nov. 1768–Mars 1786)', *La burguesía de negocios en la Andalucía de la ilustración*, 2, ed. A. González García-Baquero (Cadiz, 1991), pp. 35–52, here pp. 35, 49.
23   Pierre Vilar, *La Catalogne dans l'Espagne moderne. Recherches sur les fondements économiques des structures nationales*, 3 vols (Paris, 1962), vol. 3, pp. 118, 126.

Proto-Industry in Silesia

Merchants from Nuremberg and Augsburg had been ordering linens from Silesia since the early sixteenth century; Dutch buyers would soon join in. Notably following the Thirty Year's War, the number of people involved with textile production was on the rise, particularly in the mountain regions. A common explanation for this phenomenon has been refugees seeking protection in Silesia's more secluded areas, having to make their living without access to agricultural land.[24] An additional cause could be the increase in prices for staple foods, which was already in progress at that time.

From the mid seventeenth century the merchants in Silesia's linen trading towns Hirschberg, Greiffenberg (today Gryfów Śląski) and Landeshut (today Kamienna Góra) had established their own guilds (*Kaufmanns-Societäten*). Hirschberg was the most prominent place and the neighbouring villages were particularly crowded with weavers and spinners. In organising bleaching and other finishing processes, and in coordinating the transport to buyers, the guilds successfully pushed foreign merchants out of the Silesian linen sector. With their detailed knowledge of markets, the merchants instructed the workers to produce counterfeits of Western European makes: Bretannies, Cambrics and Sangallas (from the Swiss region of St Gallen). This did not go unnoticed, as substantiated by a protest of Cambrai merchants dating around 1750, who complained about 'fines toiles de Silesie', made in the style and measures of the original 'cambrics'.[25] With a diversified range of goods, Silesian merchants answered the demand from their own customers. These in turn were wholesale merchants at distant places of trade, who would order certain amounts of linen, of a specified quality and a defined degree of whiteness.[26]

Silesian industry also benefited from the institution of serfdom. By the eighteenth century, serfdom had virtually disappeared in the more westerly linen regions of Britanny, Normandy, Westphalia and Swabia. In Bohemia it was abolished in 1781;[27] in Silesia, by contrast, it remained in place into the early nineteenth century.[28] Estate ownership prevailed. Tenant farmers were obliged to work the land of their overlord for some days each week and owed

24 Lujo Brentano, 'Ueber den grundherrlichen Charakter des hausindustriellen Leinengewerbes in Schlesien', *Zeitschrift für Social- und Wirtschaftsgeschichte* 1 (1893), 318–40, p. 327; Siegfried Kühn, *Der Hirschberger Leinwand- und Schleierhandel von 1648–1806* (Breslau, 1938), p. 14–16.
25 Archiwum Państwowe w Jeleniej Górze (State Archives, Jelenia Góra), Sign. 23 Zoll- und Schiffsachen, report without date, presumably from 1749 or 1750.
26 Kühn, *Der Hirschberger Leinwand- und Schleierhandel*, pp. 40–3.
27 Arnost Klíma, 'Industrial Growth and Entrepreneurship in the Early Stages of Industrialisation in the Czech Lands', *Economic Development in the Habsburg Monarchy in the Nineteenth Century. Essays*, ed. J. Komlos (Boulder and New York, 1983), pp. 81–99, here p. 82.
28 Ernst E. Klotz, *Die schlesische Gutsherrschaft des ausgehenden 18. Jahrhunderts. Auf Grund der Friderizianischen Urbare und mit besonderer Berücksichtigung der alten Kreise*

him carriage services, or had to let him use draught animals at certain periods of the year. Serfs without arable land at their disposal had to make their living as lodgers working for their keep (*Einlieger*), farm-girls, farm-hands or household servants (*Mägde, Knechte, Gesinde*), having to toil as the overlord saw fit. Among these services spinning yarn and weaving were commonplace. Typically, *Einlieger* would also spin and weave on their own account in any free time they had. In earlier times estate owners had even acted as putters-out, dictating low prices for the purchase of the yarn or finished fabrics which they would in turn sell at a higher price.[29] Since the merchants' guilds had succeeded in establishing their own oligopoly on prices in the course of the seventeenth century, the estate owners had been squeezed out of this business.[30] Still, the landlords benefited from the industry; their tenants and lodgers owed them a fee for the permission to practise a craft. This was in place until the slow process of abolishing serfdom in Prussia was initiated with the October Edict of 1807.[31] Hence, the landless textile workers were never really able to negotiate the prices for their labour or for their product on equal terms. Further, with mobility harshly restricted, options to migrate for better-paid jobs were virtually non-existent. The Silesian merchants thus benefited from low production costs, enabling them to penetrate Atlantic markets with comparatively cheap textiles. At the beginning of the process of Silesia's proto-industrialisation, workers to some extent freely adopted industriousness, but in the course of the eighteenth century the stagnation and even decline of real wages imposed a further intensification of labour on the households of the rural population.[32] The low cost of labour must have been one of the reasons why most spinners did not even use spinning wheels but rather archaic yarn-winders.[33] Likewise, hand weaving persisted

Breslau und Bolkenhain-Landeshut (Aalen, 1978); Markus Cerman, *Villagers and Lords in Eastern Europe, 1300–1800* (New York, 2012).

29 Brentano, 'Ueber den grundherrlichen Charakter des hausindustriellen Leinengewerbes in Schlesien', p. 328.

30 Marcel Boldorf, 'Märkte und Verlage im institutionellen Gefüge der Leinenregion Niederschlesien des 18. Jahrhunderts', *Die Wirtschaftsgeschichte vor der Herausforderung durch die New Institutional Economics*, ed. K.-P. Ellerbrock and C. Wischermann (Dortmund, 2004), pp. 179–91, here p. 183.

31 Zimmermann, *Blüthe und Verfall des Leinengewerbes in Schlesien*, p. 18; Brentano, 'Ueber den grundherrlichen Charakter des hausindustriellen Leinengewerbes in Schlesien', pp. 327–8; Johannes Ziekursch, *Hundert Jahre schlesischer Agrargeschichte. Vom Hubertusburger Frieden bis zum Abschluss der Bauernbefreiung* (Darstellungen und Quellen zur schlesischen Geschichte), reprint of the 2nd edn (Aalen, 1978), pp. 42, 112; Kühn, *Der Hirschberger Leinwand- und Schleierhandel*, p. 19.

32 Jan de Vries, *The Industrious Revolution: Consumer Behavior and the Household Economy, 1650 to the Present* (New York, 2008).

33 Zimmermann, *Blüthe und Verfall des Leinengewerbes in Schlesien*, p. 60; Brentano, 'Ueber den grundherrlichen Charakter des hausindustriellen Leinengewerbes in Schlesien', p. 326.

well into the twentieth century.[34] The established elite of textile merchants did not initiate anything resembling the Industrial Revolution. It was a small group of newcomers, entering into the sector during the difficult Napoleonic years, who introduced mechanisation from the mid nineteenth century.

Demography and Living Costs in Prussian Silesia

When Prussian rule was imposed over the region in 1742, the sovereign Duchy of Silesia and the County of Glatz comprised some 37,500 square kilometres.[35] Population density in Prussia had been at ten people per square kilometre by the end of the seventeenth century; in Silesia it was already at twenty-one people per square kilometre. By 1805, the number of inhabitants per square kilometre in the southern region had reached fifty-two, whereas even in 1816 the density in Prussia as a whole did not exceed thirty-seven individuals per square kilometre.[36] Density was even more pressing in the mountainous regions of Lower Silesia, with sixty inhabitants per square kilometre by the early nineteenth century.[37]

The landless and the land-poor portion of the population grew even faster than the average, at least until 1806. Their numbers in Silesia exceeded 200,000 people by 1778, making up some 14 per cent of the province's population. In the face of this excess supply of labour, it is not really surprising that their daily wages stagnated. In contrast, the number of tenants working a larger or smaller tract of land on their own was hardly growing at all.[38] Information on daily, monthly or annual wages is very scarce, but it is worthwhile attempting an approximate assessment.

For a courier in late-fourteenth-century Silesia, the fee per mile had been 2 Silbergroschen and 6 Silberpfennig (30 Silberpfennig).[39] Pay had not improved

---

34 Joseph Partsch, *Schlesien. Eine Landeskunde für das deutsche Volk*, 2 vols (Breslau, 1911), vol. 2, pp. 504, 518; Heinz Pohlendt, *Die Landeshuter Paßlandschaften: Beiträge zur Landeskunde der westlichen Mittelsudeten unter besonderer Berücksichtigung der dörflichen Siedlungs- und Hauslandschaft*, Veröffentlichungen der Schlesischen Gesellschaft für Erdkunde und des Geographischen Instituts der Universität Breslau 25 (Breslau, 1938), p. 81.

35 Silesia and the far smaller territory of Glatz were jointly ceded to Prussia, and they are usually treated jointly in the literature: Friedrich G. Leonhardi, *Erdbeschreibung der Preußischen Monarchie*, 6 vols (Halle, 1792), vol. 2, p. 7; Ziekursch, *Hundert Jahre schlesischer Agrargeschichte*, p. 61.

36 Calculation based on Leonhardi, *Erdbeschreibung der Preußischen Monarchie*, pp. 7, 16; Otto Behre, *Geschichte der Statistik in Brandenburg-Preussen bis zur Gründung des Königlichen Statistischen Bureaus* (Berlin, 1905), p. 408.

37 Ziekursch, *Hundert Jahre schlesischer Agrargeschichte*, p. 134.

38 Ibid., pp. 73–6.

39 One Reichsthaler was equal to 30 Silbergroschen or 360 Silberpfennig. One Prussian mile was equal to 7.532 kilometres.

Figure 4.1. Population in Silesia, 1663–1805

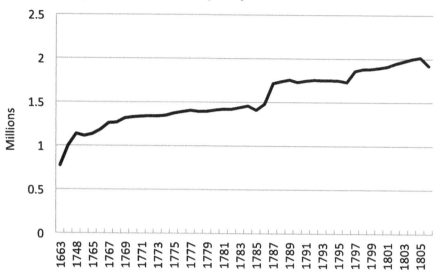

Sources: Leonhardi, *Erdbeschreibung der Preußischen Monarchie*, pp. 7, 16–17, 22, 24–5;
Schlesische Provinzialblätter 5 (1787), 59; *Schlesische Provinzialblätter* 17 (1793), 411–13,
here p. 411; Behre, *Geschichte der Statistik in Brandenburg-Preussen*, p. 462.

by the 1780s, when such a messenger still received only 3–4 Silbergroschen
(approximately 36–48 Silberpfennig) per mile.[40] The figures seem reliable, as
other sources mention similar wage levels for unskilled workers at the end
of the eighteenth century. For example, one thresher (*Dreschgärtner*) could
make 1–3 Silbergroschen (12–36 Silberpfennig) per day. A male farm-servant
owing bonded labour received 12 Reichsthaler annually; a farm-girl obtained
only 5 Reichsthaler per year.[41] Assuming 365 working days, this equates to 12
Silberpfennig for one day of male labour and only 5 Silberpfennig for one day
of female labour – even though the Prussian Servants' Law (*Gesindeordnung*,
1676) had already mandated a minimal daily wage of 18 Silberpfennig for
male farm-servants.[42] In contrast, day labourers not bound to serfdom could
make up to 5 Silbergroschen (60 Silberpfennig) per day – but they could not
count on any support from an overlord.[43]

---

40 *Schlesische Provinzialblätter* 15 (1792), 429–40, here pp. 434–9.
41 *Schlesische Provinzialblätter* 8 (1788), 233–50, here pp. 235–6.
42 'Der Herren Fürsten und Stände verneuerte Gesinde-Ordnung Anno 1676 d. 9. Novembr.',
in *Käyser- und Königl. Das Erb-Hertzogthum Schlesien concernirende Privilegia, Statuta und
Sanctiones Pragmaticæ* (Breslau, 1713), pp. 178–202, here p. 188.
43 Klotz, *Die schlesische Gutsherrschaft des ausgehenden 18. Jahrhunderts*, p. 100.

Costs of (Barely) Living

Highly valuable data from the periodical *Schlesische Provinzialblätter*[44] indicate that the income of landless and land-poor people was lagging behind the slow but steady rise of prices for grain, meat or items like shoes, and this applies from the Middle Ages to the end of the eighteenth century (Fig. 4.2). With the 1796 price for one pound of beef or pork a little over 2 Silbergroschen (25–28 Silberpfennig), it is evident why the lower classes were not consuming meat on a regular basis. Fish was even more expensive. Herring, the cheapest on the market, cost 2 Silbergroschen (24 Silberpfennig). Eel, at the top of the price range, was at 1 Reichsthaler (360 Silberpfennig). The prices for the cheapest bread oscillated around 1 Silbergroschen (12 Silberpfennig) per pound (just under 500 grams).[45] Bread was the main source of nutritional energy and it is reasonable to believe that the information that adult consumption was approximately two pounds per day is correct.[46] Hence, to cover the minimal nutritional supply with bread only absorbed up to 40 per cent of the daily earning of an unbonded male day labourer – provided he obtained the highest possible pay. Bonded farm-hands were usually provided with basic provisions by their employers, though very often of poor quality. The director of the Royal Credit Institute, Ernst Heinrich, observed that such budgeted provision might include only three dishes of meat per year.[47] It seems that the working poor were particularly impoverished in Silesia, to the point that their physical strength was perceptibly affected. According to the Prussian statesman Theodor von Schönau, for a comparable task 33 per cent more labourers were required on Silesian estates than on estates in the area surrounding Magdeburg.[48] It may even be claimed that from the 1770s many of those enslaved on plantations in the French Caribbean and in British North America were enjoying better material living conditions than Silesian cottagers.[49]

With population density higher but harvests poorer than in the lowlands

---

44   Michael R. Gerber, *Die Schlesischen Provinzialblätter 1785–1849* (Sigmaringen, 1995).

45   *Schlesische Provinzialblätter* 23 (1796), 488–91.

46   *Schlesische Provinzialblätter* 29 (1799), 525–51, here p. 539. Klotz even considers three pounds of bread necessary for one male farm-servant per day: Klotz, *Die schlesische Gutsherrschaft des ausgehenden 18. Jahrhunderts*, p. 64.

47   The Royal Credit Institute was established to provide loans to keep struggling estates in operation; Heinrich's statement dates from the very end of the eighteenth century. Cited according to Ziekursch, *Hundert Jahre schlesischer Agrargeschichte*, p. 116.

48   Ibid., p. 116.

49   Dale Tomich, 'The Other Face of Slave Labour: Provision Grounds and Internal Marketing in Martinique', *Caribbean Slavery in the Atlantic World. A Student Reader*, ed. H. Beckles and V. A. Shepherd (Kingston, Jamaica, 2000), pp. 743–57; David Eltis, 'Free and Coerced Transatlantic Migrations: Some Comparisons', *The American Historical Review* 88/2 (1983), 251–80, here pp. 279f; Robert W. Fogel and Stanley L. Engerman, *Time on the Cross. The Economics of American Negro Slavery* (Boston, MA, 1974), p. 122.

Figure 4.2. Prices in Silesia for grain, other foodstuffs, leather boots and messenger's fee per mile, 1377–1796

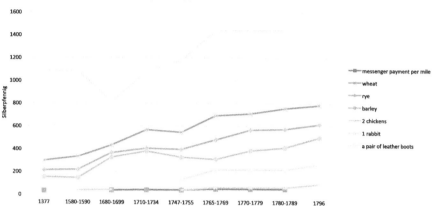

Sources: Schlesische Provinzialblätter 12 (1790), 406–12, here pp. 407–10; *Schlesische Provinzialblätter* 15 (1792), 429–40, here pp. 434–9; *Schlesische Provinzialblätter* 23 (1796), 488–91; *Schlesische Provinzialblätter* 83 (1826), 235–60, here pp. 237–8, 242; *Schlesische Provinzialblätter* 102 (1835), 207–16, here pp. 211–13.

Figure 4.3. Grain prices in Silesia, 1781–1810

Prices for grain per bushel, in Reichsmark		1781–1790	1791–1800	1801–1810
Wheat	Hirschberg	5.31	5.33	10.06
	Breslau	4.25	4.25	8.04
Rye	Hirschberg	4.07	4.13	7.52
	Breslau	3.24	3.39	6.09
Barley	Hirschberg	3.16	3.04	6.08
	Breslau	2.53	2.97	4.82

Source: Zimmermann, *Blüthe und Verfall des Leinengewerbes in Schlesien*, p. 474.

of the province, the town and valley of Hirschberg relied on grain supplies from outside – which meant that prices for bread were usually above average (Fig. 4.3).[50]

Contemporaries saw yet another reason for the long-term rise in prices: the increase of the volume of coined money in circulation. According to the *Neue Bunzlauische Monatschrift zum Nutzen und Vergnügen* (published in Bunzlau, today Bolesławiec), the monetary expenses of a family of five had increased thirtyfold during a 250-year period: they had risen from 5 Reichsthaler and 15 gute Groschen[51] per annum in 1500 to 150 Reichsthaler per annum in 1750. The authors saw a direct nexus of this inflation with the increase of the volume of cash in German lands, assuming a sixtyfold multiplication from approximately 7 million Reichsthaler in 1500 to roughly 429 million Reichsthaler in 1750.[52] Those provincial eighteenth-century economists accurately described Earl Hamilton's 'Price Revolution' – avant la lettre.

Making Ends Meet

A very detailed picture of the expenses of a peasant in the last quarter of the eighteenth century has been provided by the *Schlesische Provinzialblätter* from 1788. It draws on the example of a farm in the mountains of Lower Silesia, rented by a seignorial peasant, with its modest revenues from crop cultivation corresponding with most of the farms in the region. The farm housed six persons: the farmer, his wife and their two children (who counted as one adult), one male farm servant, one maidservant and a boy groom. Besides two horses, the farm had two cows, two goats, two draught oxen and four chickens. The farm's annual revenue of about 186 Reichsthaler was essentially generated by farming, supplemented by the yarn spun by the maidservant and the farmer's wife during the off-peak farming months. In turn, the total expenses for maintaining the farm, paying the farm-hands, the provisioning and the clothing of the wider family, plus taxes and the rent to the landlord added up to 353 Reichsthaler per annum. The deficit amounted to 167 Reichsthaler. The farm itself required at least 136 days of labour. Apart from that, at least forty-two days of labour (including horses and oxen) were owed to the overlord. The shortfall of 167 Reichsthaler had to be earned

50 Max Müller, *Die Getreidepolitik, der Getreideverkehr und die Getreidepreise in Schlesien während des 18. Jahrhunderts* (Weimar, 1897), p. 154; Zimmermann, *Blüthe und Verfall des Leinengewerbes in Schlesien*, p. 78.
51 One Reichsthaler was equal to 24 gute Groschen or 288 gute Pfennig.
52 *Neue Bunzlauische Monatschrift zum Nutzen und Vergnügen* 4 (1787), 301f. The *Schlesische Provinzialblätter* provides different figures, the general assertion remains the same: *Schlesische Provinzialblätter* 41 (1805), 31–7.

with additional work by all farm members during the remaining 187 days of the year.[53] Farmers would typically offer carriage services or let their oxen or horses in exchange for money, but rarely took to weaving. It was rather the landless people who practised both spinning and weaving, not for an additional income but as the mainstay for survival.[54]

According to the sources, by the end of the eighteenth century up to one-third of the Silesian population was involved in one way or another with the linen trade.[55] If the overall population of the province was close to 1,800,000 at that time,[56] this would equate to about 600,000 people. Production was complex: cultivating flax, breaking and heckling it, spinning yarn and bleaching it, collecting the yarn and selling it to the weavers who then manufactured panels of ordinary fabrics or wove delicate, elaborately patterned batistes. Then the finished pieces had to be brought to the merchants in the urban trade centres, often by middle-women (*Mäklerinnen*, *Umtrag-Weiber*). They collected the bales from the scattered dwellings of the weavers and carried it to sale in town. Having thus been spared a time-consuming walk, the weavers paid them a small fee.[57] In each of the linen-trading towns, the historic market square is surrounded by a walkway, protected by the columns and arches of the patrician houses. There, the merchants could exercise quality control of the fabrics, in any weather and all year round. And there were other groups making an income from this trade: the finished merchandise was loaded on horse carts and hauled to reloading points on the waterways of the region or to more distant destinations. Tenant farmers would provide some of these services, but the boatmen on the rivers and canals, and the men at the watergates, had to be paid. Finally, we need to bear in mind the smuggling that was flourishing along the borders and which supported quite a number of families. Trading restrictions like the ban on yarn exports encouraged illicit trade: while the Prussian ruler wanted the yarn to be woven in his own lands in order to keep weavers employed and to increase the state revenues, weavers in Saxony and Bohemia were always hungry for cheap yarns.[58]

53 *Schlesische Provinzialblätter* 8 (1788), 223–50.

54 See also Brentano, 'Ueber den grundherrlichen Charakter des hausindustriellen Leinengewerbes in Schlesien', p. 325; Ziekursch, *Hundert Jahre schlesischer Agrargeschichte*, p. 94; Heinz Pohlendt, *Die Landshuter Paßlandschaften*, pp. 6of.

55 *Schlesische Provinzialblätter* 29 (1799), p. 538.

56 *Schlesische Provinzialblätter* 17 (1793), 411–13, here p. 411; *Schlesische Provinzialblätter* 47 (1808), 440–2, here p. 442; Ziekursch, *Hundert Jahre schlesischer Agrargeschichte*, p. 61.

57 Zimmermann, *Blüthe und Verfall des Leinengewerbes in Schlesien*, p. 24; Kühn, *Der Hirschberger Leinwand- und Schleierhandel*, pp. 22–6.

58 Burkhard Nolte, *Merkantilismus und Staatsräson in Preußen. Absicht, Praxis und Wirkung der Zollpolitik Friedrichs II. in Schlesien und in westfälischen Provinzen (1740–1786)* (Marburg, 2004), pp. 101–22, 143–7.

Combining Micro and Macro Levels

During the period between 1747 and 1805 the total of Silesia's officially registered exports averaged almost 10 million Reichsthaler per annum, with linen goods contributing 45–54 per cent of this annual amount. Three-quarters of all those linens were destined for port cities in Western Europe (and some of it even straight for the Americas).[59] By the end of the eighteenth century, exports of Silesian linens accounted on average for 23 per cent of the total Prussian exports, which averaged 27.3 million Reichsthaler annually, and for 65 per cent of the total Silesian export value.[60]

Despite these impressive figures, the average Silesian remained poor in comparison with the regular townsfolk in places like Halberstadt and Magdeburg (the more recent acquisitions of Prussia), with the common people living in Prussia's western exclaves of Minden, Ravensberg, Tecklenburg and Lingen, or with those in its core lands of Kurmark. In 1775–76, the per capita income in the most populous region of Prussia, Silesia, added up to 2.6 Thaler, whereas the average income in Halberstadt was 4.7 Thaler. Within Prussia, only the subjects living in the Neumark and in Pomerania, with only 1.96 and 2.28 Thaler per capita, were poorer than the Silesians.[61]

The total value of linen exports from Silesia averaged around 4.4 million Reichsthaler per annum. With one full-time weaver producing a three-score (some 58–60 ells) of ordinary linen cloth weekly,[62] and each three-score valued at 7 Reichsthaler,[63] a workforce of some 12,000 Silesians would have had to have been employed in full-time weaving during the years 1747–1805 to generate that annual sum. Yet, taking into consideration that the exports also comprised a portion of the more delicate and much more expensive linen batistes (40 Reichsthaler per piece at the top of the range),[64] the number of weavers must have been smaller than that figure. Other sources do mention

59   Calculation based on statistical data found in Leonhardi, *Erdbeschreibung der Preußischen Monarchie*, pp. 58, 68; *Schlesische Provinzialblätter* 15 (1792), 265; *Schlesische Provinzialblätter* 20 (1794), 385–6, here p. 385; *Schlesische Provinzialblätter* 32 (1800), 575–6; *Schlesische Provinzialblätter* 34 (1801), 376; *Schlesische Provinzialblätter* 36 (1802), 144–7, here p. 145; *Schlesische Provinzialblätter* 39 (1804), 36–8; *Schlesische Provinzialblätter* 40 (1804), 444–6; *Schlesische Provinzialblätter* 42 (1805), 561–3; Zimmermann, *Blüthe und Verfall des Leinengewerbes in Schlesien*, pp. 460–7; Behre, *Geschichte der Statistik in Brandenburg-Preussen*, pp. 346–8.
60   Calculation based on data regarding three years (1781, 1785/6, and 1793): Behre, *Geschichte der Statistik in Brandenburg-Preussen*, pp. 346, 351.
61   Ibid., p. 102.
62   Ernst Michael, *Die Hausweberei im Hirschberger Tal* (Jena, 1925), p. 29, Marcel Boldorf, 'Märkte und Verlage im institutionellen Gefüge der Leinenregion Niederschlesien des 18. Jahrhunderts', p. 181.
63   Leonhardi, *Erdbeschreibung der Preußischen Monarchie*, p. 52.
64   Ibid., pp. 52f.

a range of 8,841–10,888 weavers for the period 1778–95.[65] An estimate of around 10,000 weavers may be assumed to be realistic, at least for the late eighteenth century. The discrepancy between the three figures may be explained with the fact that part-time spinning and part-time weaving were widespread.[66] Even when taking the unlikely number of 13,000 weavers as a basis, and estimating Silesia's population at around 1.5 million during the period 1747–1805 (Fig. 4.1), it becomes clear that during those decades, the labour of less than 1 per cent of the total population accounted for more than half of the province's export value.

It is thus relevant to have an even closer look at this small but important group of weavers and at their living conditions. The modest number of weavers seems surprising at first glance, but is actually not so remarkable after all. The persistence of estate ownership and hereditary serfdom explains why not just anybody could take up weaving, even if this occupation seemed profitable at certain periods. Redemption from hereditary subservience had been possible even before 1807, the year of reform, but it was not extensively practised because of prohibitive costs: a so-called *Lytrum personale* had to be paid for the release of persons; a *Lytrum reale* paid for all belongings. Around 1748, the ransom was in the range of 10–18 Reichsthaler per capita. Given the low income noted above – one, a maximum of 3 Silbergroschen per day for a male servant – and the considerable cost of food, the accumulation of such sums was more than burdensome, let alone the ransom for a whole family. Three per cent of the people bound to a landlord were able to redeem themselves in 1785.[67] Assuming the same rate of redemption for a time span of thirty years, hardly any serfs would have been left. Yet, if a freed person took residence as peasant or cottager on a piece of land owned by another proprietor, he fell back into subservience. The same occurred if a freedman or freedwoman married a subservient partner.[68] In the long run, redemptions did not increase the portion of freedmen and freedwomen, but rather were just another lucrative source of income for the feudal overlords. Less costly was the permit for a tenant's temporary departure from the estate. Upon payment of a fee (*Schutzgeld*) he was allowed to seek a better-paid job. In case he relied on lodging provided by his temporary employer, he owed him another fee.[69] The mover also had to pay the spinning or weaving licence (*Weberzins*) if he joined any of these crafts. As small as this group of weavers was, they were ill-placed to maintain a high standard of living.

65   Ziekursch, *Hundert Jahre schlesischer Agrargeschichte*, p. 43.
66   Kühn, *Der Hirschberger Leinwand- und Schleierhandel*, p. 19.
67   Calculation based on the details provided by Ziekursch. He states that the ransom payments became a main source of income for the landlords: Ziekursch, *Hundert Jahre schlesischer Agrargeschichte*, pp. 104f.
68   Ibid., p. 107.
69   Ibid., p. 113; Kühn, *Der Hirschberger Leinwand- und Schleierhandel*, p. 20.

The Industrious Poor

To be sure, a weaver could still earn much more money than a common farm-hand – but only as long as the economic situation in Western Europe and in the wider Atlantic world favoured the linen trade. Peter Hasenclever, a prominent linen merchant from the Rhenish Duchy of Berg, who had made a career in the Atlantic world before settling in Landeshut, was also an expert in political economy. In 1787, he estimated that out of the 5–7 Reichsthaler a weaver was paid for one three-score piece of linen (which it took him a week to weave), only 2 Reichsthaler (60 Silbergroschen) were left once the worker had paid all the inevitable expenses: the weaving licence, costs for the finished yarn, rewards for the yarn carriers (*Garnsammler*), and the pay for the middle-woman who brought the produce to town. The weavers of batistes certainly obtained more money per piece, but had to rely on better and more expensive yarns.[70] On the one hand, as the wage figures cited above indicate, 2 Reichsthaler amounted to almost the twice the pay of a common day labourer and just over eight times the pay of a bonded male farm-hand. On the other hand, Silesia's close economic entanglements with the wider world entailed risks which were more threatening to the weavers than to the merchants: maritime and continental wars, increases in customs duties for one or other of the places of destination, import bans on certain textiles and the like had immediate repercussions in the province and could easily lead to underemployment or even unemployment. On top of this came the high volatility of prices for staple foods.[71]

Hirschberg may serve as an indicator of such dependencies. During the relatively stable and prosperous period from 1752 to 1790, the value of linen exported from Hirschberg and the surrounding villages averaged up to 1.5 million Reichsthaler per annum. The value of linen exported per week thus added up to approx. 31,250 Reichsthaler. This implies that in the town and the wider valley of Hirschberg, approximately 5,300 full-time and part-time weavers were needed to manufacture the corresponding volume of fabrics. Yet, during the difficult years from 1802 to 1822, export figures nosedived to an average of 505,000 Reichsthaler per annum. This meant that no more than 1,800 weavers were needed to meet the demand. Even in times of peace and thriving commerce, the poorer strata of Silesian population had just about managed to scrape through.[72] In these lean years, the evidence is that two-thirds of the weavers became redundant, and those still in business had to

70   *Schlesische Provinzialblätter* 5 (1787), 214–36, here p. 224; see also Leonhardi, *Erdbeschreibung der Preußischen Monarchie*, p. 52. On Hasenclever: Adolf Hasenclever, *Peter Hasenclever aus Remscheid-Ehringhausen, ein deutscher Kaufmann des 18. Jahrhunderts* (Gotha, 1922).

71   Müller, *Die Getreidepolitik*, pp. 153–79.

72   Brentano, 'Ueber den grundherrlichen Charakter des hausindustriellen Leinengewerbes in Schlesien', p. 335.

fear for their sheer survival.[73] The outmigration beginning with the process of the liberation of the peasants in 1807 reveals that the linen production in this province had at least to some extent been built on a coercion which resulted from the restriction of choices and opportunities. In the ten years following the October Decree, 7 per cent of the inhabitants left the mountainous region of Lower Silesia; as much as 12 per cent left the villages in the immediate vicinity of Hirschberg (Hirschberger Kreis).[74]

The intensification of labour in this part of Central Europe does not fit with Jan de Vries' concept of an 'Industrious Revolution', nor with Roman Sandgruber's model of the origins of consumer society in the eighteenth century.[75] Both authors emphasised the desire of individuals for new choices and their capacity to increase their own spending power, and this is certainly appropriate for eighteenth-century Britain and the Netherlands. But the Silesians described here did not increase their working hours in order to exploit new opportunities for consumption. They did so because an exploitative labour regime and the high price of staple foods forced them to do so – otherwise they would have starved.

The consumption of colonial foodstuffs may serve as an indicator of access to such new opportunities. Taking into consideration Silesia's imports and exports of sugar, and the demographic growth, it may be assumed that during the 1740s the average Silesian had 2.25 pounds (approximately 1 kilogram) of sugar in his diet. By 1805 consumption had risen to no more than 2.75 pounds (approximately 1.25 kilograms).[76] This lagged far behind the per capita consumption of 9 kilograms in Britain and the 4–5 kilograms consumed in the Netherlands during the decades around 1800.[77]

The wealth which was generated by proto-industrial textile production and the far-flung export trade was mostly skimmed off by the merchant elite. The more successful traders accumulated fortunes which allowed for the

---

73 Calculation based on figures extracted from Leonhardi, *Erdbeschreibung der Preußischen Monarchie*, p. 434; *Schlesische Provinzialblätter* 15 (1792), p. 265; Daniel Hensel, *Historisch-Topographische Beschreibung der Stadt Hirschberg in Schlesien seit ihrem Ursprunge bis auf das Jahr 1797* (Hirschberg, 1797), pp. 621–718; Michael, *Die Hausweberei im Hirschberger Tal*, pp. 18f, 36; Rolf Straubel, 'Breslau als Handelsplatz und wirtschaftlicher Vorort Schlesiens (1740–1815)', *Jahrbuch für die Geschichte Mittel- und Ostdeutschlands. Zeitschrift für vergleichende und preußische Landesgeschichte* 49 (2003), 195–299, here p. 287.

74 Ziekursch, *Hundert Jahre schlesischer Agrargeschichte*, pp. 303–4.

75 De Vries, *The Industrious Revolution*, pp. 122–77; Roman Sandgruber, *Die Anfänge der Konsumgesellschaft. Konsumgüterverbrauch, Lebensstandard und Alltagskultur in Österreich im 18. und 19. Jahrhundert* (Vienna, 1982).

76 Leonhardi, *Erdbeschreibung der Preußischen Monarchie*, pp. 75–6.

77 Jonathan Hersh and Hans-Joachim Voth, *Sweet Diversity: Colonial Goods and the Rise of European Living Standards after 1492* (C.E.P.R. Discussion Paper, 2009), p. 14; see also de Vries, *The Industrious Revolution*, p. 160.

purchase of noble titles, and of landed estates with their adherent villages (and inhabitants), from declining families of the older nobility. Daniel von Buchs (1707–79) was granted a title in recognition of his commercial success; Christian Mentzel (1667–1748) acquired a substantial residential estate, but out of civic pride he declined the imperial offer to raise him to the nobility.[78] Most of the small but opulent baroque palaces around Hirschberg ended up in the hands of this new commercial elite.[79]

Only during the first decades of the nineteenth century did their strategy become obsolete. Napoleon's Continental System had dealt a blow to Silesia's commercial networks in the western hemisphere. In the following years, increasing volumes of linen yarns and linen fabrics came from new textile mills in England, Ireland and Westphalia. The Silesian linen merchants never became 'modern' entrepreneurs or factory owners. The mode of production and the labour regime they had established turned out to be a dead end, with disastrous effects on the textile workers.[80]

Conclusion

According to Karl Polanyi and Eric Hobsbawm, the Old English Poor Law offered outdoor relief for agricultural workers during the poorer winter months, in order to prevent them from moving temporarily into urban regions (from where they would probably not return in spring, when labour demand peaked). It was designed 'to stop the development of a capitalist labour market'.[81] When slavery was abolished in the Caribbean and in the American South, this was achieved by Apprenticeship Laws and Black Codes.[82] In Silesia,

---

78 Gerhard Schiller, 'Christian Mentzel (1667–1748). Das Leben eines Hirschberger Schleierherrn als Kaufmann, Bankier und Mäzen seiner Heimatstadt', *Leben in Leichenpredigten* 12, ed. Forschungsstelle für Personalschriften (Marburg, 2011), http://www.personalschriften. de/leichenpredigten/artikelserien/artikelansicht/details/christian-mentzel-1667-1748.html (accessed 28 February 2016).

79 Arno Franke, *Das schlesische Elysium. Burgen, Schlösser, Herrenhäuser und Parks im Hirschberger Tal*, Deutsches Kulturforum östliches Europa, 3rd edn (Potsdam, 2008), pp. 39f, 48–51, 68f, 123–9, 135f, 150–4, 169f; Kühn, *Der Hirschberger Leinwand- und Schleierhandel*, pp. 120–4.

80 Kühn, *Der Hirschberger Leinwand- und Schleierhandel*, p. 126; Marcel Boldorf, 'Weltwirtschaftliche Verflechtung und lokale Existenzsicherung. Die schlesischen Kaufmannsgilden im internationalen Leinenhandel des 18. Jahrhunderts', *Praktiken des Handels. Geschäfte und soziale Beziehungen europäischer Kaufleute in Mittelalter und früher Neuzeit*, ed. M. Häberlein and C. Jeggle (Konstanz, 2010), pp. 127–44, here pp. 143f.

81 George Boyer, *An Economic History of the English Poor Law 1750–1850* (Cambridge, 1990), p. 75.

82 Douglas A. Blackmon, *Slavery by Another Name. The Reenslavement of Black Americans from the Civil War to World War II* (New York, 2008).

the workforce was immobilised by serfdom and upward social mobility was minimised by the trade monopolies of the guilds. This feudal order secured a considerable elasticity in labour supply. With labour so readily available, entrepreneurs were able to freeze the wages of textile workers at the level of mere subsistence. Low wages, in turn, were no incentive for investment in mechanisation. The volatility of export markets was yet another factor which worked against technological innovation. The proto-industrial mode of production allowed for swift responses to the ups and downs of commerce. Workers were employed according to demand, and with minimal investment of capital into industrial equipment there was no surplus capacity lying dormant on which to draw during periods of crisis. For the merchant elite it was an economically sound strategy to instead invest their profits in real estate, in noble titles and in the manors that went with their new status.[83]

The cheapness of labour must also be seen in a wider Atlantic context. Wages in Central Europe generally lagged behind those in North-Western Europe.[84] Ulrich Pfister has recently claimed that real wages in German lands were even in decline during eighteenth century.[85] This case study on Silesia would confirm his results. The effects of low wages on the price of manufactures were significant, in particular with regards to labour-intensive products such as textiles. As early as the 1620s, the British economist Thomas Mun, a major shareholder of the East India Company, complained that 'Cambricks' and other linen from Continental Europe were competing in price with the calicoes the Company brought in from India.[86] Both calicoes and linen were in demand in West Africa, which implies that Central European and Indian textile producers were in direct competition on these markets – which were essentially slave markets. This competition helped to check price levels for textiles within the wider Atlantic basin, and thus to attenuate the rise of prices demanded for slaves from Africa. In short, low costs for labour in Silesia lowered the costs for slave labour on the plantations in the 'New World'. This Prussian province, with its extremely low wages, is the most striking example, but Silesian conditions put pressure on pay rates in Germany's more westerly linen regions as well. Silesian linen was also bleached or dyed in Rhenish territories before being exported – thus mixing free and unfree labour within one

83   Kühn, *Der Hirschberger Leinwand- und Schleierhandel*, p. 120.
84   Jan Luiten van Zanden, *The Long Road to the Industrial Revolution: The European Economy in a Global Perspective, 1000–1800* (Leiden, 2009), p. 98.
85   Ulrich Pfister, *Great Divergence, Consumer Revolution and the Reorganization of Textile Markets: Evidence from Hamburg's Import Trade, Eighteenth Century* (Discussion Paper, 1st draft, Westfälische Wilhelms-Universität, June 2012).
86   Thomas Mun, 'A Discourse of Trade, from England unto the East-Indies (1621)', *Mercantilism*, vol. 1: *The Rise of Mercantilist Discourse*, ed. L. Magnussen (London/New York, 1994), pp. 49–80, here p. 52.

product. These effects and practices, and the general decline of wages from Western to Eastern Europe provided all German linen regions with relatively low labour costs. Their overall competitiveness is exemplified by with the numbers of 'sletias' on African slave markets, and by the omnipresence of 'Osnabrughs' in the Caribbean.

5

There Are No Slaves in Prussia?[1]

REBEKKA VON MALLINCKRODT

Translated by Elizabeth Bredeck

In 1996 Sue Peabody published her research on slavery in France in the Early Modern Period. The title of her study – *'There Are No Slaves in France'* – reflected the contemporary belief that slaves were automatically emancipated upon reaching French soil, a belief whose roots went back as far as the sixteenth century. It also suggested the implications that this and related beliefs had for research up until the present day: slavery was long seen as a phenomenon unique to colonies outside of Europe.[2] It was possible to maintain this viewpoint because most European countries only passed laws on the status of slaves on the European continent and in the British Isles in the late eighteenth century; operating in a legal grey area benefited European owners (but also unsettled them), and helped to conceal the contradiction between slavery and contemporary notions of freedom. Hence in Great Britain 'black servants' were advertised for sale in eighteenth-century newspaper announcements, yet the term 'slave' did not appear.[3] Similarly, French and Dutch sources often deliberately avoided the term 'slavery'.[4] Research on enslavement practices on

---

1 This project has received funding from the European Research Council (ERC) under the European Union's Horizon 2020 research and innovation programme (grant agreement No. 641110 *The Holy Roman Empire of the German Nation and its Slaves*, 2015–20). It still reflects only the author's view and the ERC is not responsible for any use that may be made of the information it contains.
2 Sue Peabody, *'There Are No Slaves in France': The Political Culture of Race and Slavery in the Ancien Régime* (New York, 1996), pp. 3, 12, 14, 21, 28–9, 90. Similar notions of a 'free soil ideology' were also developed in England and the Netherlands (ibid., pp. 4–5). See also the special issue on 'Free soil' of *Slavery & Abolition* 32/3 (2011).
3 Kathleen Chater, *Untold Histories. Black People in England and Wales During the Period of the British Slave Trade c.1660–1807* (Manchester, 2009), pp. 86–7.
4 At the end of the eighteenth century Dutch jurists who were preparing the constitution still agreed not to mention slavery explicitly: Dienke Hondius, 'Access to the Netherlands of Enslaved and Free Black Africans: Exploring Legal and Social Historical Practices in the

the European continent has thus always confronted the problem that contemporaries preferred not to speak explicitly about slavery, even in situations that from an analytical-historiographical perspective clearly involved slavery.

Since the publication of Peabody's book, research on the phenomenon of slavery on the European continent has grown significantly, though with clear areas of concentration and equally visible gaps. While numerous publications have appeared in and about Western Europe and the Mediterranean, research on the less-affected areas of Northern and Central Europe – and in particular, those German-speaking countries without 'successful' colonial policy – is still in the early stages, although these countries too are now receiving increasing attention (starting with the exploration of their economic involvement).[5] In recent years we thus find a growing number of essays and books on trafficked people in the Holy Roman Empire of the German Nation (HRE), individuals abducted either from the Ottoman Empire or the Mediterranean region, or in the context of the transatlantic slave trade.[6] Even so, researchers are noticeably

Sixteenth–Nineteenth Centuries', *Slavery & Abolition* 32/3 (2011), 377–95, here p. 379; Dienke Hondius, 'Black Africans in Seventeenth-Century Amsterdam', *Renaissance and Reformation* 31/2 (2008), 87–105, here pp. 89f; Arend H. Huussen, Jr, 'The Dutch Constitution of 1798 and the Problem of Slavery', *Legal History Review* 67/1–2 (1999), 99–114, here p. 113.

5 See on this topic the research of Klaus Weber, 'Deutschland, der atlantische Sklavenhandel und die Plantagenwirtschaft der Neuen Welt (15. bis 19. Jahrhundert)', *Journal of Modern European History* 7/1 (2009), 37–67; Klaus Weber, *Deutsche Kaufleute im Atlantikhandel 1680–1830: Unternehmen und Familien in Hamburg, Cádiz und Bordeaux* (Munich, 2004). See also Karl H. Schwebel, *Bremer Kaufleute in den Freihäfen der Karibik. Von den Anfängen des Bremer Überseehandels bis 1815* (Bremen, 1995); Thomas David, Bouda Etemad and Janick Marina Schaufelbuehl, *Schwarze Geschäfte. Die Beteiligung von Schweizern an Sklaverei und Sklavenhandel im 18. und 19. Jahrhundert* (Zurich, 2005); Hans Werner Debrunner, 'Basel und der Sklavenhandel – Fragmente eines wenig bekannten Kapitels der Basler Geschichte', *Basler Stadtbuch 1993* (Basel, 1994), pp. 95–101; Hans Fässler, *Reise in Schwarz-Weiss: Schweizer Ortstermine in Sachen Sklaverei*, 2nd edn (Zurich, 2006); Konrad J. Kuhn and Béatrice Ziegler, 'Die Schweiz und die Sklaverei. Zum Spannungsfeld zwischen Geschichtspolitik und Wissenschaft', *Traverse* 16 (2009), 116–30; Niklaus Stettler, Peter Haenger and Robert Labhardt, *Baumwolle, Sklaven und Kredite. Die Basler Welthandelsfirma Christoph Burckhardt & Cie. in revolutionärer Zeit (1789–1815)* (Basel, 2004).

6 Publications from the last ten years include: Anne Kuhlmann-Smirnov, *Schwarze Europäer im Alten Reich. Handel, Migration, Hof* (Göttingen, 2013); Mischa Honeck, Martin Klimke and Anne Kuhlmann, eds, *Germany and the Black Diaspora: Points of Contact, 1250–1914* (New York, 2013); Stephan Theilig, *Türken, Mohren und Tataren. Muslimische (Lebens-) Welten in Brandenburg-Preußen im 18. Jahrhundert* (Berlin, 2013); Andreas Becker, 'Preußens schwarze Untertanen. Afrikanerinnen und Afrikaner zwischen Kleve und Königsberg vom 17. Jahrhundert bis ins frühe 19. Jahrhundert', *Forschungen zur Brandenburgischen und Preußischen Geschichte* 22 (2012), 1–32; Philipp Blom and Wolfgang Kos, eds, *Angelo Soliman. Ein Afrikaner in Wien* (Vienna, 2011); Simon Mougnol, *Amo Afer. Un noir, professeur d'université en Allemagne au XVIIIe siècle* (Paris, 2010); Iris Wigger and Katrin Klein, '"Bruder Mohr". Angelo Soliman und der Rassismus der Aufklärung', *Entfremdete Körper. Rassismus als Leichenschändung*, ed. W. D. Hund (Bielefeld, 2009), pp. 81–115; Ulrich van der Heyden, ed., *Unbekannte Biographien. Afrikaner im deutschsprachigen Europa vom 18. Jahrhundert bis zum Ende des Zweiten*

reluctant to speak explicitly of slaves.[7] This is due in part to the situation itself, as complex as it is diffuse: neither skin colour nor (often indeterminate) place of origin gives a clear indication of legal status. The coexistence of free, bonded, and enslaved dark-skinned people together with prisoners of war meant that in the HRE there was no direct correlation between physical appearance or place of origin and legal status.[8] In addition, it is harder to determine the status of slaves in societies that are not slave-holding societies, and it requires us to adapt the use of the term 'slavery' accordingly. This of course applies to the situation in all European countries equally and independent of whether or not they were directly involved in the slave trade. We thus often find what Claude Meillassoux has termed the first two indispensible criteria of slavery: abduction and hence foreignness in the society (in contrast to serfdom), and sale to an owner (in contrast to war captivity). However, the degree of dependence – and hence the absolute dependence on an owner, Meillassoux' third and final essential criterion[9] – is often hard to pinpoint given the lack

---

Weltkrieges ([Berlin], 2008); Anne Kuhlmann-Smirnov, 'Globalität als Prestigemerkmal? Die Hofmohren der Cirksena und ihres sozialen Umfeldes', *Adel und Umwelt. Horizonte adeliger Existenz in der Frühen Neuzeit*, ed. H. Düselder, O. Weckenbrock and S. Westphal (Cologne, 2008), pp. 287–309; Walter Sauer, ed., *Von Soliman zu Omofuma. Afrikanische Diaspora in Österreich 17. bis 20. Jahrhundert* (Innsbruck, 2007); Jacob Emmanuel Mabe, *Anton Wilhelm Amo interkulturell gelesen* (Nordhausen, 2007); Paul Raabe, *Anton Wilhelm Amo, ein Schwarzer am Wolfenbütteler Hof*, exhibition catalogue (Wolfenbüttel, 2006); Mark Häberlein, '"Mohren", ständische Gesellschaft und atlantische Welt', *Atlantic Understandings: Essays on European and American History in Honor of Hermann Wellenreuther*, ed. C. Schnurmann and H. Lehmann (Hamburg, 2006), pp. 77–102; Markus Friedrich, '"Türken" im Alten Reich. Zur Aufnahme und Konversion von Muslimen im deutschen Sprachraum (16.–18. Jahrhundert)', *Historische Zeitschrift* 294 (2012), 329–60; Manja Quakatz, '"Gebürtig aus der Türckey". Zu Konversion und Zwangstaufe osmanischer Muslime im Alten Reich um 1700', *Europa und die Türkei im 18. Jahrhundert*, ed. B. Schmidt-Haberkamp (Göttingen, 2011), pp. 417–30.

7   Peter Martin writes of a 'no man's land between free and unfree' (Peter Martin, *Schwarze Teufel, edle Mohren. Afrikaner in Geschichte und Bewußtsein der Deutschen* (Hamburg, 2001), p. 129), while Uta Sadji proposes that blacks in eighteenth-century Germany were 'legally speaking free, but still mostly lived like slaves' (Uta Sadji, '"Unverbesserlich ausschweifende" oder "brauchbare Subjekte"? Mohren als "befreite" Sklaven im Deutschland des 18. Jahrhunderts', *Komparatistische Hefte* 2 (1980), 42–52, here p. 50).

8   Anne Kuhlmann has recently noted the diverse living situations of people of African origin in the HRE: Anne Kuhlmann, 'Ambiguous Duty, Black Servants at German Ancien Régime Courts', *Germany and the Black Diaspora: Points of Contact, 1250–1914*, ed. M. Honeck, M. Klimke and A. Kuhlmann (New York, 2013), pp. 57–73, here pp. 58, 63. Stephan Theilig has demonstrated the presence of dark-skinned Ottoman prisoners of war well into the eighteenth century: Theilig, *Türken, Mohren und Tataren*, p. 37.

9   Claude Meillassoux, 'Postface: Esclaves, vénacles, captifs et serfs', *Esclavage et dépendances serviles. Histoire comparée*, ed. M. Cottias, A. Stella and B. Vincent (Paris, 2006), pp. 367–73, here pp. 368–9. From a legal standpoint, he argues, such dependent people do not count as persons and thus have no rights; correspondingly, all concessions are precarious privileges that can be revoked at any time. Hence there can be extreme variations in work, working and living conditions. Even in the case of manumission a former slave often remained heavily dependent

of source materials, or more specifically the lack of legal texts concerning the status of slaves. This problem is compounded by the manifold and tiered forms of dependency in the estate-based societies of early modern Europe. Due to the often isolated and clearly minority status of trafficked people on the European continent, precise legal distinctions apparently seemed less necessary than in the context of slave plantations where they represented a threatening majority. Even plantation slavery differed from the definition of slavery found in Roman law, since the arbitrary killing of a slave was (theoretically) not allowed in the former system. Therefore, an (apparently) ahistorical, analytical concept of slavery is also inadequate for variations like the ones just mentioned that in the literature are generally acknowledged as slavery.[10] Resale, presentation as a gift and, of course, the (rarely documented) manumission of trafficked people on the European continent are nonetheless clear indications that these relationships of dependency were not compatible with concepts of war captivity, serfdom and domestic service, but clearly extended beyond them and support the notion of slavery. Conversely, conditions of (non-)payment,[11] marital status,[12] occupation or – as I argue below – conformity with certain religious practices do not in themselves allow us to draw conclusions about whether a person was enslaved or free.

Finally, this reticence concerning the term 'slavery' in reference to the HRE also reflects a notion that dates back to the eighteenth century and is often apologetically formulated: the notion that Germany was not involved in the slave trade. Thus when Monika Firla, one of the first German-language scholars

on his/her former owner, be it through contractual agreements or socio-economic dependency. Above all, the dark-skinned former slaves were still recognisable as 'foreigners', or, if they had to remain in the same social environment, were known to be former slaves. Enslaved people of the second and later generations born into the slave-owning society could partially regain their social existence by expanding their privileges and making them permanent (pp. 367, 371–3).

10   Peter Kolchin accordingly calls for a concept of slavery that is historically and geographically variable: Peter Kolchin, 'L'approche comparée de l'étude de l'esclavage. Problèmes et perspectives', *Esclavage et dépendances serviles. Histoire comparée*, ed. M. Cottias, A. Stella and B. Vincent (Paris, 2006), pp. 283–301, here p. 293.

11   Many non-enslaved workers were not paid with money, while some slaves received at least partial compensation: Chater, *Untold Histories*, pp. 85–6, 89; Alessandro Stella, *Histoires d'esclaves dans la péninsule ibérique* (Paris, 2000), pp. 21, 135, 138. On the transition to paid labour as a trend in society as a whole in the eighteenth century: Walter Sauer and Andrea Wiesböck, 'Sklaven, Freie, Fremde. Wiener "Mohren" des 17. und 18. Jahrhunderts', *Von Soliman zu Omofuma. Afrikanische Diaspora in Österreich 17. bis 20. Jahrhundert*, ed. W. Sauer (Innsbruck, 2007), pp. 23–56, here p. 49; Salvatore Bono, 'Sklaven in der mediterranen Welt. Von der Ersten Türkenbelagerung bis zum Wiener Kongress (1529–1815)', *Angelo Soliman. Ein Afrikaner in Wien*, ed. P. Blom and W. Kos (Vienna, 2011), pp. 35–49, here p. 43; Theilig, *Türken, Mohren und Tataren*, p. 38.

12   In Spain the church officially recognised marriages between slaves: Stella, *Histoires d'esclaves*, p. 130. For the Mediterranean region see also Bono, 'Sklaven in der mediterranen Welt', p. 45.

to have addressed the topic, writes that German dealers released enslaved
Africans by purchasing them, the statement must be read as a euphemistic interpretation.[13] When Andreas Becker claims that without exception slaves brought
to Brandenburg-Prussia were baptised and thereby given the same status as
servants, since according to canon law Christians could not be slaves,[14] we need
to ask what legal standing canon law could have possibly had in Protestant
Prussia, and also why normative concepts should be taken more seriously in this
case than in others. Certainly, the principle that baptism liberated was known
in France as early as the sixteenth century. It was also in circulation in Great
Britain, though often dismissed, as in court rulings of 1729 and 1749 as well as
in the notorious judgment of Lord Mansfield. In the colonies, however, people
saw no contradiction in any case between Christianisation and enslavement:
The Code Noir of 1685 prescribed the baptism of slaves, but this did not mean
that they became free as a result, and for Nikolaus von Zinzendorf and the
Moravian Brethren congregations, Christianisation and slavery were likewise
not mutually exclusive. Early modern Europe provides numerous examples
to show that baptism did not automatically lead to freedom. Instead, that
hope cherished by many enslaved men and women was dashed time and time
again. In the eighteenth century, galley slaves were freed through baptism in
the Papal States, but not in Marseilles. In Austria well into the first half of
the century, baptism did not lead to liberation and the first part of the 1758
Codex Theresianus declared the suspension of 'servile subserviance among
Christians', but it never took effect.[15] Furthermore, in Europe slaves were by no
means all baptised;[16] in short, there was nothing automatic about any of these
processes, and in fact, the notion that baptism led to freedom was repudiated
in Prussia as a papal doctrine.

In this chapter I propose not to apply the notion of slavery generally to
all trafficked people in the HRE, but to use the term specifically and in a
case-related way, taking Brandenburg-Prussia during the second half of the
eighteenth century as example. At that time, the Central European territorial
power looked like the epitome of a failed colonial power: Brandenburg-Prussia

---

13   Monika Firla, 'AfrikanerInnen und ihre Nachkommen im deutschsprachigen Raum',
AfrikanerInnen in Deutschland und schwarze Deutsche – Geschichte und Gegenwart, ed.
M. Bechhaus-Gerst and R. Klein-Arendt (Berlin, 2004), pp. 9–24, here p. 15.

14   Becker, 'Preußens schwarze Untertanen', pp. 15–16, 28.

15   Peabody, *'There Are No Slaves in France'*, pp. 13, 31, 80; Chater, *Untold Histories*, pp. 84,
91; Häberlein, '"Mohren", ständische Gesellschaft und atlantische Welt', p. 101; Wipertus Rudt
de Collenberg, 'Le baptême des musulmans esclaves à Rome aux XVIIe et XVIIIe siècles. Le
XVIIIe siècle', *Mélanges de l'École française de Rome. Italie et Méditerranée* 101/2 (1989),
519–670, here pp. 535, 537; Sauer and Wiesböck, 'Sklaven, Freie, Fremde', p. 47. For the
Mediterranean region see also Bono, 'Sklaven in der mediterranen Welt', p. 45.

16   In Paris, for example, only 28.3 per cent of the registered 'blacks' in 1762 were baptised:
Peabody, *'There Are No Slaves in France'*, p. 82.

had already (1718) sold its few colonies to the Dutch West India Company (WIC),[17] the Brandenburg African Company had long since been dissolved,[18] and attempts to build a seaport in Emden and establish a 'Royal Prussian Asian Company in Emden to Canton and China' in the 1740s and 1750s had met with only marginal success. After the Seven Years War those efforts were not renewed.[19] At the same time, the research of Klaus Weber and others has shown the deep economic involvement not only of German, but more specifically also of Prussian merchants, bankers and ship-owners as partners, producers and suppliers of trade goods as well as consumers of plantation products. Copper from the Harz, linen from Silesia (which then belonged in large part to Prussia) and Westphalia were among the most highly sought-after items to be traded for slaves, and were mass-produced in large quantities for this purpose.[20] The following will focus not on this form of participation in the slave trade, however, but instead on enslaved people in Brandenburg-Prussia itself. Using as a starting point the 'Legal History of a Purchased Moor' ('Rechtsgeschichte eines erkauften Mohren') that appeared in 1780 in the journal *Beyträge zur juristischen Litteratur in den Preußischen Staaten* (Contributions to Legal Literature in the Prussian States),[21] I aim to show:

<hr/>

17   Berlin, Geheimes Staatsarchiv Preußischer Kulturbesitz (GStA PK), I. HA Geheimer Rat, Rep. 65 Marine und Afrikanische Kompagniesachen, No. 117 Afrikanische Kompagniesachen, 1718 (Sale of African possessions to the Dutch West India Company, honorary gift of 12 'Negro boys').
18   Ulrich van der Heyden, *Rote Adler an Afrikas Küste. Die brandenburgisch-preußische Kolonie Großfriedrichsburg in Westafrika*, 2nd edn (Berlin, 2001); Ulrich van der Heyden, 'Benjamin Raule und Berlin', '... *Macht und Anteil an der Weltherrschaft': Berlin und der deutsche Kolonialismus*, ed. U. van der Heyden and J. Zeller (Münster, 2005), pp. 63–8; Adam Jones, *Brandenburg Sources for West African History 1680–1700* (Wiesbaden, 1985); Sven Klosa, *Die Brandenburgische-Africanische Compagnie in Emden. Eine Handelscompagnie des ausgehenden 17. Jahrhunderts zwischen Protektionismus und unternehmerischer Freiheit* (Frankfurt a.M., 2011); Malte Stamm, 'Das Koloniale Experiment. Der Sklavenhandel Brandenburg-Preußens im transatlantischen Raum 1680–1718' (unpublished dissertation, University of Düsseldorf, 2011), http://d-nb.info/1036727564/34 (accessed 10 May 2014); Andrea Weindl, *Die Kurbrandenburger im "atlantischen System", 1650–1720*, Arbeitspapiere zur Lateinamerikaforschung, II/3 (2001), http://lateinamerika.phil-fak.uni-koeln.de/fileadmin/sites/aspla/bilder/arbeitspapiere/weindl.pdf (accessed 5 May 2015).
19   Thomas Biskup and Peter H. Wilson, 'Großbritannien, Amerika und die atlantische Welt', *Friederisiko – Friedrich der Große*, ed. Stiftung Preußische Schlösser und Gärten Berlin-Brandenburg, 3 vols (Munich, 2012), vol. 1, pp. 146–62, here pp. 158–9.
20   Weber, 'Deutschland, der atlantische Sklavenhandel und die Plantagenwirtschaft der Neuen Welt'; Weber, *Deutsche Kaufleute im Atlantikhandel 1680–1830*. See also chapter 4 by Anka Steffen and Klaus Weber in this book. In the eighteenth century Brandenburg-Prussia included: the County of Mark (from 1609), the County of Ravensberg (from 1614/47), the principalities of Halberstadt and Minden (from 1648), the County of Lingen (from 1702) and the County of Tecklenburg (from 1707).
21   Anonymous, 'Rechtsgeschichte eines erkauften Mohren', *Beyträge zur juristischen Litteratur in den Preußischen Staaten*, 6. Sammlung, 4. Abschnitt (Berlin, 1780), 296–311.

1. that it is accurate to use the term 'slavery' in connection with German-speaking areas in the early modern period,
2. that it is heuristically useful and important to apply the concept of slavery in order to illustrate how the debate about the abolition of slavery and the dispute over the elimination of serfdom were interconnected, and
3. that applying the concept of slavery to the HRE enriches international research on slavery in that it explores 'small slaveries' and 'slaveries without the name of slavery', focusing on agents (slaves, owners, traders and intermediaries) rather than the institution of slavery, and on enslavement practices ('slaving') rather than slave-holding societies or systems of slavery, as recently urged by Michael Zeuske and Joseph C. Miller.[22]

I

In 1780 the periodical *Contributions to Legal Literature in the Prussian States* published an essay entitled 'Legal History of a Purchased Moor'. In the report, written by an unidentified member of the Berlin Superior Court to the Ministry of Justice, the facts of the case were summarised as follows:

> A Moor purchased in Copenhagen by the chamberlain von Arnim and brought by him to our country has dared to most humbly beseech Your Royal Majesty by means of this petition dated 19 April of this year [1780]: That he might be freed from the yoke of bondage, and that von Arnim might be enjoined not to re-sell him to another party as planned. He claims in the eloquent petition that as a current subject of Your Royal Majesty he has an entitlement to freedom, which is even more his due since von Arnim purchased him 7 years ago in Denmark from Privy Councillor Wurm on the condition that he must serve as his subject for only two more years, since he had already served 8 years, and was originally required to serve only 10 years, at which time he must be set free. Nevertheless, von Arnim has already kept him 5 years past this time, and moreover has treated him most cruelly, and did not want to permit him to receive instruction in the Christian religion.[23]

22 Michael Zeuske, 'Historiography and Research Problems of Slavery and the Slave Trade in a Global-Historical Perspective', *International Review of Social History* 57 (2012), 87–111, here pp. 87, 105, 110; see also Michael Zeuske, *Handbuch Geschichte der Sklaverei. Eine Globalgeschichte von den Anfängen bis zur Gegenwart* (Berlin, 2013); Joseph C. Miller, 'Slaving as Historical Process: Examples from the Ancient Mediterranean and the Modern Atlantic', *Slave Systems: Ancient and Modern*, ed. E. Dal Lago and C. Katsari (Cambridge, 2008), pp. 70–102; Joseph C. Miller, *The Problem of Slavery as History. A Global Approach* (New Haven, 2012).
23 Anonymous, 'Rechtsgeschichte eines erkauften Mohren', p. 296.

While the unnamed petitioner apparently thought that he had been
engaged as an indentured servant, that is, required to serve only for a limited
period of time, von Arnim assumed that he had acquired the 'Moor' as
property. The reporting court official likewise spoke explicitly of a 'slave
introduced in these local states'.[24] Since in source materials of the time the
term 'Moor' was applied indiscriminately to dark-skinned people of different
origins,[25] it is only the place of purchase that suggests it was an African slave
who had come to Denmark via the transatlantic slave trade. What the author
thought of the petitioner's request is evident in the phrase 'has dared'.

On the other hand, Joachim Erdmann von Arnim's prior history could not
lead him to expect especially privileged treatment. Born in 1741, he became
Royal Prussian Chamberlain in 1763, served from 1771 to 1774 as a Prussian
emissary in Copenhagen, and starting in 1776 was director of the Royal
Opera and the French Comedy in Berlin; he was also the father of the writer
Achim von Arnim. However, as emissary he had failed to attend a dinner with
the royal widow Juliane Marie and had been removed from Copenhagen,
and only one year after his transfer to the court in Dresden he was likewise
recalled.[26] When as theatre director he intervened on behalf of a singer,
Frederick firmly put him in his place: 'You however should not imagine that
you are my privy councillor, I have not engaged you as such; it would behoove
you instead to apply yourself to carrying out my orders.'[27]

At the time the petition was submitted Frederick had closed the French
theatre and Joachim Erdmann von Arnim was spending most of his time at
his Friedenfelde estate.[28] Decorated as a prestigious Rococo manor house, its
inventory and garden design suggest that despite the rural setting Joachim
Erdmann attached great importance to the display of worldliness and wealth.
This included (among other things) six cannons on weapon mounts as well
as nine statues of Roman emperors in the garden, the lavish use of 'Peking'
– a Chinese-style fabric painted with blossoming branches – for wallpapers,

---

24   Ibid., p. 298.
25   Kuhlmann, 'Ambiguous Duty', p. 64; Theilig, *Türken, Mohren und Tataren*, pp. 36, 51.
26   *Fortgesetzte Neue Genealogisch-Historische Nachrichten von den Vornehmsten
Begebenheiten, welche sich an den Europäischen Höfen zutragen, worinn zugleich vieler Stands-
Personen Lebens-Beschreibungen vorkommen.* Der 25. Theil (Leipzig, 1764), p. 547; Stefan
Hartmann, *Die Beziehungen Preußens zu Dänemark 1688 bis 1789* (Cologne, 1983), pp. 287, 298;
Hans Kiefner, 'Zur "Rechtsgeschichte eines erkauften Mohren". Das Berliner Kammergericht
und Friedrich der Große über Sklaverei – ein Supplikationsverfahren im Jahr 1780', *Recht der
Persönlichkeit*, ed. H.-U. Erichsen, H. Kollhosser and J. Welp (Berlin, 1996), pp. 105–39, here
pp. 109f; Carl Nagel, *Achim von Arnims Eltern in Friedenfelde. Zweihundert Jahre Geschichte
eines uckermärkischen Gutes und seiner Besitzer sowie ein Inventarium des Herrenhauses aus
dem Jahre 1778* (Bochum, 1966), pp. 14–15.
27   Nagel, *Achim von Arnims Eltern*, p. 17.
28   The source for this and subsequent information is ibid., pp. 18, 21, 41.

upholstery and draperies, a coffee service, and special cups for hot chocolate. In his view, a black valet apparently also belonged in this ensemble.

As head of both the house and estate, von Arnim held all the local legal power in his own hands, including the low jurisdiction and the church patronate. It is remarkable, therefore, that the petition of the 'Moor' ever reached Frederick. The opportunity for submission may have arisen when the black servant accompanied Joachim Erdmann on one of his trips to Berlin, where von Arnim still maintained an apartment.[29] The servant may also have used the services of a professional writer. The argument about being prevented from practising his religion could have proven quite dangerous for von Arnim, who as master of the house and lord of the manor was responsible for the spiritual well-being of his subjects, and suggests that the writer may have had some experience devising particularly effective arguments.[30]

Since thousands of petitions were addressed to the Prussian king at the end of the eighteenth century, but he himself only processed a fraction of them, as for example 128 petitions between 1 July 1779 and 30 June 1780,[31] it is astonishing in several respects that this particular text found its way to him. This ratio alone led David M. Luebke to conclude: 'Even under the best of conditions, therefore, the odds against obtaining a royal hearing, let alone a favorable one, were overwhelming.'[32] It is thus a great stroke of luck for historians, since this instance of conflict forced each person involved to take a stance on the issue of slavery. At the same time, there are indications that the case in question was not some rare exception, but merely the serendipitous documentation of what may well have been a more frequently recurring phenomenon. We know from other countries that given the framework of limited and tiered liberties within the early modern estate-based society, and given the often dire living conditions of the lowest classes, slaves carefully weighed the 'costs' and benefits of manumission, and did not necessarily ask to be released unless their situation proved absolutely unbearable.[33]

In his rescript of 24 April 1780 Frederick ordered a more thorough investigation of the case, which in turn prompted von Arnim himself to make a

29 Ibid., p. 27.
30 On the strategic organisation of petitions and the possible influence of professional writers see Janine Rischke and Carmen Winkel, '"Hierdurch in Gnaden ...". Supplikationswesen und Herrschaftspraxis in Brandenburg-Preußen im 18. Jahrhundert', *Jahrbuch für die Geschichte Mittel- und Ostdeutschlands* 57 (2011–12), 57–86, here pp. 62–3.
31 David M. Luebke, 'Frederick the Great and the Celebrated Case of the Millers Arnold (1770–1779). A Reappraisal', *Central European History* 32/4 (1999), 379–408, here p. 404. In the first two months following the Millers Arnold case, 1,800 petitions from peasants alone were supposedly submitted (ibid., p. 405). Rischke and Winkel calculated 2,922 petitions for the year 1753: Rischke and Winkel, '"Hierdurch in Gnaden ..."', p. 62, see also p. 68.
32 Luebke, 'Frederick the Great and the Celebrated Case of the Millers Arnold', p. 404.
33 See e.g. Peabody, *'There Are No Slaves in France'*, p. 51.

statement.[34] He responded that he had purchased the Moor six years earlier from the Bargum dealership in Copenhagen; he had paid 200 Reichsthaler 'without entering into a written contract, and without the slightest restriction that he would keep him only for a specific time and then grant him his freedom'. Henning Frederik Bargum (1733–c.1800) was the director of the Danish Guinea Company founded in 1765 that managed the Danish slave trade with the Gold Coast of Africa.[35] Von Arnim therefore demanded 'unrestricted possession of the same, and the permission to sell him again, which he also planned to do'. He also countered the charge that he had prevented the man from practising his religion by claiming that the slave was 'a wild, ill-mannered and disreputable person who was as little interested in religion as in other forms of knowledge, but solely giving free rein to his sensual drives and passions, which no means of force could keep him from doing'. This assertion was scarcely credible, however: had the servant really been so unruly, von Arnim would hardly have kept him for six years. The reporting court official then summarised the legal dilemma as follows:

> On the one hand it seems inequitable to prevent an owner from taking actions that his property rights over a legally acquired slave allow: on the other hand it has the appearance of severity and cruelty to place a human being, the noblest creature, so far beneath his true worth that he be treated like an animal devoid of reason and sold from one hand to the next.

It was precisely the unusual character of the case that moved the court official to continue at greater length than usual, since 'in His Royal Majesty's states no special law on this matter exists; nor has such an instance ever been decided in our court of law'.[36] This was most likely the reason that the opinion was published in the *Contributions to Legal Literature in the Prussian States*, thereby preserving the case for posterity.[37]

While the survival of the record of the Arnim case is extraordinary for a number of reasons, the practice of purchasing human beings in other European countries or transporting them to the HRE from other European colonies was far less uncommon than earlier research presumed on the basis of the story's apparently exceptional character. In 1740 Frederick himself had 'ordered' two black Africans from the Netherlands through his senior civil servant Johann Peter von Raesfeld in Cleve and the Prussian Resident in Amsterdam Philip

34   The source for this and subsequent information is Anonymous, 'Rechtsgeschichte eines erkauften Mohren', pp. 297–8.
35   Bertil Haggmann, 'Danish Africa Companies', *The Historical Encyclopedia of World Slavery*, ed. J. P. Rodriguez, 2 vols (Santa Barbara, 1997), vol. 1, p. 208.
36   Anonymous, 'Rechtsgeschichte eines erkauften Mohren', p. 309.
37   For this case neither the petition itself nor the archival materials pertaining to it have survived.

Anthony d'Erberfeld.[38] He did, however, find the 'well-made young negro' named Coridon quite expensive ('But since the price seems excessive to me you need not look for any others').[39] Frederick paid 510 Dutch gulden for one of the two Africans. Since Raesfeld was paid for the delivery of two Moors in 1742, it was most likely actually two persons. The name of the second African was not mentioned in the files, but it is possible that he was the 'Moor William' who from 1743 until 1749 received four Thaler each year from Frederick II as a New Year's gift.[40] No further records exist for either Coridon or William, but the naming itself suggests that at least William had been already baptised when purchased or was baptised in Prussia. In subsequent years neither William nor Coridon appear among the gift recipients. Either Coridon had never reached the court alive or both had died at this point, or perhaps they were serving in the military from that point on.

Both in the military and in Frederick II's personal surroundings there are many documented male and female 'Moors' during the second half of the eighteenth century. Frederick's brother Prince Ferdinand of Prussia (1730–1813) retained court Moors continuously until the end of the century, possibly using the opulence of his court to compensate for the fact that he himself was not king.[41] The princess had a Moor named Azor at her disposal, too. Beginning in 1780–81, Frederick II took responsibility for the pension of the 'Moor Caroline', whose aristocratic master had died.[42] Although Frederick apparently no longer had court Moors as part of his personal entourage after 1749, he increased the number of black Africans in the Prussian military. Because this took place over a period of at least ten years, it was not simply a case of transferring the court Moors into the military; instead it involved additional recruitments, purchases and/or 'gifts' of human beings. It is not possible to determine where these people came from since the Prussian army archive in Potsdam was destroyed in World War II, but in earlier research that was still able to draw on this archive their service and the increase in their number are well documented.

When the large Potsdam Royal Regiment was dissolved in 1740, Frederick transferred its 'Moorish pipers' to the artillery. In 1747 a total of sixteen such

38   Berlin, GStA PK, I. HA Geheimer Rat, Rep. 34, No. 866 Rechts- und Besitzverhältnisse der Familie von Raesfeld, Erstattung von Geldern für die Übersendung zweier Mohren 1742, fol. 9.
39   Berlin, GStA PK, I. HA Geheimer Rat, Rep. 36 Hof- und Güterverwaltung, No. 304. Frederick was supposed to pay 510 gulden for the slave plus 123 gulden 12 *sols argent d'Hollande* for his clothing and transportation. By his own account, von Arnim had paid 200 Reichsthaler for 'his' slave in Copenhagen in 1774: Anonymous, 'Rechtsgeschichte eines erkauften Mohren', p. 297.
40   Berlin, GStA PK, BPH, Rep. 47 (Friedrich II.), No. 939 (receipts for New Year's gifts 1743–49).
41   Berlin, GStA PK, I. HA, Rep. 133, No. 262.
42   Berlin, GStA PK, I. HA Geheimer Rat, Rep. 36 Hof- und Güterverwaltung, No. 426, p. 56.

pipers were serving there and, according to Prussian budget records, each received '4 Thaler in wages' per month.[43] In 1759 Frederick II even increased the number of black artillerymen to thirty-two.[44] 'Moors' also served in the infantry: in 1741 four companies of Prussian grenadiers came through Breslau, and a 'Moorish piper' played in each one.[45] The First Grenadier Company of the I. Bat. Guard No. 15 had dark-skinned pipers up until 1806. In the Prussian cuirassier regiment of Margrave Frederick William of Brandenburg-Schwedt (1731–71), the timpanist and all buglers were of black African descent until 1771. A painting by Georg Lisiewski shows Margrave Karl of Brandenburg-Schwedt (1705–62) in his military camp with his two brothers and two court Moors.[46] In 1755 a black piper named Epoli has also been confirmed as a member of the infantry regiment under Margrave Karl of Brandenburg. Indicted for baptising the terminally ill 'Moor' who died shortly thereafter, the Catholic priest Father Riepe testified at his questioning that the man had come from France (though he was not certain), but in any case spoke French.[47]

Given that the number of African men and women who reached the HRE through abduction, sale or as gifts was so large, and that the number of free blacks in Europe during this same time was still (as far as we can tell) so small, it seems highly likely that the Africans in Brandenburg-Prussia for the most part also reached the country in this way. As early as 1714/15 Frederick's father Frederick Wilhelm I had used a London intermediary to purchase two dark-skinned youths;[48] in the 1720s and 1730s he tried once again to make acquisitions via Amsterdam, The Hague and London.[49] In 1729 the Danish King Christian VI sent an eight-year-old boy from the West Indian island of

43   M. Rischmann, 'Mohren als Spielleute und Musiker in der preußischen Armee', *Zeitschrift für Heeres- und Uniformkunde* 85/87 (1936), 82–4, here p. 83.
44   Martin, *Schwarze Teufel, edle Mohren*, p. 125; Peter Panoff, *Militärmusik in Geschichte und Gegenwart* (Berlin, 1938), p. 79.
45   The source for this and subsequent information is Rischmann, 'Mohren als Spielleute und Musiker in der preußischen Armee', pp. 83–4.
46   Daniel Hohrath, *Friedrich der Große und die Uniformierung der preußischen Armee von 1740–1786*, 2 vols (Vienna, 2011), vol. 1, p. 39.
47   Berlin, GStA PK, I. HA Geheimer Rat, Rep. 47 Geistliche Angelegenheiten, Tit. 23, Fasz. 3. Theilig, *Türken, Mohren und Tataren*, pp. 73–4. writes that Epoli had been sold at auction after the death of his owner in France, but I could not find this information in the source. The case was problematic not only because it was the responsibility of the military chaplain (who as a result had also missed out on the fees involved), but also because the cleric was a Catholic priest.
48   Berlin, GStA PK, II. HA Abt. 4 Tit. 42, No. 3 from 6 November 1714 and 19 January 1715; Theilig, *Türken, Mohren und Tataren*, pp. 50–1, 106; Kuhlmann-Smirnov, *Schwarze Europäer*, p. 67.
49   Jürgen Kloosterhuis, ed., *Legendäre 'lange Kerls'. Quellen zur Regimentskultur der Königsgrenadiere Friedrich Wilhelms I., 1713–1740* (Berlin, 2003), pp. 161–2; Theilig, *Türken, Mohren und Tataren*, p. 53; Kuhlmann-Smirnov, *Schwarze Europäer*, pp. 67–8.

St Thomas as a gift from Copenhagen to his sister-in-law at the Aurich court.[50] In 1752 two twelve-year-old 'Moorish' boys were 'sent as a gift from Holland' to the ruling Count of Berleburg;[51] in 1756 a Lübeck merchant gave the Duke of Saxony-Weimar-Eisenach a 'Moor' as a gift;[52] in 1764 a blacksmith sent Duke Carl Eugen of Württemberg a young black slave he had 'brought along' from the Dutch colony of Suriname;[53] one year later (1765) Franz von Borries bought Yunga, a fourteen-year-old West African, in London;[54] in 1771 a doctor living in Amsterdam offered the landgrave Frederick II of Hessen-Kassel 'a Surinamese Moor' he had 'purchased very young'; from 1773 until 1775 (probably even more often) the Hessian landgrave actually 'imported' black minstrels from the Netherlands. In other words, what we see here are not merely individual cases but a system in which not only the Netherlands, but also London and Copenhagen, apparently played a key role as trading centres.

This 'grey' market required that in Europe the trade in human beings, even if not explicitly allowed, would at least still be tolerated. In Great Britain this was possible until at least 1772, when Lord Mansfield, the Lord Chief Justice, ruled in the famous Somerset case that because no law concerning slavery existed in England, slavery consequently did not exist there, and hence the slave Somerset should be set free.[55] Yet even after this ruling, black servants continued to be taken back to the Caribbean colonies against their will. The example of the doctor and naturalist Dr Joachim von Exter, who in 1793 brought with him a seven-year-old black boy from London to Hamburg and made a present of him there to Dr Kellinghusen,[56] also shows that for interested parties from the HRE, this source had not dried up.

In many European countries, moreover, the legal status of imported slaves worsened in the course of the eighteenth century. In 1776 in the Netherlands it was determined by law that slaves would not automatically be freed upon

50   Kuhlmann, 'Ambiguous Duty', p. 60.
51   Häberlein, '"Mohren", ständische Gesellschaft und atlantische Welt', pp. 88–9. The two boys named Caspar and Coridon came from Suriname and Berbice. Although he had the same name, this was not the Coridon that Frederick II of Prussia had purchased in 1740, as he would have still been an infant at the time he was transported halfway across Europe. The Prussian source instead refers to a 'jeune negre bien fait' ('well-made young negro'; see above).
52   Alexander Niemann, 'Ein Mohr am Weimarer Hof der Goethezeit. Nachkommen, Herkunft der Ehefrauen, familiäres und soziales Umfeld', *Genealogisches Jahrbuch* 33/34 (1993/4), 57–90, here pp. 58–9.
53   The source for this and subsequent information is Häberlein, '"Mohren", ständische Gesellschaft und atlantische Welt', pp. 87, 96; Kuhlmann-Smirnov, *Schwarze Europäer*, pp. 54–5; Sadji, 'Unverbesserlich ausschweifende', pp. 43–4.
54   Sadji, 'Unverbesserlich ausschweifende', pp. 43, 46.
55   The source for this and subsequent information is Chater, *Untold Histories*, pp. 91–2.
56   Wilhelm Albers and Armin Clasen, 'Mohren im Kirchspiel Eppendorf und im Gute Ahrensburg', *Zeitschrift für Niederdeutsche Familienkunde* 41 (1966), 2–4, here p. 3.

arrival in that country;[57] indeed, after abortive attempts in the eighteenth
century, slavery on Dutch soil was not abolished until 1838.[58] In France, up
until 1716, slaves were freed if their owners had neglected to register them,
but according to the law of 1738 this was no longer the case: the length of
their stay in France was restricted to three years, and failure to register them
meant that the slaves would be confiscated and returned to the colonies.[59] In
1777, slaves from the colonies were no longer allowed to enter the country at
all: they had to remain in a special depot at the harbour and were sent back
on the next ship.[60]

The countries without colonies profited from the colonial powers, and
through them participated not only in the exchange of goods but also in the
slave trade. This was true, for example, not merely in the sense of involvement
as a 'hinterland' supplier, but quite literally: it was not an exceptional case that
slaves were 'imported' via European third countries into the HRE, after the
sale of the short-lived German colonies and slave-trading company it was the
rule. Since abduction and sale are characteristics of slavery, we must assume
that most blacks had not come of their own free will to Brandenburg-Prussia.
It was not until 1783/4 with the arrival of black Hessian army members
who had fought in the American Revolution that for the first time a sizeable
number of African-Americans who were either free(d) or had escaped slavery
came to the HRE. According to current research this group remained exclusively in Hessen-Kassel, and consisted of free soldiers together with accompanying, i.e. purchased, stolen, and confiscated slaves.[61]

In research to date, though, arguments against slave status have usually
been based not on place of origin and form of acquisition, but on subsequent
treatment: in fact, the absence of written records of emancipation is often a
problem when working with primary sources. Payment for work, marriage
and certain activities are insufficient evidence, however, that a person's slave
status was lifted upon entering the country or through baptism. Among
musicians, for example, only those who belonged to the small group of guild

57 Hondius, 'Access to the Netherlands', pp. 385–6.
58 Kwame Nimako and Glenn Willemsen, *The Dutch Atlantic. Slavery, Abolition and
Emancipation* (London, 2011), p. 33. In 1814 the Dutch prohibited the slave trade.
59 Peabody, *'There Are No Slaves in France'*, pp. 5–6, 17–18, 38. Neither of the two laws was
registered by the Parliament of Paris, however, so although slaves often successfully appealed for
their freedom there, sometimes they were re-enslaved by royal fiat (ibid., pp. 23–36, 39, 49–56,
88).
60 Peabody, *'There Are No Slaves in France'*, pp. 7, 106, 120. Now, however, the number of
requests from owners trying to legalise their slaves through manumission increased (ibid.,
p. 135).
61 Maria I. Diedrich, 'From American Slaves to Hessian Subjects. Silenced Black Narratives of
the American Revolution', *Germany and the Black Diaspora: Points of Contact, 1250–1914*, ed.
M. Honeck, M. Klimke and A. Kuhlmann (New York, 2013), pp. 92–111, especially pp. 93–4,
107.

Figure 5.1. Portrait showing Wilhelmina of Prussia and her brother Frederick with a 'court Moor' wearing a silver slave collar. Oil, Antoine Pesne, 1714

musicians and those who attained citizenship were 'free' in the full legal
sense, while this was not necessarily the case for musicians in the military.[62]
One piece of evidence against automatic emancipation can be found in the
depiction of court Moors wearing silver slave collars,[63] clearly visible for
instance in the 1714 portrait by Antoine Pesne of Wilhelmina of Prussia
and her brother Frederick (later Frederick the Great) (Fig. 5.1). Even if one
interprets this as a visual topos the question still remains: Why did Pesne or
his noble client respectively choose to depict the court Moor as a slave?

The legal case in question here even shows explicitly that emancipation upon
crossing the border or through baptism cannot be assumed; as a 'normal
exceptional case' (Edoardo Grendi) it instead casts new light on the complex
relationship between slavery and serfdom.

II

It is unclear whether the court official who wrote the legal opinion on the
petition was aware of Frederick's own slave purchases. A few years earlier
in 1768, the Prussian king had indeed extradited a 'Moor' who had fled to
Prussia from the Electorate of Saxony, apparently unwilling to accept his
fate.[64] In his written assent Frederick noted only that the black servant had
once belonged to the empress of Russia. Faced with runaway subjects and
soldiers regardless of skin colour, this was a matter of maintaining something
of vital importance to the Prussian king through cooperative behaviour,
since in return he was promised 'la reciprocité la plus exacte dans tous les
cas pareils'.[65] This incident alone gave no clear indication yet of attitudes
towards enslavement practices. In the Arnim case, the court official began his
detailed discussion on a note of preserving estate-based society in general:
'We believe we have good reason to claim that servitude (servitus) does not
run contrary to natural law, but instead is actually founded upon it.'[66] In what
followed, however, he appealed to natural law to justify not only estate-based
society in general, but slavery in particular. Though all human beings were
admittedly free in their natural state, there were four possible ways to legally

---

62   Kuhlmann, 'Ambiguous Duty', pp. 64–5.
63   Theilig, *Türken, Mohren und Tataren*, p. 39; Elizabeth McGrath, 'Sklaverei', *Handbuch
der politischen Ikonographie*, ed. U. Fleckner, M. Warnke and H. Ziedler, 2 vols (Munich, 2011),
vol. 2, pp. 350–7, here p. 353.
64   The source for this and subsequent information is Berlin, GStA PK, I. HA Geheimer Rat,
Rep. 41 Beziehungen zu Kursachsen, No. 1759, Auslieferung eines aus Kursachsen geflüchteten
Mohren, 1768.
65   Ibid.
66   Anonymous, 'Rechtsgeschichte eines erkauften Mohren', p. 298.

acquire slaves in what the author described as increasingly complex and differentiated societies that relied on the work of labourers: a person could become enslaved (1) by subjugation in war, (2) by contract, especially in cases of extreme poverty, (3) by birth to enslaved parents, and (4) as punishment for such crimes as theft or debt. 'Still today among several savage peoples, especially in Guinea, it is the prevailing custom to punish even the smallest crimes by slavery', the official continued, thereby using African slavery to casually and indirectly justify the practice of transatlantic slavery. Notably, the official did not proceed to check whether one of the four above-mentioned conditions applied to the petitioner. Instead he concluded more generally that the acquisition of slaves was permitted under natural law and that a ban on slavery and/or the slave trade would illegitimately curtail the property rights of the individual.[67]

In the historical overview that followed he explained that Brandenburg-Prussia had withdrawn from the slave trade practised by Christian nations for the past three hundred years, despite the fact that the trade would make those other countries very rich. For all the criticism of the slave trade, though, 'the lot of prisoners of war, even slaves, when they came over from those barbarian regions to European nations, [had become] more tolerable'. There were exceptions, however: 'the Turks, Tartars and Moors, who force into slavery captured Christians, who in turn *jure retorsionis* do the same to them'. This was allowed by the recess of the Imperial Diet in 1542.

> They feel all the effects of the harshest rule even today; they can be sold, given as gifts and bequeathed, which does not change even if they accept the Christian faith, though Pope Pius V wishes them declared free in such cases.[68]

Notably, the official did not mention (or did not know) the considerably more lenient regulations concerning the treatment of prisoners of war following the Peace of Karlowitz in 1699 and reaffirmed by the Peace of Passarowitz in 1718.[69]

Following this emphatic, pages-long justification of slavery based on natural law and the defence of European enslavement practices as comparatively humane or at least legitimate in the sense of retributive justice, the official turned to the current legal situation in neighbouring European countries. According to his information, slaves in France were emancipated if they registered with the court of the admiralty; he referenced the Somerset case in England, and noted that in the Netherlands slaves could apply for

---

67   Ibid., pp. 299–303.
68   Ibid., pp. 304–6.
69   Cf. Theilig, *Türken, Mohren und Tataren*, p. 37.

their freedom as soon as they touched the soil of the Republic, even against
their owners' will. Indeed, the official described the situation of slaves as
more positive than was actually the case, as we know from current research,
in part because he referred to older legal decisions and was unaware that the
status of slaves had worsened in France and the Netherlands. Even so, this
look at neighbouring European countries presented the idea of emancipation
as a possible alternative in the current case. As if suddenly realising the consequences of such a decision for Brandenburg-Prussia, the author abruptly
shifted his argumentation:

> Interpreters of Roman law therefore have many different opinions about
> applying the tenet of servitude to the present day. Some reject all use thereof,
> since the servitude found among the Germans has never been like that of
> Roman times, as noted above. Others apply it to serfs *glebae ascriptores*
> and others who, while not actually for their person, *cum fundo*, may still
> be sold. ... Nevertheless, there is still a world of difference between these
> serfs and Roman slaves, and these legal scholars can provide no judgment
> on the present case.[70]

He was apparently concerned that a decision about enslavement practices
might conversely set a legal precedent regarding serfdom.

He then went on to reject the so-called 'free soil ideology' that granted
emancipation upon arrival on European soil, claiming it was not 'supported
by sufficient reasons'. He likewise dismissed the decree of Pope Pius V
granting slaves their freedom once baptised as non-binding for Protestant
churches; it should be applied only to Jewish slave-owners. Thus, even though
the concept of freedom through baptism was in circulation also in Protestant
countries,[71] the court official effectively eliminated all possible reasons for
emancipating the slave and, in addition, drew a firm dividing line between
slavery and serfdom. Citing natural law, he concluded that von Arnim was
allowed to resell his slave, unless slaves in Copenhagen were freed after ten
years in accordance with the law or the contract mentioned by the slave
really did exist, 'which there is little likelihood of proving, since prior to the
appointed date, von Arnim denied the existence of a concluded contract'.
Von Arnim was thus granted greater credibility and the slave given the entire
burden of proof.[72]

After taking a clear stand and supporting his decision with considerable
intellectual effort in over ten pages of argument, the official suddenly qualified
his position in the closing paragraph:

70   Anonymous, 'Rechtsgeschichte eines erkauften Mohren', pp. 306–8, and cf. p. 309.
71   See note 15 as well as, for example, *The Interesting Narrative of the Life of Olaudah
Equiano, or Gustavus Vassa, the African*, ed. A. Costanzo (Peterborough, 2002), p. 109.
72   Anonymous, 'Rechtsgeschichte eines erkauften Mohren', pp. 308–10.

> Whereas Your Royal Majesty in his innate grace and magnanimity has
> deigned to eliminate the harsh serfdom still occurring in several of His
> provinces, and thereby seems to express that that same Most Exalted One
> would not tolerate an even harsher yoke of servitude in His lands; and
> whereas, further, Your Royal Majesty extends his patrimonial care not only
> to the children born in his land, but to each and every person who places
> himself under the same Most Exalted One's protection: we therefore most
> humbly submit: whether it would be possible to introduce a law in His lands
> concerning slavery that would grant the above-mentioned Dutch rights?[73]

Here he was referring to the concept – never codified in actual law – of
liberation upon entering the Republic of the Netherlands. Why this manoeu-
vring, and why the insistent separation of slavery from serfdom in the
preceding pages? Just a year earlier (1779), Frederick had sided with the millers
Christian and Rosine Arnold in their suit against their landlord who had
diverted their water to fill his own carp pool, leaving the Arnolds unable to
pay in grain for their lease. After the millers had lost their case at every judicial
level, Christian submitted a petition to Frederick II. The king decided that the
manorial lord could not simply claim all the water for himself, as water was a
shared or public good. Frederick then dismissed a number of judicial officers
and placed others under arrest.[74] This course of action shocked the nobility
and bureaucracy alike,[75] and helps explain why the court official handling the
petition took such a cautious, deliberate approach. He did not wish to meet
the same fate as his colleagues in the Berlin Superior Court: they, too, had
heard the Arnolds' case, and had landed in prison. These interconnections
between slavery, the manorial system and serfdom make the slave's petition
particularly interesting with regard to the repercussions of the transatlantic
slave trade for Prussian history in the sense of 'entangled histories'.

Even earlier than this, Frederick had clearly shown that he supported the
peasants: according to the basic instructions for the General Directory of
1748 (i.e. the central Prussian agency for the interior and finance), domain
peasants should be released to the extent that it was possible; those 'subjects'
working for cities and the nobility should be required to perform manual
labour and unpaid horse-and-cart work for a maximum of three or four days
per week, not for the entire week as they had before.[76] Domain officers who
beat peasants with sticks would be sentenced to six years' imprisonment.

---

73   Ibid., p. 310.
74   Gerd Heinrich, *Friedrich II. von Preußen. Leistung und Leben eines großen Königs* (Berlin,
2009), pp. 256–8; Luebke, 'Frederick the Great and the Celebrated Case of the Millers Arnold'.
75   Peter Weber, 'Das Allgemeine Gesetzbuch – ein Corpus Juris Fridericianum?', *Friedrich II.
und die europäische Aufklärung*, ed. M. Fontius (Berlin, 1999), pp. 103–11, here p. 109.
76   The source for this and subsequent information is Walther Hubatsch, *Friedrich der Große
und die preußische Verwaltung*, 2nd rev. edn (Cologne, 1982), pp. 175–6.

The 1766 regulations for district officers required them to report immediately to the court every offence against peasants committed in their jurisdiction. However, it was difficult to have a unified legal code concerning peasants in the Prussian state since existing privileges had to be respected and the legal status of the peasants varied widely from one part of the country to another.

With the cabinet order of 16 April 1754, Justice Minister Samuel von Cocceji had been told that 'the slavery of serfdom still common in Pomerania seems so harsh to me, and to have such a deleterious effect on the entire district, that I wished it could be abolished completely'.[77] Frederick repeatedly linked serfdom with slavery linguistically, as in this 1772 reply to a request submitted by a serf from the Kurmark: 'Slavery has ended, the fellow must be protected.'[78] Or in a later text (1777) when writing about how peasants were bound to the soil:

> Of all situations this is the most unfortunate, and must appall human feeling most profoundly. Surely no one is born to be the slave of one of his own kind. We abhor this abuse for good reason and think that we need only to want it thus in order to eliminate this deplorable barbarian custom. But that is not the case; it is supported by contracts of old between the landlord and the settlers. Farming is tailored to the compulsory labour of the peasants. Were we to eliminate this abhorrent institution with one stroke, we would be doing away with farming altogether. The nobility would then have to receive compensation for the partial loss of income they would experience.[79]

This was actually a polemical conflation of slavery and serfdom on Frederick's part, one that had already enjoyed a long tradition and was still common among Frederick's contemporaries.[80] That he did not imply the elimination of slavery in the narrower sense becomes apparent when we look at Frederick's own brief response to the Moor's petition: he clearly rejected freeing the slave on the basis of the free soil ideology, but should there actually

---

77   Quoted from ibid., p. 177 (source not named).
78   *Acta Borussica. Die Behördenorganisation und die allgemeine Staatsverwaltung Preußens im 18. Jahrhundert*, 16/1 (1970), p. 22, cited by Kiefner, 'Zur "Rechtsgeschichte eines erkauften Mohren"', p. 116.
79   Friedrich der Große, 'Regierungsformen und Herrscherpflichten (1777)', *Die Werke Friedrichs des Großen in deutscher Übersetzung*, ed. G. Berthold Volz, 10 vols (Berlin, 1912), vol. 7, pp. 225–37, here p. 233. The nobility did receive compensation following the abolition of serfdom in Prussia in the nineteenth century.
80   Cf. Renate Blickle, 'Leibeigenschaft. Versuch über Zeitgenossenschaft in Wissenschaft und Wirklichkeit, durchgeführt am Beispiel Altbayerns', *Gutsherrschaft als soziales Modell*, ed. J. Peters (Munich, 1995), pp. 53–80, here p. 61: 'Beginning around 1700 serfdom was used as a battle cry, and was not only compared with slavery but equated with it.'

be a contract as the petitioner claimed, the latter could have recourse to legal action.[81] Apparently the slave was unable to produce such a contract, so the files contain no further mention of the case. As in issues of serfdom, here too 'ancient contracts' and property rights served as the basis for his decision, and it seems that above all else, Frederick wished to convey an image of legal certainty and the rule of law. By reassuring the aristocracy in this way the Prussian king may have also been reacting against the nobility's opposition to the abolition of serfdom, a project which during the entire period of Frederick II's reign made only slow and halting progress.[82] In contrast, acceptance of the free soil principle would have led logically to the complete elimination of serfdom in Prussia. Thus both forms of dependency – slavery and serfdom – were intertwined, even though Brandenburg-Prussia had no slave trade at the time and as a Central European land power appeared to stand only at the margin of the traffic in people.

Apparently the need for regulation in such cases was recognised in the following years, and this also indicates that they were not so infrequent or unusual as the research to date suggests. Work began that same year (1780) on the General Law Code for the Prussian States (ALR, Allgemeines Landrecht für die Preußischen Staaten), though Frederick II (1712–86) died before it took effect in 1794, and it was valid only subsidiary to local rights. According to this general code:[83]

§ 196 Slavery shall not be tolerated in royal lands.
§ 197 No royal subject can and may obligate himself to slavery.
[But:]
§ 198 Foreigners who are in royal lands for a limited time retain their rights over accompanying slaves.
§ 200 When such foreigners settle permanently in royal lands; or when royal subjects bring slaves purchased elsewhere into these lands, slavery ceases to exist.

Nonetheless, slaves had to work without payment until their owner had been reimbursed for the purchase price (§ 202, see also §§ 203–5) which meant that in most cases the slaves' actual circumstances initially did not change. 'The lord [could] also add a former slave to a country estate as a subject' (§ 207), which meant: transform him into a subject of the estate with an obligation to remain on-site (*Schollenpflicht*) and perform compulsory labour. Were any children conceived while the person was still in a state of

---

81   Anonymous, 'Rechtsgeschichte eines erkauften Mohren', p. 311.
82   Hubatsch, *Friedrich der Große*, pp. 177–9.
83   The source for this and subsequent information is *Allgemeines Landrecht für die Preußischen Staaten von 1794*, with an introduction by Hans Hattenhauer and a bibliography by Günther Bernert, 2nd expanded edn (Berlin, 1994), Theil II, Titel V.

slavery, they were required to provide services just like 'other abandoned children who were being cared for and educated' (§ 206); in other words, the children of slaves were viewed as orphans. Accordingly, they were required to work without pay for their foster parents for the same length of time as those parents had spent raising them.[84] Had there been no slaves in Brandenburg-Prussia, such detailed regulations would have been superfluous.

The same legal document abolished 'former serfdom, as a form of personal slavery',[85] but the *Schollenpflicht* of peasants and their children posed an obstacle to this rhetorical formula since it was by no means lifted and was enforced by the use of corporal punishment.[86] The emancipation of the peasants, like the abolition of slavery, was in fact a protracted process that continued well into the nineteenth century.

III

In the long run the petitioning slave achieved a certain success, but in the short run – which was biographically relevant – he had to accept defeat in 1780. Despite this failure the case is significant. Here for the first and, according to current research, only time in a German-speaking region, and if we set aside other tacit or 'silent' practices and forms of protest such as escape, desertion or suicide, an African slave raised his voice in protest against his enslavement. From the perspective of subaltern studies this case allows us to move away from a reconstruction of the 'Moor' as exotic item or the object of aristocratic and bourgeois prestige culture and mercantile interests, and see slaves as agents instead, not only in the sense that they shaped their lives, developed relationships, and negotiated social and economic opportunities, but also insofar as they openly thematised and criticised their condition.

At the same time, in this conflict two comparative perspectives converge, as debates about the status of slaves on the European continent that look beyond national borders meet up with the comparison of slavery and other forms of bondage like serfdom that should be seen not only as separate systems, but also in terms of how they intersect and influence one another. These interrelations as well as efforts to distinguish between different kinds of dependency did not take place detached from social practices. They were embedded in negotiation processes between the monarch, the administrative apparatus, aristocratic land owners, peasant subjects and slaves who were brought into the country.

84   Ibid., Theil II, Titel II, §§ 754–5.
85   Ibid., Theil II, Titel VII, § 148.
86   Ibid., Theil II, Titel VII, §§ 150, 155, 185.

Therefore the notion that on the European continent slavery quietly 'evolved into the social reality of domestic service',[87] or that baptism and/or crossing borders automatically led to emancipation should be used only cautiously. Contemporaries spoke of slavery not only polemically and figuratively, but also in reference to actual people and legal conditions. A servant or serf could not have been sold (legally) by von Arnim in 1780. If we approximate slavery on the European continent too closely to other forms of dependency we run the risk of downplaying or trivialising the legal status of slaves; for example, their passage from hand to hand cannot be compared with the practice of sending aristocratic children, servants and cooks unasked from one aristocratic court to another.[88] At the same time, the many-tiered forms of compulsory labour and dependency in early modern society might have meant that slavery was not necessarily perceived as something radically foreign or different by contemporaries.[89] Yet if we ignore the moment of irritation and ambiguity that stirred debate at the time, we miss an opportunity to view Central European society in the early modern period as part of the transatlantic world. In the second half of the eighteenth century, holding slaves was still part of the contemporary European horizon, even in a Central European land power such as Prussia. This perspective makes it possible to view the process of eliminating serfdom not as an isolated one, but embedded in global interactions. Until now, slavery and serfdom on the European continent were considered two distinct systems that 'appeared to be so different in time and place that it was impossible that one had influenced the other'.[90] But as the case discussed here suggests, both legal concepts should be viewed as less isolated than slavery experts on the one hand and Prussian history experts on the other have supposed.

87   This is the conclusion drawn by Sauer and Wiesböck, 'Sklaven, Freie, Fremde', pp. 48–9.
88   Thus Kuhlmann, 'Ambiguous Duty', p. 60.
89   Sauer and Wiesböck, 'Sklaven, Freie, Fremde', p. 47.
90   Robert M. Berdahl and later Claus K. Meyer identified paternalist arguments as a shared feature of slavery in the American South and the form of subservience found in the manorial system. However, since the institutions in the American South and on estates east of the Elbe differed in so many ways, neither Berdahl nor Meyer looked for possible reciprocal influences; Meyer wrote of 'institutions that were separated from one another in time and space, existed in completely different circumstances, and reflected fundamentally different structures': Claus K. Meyer, 'Ein zweischneidiges Schwert. Ordnung und Reglementierung auf Rittergut und Sklaven-Plantage', *Leibeigenschaft. Bäuerliche Unfreiheit in der frühen Neuzeit*, ed. J. Klußmann (Cologne, 2003), pp. 241–72, here p. 242. See also Shearer Davis Bowman, *Masters & Lords. Mid-19th Century U.S. Planters and Prussian Junkers* (New York, 1993).

6

Julius von Rohr, an Enlightenment Scientist of the Plantation Atlantic[1]

DANIEL HOPKINS

The career of Julius Philip Benjamin von Rohr, a German botanist in Danish colonial service, embodied many of the scientific, economic, and moral concerns of his times. He was born in Merseburg, in Prussia, in the 1730s, studied natural history and medicine in Halle, and emigrated to Denmark as a young man, apparently to escape the Seven Years' War.[2] In 1757 the Danish government sent him to the Danish West Indies (which are now the US Virgin Islands) to serve as public land surveyor.[3] His rather unusual commission also called on him to study the islands' natural history. The Crown had lately taken over the administration of the colony from the Danish West India and Guinea Company, and the slave-plantation economy of St Croix, the largest of the islands, which had been settled by the Danes in the 1730s, was beginning to boom when von Rohr arrived.[4] The island was transformed in his time there: in 1750, perhaps half the

1   The author is exceedingly grateful for the very material assistance, including readings of manuscript sources in German and Latin, of Ulla Mark Svensson, Erik Gøbel, Peter Wagner, Per Nielsen, Niklas Thode Jensen and Lise Groesmeyer, as well as of the editors. Translations from Danish are the author's.

2   'von Rohr, Julius Philip Benjamin', *Dansk biografisk leksikon*, ed. C. F. Bricka (Copenhagen, 1887–1905), http://runeberg.org/dbl/ (accessed 1 March 2016); Carl F. Christensen, *Den danske botaniks historie*, 3 vols (Copenhagen, 1924–26), vol. 1, p. 116; Kai L. Henriksen, *Oversigt over dansk entomologis historie* (Copenhagen, 1921), pp. 125–6; Thorkel Dahl and Kjeld de Fine Licht, *Surveys in 1961 on St. Thomas and St. Croix* (Copenhagen, 2004), p. 276.
3   Rigsarkivet (The Danish National Archives, here abbreviated RA), Copenhagen, Rentekammeret (Rtk.) 2249.2, Vestindisk-Guineisk Renteskriverkontor, 1754–1760, Kongelige Resolutioner, Julius Philip Benjamin von Rohr, of Merseburg, n.d., and royal resolution, 12 April 1757; Rtk. 2249.10, Amerikansk og Afrikansk Kopibog, or letter copy-book, 19 April 1757, to von Rohr.
4   See Waldemar Westergaard, *The Danish West Indies under Company Rule (1671–1754)* (New York, 1917), pp. 71–94.; J. O. Bro-Jørgensen, *Vore gamle tropekolonier*, vol. 1: *Dansk Vestindien indtil 1755*, ed. J. Brøndsted, 2nd edn (Copenhagen, 1966); and Jens Vibæk,

acreage of the island remained in woods and bush; thirty-five years later, the island was cultivated essentially from end to end.[5] Von Rohr also served as the island government's architect, building engineer, and construction supervisor;[6] he spent most of the rest of his life in the West Indies.

Although von Rohr's career was launched out of an elite Copenhagen circle of German expatriates and German-speaking Danes from the kingdom's southern duchies, he became a true citizen of the Atlantic, an Enlightenment scientist of international repute, with extraordinary personal experience of the tropical world and far-flung intellectual connections. He was an enthusiastic natural historian, but he was also a diligent and trusted government official, and some of the main colonial ideas and ambitions of the Danish state at this period found expression in the work he was asked to do. An examination of the last decade or so of his life, in particular, opens unusual new North-Western European perspectives on the plantation world of the Atlantic at the start of a period of profound transformation, when societies began to turn away from slavery and its fruits.

Natural History in a Colonial World

The study of natural history in the eighteenth century encompassed far more than botany and zoology and mineralogy. It concerned itself with every aspect of the natural constitution and condition of countries and regions – with physical resources; with climatic limitations and opportunities; with agriculture, fisheries, forestry, and mining; with techniques and manufactures; with transportation and trade; with political structures and religious practices – in sum, with the rigorous characterisation of places and how they worked. It was the stuff of public affairs and administration and, of course, of colonialism.[7] Natural history was also a highly international

Vore gamle tropekolonier, vol. 2: *Dansk Vestindien 1755–1848*, ed. J. Brøndsted, 2nd edn (Copenhagen, 1966).

5   Johann Cronenberg and Johann Christoph von Jægersberg, 'Charte over Eilandet St. Croix', 1750, Copenhagen, National Cadastre and Survey – Denmark, Hydrographic Division, manuscript map no. A/18–49; P. L. Oxholm, *Charte over den Danske Øe St. Croix i America forfærdiget i Aaret 1794, og udgivet i Aaret 1799* (Copenhagen, 1799); and Daniel Hopkins, Philip Morgan and Justin Roberts, 'The Application of GIS to the Reconstruction of the Slave-Plantation Economy of St. Croix, Danish West Indies', *Historical Geography* 39 (2011), 85–104, p. 88.

6   C. G. A. Oldendorp's *History of the Mission of the Evangelical Brethren on the Caribbean Islands of St. Thomas, St. Croix, and St. John*, ed. J. J. Bossard, English edition and translation by Arnold R. Highfield and V. Barac (1777; Ann Arbor, 1987), p. xxxiii.

7   See Londa Schiebinger, *Plants and Empire: Colonial Bioprospecting in the Atlantic World* (Cambridge, MA, 2004), pp. 5–12; Susan Scott Parish, *American Curiosity: Cultures of Natural History in the Colonial British Atlantic World* (Chapel Hill, 2006), pp. 103–8.

field, and it was in part its global networks of scientific correspondence that carried von Rohr so far in the world. It is likely that Christian Kratzenstein, a German scientist at the University of Copenhagen who had also studied and taught at Halle, helped von Rohr secure his position.[8] Kratzenstein had himself been recruited to the University of Copenhagen while on a scientific voyage from Archangel around the North Cape and through the Sound and so back to St Petersburg. The two men were compatriots and contemporaries, and undoubtedly friends, but perhaps what they had most significantly in common was the study of natural history. Kratzenstein, a scientist of some prominence, thought fit to mention von Rohr more than once in letters to Carl Linnaeus himself in the late 1750s. He lamented in one of them, perhaps facetiously, that von Rohr was obliged to eat some of the specimens he had collected, instead of preserving them and sending them home to Europe, for von Rohr's salary did not go far in the rather opulent plantation society of the islands.[9] Von Rohr was not alone in the study of natural history in his early years in the Danish West Indies: he had obtained his medical degree while in Copenhagen and in the mid-1760s sat on a medical review board on St Croix with Patrick Browne, the distinguished Irish botanist, who resided on the island for a decade or so.[10] It is a suggestive intellectual connection, although little else is known of the two scientists' association. In his early botanical descriptions, von Rohr repeatedly cited Browne's *Civil and Natural History of Jamaica*, a broad treatment typical of the day, published the year before von Rohr went to St Croix.[11]

Von Rohr also drew on important cultural connections. A number of German-speaking families – the Schimmelmanns, the Bernstorffs, the Reventlows, the Moltkes, and others – enjoyed great influence in Denmark at this period.[12] Von Rohr, whose noble birth and advanced education doubtless helped him negotiate the upper ranks of Danish society, in time found himself connected, in particular, to the Schimmelmann family, which was heavily

8   Rtk. 2249.2, Kongelige Resolutioner, Christianus Gottlieb Kratzenstein, Copenhagen, 26 October 1759, and royal resolution, 17 November 1759, and Amerikansk og Afrikansk Kopibog, 19 April 1757, to von Rohr; 'Kratzenstein, Christian Gottlieb', *Dansk biografisk leksikon*, ed. P. Engelstoft, 2nd edn (Copenhagen, 1933–44); Dahl and de Fine Licht, *Surveys* in 1961, p. 276.
9   Henriksen, *Oversigt*, p. 125; J. C. Schiødte, 'Af Linnés brevvexling: actstykker til naturstudiets historie i Danmark', *Naturhistorisk Tidsskrift* Series 3, vol. 7 (1870–71), 333–522, here pp. 379–403, especially pp. 381, 384–5, 391–3, 394.
10   Kristian Carøe, *Den danske Lægestand, doktorer og licentiater 1479–1788* (Copenhagen, 1909), pp. 18f; E. C. Nelson, 'Patrick Browne M.D. (c.1720–1790), an Irish Doctor in the Caribbean: His Residence on Saint Croix (1757–1765) and his Unpublished Accounts of Volcanic Activity on Montserrat', *Archives of Natural History* 28/1 (2001), 135–48.
11   Published by the author in London in 1756; Julius von Rohr, 'Natur-Historie von St. Croix', typed transcript by Lise Groesmeyer; Daniel Hopkins, *Peter Thonning and Denmark's Guinea Commission: A Study in Nineteenth-century African Colonial Geography* (Leiden, 2013), p. 23.
12   Erik Gøbel, *De styrede rigerne* (Odense, 2000), pp. 96–8.

invested in the slave trade and owned several of the largest slave plantations in the Danish West Indies.[13] Heinrich Carl Schimmelmann had come to
Denmark in 1761 and became the kingdom's leading financial officer; his son
Ernst Schimmelmann (von Rohr's contemporary) served the Danish state in
many high capacities. A man of enormous power and wealth, Schimmelmann
was also a great supporter of the arts and sciences.[14]

The natural history of the Danish West Indies was essentially unknown to
science at this period, and von Rohr collected assiduously, finding fifty new
genera of plants in his first year in the islands.[15] His survey work as a matter
of course placed him out in the field in a great variety of local environmental
conditions, and his machete-wielding survey slaves doubtless became quite
attuned to his interest in natural history specimens. On the whole, however,
the documentary record of his scientific work in his early years in the islands
is quite limited and of rather a technical character. A manuscript of about 150
pages, consisting of the journal of his voyage across the Atlantic in 1757 and
descriptions of a number of natural history specimens, all of it in German, is
preserved at the Royal Library in Copenhagen; it is illustrated with a number
of rather fine watercolours of insects and shells.[16] On the other hand, the
archives of the Danish West Indian surveyor's office are full of his point-
to-point survey reports, which he kept in German; von Rohr seems never
to have forsaken his native tongue in his written dealings with the rest of
Danish officialdom. His English, in a society dominated by planters of British
extraction, came to be very passable.[17] Latin was, of course, indispensable in
his scientific correspondence.

13   Dahl and de Fine Licht, *Surveys in 1961*, p. 278; Erik Gøbel, *Det danske slavehandelsforbud
1792* (Odense, 2008), pp. 24, 27–8, 30–1; RA, Privatarkiv no. 6284, Carl Heinrich Schimmelmann,
box 1, A. I. 1–2, Breve fra Institutioner og Private, three letters from von Rohr in the Danish
West Indies; Christian Degn, *Die Schimmelmanns im atlantischen Dreieckshandel. Gewinn und
Gewissen* (Neumünster, 1974); Danske Kancelli, I Almindelighed, A, IV, 3, Koncepter og Indlæg
til Christian VII's adelig Patenter, II (1780–1809), no. 97, regarding the naturalisation of von
Rohr's nobility, 21 August 1782.
14   'Schimmelmann, Heinrich Carl' and 'Schimmelmann, Heinrich Ernst', *Dansk biografisk
leksikon*, 2nd edn; Gøbel, *Det danske slavehandelsforbud*, pp. 22–4, 25–7, 36–7; Pernille Røge,
'L'expérimentation coloniale britannique, danoise et française sur la côte ouest africaine dans
les années 1780 et 1790', *Africains et Européens dans le monde atlantique, XVe–XIXe siècle*, ed.
G. Saupin (Rennes, 2014), pp. 217–35, here p. 223.
15   Christensen, *Den danske botaniks historie*, vol. 1, p. 116.
16   The Royal Library, Copenhagen, manuscript section (Thott, 1299, 4to), Julius von Rohr,
'Natur-Historie von St. Croix, erste Sammlung'; Christensen, *Den danske botaniks historie*,
vol. 1, p. 116 and vol. 2, p. 91; *Catalogus herbarii J. Ryani M.D.* (Copenhagen, 1809).
17   RA, Vestindiske lokalarkiver, St. Croix stadskonduktør og landmåler, landbreve og
landmålerprotokol for St. Croix 1759–1811; Neville A. T. Hall, *Slave Society in the Danish West
Indies: St. Thomas, St. John, and St. Croix*, ed. B. W. Higman (Baltimore, 1992), pp. 15–17;
Daniel Hopkins, 'The Eighteenth-Century Invention of a Measure in the Caribbean: The
Danish Acre of St. Croix', *Journal of Historical Geography* 18/2 (1992), 158–73, here pp. 160–1.

By 1773, von Rohr had established a botanic garden on the edge of Christiansted, the main town on St Croix.[18] On a map drawn in 1779, the garden is shown to have occupied a plot almost the size of two city blocks.[19] Such gardens were important scientific and administrative instruments, both at home in Europe and on colonial frontiers; the Danish intellectual and governmental environment out of which von Rohr had come to the West Indies put a great deal of emphasis on the economic significance of the science of plants. A royal botanic garden had been founded in Copenhagen only a few years before von Rohr had been sent out, and in 1753, Adam Gottlob Moltke, the confidant of King Frederik V and president of the Danish West India and Guinea Company, had ordered live West Indian plants sent home for this garden.[20] In 1759, an educational institute was established in connection with the garden, with the royally stated object that 'Our dear subjects might be able to ... seek out, properly investigate, and correctly make use of all the treasures and riches of nature with which God has blessed our kingdoms', especially such useful plants 'as either grow wild in or at least can stand our climate'.[21] The government's intent was also to advance the study of the natural sciences in general, for the University of Copenhagen had been remiss in incorporating the sciences – which were regarded in some academic quarters as atheistic – in its programmes of instruction.[22] Late that year, von Rohr was ordered on royal authority to send home carefully preserved seeds and live specimens of rare or useful West Indian plants, with instructions for their care.[23]

18 Dahl and de Fine Licht, *Surveys in 1961*, p. 277.
19 RA, Maps and Drawings Collection, Rtk. 337,303, P. L. Oxholm, 'Grundriss af Byen Christianstæd', manuscript map, surveyed in 1779.
20 'Moltke, Adam Gottlob', *Dansk biografisk leksikon*, 2nd edn; Dahl and de Fine Licht, *Surveys in 1961*, pp. 276–7; Westergaard, *The Danish West Indies*, p. 238.
21 Axel Garboe, *Geologiens historie i Danmark*, 2 vols (Copenhagen, 1959 and 1961), vol. 1, pp. 140–1. The acclimatisation of plants native to foreign climes was a central element in natural history. Linnaeus himself stoutly maintained that tea could be cultivated at the latitude of Uppsala, the university town a short distance north of Stockholm, thereby sparing Sweden considerable outflows of coin to the Far East: Daniel Hopkins, 'Danish Natural History and African Colonialism at the Close of the Eighteenth Century: Peter Thonning's "Scientific Journey" to the Guinea Coast, 1799–1803', *Archives of Natural History* 26/3 (1999), 369–418, here p. 376; Lisbet Koerner, *Linnaeus: Nature and Nation* (Cambridge, MA, 1999), pp. 135–8, 150–1; Londa Schiebinger and Claudia Swan, 'Introduction', *Colonial Botany: Science, Commerce, and Politics in the Early Modern World*, ed. L. Schiebinger and C. Swan (Philadelphia, 2005), pp. 1–16, here p. 2; Tore Frängsmyr, 'Editor's Introduction', *Linnaeus, the Man and his Work*, rev. reprint, ed. T. Frängsmyr (Canton, MA, 1994), pp. vii–xiv, here pp. x–xi.
22 Christensen, *Den danske botaniks historie*, vol. 1, pp. 71–4; Peter Wagner, 'The Royal Botanical Institution at Amalienborg. Sources of Inspiration', *Botanical Journal of Scotland* 46/4 (1994), 599–604, here p. 599.
23 Rtk. 2249.10, Amerikansk og Afrikansk Kopibog, 1755–1760, 20 November 1759 (no. 343), to von Rohr.

The world's local and transoceanic economies in this era were largely driven by commerce in cultivated and wild plant products. More particularly, Atlantic commerce depended on important tropical and subtropical agricultural products, especially sugar and cotton (which simply could not be produced in more northerly climates), on supplying the enslaved African labour force to cultivate them in the Americas, and on the manufacture of the goods with which to purchase the slaves.[24] Another vital spoke of this great wheel of commerce was the sustenance and support of those slave labourers and the plantations they worked with foodstuffs, tools and supplies: the development of the great cities of the North American east coast in the eighteenth century was inseparable from their trade with the West Indies, for they supplied the all but monocultural slave-plantation islands of the Caribbean with their every necessity, importing in return huge quantities of rum or its essential ingredient, molasses.[25]

It was an age (and had been since the time of Columbus) not only of the colonial exploitation of exotic agricultural commodities but of transfers of all manner of useful plants and the methods of their cultivation up and down the latitudes, and from one hemisphere to the other – grains, spices, sugar cane, potatoes, medicinal plants, fruits, tea, coffee, dye plants, tomatoes, vanilla beans.[26] The movements of plants across the sea in the colonial era – as much

24   Eric Williams, *Capitalism and Slavery* (Chapel Hill, 1944), pp. 98–106; Barbara L. Solow and Stanley L. Engerman, eds, *British Capitalism & Caribbean Slavery: The Legacy of Eric Williams* (Cambridge, 1987); Walter Minchinton, 'Abolition and Emancipation: Williams, Drescher and the Continuing Debate', *West Indies Accounts: Essays on the History of the British Caribbean and the Atlantic Economy in Honour of Richard Sheridan*, ed. R. A. McDonald (Kingston, Jamaica, 1996), pp. 253–73; Richard Drayton, *Nature's Government: Science, Imperial Britain, and the 'Improvement' of the World* (New Haven, 2000), pp. 62–3; David Eltis, *The Rise of African Slavery in the Americas* (Cambridge, 2000), pp. 271–2; Kenneth Morgan, *Slavery, Atlantic Trade and the British Economy, 1660–1800* (Cambridge, 2000), pp. 47–50; and Hopkins, *Peter Thonning and Denmark's Guinea Commission*, pp. 2–3.
25   Herbert C. Bell, 'The West India Trade before the American Revolution', *American Historical Review* 4/2 (1917), 272–87, esp. on pp. 286–7; Richard Pares, *Yankees and Creoles; the trade between North America and the West Indies before the American Revolution*, reprint (Hamden, CT, 1968), pp. 25, 161–2; David Watts, *The West Indies, Patterns of Development, Culture and Environmental Change since 1492* (Cambridge, 1987), p. 173; Richard B. Sheridan, *Sugar and Slavery: An Economic History of the British West Indies, 1623–1775* (Baltimore, 1973), pp. 314–16, 352–9; Drayton, *Nature's Government*, pp. 106–7.
26   Alfred W. Crosby, Jr, *The Columbian Exchange: Biological and Cultural Consequences of 1492* (Westport, 1972), pp. 64–74, 106–8; Daniel P. Hopkins, 'Peter Thonning, the Guinea Commission, and Denmark's Postabolition African Colonial Policy, 1803–1850', *William and Mary Quarterly*, 3rd Series, 64/4 (2009), 781–808, here pp. 782–3; Christopher P. Iannini, *Fatal Revolutions: Natural History, West Indian Slavery, and the Routes of American Literature* (Chapel Hill, 2012), pp. 186–7; see also Amy R. W. Meyers, 'Picturing a World in Flux: Mark Catesby's Response to Environmental Interchange and Colonial Expansion', *Empire's Nature: Mark Catesby's New World Vision*, ed. A. R. W. Meyers and M. Beck Pritchard (Chapel Hill, 1998), pp. 228–61, here pp. 240–1, 243, 246.

as of people, free or enslaved – transformed the world.[27] It is not for nothing that Thomas Jefferson, an upstanding figure of the American Enlightenment (with its indispensable baggage, on the edge of an unexplored continent, of natural history), wrote, 'the greatest service which can be rendered any country is to add an useful plant to its culture'.[28]

Botanic gardens, through which exotic specimens could be introduced under expert care, had become crucial public institutions in these remarkable global exchanges of live plant material.[29] There had been botanic gardens on the French Caribbean islands of Guadeloupe and Cayenne in the first decades of the eighteenth century.[30] In 1758, Britain's Royal Society of Arts offered prizes for the introduction and cultivation in the West Indies of valuable non-native food crops and spice and dye plants.[31] In 1765, the first British botanic garden in the West Indies was established, on the island of Saint-Vincent.[32] A few years after von Rohr had commenced work on his garden at Christiansted, Jamaica's first botanic garden was laid out, with the goal of introducing into a British territory the production of cochineal, a brilliant red dye derived from the tiny insects that infest a Central American cactus.[33]

Hans West, a school rector and amateur botanist, whose book on the Danish West Indies appeared in 1793, wrote that von Rohr's garden, 'resplendent with the plants of all climes, from the cedar to the ice-plant, would be a rich school for the European botanist'.[34] Strange and beautiful

27 Judith Carney and Richard Nicholas Rosomoff, *In the Shadow of Slavery: Africa's Botanical Legacy in the Atlantic World* (Berkeley, 2009); Hopkins, *Peter Thonning and Denmark's Guinea Commission*, pp. 690, 691.

28 Thomas Jefferson, Summary of Public Service, after 2 September 1800, *The Papers of Thomas Jefferson*, vol. 32: *1 June 1800 to 16 February 1801*, ed. B. B. Oberg (Princeton, 2005), p. 124; see Meyers, 'Picturing a World in Flux', pp. 249–50.

29 Madeleine Ly-Tio-Fane, 'Botanical Gardens: Connecting Links in Plant Transfer between the Indo-Pacific and Caribbean Regions', *Islands, Forests and Gardens in the Caribbean: Conservation and Conflict in Environmental History*, ed. R. S. Anderson, R. Grove and K. Hiebert (Oxford, 2006), pp. 53–63; Schiebinger and Swan, 'Introduction', *Colonial Botany*, p. 13.

30 Susan Danforth, 'Cultivating Empire: Sir Joseph Banks and the (failed) Botanical Garden at Nassau', *Terrae Incognitae* 33 (2001), 48–58, here p. 50.

31 Richard A. Howard, 'Botanical Gardens in West Indies History', *Garden Journal* (July–August 1953), 117–20, here pp. 117–18.

32 Richard Howard, 'The St. Vincent Botanic Garden – The Early Years', *Arnoldia* 57/4 (Winter, 1997–98), 12–21, here p. 12; Drayton, *Nature's Government*, p. 65; John Gascoigne, *Science in the Service of the State: Joseph Banks, the British State and the Uses of Science in the Age of Revolution* (Cambridge, 1998), pp. 130–1; Richard H. Grove, *Green Imperialism: Colonial Expansion, Tropical Island Edens and the Origins of Environmentalism, 1600–1860* (Cambridge, 1995), pp. 281–2.

33 Danforth, 'Cultivating Empire', p. 51.

34 H. West, 'Beretning om det danske Eiland St. Croix i Vestindien, fra Juniimaaned 1789 til Juniimaaneds Udgang 1790', *Maanedskriftet Iris*, July 1791, pp. 1–88, here pp. 29–30;

plants were also being raised in the pleasure gardens of the planters of St Croix, 'who by [von Rohr's] example and assistance have gotten a taste for introducing foreign plants'.[35] Von Rohr cultivated one variety of cotton from a particularly distant clime: he had obtained the seed, by way of the botanic garden in Copenhagen, from J. C. Samuel, a German missionary (educated, like von Rohr and Kratzenstein, at Halle) in Danish service at Tranquebar, in south-eastern India.[36] Among the ornamentals von Rohr had successfully introduced was the Otaheite-tree or hibiscus, which, West wrote, shaded the graves of the Tahitians: the plant had already become common on St Croix.[37]

At least as early as 1777, von Rohr had been sending plant specimens to Sir Joseph Banks, one of the central figures of the English – and Atlantic – Enlightenment, whose scientific correspondence and support of natural history were comparable in many respects to Linnaeus's extraordinary network.[38] Banks, as director of Kew Gardens, near London, was even more interested than most in the economically advantageous transfers of plants that botanical gardens were intended to facilitate. Perhaps the most famous of his economic botanical undertakings was his support of Captain William Bligh's voyages to transport live breadfruit trees – an important food crop – to the West Indies from the Pacific islands; having failed in 1789 because of the mutiny on his vessel *Bounty*, Bligh delivered breadfruit trees safely to the botanic garden at Saint-Vincent in 1793. In the meantime, the French had also introduced the plant on Martinique,[39] and in 1794 Hans West wrote to the great Danish botanical authority Martin Vahl (one of the last of Linnaeus's students) that the breadfruit had recently been introduced into St Croix from Martinique. 'It is coming up in several gardens,' he said, 'but takes 5 years to bear, and at Kew, I heard, 7.'[40] This was no mere botanical curiosity, but substantial economic news.

Naturforskeren, Apoteker på St. Croix Peder Eggert Benzon's efterladte dagbøger og breve (1816–1840), ed. A. Schæffer (Copenhagen, 1967), pp. 57, 83–4, 107, 146, 252–3.
35   Hans West, *Bidrag til beskrivelse over St. Croix* (Copenhagen, 1793), p. 264.
36   'John, Christoph Samuel', *Dansk biografisk leksikon*, 2nd edn; J.-P.-B. de Rohr, *Observations sur la culture du coton …* (Paris, 1807), p. 62; Paul A. Fryxell, 'The West Indian Species of Gossypium of von Rohr and Rafinesque', *Taxon* 18/4 (1969), 400–14, here p. 402.
37   West, *Bidrag til beskrivelse over St. Croix*, pp. 269, 297.
38   British Library, Department of Manuscripts, Add. MS 8094.185, Julius von Rohr, St. Croix 24 June 1777, to Joseph Banks; *The Banks Letters*, ed. W. R. Dawson (London, 1958), p. 709.
39   John Gascoigne, *Joseph Banks and the English Enlightenment: Useful Knowledge and Polite Culture* (Cambridge, 1994); Lucile H. Brockway, *Science and Colonial Expansion: the Role of the British Royal Botanic Gardens* (New York, 1979); Howard, 'Botanical Gardens in West Indies History', pp. 119–20; Grove, *Green Imperialism*, p. 339.
40   Botanisk Centralbibliotek, Copenhagen, letters collection, Hans West, St. Croix, 13 June 1794, to Martin Vahl.

A Caribbean Odyssey

In 1782, the Danish Commerce Collegium (the department of commerce), which was headed by Ernst Schimmelmann,[41] wrote to the Chamber of Customs, the branch of the central government that administered the Danish West Indies, that it had received complaints from industrialising textile manufacturers regarding the quality of the cotton imported from the islands, which, its letter said, was considerably inferior to fibre from Martinique, Guadeloupe and the Guianas. The Commerce Collegium presumed that the discrepancy could not be accounted for by significant differences in climate and soils, and that the Danish West Indian planters' methods and plant stock must be in some way deficient.[42] The Collegium knew of no one better suited to investigate the matter than Julius von Rohr and recommended that he be ordered to travel to other West Indian colonies to study techniques of cultivation and production, and to collect the best cotton seed for distribution to planters in the Danish islands. The Commerce Collegium asked that von Rohr's task should include the preparation of a manual of cotton cultivation. St Croix planters who improved their production, the Collegium promised, could count on purchases by the Royal Danish Cotton Manufacture, an administrative arm of the Commerce Collegium that had been established in 1779 and transferred to private hands only a few months before the Collegium's approach to the colonial office of the Chamber of Customs.[43] With the Crown's approval, von Rohr was relieved of his regular duties and dispatched on a year's expedition down the Antilles to South America.[44]

It was an extraordinary opportunity. Von Rohr wrote to Joseph Banks in some elation in July 1783:

41   Gøbel, *Det danske slavehandelsforbud*, p. 25.

42   RA, Generaltoldkammer or Chamber of Customs (GTK), West Indian correspondence journal (VJ) 616/1782, from the Commerce Collegium (CC), 3 September 1782; CC, kopibog, 3 September 1782, to the GTK; VJ 244/1784, the Danish West Indian administration, 7 October 1783; RA, Fonden ad Usus Publicos, Forestillinger & Resolutioner, pro memoria from the CC to the Directors of Fonden ad Usus Publicos, 25 November 1786.

43   CC, kopibog, 14 December 1782, to von Rohr; Morten Westrup, 'Kommercesagernes bestyrelse', *Rigsarkivet og hjælpemidlerne til dets benyttelse*, ed. W. von Rosen (Copenhagen, 1983), pp. 441–68, here pp. 464–6; J. O. Bro-Jørgensen, *Industriens historie i Danmark*, vol. 2: *Tiden 1730–1820*, ed. A. Nielsen (Copenhagen, 1943), p. 174.

44   CC, Diverse, Varia, 1774–92 og udat., Korrespondance vedrørende v. Rohrs undersøgelser angående bomuldskulturen i Vestindien, 1786–87; CC, correspondence journal (CCJ) and journaled files (CCJS) 1027/1782, GTK, n.d. (CCJS contains the full text of letters and CCJ an index to the correspondence with abstracts and notes on actions taken; individual letters appear or are cited under the same reference numbers in both files); VJ 844/1782, royal resolution, 2 December 1782; CC, kopibog, 14 December 1782, to von Rohr; VJ 244/1784, the West Indian administration, 7 October 1783.

Nothing, but the Duty and Care of my Post in the Kings Services has hinder'd me in the Pursuance of my Passion for natural History. At last the Reward for the first came, and free of all other Business, I am going next Week to St: Domingo, upon the Kings' [sic] Account: from there to Cajenne to which purpose Mr. Ryan len[t] me his Fusée Aublet.[45]

John Ryan was a wealthy planter and amateur botanist, with plantations on both St Croix and Montserrat, to whom von Rohr was evidently quite close; von Rohr had sent a shipment of dried plants and a letter of introduction for Ryan to Banks in 1777, and one of von Rohr's letters to Banks was posted in Montserrat.[46] 'His Fusée Aublet' refers to the *Histoire des plantes de la Guiane françoise* recently published by Jean Baptiste Christofore Fusée-Aublet, who after spending many years in the French colony of Isle de France (Mauritius), in the Indian Ocean, had for a time been the director of the botanic garden at Cayenne.[47]

'There after', von Rohr went on in his letter to Banks, 'I intend to Surinam and along that Coast, as far as I can come, and the Kings and my own Money will [let] me reach … The List You dit give to Mr. Ryan, of Jacquin's Plants I take also with me, in order to collect them for You.' (Nikolaus Joseph Jacquin had collected in the Caribbean and on the South American coast for Francis I of Austria in the late 1750s.)[48] Von Rohr enclosed with this letter thirty dried herbarium specimens, with his regrets that, after so many years, he was not sending more. 'When I return to my Garden again', he wrote, 'I will be so bold as to beg You for some seeds, who could make it a Garden of consequence.'

It seems remarkable that von Rohr made no mention whatsoever of cotton in this letter to Banks. There prevailed a certain tension between science (and its aesthetics) for its own sake and its application to the improvement – so characteristic of Enlightenment-era scientific and governmental ambitions – of crops, techniques, and the workings of the economy and society in general, but von Rohr's errand, although he here ignored it in his eagerness to convey his great botanical news to Banks, reflected perfectly the age's sense of the breadth of natural history and of the state's interest in putting it to practical use.[49]

45   British Library, Department of Manuscripts, Add. MS 8094.185, Julius von Rohr, St. Croix, 19 July 1783, to Joseph Banks; *The Banks Letters*, p. 709.
46   *The Banks Letters*, p. 709; see Orla Power, 'Beyond Kinship: A Study of the Eighteenth-century Irish Community at St. Croix, Danish West Indies', *Irish Migration Studies in Latin America* 5/3 (2007), 207–14, here p. 208, and *The Diary of John Baker*, ed. P. C. Yorke (London, 1931), pp. 10–12.
47   Published in London by P. F. Didot in 1775; Madeleine Pinault Sørensen, 'Les voyageurs artistes en Amérique du Sud aux xviiie siècle', *Les naturalistes français en Amérique du Sud XVIe–XIXe siècles*, ed. Y. Laissus (Paris, 1995), pp. 43–55, here p. 51; Ly-Tio-Fane, 'Botanical Gardens: Connecting Links', p. 58.
48   Santiago Madriñán, *Nikolaus Joseph Jacquin's American Plants* (Leiden, 2013).
49   Hopkins, 'Danish Natural History and African Colonialism', pp. 380–1.

Von Rohr's Caribbean odyssey in the end lasted twenty-five months. In a long, rather uneven report to the Commerce Collegium, the scientist related that he had visited Puerto Rico, Martinique, Saint-Domingue, Curaçao, Jamaica, Guadeloupe, Cayenne, Suriname, Paramaribo, Trinidad, and the cities of Cartagena and Santa Marta in what is today Colombia.[50] (In a letter to Banks written along the way, he regretted that Jacquin had published no journal of his travels: it would have been useful to be able to follow in the Dutchman's botanical footsteps near Cartagena, where Jacquin had collected extensively.)[51] On the other hand, von Rohr wrote in a separate account of his expedition among the Amerindians of the region around Mazinga, not far from Santa Marta, that he presumed that he must be the first European scientist to see the rich fauna and flora in these mountains.[52] Von Rohr was travelling with three local Amerindian guides and two black slaves of his own, he wrote; one of his slaves specialised in collecting insects, the other in plants. It is to be noted that a copy of this account is to be found among Ernst Schimmelmann's papers: it is clear that he was closely interested in von Rohr's expedition.

Even from the sea, on the approaches to Santa Marta, von Rohr had seen remarkably straight lines cutting across the landscape; his first thought, as a surveyor, was that these must be the recently demarcated boundary lines of plantations, but they proved to be great granite stairways, sixteen feet wide, up the mountainsides, constructed, he was given to understand, by an Amerindian civilisation that had flourished in this area three centuries earlier.[53] He had botanised happily here for six weeks, he wrote to Banks, sometimes spending nights in meadows where once there had been large towns.[54]

The Amerindians raised and smoked tobacco, and von Rohr had been interested to see what he took to be wild vanilla vines in some profusion.[55] He particularly inquired of his Amerindian guides about the valuable antimalarial chinabark; he hoped that it might be found somewhere closer than in the environs of 'Loxa' (or Loja), in what is now Ecuador. There almost forty

50   CCJS 854/1786, Julius von Rohr, Ste. Croix, 31 May 1786.
51   British Library, Department of Manuscripts, Add. MS 8095.226, Julius von Rohr, Kingston, Jamaica, 16 September 1783, to Joseph Banks; Madriñán, *Jacquin's American Plants*, pp. 37, 39.
52   RA, Privatarkiv no. 6285, Heinrich Ernst Schimmelmann, archival dates 1751–1848, bundle 11, Koncepter ang. Slavehandelen og Negervæsenet i Vestindien og Kopier vedr. Sierra Leone Kolonien, Julius von Rohr, Bericht über meine Reise nach den Gebürgen bey Mazinga vieje, oder Alt-Mazinga, ohnweit St. Martha, und die über die Berge gehenden Indianer Treppen, 20 November 1786; copy in RA, Privatarkiv no. 2564, J. F. Heinrich.
53   Von Rohr, Bericht über meine Reise nach den Gebürgen bey Mazinga vieje.
54   British Library, Manuscripts Collection, Add. MS 8096.170–171, Julius de Rohr [*sic*] to Joseph Banks, Cayenne, 30 August 1784.
55   Von Rohr, Bericht über meine Reise nach den Gebürgen bey Mazinga vieje.

years earlier Charles-Marie de La Condamine had collected live specimens of
cinchona, which he had transported to Cayenne in the hope that they could
be acclimatised there in a French colonial territory.[56] Von Rohr related that
he had shown his guides a printed image (in the engraving of which Banks
had had a part) of the cinchona tree.[57] The Mazingans knew the plant but
informed him that it grew higher up on the Nevada de Santa Marta. Von Rohr
speculated in his report to the Commerce Collegium that cinchona might do
well in Denmark's cool climate, just as the potato, another plant adapted to
the cool soils and climate of the Andes, to which it was native, had become
acclimatised after it arrived in the northern lowlands of Europe. Thinking
along the same lines, La Condamine, in his day, had sent seeds of '*Quinquina*'
to a Jesuit mission high up the Oyapock River, on the border between French
Guiana and Brazil, where, he said, the 'less ardent' climate and terrain better
resembled those of Loxa than did Cayenne.[58]

Von Rohr spent the best part of a year in Cayenne, a thousand miles east
of Santa Marta, 'among erudite friends and flowers', as he wrote to Banks.[59]
He had already heard of the south-east Asian spice plants that had lately been
introduced into cultivation in Cayenne and, a few months after he arrived,
he was in attendance when a monument was raised to 'Mr. Poivre', who, von
Rohr wrote, had smuggled clove plants out of the East Indies and introduced
them into Mauritius; he had subsequently sent live clove seedlings, as well
as nutmeg and other spice plants, to the Antilles.[60] Von Rohr was doubtless
learning a great deal about the wider world of colonial botany in the
company he was keeping in Cayenne. Nonetheless, in dropping the names of
Pierre Poivre, the celebrated Indian Ocean botanical adventurer and colonial

56 CCJS 854/1786, Julius von Rohr, Ste. Croix, 31 May 1786; Schiebinger and Swan,
'Introduction', *Colonial Botany*, pp. 1–2; and Charles-Marie de La Condamine, *Relation
abrégée d'un voyage fait dans l'intérieur de l'Amérique Méridionale* (Maestricht, 1778), pp. 26,
198–9.
57 Von Rohr, Bericht über meine Reise nach den Gebürgen bey Mazinga vieje; Aylmer
Bourke Lambert, *A Description of the Genus Cinchona, Comprehending the Various Species
of Vegetables from which the Peruvian and other Barks of a Similar Quality are Taken,
Illustrated by Figures of all the Species hitherto Discovered, to which is prefixed Professor
Vahl's Dissertation on this Genus, Read before the Society of Natural History at Copenhagen*
(London, 1797), dedication by the author, the vice-president of the Linnean Society, to Sir
Joseph Banks, n.p.
58 La Condamine, *Relation abrégée*, p. 199.
59 Von Rohr to Banks, Cayenne, 30 August 1784; see also n. 54.
60 CCJ and CCJS 854/1786, von Rohr, Ste. Croix, 31 May 1786; Thomas Zumbroich,
'The Introduction of Nutmeg (*Myristica fragrans* Houtt.) and Cinnamon (*Cinnamomum
verum* J. S. Presl.) to America', *Acta Botánica Venezuelica* 28/1 (2005), 155–60; E. C. Spary,
'Of Nutmeg and Botanists: The Colonial Cultivation of Botanical Identity', *Colonial Botany.
Science, Commerce, and Politics in the Early Modern World*, ed. L. Schiebinger and C. Swan
(Philadelphia, 2005), pp. 187–203, here p. 200.

administrator, and of Poivre's collaborator at Mauritius, the botanist Philibert Commerson, he appears to have assumed that the transoceanic connections he was making in his official report would also be appreciated in the social and administrative environments in which Ernst Schimmelmann moved and worked in Copenhagen.[61] Von Rohr's cotton research was a strand in a larger intellectual and economic fabric.

With the permission of the governor of Cayenne, who declared magnani- mously that when it came to science, all nations were one (but who kept armed guards on the clove trees introduced at such trouble and expense by the French government), von Rohr travelled by river up into French Guiana with Louis Richard, a naturalist sent out to the West Indies by the French Academy of Sciences in 1781 expressly to work on the wider propagation of Poivre's plants.[62] The expedition carried them some two hundred miles through the country.

When they returned to Cayenne, von Rohr related, the clove trees were in bloom. He managed to obtain a quantity of the seeds and sowed them discreetly among the roots of potted specimens of many other useful and interesting plants he had found, including a couple of cinnamon trees. These he forwarded to St Croix. He had also acquainted himself with the cultivation and processing of the cloves, he wrote. Unfortunately, by the time he himself arrived home, a hurricane had destroyed his seedlings.[63]

Von Rohr's botanical collections on his long journey were of great scientific value. He later wrote to Banks, 'I have been very much flatter'd by Your last Letter, that the Cayenne Plants, I had the Honour to send … dit please You'.[64] Herbarium specimens he sent back to Denmark reached Martin Vahl, who later published descriptions of quite a number of von Rohr's plants, with expensive copperplate illustrations.[65] The publication was financed by von Rohr's friend John Ryan, the Montserrat planter, who wrote to Vahl, 'I will tell you beforehand, that I shall not mind a little Sacrifice on this occasion'.[66] Vahl, in 1791, having published the first volume of his great *Symbolae Botanica*, sent von Rohr a copy of it, notifying him that he was

61   Madeleine Ly-Tio-Fane, *The Triumph of Jean Nicolas Céré and his Isle Bourbon Collaborators* (Paris, 1970), pp. 62–4; Ly-Tio-Fane, 'Botanical Gardens: Connecting Links', pp. 58–9; Grove, *Green Imperialism*, pp. 8–9.
62   CCJ and CCJS 854/1786, von Rohr, Ste. Croix, 31 May 1786; Sørensen, 'Les voyageurs artistes', p. 51.
63   CCJS 854/1786, von Rohr, Ste. Croix, 31 May 1786.
64   British Library, Department of Manuscripts, Add. MS 8098.170–171, Julius von Rohr, Montserrat, 25 April 1788.
65   Fryxell, 'The West Indian Species of Gossypium', pp. 401–2; Christensen, *Den danske botaniks historie*, vol. 2, pp. 86–8.
66   Botanisk Centralbibliotek, Copenhagen, letters collection, John Ryan, London, 28 March 1798, to Martin Vahl.

inserting descriptions and images of some of von Rohr's plants in the second volume; he enclosed some plate proofs. Vahl also related that descriptions of some of von Rohr's plants, passed along by Joseph Banks, had recently been published by Olof Swartz, the Swedish botanist, who had himself botanised in the West Indies.[67]

Von Rohr's material, including not merely plant specimens but also information on pests in sugar cane and cotton (controlled lately, by von Rohr's account, with the help of flocks of turkeys), was also drawn upon in articles by metropolitan scientists in the *Skrivter* of the highly prestigious Natural History Society, whose membership, besides counts Schimmelmann, Bernstorff and Moltke, included a startling range of prominent members of Danish society – scientists, government ministers, merchant shippers, doctors, religious leaders and jurists.[68] Natural history was all the rage – wealthy elites indulged themselves in ornate gardens and gracious cabinets of pressed flowers, gleaming insects, and spectacular seashells from the South Seas – but this fascination with the natural world was enmeshed in material concerns and extended to the undertakings of the state.[69]

A formal proposal to organise a Danish natural history society had been issued in 1789 by no less a figure than P. C. Abildgaard, the founder of the Royal Veterinary School, president of the Agricultural Society and secretary of the Royal Danish Academy of Sciences and Letters. Abildgaard's prospectus artfully and succinctly sketched out a well-balanced philosophy of nature and humanity's place in it.[70] 'Where else than in nature', he wrote, 'and its wise, glorious organisation, can humanity find models and strongly eloquent examples of order, beauty, industry without bondage, frugality in the midst of plenty, and the most perfect unity in untold multiplicity?' Rather more concretely, 'from the three kingdoms of nature we have our food, our

67   GTK, Vestindiske og Guineiske Sager, Diverse Dokumenter, Schimmelmannske papirer vedk. Kommissionerne betræffende Guinea og Negerhandelen, samt forskellige Vestindiske papirer, Martin Vahl, Copenhagen, 29 March 1791, to von Rohr; Christensen, *Den danske botaniks historie*, vol. 1, p. 168; 'Swartz, Olof', *Dictionary of Scientific Biography*, ed. C. Coulston Gillispie (New York, 1970–80).
68   N. Tønder Lund, 'Om den rette *Qvassia amara*, og om den falske, efter Herr von Rohr', *Skrivter af Naturhistorie-Selskabet* 1/2 (1791), 68–72; [Tønder Lund], 'Plante-slægter beskrevne af Hr. Oberst-Lieutenant von Rohr, med tilføiede Anmærkninger af Hr. Professor Vahl', *Skrivter af Naturhistorie-Selskabet* 2/1 (1792), [205]–221; Joh. Chr. Fabricius, 'Beskrivelse over den skadelige Sukker- og Bomulds-Orm i Vestindien, og om *Zygænæ Pugionis* Forvandling', *Skrivter af Naturhistorie-Selskabet* 3/2 (1794), 63–7, here p. 66; 'Rohr, Julius Philipp Benjamin von', Frans A. Stafleu and Richard S. Cowan, *Taxonomic Literature*, 2nd edn (Boston, MA, 1983); Hopkins, 'Danish Natural History and African Colonialism', pp. 373–8.
69   See Daniel Hopkins, 'Peter Thonning and the Natural Historical Collections of Denmark's Prince Christian (VIII), 1806–07', *Nordisk Museologi* 2 (1996), 149–64.
70   For details on Abildgaard's proposal and full source details, see Hopkins, 'Danish Natural History and African Colonialism', pp. 374–6.

clothing, our domestic conveniences, our remedies in sickness, and all the things that in the arts and trades are employed to such great advantage to the society'.

The Natural History Society's aims were intellectually and spiritually ambitious and at the same time down to earth. Articulating for another generation the worrisome lack of such instruction in the nation's educational institutions, Abildgaard's *Invitation* to subscribe to the society argued vigorously that the formal study of nature was indispensable, in those enlightened times, for it

> has such a beneficial influence on the human intellect ...; it teaches man to read in the book of Nature; it accustoms him to be sensible of the elevated, embrace the great, think about the wonders of creation, and through such thoughts raise himself from the bestial to the nobility of reason; and finally because it ... has such an important influence on other sciences, as well as in the workings of civil life, in economy, in trade, in agriculture and manufacturing.

The Society's museum would serve the purposes of 'utility and instruction', and its botanic garden would specialise in economic botany.

Martin Vahl wrote the first article in the Natural History Society's *Skrivter* – a piece on chinabark – in which he mentioned specimens sent him from St Croix.[71] In another long article, Vahl published 'Plant genera described by Mr. Lieutenant Colonel von Rohr'. This article was introduced by Niels Tønder Lund, to whom von Rohr had sent the plants. Tønder Lund was one of the founding members of the Natural History Society, a noted amateur entomologist and a high-ranking officer in the Chamber of Customs. 'These descriptions and observations', he wrote:

> made on the spot from the living plants by so knowledgeable and observant a practitioner of the science, which distinguish themselves by their preciseness and are entirely in the spirit of Linné, I could not serve better, although without the author's permission, than to lay them before the Natural History Society.[72]

A manuscript abstract of Abildgaard's *Invitation* that was circulated in the halls of the civil administration in Copenhagen noted that the Society proposed to fund young scientific travellers, on the Linnean model,[73] who 'will be instructed to not only concern themselves with natural history proper, but

71   Martin Vahl, 'Om slægten Cinchona, og dens arter', *Skrivter af Naturhistorie-Selskabet* 1/1 (1790), [1]–25, esp. on p. 15 (three plates are bound in at the back of the number).
72   [Niels Tønder Lund], 'Plante-slægter beskrevne af Hr. Oberst-Lieutenant von Rohr', [p. 205].
73   Hopkins, 'Danish Natural History and African Colonialism', p. 374.

also with the natural and economic constitution of the land through which they travel'. The government could hope that these 'young students, in these journeys about the Fatherland, can obtain the knowledge of the country so necessary for civil servants'. Ernst Schimmelmann's signature stands out on the list of subscribers attached to this document. Many threads bound Schimmelmann – and the interests and aspirations of the upper ranks of Danish society more generally – to the work of Julius von Rohr in the West Indies. This was no marginal scientific figure, but the kingdom's most important practitioner of tropical – which is essentially to say colonial – natural history, in the full Linnaean, improving, economic sense of the word.

Von Rohr had collected the seeds of many varieties of cotton on his journeys and, at home on St Croix, he cultivated test plots of cotton not only in his own garden but in other environmental settings, including at La Grange, Count Schimmelmann's large plantation in the West End Quarter.[74] The supervision of repairs to public buildings damaged in the recent hurricane consumed most of his time, however, and the Commerce Collegium was eventually obliged to remind him of his commitment to produce a manual on cotton cultivation. The Danish West Indian government warmly supported his application for another year's leave to complete this work and, indeed, he was soon thereafter allowed to retire at full pay – quite a rare distinction – to devote himself entirely to the pursuit of natural history.[75] In 1791, the first part of his treatise on cotton was published in Altona, near Hamburg.[76] In truth, since the book was in German, it is likely to have been of limited use to the mainly English-speaking planters of the Danish West Indies. (A French translation appeared in 1807.)[77] Von Rohr's work in any case had little impact on the production of cotton on St Croix, where the land was largely given over to sugar cane.[78]

74   [Von] Rohr, *Observations sur la culture du coton*, pp. 54, 56–7, 175, 178; West, *Bidrag til beskrivelse over St. Croix*, p. 297.

75   CC, Diverse, Varia, 1774–92 og udat., Korrespondance vedrørende v. Rohrs undersøgelser angående bomuldskulturen i Vestindien, 1786–87, Schimmelmann, Lindemann, Laurberg, and Colbiørnsen, St. Croix, 15 May 1786, to Det Kongelig Westindiske Kammer, copy; VJ 632/1786, Heinrich, 12 September 1786; RA, Finansdeputationen, correspondence journal, 506/1791, GTK, 4 April 1791; GTK, Vestindiske forestillinger og resolutioner, 1791 and 1792, 13 April 1791; Hopkins, *Peter Thonning and Denmark's Guinea Commission*, p. 542.

76   Julius Philip Benjamin von Rohr, *Anmerkungen über den Cattun Bau* (Altona, 1791–93).

77   [Von] Rohr, *Observations sur la culture du coton*.

78   Peter Lotharius Oxholm, *De Danske Vestindiske Øers Tilstand i henseende til Population, Cultur og Finance-Forfatning* (Copenhagen, 1797), p. 67; Hopkins, Morgan and Roberts, 'The Application of GIS to the Reconstruction of the Slave-Plantation Economy of St. Croix, Danish West Indies', p. 96; George F. Tyson, Jr, 'On the Periphery of the Peripheries: The Cotton Plantations of St. Croix, Danish West Indies, 1735–1815', *Bondmen and Freedmen in the Danish West Indies, Scholarly Perspectives*, ed. G. Tyson (1991; St Thomas, 1996), pp. 1–36.

A Colonial Turn Towards Africa

Von Rohr was not given long to enjoy his retirement. Late in 1791, the Danish Crown, at the instigation of Ernst Schimmelmann, called upon him to undertake a new agronomic and colonial investigation of particular significance, this time on the Guinea Coast of Africa.[79] The Danes, through a series of private slave-trading companies, had for a century or more maintained a string of castles and slave-trading lodges along a hundred-mile stretch of the African coast between Accra and the mouth of the Volta River, in what is now southeastern Ghana.[80] In 1788, a German-born physician, Paul Isert, had published a memoir of several years' service in the Danish slave forts and of a long visit to the West Indies, where he appears to have made the acquaintance of Julius von Rohr. He succeeded in interesting Ernst Schimmelmann in a Danish colonial project in West Africa: the idea was to cultivate cotton and sugarcane and other typical West Indian crops in West Africa, thereby rendering West Indian production superfluous and eliminating the economic motivation for the Atlantic slave trade that supplied the plantations of the West Indies.[81]

Isert drew up elaborate plans for a small plantation colony with Ernst Philip Kirstein, Schimmelmann's German-born private secretary.[82] Schimmelmann himself warned Jens Adolf Kiøge, the governor of the Danish trading establishments on the Guinea Coast, that he preferred that the matter be kept quiet, for the time being, but wrote that Isert's experiment might prove significant; any nation, he said, that could obtain the products of the West Indies in Africa, without depending on the Atlantic slave trade, might find itself rather advantageously placed in the markets in the prevailing new climate of abolitionism.[83] Schimmelmann accepted from the start, however, that Isert's

79   Ray A. Kea, 'Plantations and Labour in the South-East Gold Coast from the Late Eighteenth to the mid Nineteenth Century', *From Slave Trade to Legitimate Commerce: The Commercial Transition in Nineteenth-Century West Africa*, ed. R. Law (Cambridge, 1995), pp. 119–43; Hopkins, *Peter Thonning and Denmark's Guinea Commission*, pp. 49–50, 57.

80   Georg Nørregård, *Danish Settlements in West Africa 1658–1850*, transl. Sigurd Mammen (Boston, MA, 1966); *Danish Sources for the History of Ghana, 1657–1754*, ed. O. Justesen, transl. James Manley (Copenhagen, 2005); Hopkins, *Peter Thonning and Denmark's Guinea Commission*.

81   Paul Erdmann Isert, *Reise nach Guinea und den Caribäischen Inseln in Columbien* (Copenhagen, 1788), translated in *Letters on West Africa and the Slave Trade. Paul Erdmann Isert's Journey to Guinea and the Caribbean Islands in Columbia (1788)*, transl. Selena Axelrod Winsnes (Oxford, 1992), pp. 184, 190, in Winsnes's edition; Per Hernæs, 'A Danish Experiment in Commercial Agriculture on the Gold Coast, 1788–93', *Commercial Agriculture: The Slave Trade and Slavery in Atlantic Africa*, ed. R. Law, S. Schwarz and S. Strickrodt (Woodbridge, 2013), pp. 158–79.

82   Joseph Evans Loftin, Jr, 'The Abolition of the Danish Atlantic Slave Trade' (unpublished dissertation, Louisiana State University, 1977), p. 86.

83   Joseph C. Miller, 'Introduction: Atlantic Ambiguities of British and American Abolition', *William and Mary Quarterly*, 3rd Series, 64/4 (2009), 677–704, here pp. 684–5.

colony would depend on local slave labour.[84] The Danish government sent
Isert back to Africa with a party of craftsmen in 1788. He succeeded in establishing the modest seat of the colony he envisaged in the well-watered hills of
Akuapem, a few miles north of Accra, but died two months after arriving on
the Guinea Coast. The little colony then languished, but Schimmelmann did
not abandon this African colonial ambition.[85]

African commercial and colonial schemes figured heavily in this era of
abolitionism.[86] The Danish government was aware of British colonial undertakings in Sierra Leone, as was the educated public;[87] it was reported from
England in the Danish press that abolitionists, encountering insurmountable
political obstacles to passing legislation to end the Atlantic slave trade, had
resolved to attempt:

> to undermine it like a stronghold it is not advisable to storm; a colony
> in Africa, where by free hands there could be planted and produced the
> greatest part of the necessaries for which slaves are used in the West Indies,
> [would] little by little cut the slave trade off at the root.

This Danish reporter went on:

> To this was linked the philanthropic idea of spreading from such a colony
> knowledge, religion, and better morals among the blacks and showing them

84 Hopkins, *Peter Thonning and Denmark's Guinea Commission*, pp. 21, 23–6, 33–4.
85 Daniel Hopkins, 'The Danish Ban on the Atlantic Slave Trade and Denmark's African
Colonial Ambitions, 1787–1807', *Itinerario* 25/3–4 (2001), 154–84, here pp. 156–9, 164; Hopkins,
Peter Thonning and Denmark's Guinea Commission, pp. 34–9, 40–3.
86 See Hopkins, 'The Danish Ban on the Atlantic Slave Trade', pp. 164–7, and, for example,
Jean-Paul Nicolas, 'Adanson et le mouvement colonial', English abstract, in *Adanson: The
Bicentennial of Michel Adanson's 'Familles des plantes'*, part 2, ed. G. H. M. Lawrence
(Pittsburgh, 1964), pp. 436–49, here p. 444; Eveline C. Martin, *The British West African
Settlements, 1750–1821* (1927; repr. New York, 1970), pp. 153–4; Christopher Fyfe, *A History
of Sierra Leone* (London, 1962), pp. 46, 7–8, 94; A. G. Hopkins, *An Economic History of West
Africa* (London, 1973), p. 137; Vincent Carretta, *Equiano, the African: Biography of a Self-Made
Man* (Athens, GA, 2005), pp. 221–2; Edward E. Reynolds, 'Abolition and Economic change on the
Gold Coast', *The Abolition of the Atlantic Slave Trade: Origins and Effects in Europe, Africa,
and the Americas*, ed. D. Eltis and J. Walvin (Madison, WI, 1981), pp. 141–51; Deirdre Coleman,
Romantic Colonisation and British Anti-Slavery (Cambridge, 2005), especially pp. 28–62;
Christopher Leslie Brown, *Moral Capital: Foundations of British Abolitionism* (Chapel Hill,
2006), on, for example, pp. 314–21; Christopher Leslie Brown, 'The Origins of "Legitimate
Commerce"', *Commercial Agriculture: The Slave Trade and Slavery in Atlantic Africa*, ed.
R. Law, S. Schwarz and S. Strickrodt (Woodbridge, 2013), pp. 138–57, here pp. 138–40.
87 See C. A. Trier, 'Det dansk-vestindiske Negerindførselsforbud af 1792', *Historisk Tidsskrift*,
7th series, 5 (1904–05), 405–508, here p. 447; Henning Højlund Knap, 'Danskerne og slaveriet.
Negerslavedebatten i Danmark indtil 1792', *Dansk kolonihistorie. Indføring og studier*, ed.
P. Hoxcer Jensen, L. Haar, M. Hahn-Pedersen, K. U. Jessen and A. Damsgaard-Madsen (Århus,
1983), pp. 153–74; Hopkins, 'The Danish Ban on the Atlantic Slave Trade', p. 154.

the loathsomeness of the slave trade, as well as of their mutual enmity, two calamities that stand in relation to one another as cause and effect.[88]

In 1791, the progress through the British parliament of an ultimately unsuccessful bill abolishing the Atlantic slave trade was followed closely in Denmark, and Crown Prince Frederik set up a commission to study the Danish slave trade and the feasibility of abolishing it.[89] Ernst Schimmelmann headed this Slave-Trade Commission, as it was commonly called, and apparently drafted its recommendation to the Crown. Niels Tønder Lund, of the Chamber of Customs, was among the commission's high-ranking members, and Ernst Kirstein managed its paperwork.[90]

Late in October 1791, when the Slave-Trade Commission was still in the midst of its deliberations, Schimmelmann secured from the regent an order sending Julius von Rohr to the Guinea Coast to determine whether conditions in the area around the Danish forts might favour the establishment of a plantation colony there.[91] The archival record indicates that Schimmelmann personally communicated the royal will in this matter to von Rohr and the West Indian administration. A few days later, the Fonden ad Usus Publicos (The Fund for Public Purposes), another of the agencies Schimmelmann controlled, ordered the necessary money disbursed.[92] Schimmelmann appears to have been operating outside the usual colonial administrative channels; in his eagerness, he himself advanced considerable sums towards von Rohr's expedition.[93]

It also appears that, as in the case of Isert's colonial experiment, Schimmelmann attempted to keep this new African colonial undertaking quiet. The Slave-Trade Commission's recommendation that the Danish slave trade be abolished (the commission's formal opinion was in any case not a public matter) permitted itself only a few lines about the African slaving forts; the commission was aware, it wrote, in an oblique reference to von Rohr's mission, that the Crown was just at that time investigating the feasibility of

88   [Frederik Sneedorff], 'Breve fra en dansk reisende' No. XXIX, London, 4 May 1792, *Minerva* 2 (May, 1792), 257–72, here pp. 257–8; see also Hopkins, *Peter Thonning and Denmark's Guinea Commission*, pp. 60–8.

89   Gøbel, *Det danske slavehandelsforbud*, pp. 41–52; Hopkins, *Peter Thonning and Denmark's Guinea Commission*, pp. 49, 61, 64, 224.

90   Gøbel, *Det danske slavehandelsforbud*, pp. 52–4.

91   Hopkins, *Peter Thonning and Denmark's Guinea Commission*, pp. 50, 55–7, 69; see P. G. Hensler, 'Préface de l'Éditeur', [Von] Rohr, *Observations sur la culture du coton*, part 2, pp. lxxxiii–lxxxvi, on p. lxxxvi.

92   RA, Fonden ad Usus Publicos, Missive-Protokol, April 1781–June 1796, 7, 11, 18 and 25 November and 6 December 1791, to Falbe.

93   *Fonden ad Usus Publicos: Aktmæssig Bidrag til Belysning af dens Virksomhed, udgivne af Rigsarkivet*, vol. 1: *1765–1800* (Copenhagen, 1897), pp. 140–1.

cultivating the typical products of the West Indies in a West African colony and therefore deferred any recommendation on this subject.[94]

Schimmelmann's administrative caution notwithstanding, the thinking was ambitious: the plan envisaged, if still rather nebulously, the transplantation of a huge economic structure, an entire way of life, back across the Atlantic to Africa from the New World, which was itself such a compelling colonial example, with its legendary history – not, at the time, at all remote – of unheard-of territorial expansion and development, and the rapid creation of fabulous wealth. The science of the relationships among plants, climates and soils in various parts of the world was not yet well worked out, however; it remained a matter of surmise that the great commodity crops of the West Indies might thrive in the natural environs of the Danish forts in West Africa. A young metropolitan scientist, were such a one available, would not serve Schimmelmann's purposes so well as an experienced tropical plantation agronomist, and von Rohr, his distinguished servant and compatriot, was as immediate to his hand as the slow transoceanic communications of the day permitted.

Schimmelmann found another instrument in the person of Jens Flindt, a former slave-trader on the Guinea Coast who had for a time been in charge of Isert's plantation and had himself addressed an elaborate colonial proposal to Ernst Schimmelmann early in 1791. Flindt was in Copenhagen when Schimmelmann and Prince Frederik made their decision about von Rohr, and he was ordered to the West Indies to learn something of plantation agriculture there and then to proceed with von Rohr to West Africa.[95]

Flindt took his sister abroad with him, and not for the first time. He was later characterised as 'not a very bright or knowledgeable man, but probably, together with his sister, the most active Europeans that had ever been in Guinea'. The prominent Swedish colonial promoter C. B. Wadström, in 1795, in his *Essay on Colonisation, Particularly Applied to the Western Coast of Africa*, wrote of Ms Flindt that, 'with the same zeal for the civilisation of Africa, by which Mrs. Dubois has done so much honour to the sex',[96] she had been with her brother at Isert's plantation, 'with a view to instruct the negro women in needle-work, spinning cotton and other parts of female industry; and that she has already made very considerable progress in this laudable and benevolent undertaking'. Flindt thought it important to bring to

94   RA, Dokumenter vedrørende Kommissionen for Negerhandelens bedre Indretning og Ophaevelse m. m. 1783–1806, box II, the Slave-Trade Commission's 'Allerunterthänigste Vorstellung', 28 December 1791; Loftin, 'The Abolition of the Danish Atlantic Slave Trade', pp. 128–9; Gøbel, *Det danske slavehandelsforbud*, pp. 93, 246–7; Hopkins, *Peter Thonning and Denmark's Guinea Commission*, pp. 59–60.

95   Hopkins, *Peter Thonning and Denmark's Guinea Commission*, pp. 40, 42–3, 46–8, 57–8.

96   Wadström was presumably referring to Mrs Isaac Dubois (formerly Anna Maria Falconbridge), who published a *Narrative of Two Voyages to the River Sierra Leone during the Years 1791–2–3* in London in 1794.

Schimmelmann's attention that, in the course of her efforts to apply the tenets of Scandinavian agrarian home economics to African raw materials, his sister had succeeded in 'distilling spirits and brewing beer from the land's grain, called maize'. Spirits, of course, were a vital article in the African trade.[97]

On 16 March 1792, on the Slave-Trade Commission's recommendation, Prince Frederik banned his subjects' participation in the Atlantic slave trade. The law was to take effect ten years thereafter, to allow the West Indian planters time to build up healthy and demographically balanced stocks of slaves, in the stated expectation that the population would thereafter be able to sustain itself naturally and that the profitable production of sugar could thus be maintained. Taxation on holdings of female slaves was lowered, and the Danish government offered low-interest loans for the purchase of new slaves from Africa.[98] However, it is clear that Schimmelmann could foresee the abolition of slavery itself, in time,[99] and his investment in Isert's project suggests that he already understood that, without slave labour, the sugar industry of the West Indies might ultimately be doomed. The tropical soils and climate of Africa seemed to present a significant, if radically challenging, colonial alternative.[100] It was to explore this possibility once again, and now with more urgency than ever, that Schimmelmann turned to Julius von Rohr.

News of the epoch-making edict of 16 March arrived in the Danish West Indies late in May that year. It was not wholeheartedly welcomed there. It was reported that in July, the local administration provided the burgher council on St Croix with copies of the printed decree and assured its members that the royal decision:

> most exclusively aimed at the glory of humanity, the [island's] better culti-vation, and the residents' and especially the planters' welfare, [all of] which was, of course, recognised with the most grateful awe, although one and another difficulty in putting His Majesty's most gracious will into effect was feared. However, [the council] gave the assurance, on behalf of the planters, that these would seek out every possibility of furthering

the king's wishes. The edict's 'main contents' were not published in the *St. Croix Gazette* until August.[101]

Early in October, von Rohr left St Croix for West Africa. The prevailing winds were not favourable for passage directly east across the Atlantic from the West

---

97   Hopkins, *Peter Thonning and Denmark's Guinea Commission*, pp. 62, 75, 78, 121–3, 125, 246.
98   Gøbel, *Det danske slavehandelsforbud*, pp. 84–5; Hopkins, *Peter Thonning and Denmark's Guinea Commission*, p. 59; Pernille Røge, 'Why the Danes Got There First – A Trans-imperial Study of the Abolition of the Danish Slave Trade in 1792', *Slavery and Abolition* 35/4 (2014), 576–92.
99   Gøbel, *Det danske slavehandelsforbud*, pp. 55, 69.
100 Hopkins, *Peter Thonning and Denmark's Guinea Commission*, p. 34.
101 VJ 139/1793, the Danish West Indian administration, 31 December 1792.

Indies, and he travelled first to New England.[102] Besides the Flindts, von Rohr was accompanied by five West Indians, one an experienced planter, the others either slaves or freedmen. The party also included a number of Danish craftsmen Flindt had brought with him from Copenhagen, also at public expense.[103]

Von Rohr fell ill in the USA and sent most of the rest of his crew and a good deal of baggage ahead of him to Africa; his things included survey instruments, two microscopes, a set of paints, the seeds of thirty-one varieties of cotton, and several hundred books. An inventory of the books survives: the extraordinarily cosmopolitan little library this consummate natural historian of the Atlantic had carried with him from the West Indies reflected the broad intellectual spectrum of colonialism. Many of the books were by German writers, and many others had been issued in German translation.[104]

If von Rohr followed the debates on abolitionism, they left little distinct trace in the inventory of his books, but some of the titles reflected the Christianising mission often appealed to by abolitionist promoters of African colonies at this period. Besides four Danish Bibles, his library included – also in several copies – some of the theological writings of Emanuel Swedenborg, the visionary and influential Swedish polymath who advanced the idea that a vigorous new stage in the history of Christianity, the 'Church of the New Jerusalem', would soon emerge, most likely in Africa.[105]

Von Rohr's Intellectual Encounters in the USA

Early in 1793, in Philadelphia, von Rohr presented a letter of introduction from Governor Walterstorff of the Danish West Indies, to Thomas Jefferson, the Secretary of State of the USA.[106] Walterstorff wrote that von Rohr had:

---

102   VJ 8/1793, the West Indian administration, 18 October 1792; notice in the *Royal Danish American Gazette*, 13 October 1792.

103   GTK, Guinea correspondence journal 3/1794, Generaltoldkammeret, Lieutenant Hager, Fort Christiansborg on the Guinea Coast, 14 March 1793; GTK, Vestindiske og Guineiske Sager, Diverse Dokumenter, Guineiske Uafgjorte (Journal) Sager, 1775–1803, no. 42, Hans Christophersen, Giersløv Bye under Gissegaards Gods i Sjælland, 28 October 1795, to Schimmelmann.

104   GTK, Vestindiske og Guineiske Sager, Diverse Dokumenter, Schimmelmannske papirer vedk. Kommissionerne betræffende Guinea og Negerhandelen, Flindt, Collonien Friderichstæd, 22 July 1793, to Schimmelmann; same box, no. 2, Iserts Fredriksnopel, Aquapim, Flindt, Copenhagen, 19 March 1800, to the Finance Collegium; [Von] Rohr, *Observations sur la culture du coton*, p. 66; Daniel Hopkins, 'Books, Geography and Denmark's Colonial Undertaking in West Africa, 1790–1850', *Geographies of the Book*, ed. C. Withers and M. Ogborn (Farnham, 2010), pp. 221–46, here pp. 230–3.

105   Philip D. Curtin, *The Image of Africa, British Ideas and Action, 1780–1850* (Madison, 1964), pp. 26–7; Røge, 'L'expérimentation coloniale', p. 222.

106   Ernst Frederick Walterstorff, St. Croix, 9 October 1792, to Thomas Jefferson, Secretary of State for foreign affairs, Philadelphia, Missouri Historical Society, St. Louis, Jeffersoniana,

a claim to the attention of every person who wishes success to philan-thropic undertakings and the extension of human knowledge ... [H]is botanical Garden, laid out entirely at his own expense, is hardly inferior to Dr. Anderson's at St. Vincents or to any in the french Islands ... Your Excellency knows perhaps that, besides our having taken the lead in abolishing the Slave-trade, the King has also established a new Colony on the Coast of Guinea, near the Rio Volta, with a view of promoting civilisation amongst the Negroes, and the cultivation of westindia produce, particularly cotton ... The King has therefore thought, that no person would be more capable of laying a permanent foundation for the prosperity of [said] Colony than Colonel von Rohr, whose mild and benevolent dispo-sition will reconcile to him the confidence of the natives ... Should however the endeavour of Colonel von Rohr not be attended with that success which he so eagerly anticipates, I am sure that he will increase the treasures of natural history, and that within a few years we shall see many african plants flourish in our gardens.

Your Excellency has been too zealous a promoter of arts and Sciences in America, to be uninterested in any thing which relates to their success even in remote countries.

Certainly the secretary of state will have known by this time of the royal edict of 16 March 1792, and Walterstorff had no reason not to allude to this measure that reflected so well on his nation, but it may be that he overstepped the bounds of discretion in bringing to Jefferson's notice the Danish govern-ment's African colonial enterprises, considering Schimmelmann's own circumspection about it. It appears, in any case, that Jefferson arranged a meeting between von Rohr and President Washington, of which nothing further is known.[107]

Jefferson was active in the American Philosophical Society, and von Rohr found himself on friendly terms with another of the Society's members, Benjamin Smith Barton, the Philadelphia botanist and professor of medicine, whose herbarium is recorded to have included more than a hundred specimens von Rohr had collected in the Antilles and South America.[108] Von Rohr evidently made no effort to conceal the purpose of his expedition to Africa;

Bixby Collection; *The Papers of Thomas Jefferson*, vol. 24: *1 June to 31 December 1792*, ed. J. Catanzariti *et al.* (Princeton, 1990), p. 458.

107 Jefferson, Philadelphia, 5 March 1793, to George Washington, *The Papers of George Washington*, Presidential Series, vol. 12: *16 January 1793–31 May 1793*, ed. C. Sternberg Patrick and J. C. Pinheiro (Charlottesville, 2005), pp. 266–7.

108 Francis W. Pennell, 'Benjamin Smith Barton as Naturalist', *Proceedings of the American Philosophical Society* 86/1 (1942), 108–22, here p. 108, and Francis W. Pennell, 'Historic Botanical Collections of the American Philosophical Society and the Academy of Natural Sciences of Philadelphia', *Proceedings of the American Philosophical Society* 94/2 (1950), 137–51, here pp. 140–1.

in a letter to him written after von Rohr had travelled on to New York to take passage to West Africa, Barton rather neatly plucked out for praise a number of the main threads in the intellectual and moral backdrop to von Rohr's mission. It seems likely that Barton's highly charged phrases reflect ideas that von Rohr himself had expressed in their conversations, and not the younger American scientist's own moral and intellectual projections alone:[109]

> I foresee what new beauties, what new instances of immeasurable wisdom, in the works of nature, you will discover, in a land hitherto unexplored by science. I foresee, with still greater pleasure, the benefits and the blessings that will accrue to an injured race of mankind, from the wisdom of your scheme, guided and animated by the most dignified enthusiasm. The empire of reason is to be established. Your benevolence and labours are to contribute, not a little, to the glorious event ... Adieu. May the god of nature take you under his protection.

In a postscript, Barton wrote, 'Make my friendly compliments to Julius, and Marcus.' These may have been von Rohr's enslaved collectors.

In August 1793, from New York, von Rohr wrote to Banks that he had also had the pleasure of the company of Benjamin Rush, the renowned Philadelphia scientist and political figure, as well as of 'your correspondent', Dr Samuel Mitchill (the founder, in 1791, of New York's Society for the Promotion of Agriculture, Arts and Manufactures, and decades later, of the Literary and Philosophical Society of New York, and the New York Lyceum of Natural History).[110] Rush, in his autobiography, recalls a conversation with von Rohr in April 1793: 'The doctor was on his way by order of the King of Denmark to establish a free colony on the coast of Africa in the latitude of 5° in order to introduce civilisation among the Africans.'[111] Other evidence to support this characterisation of the projected colony as 'free' has not come forth, but perhaps it represents ideals the two scientists shared. Rush went on:

> He was a German by birth, very learned and sensible, aged 59. He spoke highly of the intellectual and moral faculties of the negroes. A black man travelled with him who was his intelligencer in every strange place that he visited. [This man] was, he said, a Botanist and a philosopher. He had been taught morality by his father by means of fables, many of which the Doctor

109 Benj. Smith Barton, 13 May 1793, to Julius von Rohr, 3rd Street #119, American Philosophical Society Library, Benjamin Smith Barton Papers, B D284.d, Series I.
110 British Library, Manuscripts Collection, Add. MS 8098.280–281, Julius von Rohr, New-York, 10 August 1793, to Joseph Banks; Courtney Robert Hall, *A Scientist in the Early Republic. Samuel Latham Mitchill 1764–1831* (New York, 1962), p. 146; Iannini, *Fatal Revolutions*, p. 186.
111 *The Autobiography of Benjamin Rush: His 'Travels through Life' Together with His Commonplace Book for 1789–1813*, ed. G. W. Corner (Philadelphia, 1948), pp. 92, 304–5.

said were original and truly sublime. He gave the Doctor such an account of plants in Africa as enabled him to class them by Linnaeus.[112]

Samuel Mitchill, for his part, saw fit to mention von Rohr's treatise on cotton in 'A concise and comprehensive account of the writings which illustrate the botanical history of North and South America', in which he also named John Ellis, who published *Directions for Bringing over Seeds and Plants from the East-Indies and other Distant Countries in a State of Vegetation* in 1770 and *An Historical Account of Coffee* in 1774, Edward Bancroft, author of a 1769 *Essay on the Natural History of Guiana, in South America*, and Peter Kalm, one of Linnaeus's apostles, who had travelled in North America in the late 1740s.[113] Mitchill related in this account:

> I knew this virtuous and intelligent gentleman, when he was in New York preparing for a voyage in the gulf of Guinea. His government had determined to make a settlement there, and with a view to gratify [von] Rohr's passion for botanical and entomological researches, had appointed him to superintend the colony. I expected much from his skill and ardour; but, alas! the vessel he chartered in this port was never heard of after departure; and was supposed to have foundered in the ocean.[114]

Subsequent Danish-African Colonial Developments

Several more years elapsed before another scientist, this time a young product of the Natural History Society, was sent to the Guinea Coast to investigate the natural history and economic potential of the territory around the Danish

---

112 Von Rohr's compatriot on St Croix, the Moravian missionary Christian Georg Andreas Oldendorp, in the ethnographic sections of the monumental manuscript published in shortened form in 1777 as *Geschichte der Mission der evangelischen Brüder auf den caraibischen Inseln S. Thomas, S. Croix und S. Jan*, ed. J. J. Bossart (Barby, 1777), had similarly depended on information provided by enslaved Africans in putting together an extraordinary contemporary record of the West African societies out of which these slaves had been brought to the West Indies: Gudrun Meier, 'Preliminary Remarks on the Oldendorp Manuscripts and their History', and Karen Fog Olwig, 'African Cultural Principles in Caribbean Slave Societies: A View from the Danish West Indies', both in *Slave Cultures and the Cultures of Slavery*, ed. S. Palmié (Knoxville, 1995), pp. 67–77, esp. on p. 70, and pp. 23–39, esp. on pp. 24, 29–33; C. G. A. *Oldendorp's history*, p. xxii.

113 See *The America of 1750: Peter Kalm's Travels in North America*, transl. Adolph B. Benson (1937; New York, 1966).

114 Samuel L. Mitchill, 'A Discourse Delivered before the New York Historical Society, at their Anniversary Meeting, 6th December, 1813, Embracing a Concise and Comprehensive Account of the Writings which Illustrate the Botanical History of North and South America', *Collections of the New-York Historical Society* 2 (1814), [149]–215, quotation on p. 212; VJ 442/1795, Lindemann, Danish West Indies, 7 May 1795.

forts.[115] This was Peter Thonning, who spent several years on the Coast, from 1799 to 1803. His orders, written by Niels Tønder Lund, of the Slave-Trade Commission, spoke of identifying African articles of trade to replace the slave trade, not of a colony, but Thonning's final report embodied a well-grounded argument for a Danish agricultural colony in West Africa. It was brought to the attention of the Slave-Trade Commission, and Ernst Schimmelmann asked Thonning to prepare a detailed colonial plan.[116]

In the meantime, however, Denmark's abolition of the Atlantic slave trade had come into effect on 1 January 1803. The planters of the West Indies agitated strenuously for its repeal or suspension and, early in 1804, the Slave-Trade Commission acknowledged that an economic crisis in the Danish West Indies might be expected to result from the ban. Count Schimmelmann drew up a plan for what he called a Colonial Institute of state-owned model plantations in the West Indies, predicated on the belief that easing the slaves' lives would in time lead to the augmentation of their numbers. The commission's recommendation to the Crown more than ten years earlier had based itself on this same faith in amelioration, but Schimmelmann now seems to have been prepared to abandon much of the ground won by the edict of 16 March 1792. To keep the slave-based economy of the Danish West Indies afloat, he wrote, it might be necessary to bring African 'settlers and workers', rescued from the slave trade, to the West Indies, 'without completely cutting them off from the possibility of returning emancipated to Africa'.

As the Chamber of Customs rather reluctantly put it in the formal legislative proposal based on Schimmelmann's plan that was laid before the Crown Prince:

> when the proposed plantations on the Coast of Guinea have got a start, the population in the West Indies, if it were necessary, could be supplemented with workers from [these Africa plantations], who had there become accustomed to work, to domesticity and order. On the other hand, negroes from the plantations in the West Indies, who were practised in various branches of cultivation suitable for Guinea, could be furnished to Guinea.[117]

The pressure from the West Indies was apparently considerable, but Prince Frederik would have none of this contorted colonial policy. His administrative tack was to ask for detailed and recent demographic information from the West Indies, and by the time this had been gathered, Great Britain had itself

---

115   Hopkins, *Peter Thonning and Denmark's Guinea Commission*, pp. 95, 97–8.
116   Hopkins, 'The Danish Ban on the Atlantic Slave Trade', pp. 171–2.
117   Hopkins, *Peter Thonning and Denmark's Guinea Commission*, pp. 222–3.

abolished the Atlantic slave trade. The Danish ban was of course allowed to stand, and the nation escaped with its moral laurels unruffled.[118]

A Danish presence in Africa now seemed the most promising element in the Danish colonial office's thinking for the future, but the Napoleonic Wars and the ensuing economic ruin precluded any further measures for the time being. When an administrative position opened up, Peter Thonning was brought into the colonial office of the Chamber of Customs, from which position he advanced, with exquisite sophistication, what amounted to Schimmelmann's old African colonial policies for almost four decades. His colonial plan would have required an alarmingly large state commitment, however, and, in the mood of retrenchment that had gripped Denmark since the war and the loss of Norway at the Congress of Vienna, he was never able to force his scheme through the Danish bureaucracy.[119]

Instead, in 1850, Denmark sold its African forts for a trifling sum to Great Britain, which within a generation or two was able to turn its Gold Coast Colony to good economic account. It was not sugar cane and cotton, the dominant West Indian agricultural products in Schimmelmann's and von Rohr's time, that became the great export crops of this eastern portion of the Gold Coast, but cocoa, a Central American forest crop introduced in the 1880s in the hills of Akuapem. The plants were initially acclimatised in an agricultural community generally acknowledged to have been influenced by a small colony founded in the early 1840s, during the Danish period, by a Danish-Norwegian missionary, Andreas Riis, who brought six families of Christian former slaves from Jamaica to settle in these hills. That enterprise was supported by an English organisation, the Society for the Suppression of the Slave Trade and the Civilisation of Africa, whose president, Thomas Fowell Buxton, in 1840 published an angry denunciation of the failure of the European governments to suppress the Atlantic trade for decades after it was formally banned. The central thesis of his book, *The African Slave Trade and its Remedy*, was that the illegal trade in slaves across the Atlantic could only be ended by European agricultural colonisation in West Africa.[120]

---

118   Hopkins, 'The Danish Ban on the Atlantic Slave Trade', pp. 174–5.

119   Hopkins, *Peter Thonning and Denmark's Guinea Commission*, p. 273.

120   Thomas Fowell Buxton, *The African Slave Trade and its Remedy* (London, 1840); Edward Reynolds, *Trade and Economic Change on the Gold Coast, 1807–1874* (Harlow, 1974), pp. 177–8; M. A. Kwamena-Poh, *Government and Politics in the Akuapem State 1730–1850* (Evanston, 1973), pp. 114–15, 117–19; Polly Hill, *The Migrant Cocoa-Farmers of Southern Ghana* (Cambridge, 1963), pp. 17, 168–9, 171–3; Hopkins, 'Peter Thonning, the Guinea Commission, and Denmark's postabolition African colonial policy', p. 806; Hopkins, *Peter Thonning and Denmark's Guinea Commission*, pp. 615, 620–1, 688; Robin Law, Suzanne Schwarz and Silke Strickrodt, 'Introduction', and Robin Law, '"There's nothing grows in the West Indies but will grow here": Dutch and English projects of plantation agriculture on the Gold Coast, 1650s–1780s', both in *Commercial Agriculture: The Slave Trade and Slavery in*

The historical thread of this thinking, back through the moral, intellectual, economic and political environments in which, in the Danish case, Thonning, von Rohr, Isert, and Schimmelmann had operated, is unbroken. Although the standard periodisation holds that African colonial history commenced with the establishment of European territorial regimes towards the end of the nineteenth century, decisive impetus towards the colonisation of Africa in fact developed much earlier, in the context of late-eighteenth-century colonial projects undertaken in the era of abolitionism.

Atlantic Africa, ed. R. Law, S. Schwarz and S. Strickrodt (Woodbridge, 2013), pp. 1–27, here pp. 19–20, and pp. 116–37.

7

A Hinterland to the Slave Trade?
Atlantic Connections of the Wupper Valley
in the Early Nineteenth Century

ANNE SOPHIE OVERKAMP

'You read hideous accounts of the transport of African slaves. Ours was very much like it,' stated the German merchant Johann Wilhelm Fischer after he had experienced a most unpleasant sea voyage due to a military intervention during the Napoleonic Wars in 1813.[1] After their ship had been captured by the British, he and his fellow travellers were held in a cramped, dark room where they could neither stand up nor lie down; they were hungry and thirsty, seasickness and diarrhoea adding to their severe discomfort. In short, the journey was so terrible that according to Fischer everyone felt like dying. By highlighting lack of food and water, scarcity of space and disease, Fischer did indeed evoke features common to the excruciating experience of the Middle Passage, although he had to endure these only for one night instead of several months. Fischer and his family lived in the Duchy of Berg, one of the smaller German principalities and an area remote from the Atlantic coast, seemingly unconnected to the world of the slave trade. Nevertheless, Fischer could be sure that readers of his memoirs – friends and relatives – would be familiar with the terrors of the Atlantic slave trade and would thus sympathise with his plight on the British ship. This raises the question of how people in continental Germany knew about the slave trade and how far they were concerned by it, materially and morally.

German states had been involved in the slave trade only briefly at the end of the seventeenth century when Brandenburg-Prussia tried to become a player in the triangular trade between Europe, Africa and the Caribbean. The effort was orchestrated by the *Brandenburgisch-Afrikanische Handelscompagnie*

---

1 Johann Wilhelm Fischer, 'Nachrichten aus meinem Leben, hg. von Walther von Eynern', *Zeitschrift des Bergischen Geschichtsvereins* 58 (1929), 33–182, here p. 139.

(Brandenburg African Trade Company) which organised the shipment of 18,000 Africans to the 'New World' between 1682 and 1711.[2] German seamen participated in slaving voyages for much longer than that, with men from the Frisian Isles serving on both Dutch and Danish slavers throughout the eighteenth century.[3] Probably because of this relatively marginal involvement in the slave trade, the issue did not become a heated object of public debate as it did in Britain, but it did receive scholarly attention. In particular, professors at the two leading universities in Germany, Göttingen and Halle, devoted a series of publications to the question of slavery and the slave trade, generally dealing with it in the emerging field of anthropology and paying particular attention to the question of human race(s). Putting stress on slavery's perceived importance for the economies of both the Americas as well as Europe, these writers pleaded for the most part in favour of the maintenance of slavery, although they voiced their concern for a better treatment of slaves. Material interests therefore far outweighed moral considerations, even in the academic sphere.[4]

Merchants like Johann Wilhelm Fischer may not have followed academic debates but were ardent readers of political journals such as the *Politisches Journal* (Political Journal) or *Minerva*. Those two gave comprehensive coverage to the Haitian Revolution, one of the 'hot topics' of the time.[5] Books concerned with European colonies overseas such as the Abbé Raynal's *Histoire des deux Indes* were also received by elite society even in German backwaters. Access to newspapers, journals and books was often facilitated by membership of one of the many reading societies that sprang up all across Germany in the last third of the eighteenth century; the first one known in the Wupper Valley was founded in Elberfeld in 1775.[6]

2   Nils Brübach, '"Seefahrt und Handel sind die fürnembsten Säulen eines Etats". Brandenburg-Preussen und der transatlantische Sklavenhandel im 17. und 18. Jahrhundert', *Amerikaner wider Willen. Beiträge zur Sklaverei in Lateinamerika*, ed. R. Zoller (Frankfurt a.M., 1994), pp. 11–42. See also chapter 1 in this volume.

3   For one of the few investigations of this topic see Catharina Lüden, *Sklavenfahrt mit Seeleuten aus Schleswig-Holstein, Hamburg und Lübeck im 18. Jahrhundert* (Heide, 1983).

4   Karin Schüller, *Die deutsche Rezeption haitianischer Geschichte in der ersten Hälfte des 19. Jahrhunderts: Ein Beitrag zum deutschen Bild vom Schwarzen* (Cologne, 1992), pp. 56–73.

5   For an overview of the coverage by German journals, ibid., pp. 167–95.

6   On Germans interested in Caribbean affairs and means of information see Susan Buck-Morss, *Hegel, Haiti and Universal History* (Pittsburgh, 2009), and Florian Kappeler, 'Die globale Revolution. Forster und Haiti', *Georg-Forster-Studien* 19 (2014), 17–43. On reading societies in general Uwe Puschner, 'Lesegesellschaften', *Kommunikation und Medien in Preußen vom 16. bis zum 19. Jahrhundert*, ed. B. Sösemann (Stuttgart, 2002), pp. 193–206; on Elberfeld Eberhard Illner, *Bürgerliche Organisierung in Elberfeld, 1775–1850* (Neustadt a.d. Aisch, 1982). On the circulation of books see the advertisement in the Elberfeld journal *Bergisches Magazin* in which the solicitor Karl Wülfing asked for his copy of Abbé Raynal's work to be returned, having forgotten to whom he had lent it: *Bergisches Magazin* 40 (1789), p. 322.

But the slave trade would have been of more than academic interest to a man like Fischer, as it would to other merchants not only in port cities but also in continental Germany. As scholars like Klaus Weber and Margrit Schulte Beerbühl have demonstrated, from the seventeenth century onward merchants from inland regions such as the Rhineland or Silesia were deeply involved in (trans-)Atlantic endeavours, organising the export of goods produced in the hinterland, usually by sending members of their families to important port cities such as Bordeaux, Cadiz or London.[7] With regard to the slave trade, Klaus Weber has argued that even though German merchants invested relatively little capital into the actual trade when compared with investments made by merchants of other nations, they nevertheless profited substantially. The business of supplying low-priced textiles for barter on the African coast as well as for clothing slaves in the Caribbean generated large profits and promoted the process of proto-industrialisation in the German hinterland.[8] The resulting economic growth stimulated demand for colonial products such as sugar and coffee, even among the rural population, which again fuelled the slave trade.[9]

One of the German regions involved in this way happened to be Fischer's homeland, the Duchy of Berg.[10] In this principality, the neighbouring towns Elberfeld and Barmen in the valley of the river Wupper, a tributary of the Rhine, had specialised from very early on in the production of textile goods. Since 1527, merchants from Elberfeld and Barmen had enjoyed the so-called *Garnnahrungsprivileg* (yarn privilege) which granted them a monopoly for the bleaching of linen in the territory. Over time, merchant-manufacturers in the two towns added more and more products to their range and, by the end of the eighteenth century, they not only held almost a monopoly in Germany on the production of inexpensive tape, ribbons, braids and trimmings made from linen and cotton but also produced substantial quantities of inexpensive fabrics from a cotton-linen mix called *Siamosen*. By the end of the century,

---

7   Klaus Weber, *Deutsche Kaufleute im Atlantikhandel 1680–1830: Unternehmen und Familien in Hamburg, Cádiz und Bordeaux* (Munich, 2004); Margrit Schulte Beerbühl, *Deutsche Kaufleute in London: Welthandel und Einbürgerung (1600–1818)* (Munich, 2007). For a joint summary of their findings in English see Margrit Schulte Beerbühl and Klaus Weber, 'From Westphalia to the Caribbean: Networks of German Textile Merchants in the Eighteenth Century', *Cosmopolitan Networks in Commerce and Society 1660–1914*, ed. A. Gestrich and M. Schulte Beerbühl (London, 2011), pp. 53–98.

8   Klaus Weber, 'Deutschland, der atlantische Sklavenhandel und die Plantagenwirtschaft der Neuen Welt (15. bis 19. Jahrhundert)', *Journal of Modern European History* 7/1 (2009), 37–67. See also chapter 4 in this volume.

9   Jörg Ludwig, 'Amerikanische Kolonialwaren in Sachsen im 18. und frühen 19. Jahrhundert', *Sachsen und Lateinamerika*, ed. J. Ludwig, B. Schröter and M. Zeuske (Frankfurt a.M., 1995), pp. 51–79.

10   Jörg Engelbrecht, *Das Herzogtum Berg im Zeitalter der Französischen Revolution. Modernisierungsprozesse zwischen bayerischem und französischem Modell* (Paderborn, 1996).

Wupper Valley merchants supervised close to eight thousand looms producing linen and cotton-linen fabrics.[11] The latter were to a large degree destined to become clothing for sailors as well as for slaves on plantations in the West Indies – a fact that was common knowledge not only among local merchants, but also among regional government officials and observant travellers, who marvelled at the rates of production achieved in the Wupper Valley.[12] The export rates of these fabrics were so important that fluctuations in demand and changing prices heavily affected the local economy, most notably the relations between merchant-manufacturers and the weavers they employed. In fact, the abolition of the local weavers' guild, numbering almost a thousand members in 1783, can also be attributed to a lack of wage elasticity in face of a highly volatile global market.[13]

This integrated system of Atlantic plantation economy, slave trade and continental manufacturing centres came to an end during the turbulent decades after 1789. The French and Haitian Revolutions, the disintegration of the Iberian empires and consequently the emergence of a whole plethora of new states with their own political economies as well as decades of warfare across the globe, resulted in a reordering of the political and mercantile landscape. The British volte-face in turning from the largest slave-trader into the champion of abolition just added another facet to this turbulent time.[14]

Despite all the changes that took place in this Age of Revolutions, it is clear that important lines of continuity lasting from the late eighteenth well into the nineteenth century can be made out, notably in developments in the integrated system of the early modern Atlantic (plantation) economy as it was manifested in the material relations between continental Germany and Latin America. As noted above, the slave trade played an important role in these relations during the early modern period. Accordingly, this chapter considers the role it played during the nineteenth century, exploring the question of whether the Wupper Valley played a similar role as hinterland to the slave trade or slave economies in the early nineteenth century as it did

11   Walter Dietz, *Die Wuppertaler Garnnahrung* (Neustadt a.d. Aisch, 1957); Herbert Kisch, 'From Monopoly to Laissez-faire: The Early Growth of the Wupper Valley Textile Trades', *Journal of European Economic History* 1 (1972), 298–407. See the image on the front cover of this volume for a visual impression of linen bleaching in the Wupper Valley landscape.
12   This observation was made among others by Philip Andreas Nemnich, 'Tagebuch einer der Kultur und Industrie gewidmeten Reise (1809)', … *und reges Leben ist überall sichtbar! Reisen im Bergischen Land um 1800*, ed. G. Huck and J. Reulecke (Neustadt a.d. Aisch, 1978), pp. 147–64, here p. 150.
13   Martin Henkel, *Zunftmissbräuche. 'Arbeiterbewegung' im Merkantilismus* (Frankfurt a.M., 1989).
14   David Armitage and Sanjay Subrahmanyam, eds, *The Age of Revolutions in Global Context, c.1760–1840* (Basingstoke, 2010).

in the eighteenth.[15] This involves considering where slavery features in the sources, and asking whether it features solely as a matter of material relations or whether it was also an issue of moral concern to the actors involved. The complex entanglements of geographically distant regions call for exploration of three planes of observation: on the level of individual actors, the impressive network of trade relations all around the American coastline built up by the Wupper Valley firm Abraham & Brothers Frowein is scrutinised. On the level of semi-public institutions, the importance is considered of the *Rheinisch-Westindische Compagnie* (Rhenish-West Indian Company), an inland-based export company established in 1821. Finally, on the political level, the contribution of the Prussian government (following the Duchy of Berg becoming part of Prussia in 1815) to Atlantic trade relations in the form of treaties, establishment of consuls and trade representatives is surveyed. While it might be going too far to call the Wupper Valley a hinterland to the slave trade, it certainly was a beneficiary of the continued trafficking of hundreds of thousands of Africans. In detail, though, the picture that emerges is one in which epochal moments like the Haitian Revolution and legislative abolition feature, if at all, as an unavoidable stimulus for a change in business practice or even as a business opportunity, against a remarkable continuity of institutional structures and globalised business horizons, without themselves provoking explicit reflection on the ethics of trading in, on or with slave economies.

Taping the World Together: The Transatlantic Network of Abraham & Brothers Frowein

The company Abraham & Brothers Frowein (A&BF) was founded in Elberfeld in 1763 by Abraham Frowein (1734–1813).[16] He came from a family of lesser means but thanks to the supportive trading network among Wupper Valley merchants, and his own business acumen and persistence, he managed to build a sizeable business over time. In 1787, he made two of his nephews, Abraham (1766–1829) and Caspar (1759–1823), partners of the company. By that year, the company was worth about 70,000 Reichsthaler. They specialised in all sorts of linen passementerie, including tape, garters and figured ribbons, as well as woollen ribbon. Most of the goods were mundane, everyday items

---

15 For a concise discussion of the term 'hinterland' and the relevant literature see the Introduction to this volume.
16 Edmund Strutz, *175 Jahre Abr. Frowein jun., Abr. [und] Gebr. Frowein, Frowein [und] Co. A.-G.* (Düsseldorf, 1938); Anne Sophie Overkamp, 'Of Tape and Ties: Abraham Frowein from Elberfeld and Atlantic Trade', *Europeans Engaging the Atlantic: Knowledge and Trade, 1500–1800*, ed. S. Lachenicht (Frankfurt a.M., 2014), pp. 127–50.

sold in large units to customers in Germany, the Netherlands, France, Spain and Portugal. The goods bought by wholesale customers on the Iberian Peninsula were mostly destined for the American colonies. This share of A&BF's trade was so important that when the Spanish government prohibited the import of textile products after committing itself to the colonists' cause in the American war of independence in 1779, the firm ventured to send its goods directly across the Atlantic. Destinations chosen were the Dutch colony Curaçao, the Danish possession St Thomas and the French colony Saint-Domingue as well as Charleston on the American mainland. Despite these varying locations, the ultimate destination for AB&F goods was continental South America. These early endeavours met with little success but since the 1780s, at the latest, knowledge about transatlantic trade as well as trading relations had been firmly established in the company.

Thanks to an advantageous marriage by the nephew Abraham as well as a prudent spread of investments and the deliberate servicing of a variety of markets, the company not only weathered well the storms of the Napoleonic period, but also increased its value significantly. When Caspar Frowein retired from the company due to ill health in 1813, the company's assets amounted to almost 430,000 Reichsthaler. More than half of these assets, however, consisted of goods in stock.[17] It comes as no surprise that as soon as relations in Europe returned to a more stable footing, A&BF sought to place these goods widely on the market. Consistent with the earlier importance of South America as an outlet for their goods, they saw this part of the world as an attractive alternative to the European markets blocked off by a system of protective tariffs. The changing political landscape, namely the spread of rebellion in the Spanish colonies as well as the recently achieved independence of the Pearl of the Antilles, Haiti, provided a number of interesting opportunities but also challenges, as A&BF were soon to learn.

Haiti became their gateway into the South American and Caribbean market. This was all the more logical as Abraham Frowein's nephew Eduard Weber had set up a business in Port-au-Prince, in which he was later joined by his brother Albert.[18] From at least 1816 onward, A&BF regularly sent barrels and chests filled with their products to their nephews overseas. Albert and Eduard proved to be good commission agents, maintaining prices at a profitable level and furnishing their relatives back home with information on both the state of the market and the political situation. Much space was also devoted to economic matters such as the debasement of the currency and its effects on the economy. However, in their letters they did not reflect on

---

17   Frowein Company Archive (FCA), No. 1342.
18   The first letter by Eduard to his uncle recorded in the Frowein Company Archive is dated 10 January 1817 but refers to earlier shipments. Eduard probably had set up business on the island by 1815 at the latest.

Haiti's particular history of a slave-led revolution nor did they remark on the fact that they were living in a predominantly black society. Rather, they kept such observations for oral communication. Considering the fact that the two brothers did not hesitate to send lengthy accounts overseas and wrote both personal as well as business letters to their uncle, all of which are recorded in the archive, this preference for personal communication is striking and invites interpretation. Both Weber brothers seem to have felt fairly at home on Haiti, both of them serving as consuls and enjoying good relations with the Haitian elite. By reserving further mention – and judgement – in their letters, they avoided committing their private opinion about Haiti and its society to the semi-public form of a letter. This omission might be interpreted as an expression of respect for this host country or simply as diplomatic tactfulness.

Similarly, slavery and the slave trade are rarely mentioned in their letters. When reporting on the differences between the kingdom in the north and the Republic in the south during the years until 1818, Eduard did comment that tyranny held sway under Christophe (King Henry), and that the 'the negro lives under the same pressure as during the time of the French', an assumption that was generally acknowledged.[19] Eduard did not qualify this impression morally in either way, maintaining his stance of impartial observer, at least when writing. Albert got directly involved with the slave trade while still employed in Havana as his principal's firm was engaged in outfitting ships that were part of the trade. His move to Haiti was prompted by a desire to work less and on his own account as the climate proved too strenuous for the long hours expected from a clerk. He voiced neither any moral concerns about being engaged in the slave trade nor any desire to live in a place where slavery was at least nominally abolished. But this omission of slavery and the slave trade as topics of discussion on both their parts was rather the rule than the exception among German overseas merchants. As Lars Maischak has shown, German merchants in the earlier nineteenth century were generally colour-blind in their condescension and paternalism towards the 'lower sorts'; the silence maintained by the Webers was more likely to have been motivated by pragmatism than by racism. Cosmopolitan German merchants were usually ready to accept non-Europeans as peers if they passed the test of refinement and character, as is shown not least by the Weber brothers' acceptance of the Haitian elite.[20]

---

19   'Dagegen herrscht die größte Tyrannei auf Christophs Seite, und der Neger lebt unter denselben Druck wie zur Zeit der Franzosen.' FCA, No. 268, Eduard Weber to Abraham Frowein, Bremen, 26 December 1818. Eduard was about to embark on a visit to Elberfeld and wrote that he would rather make any further observations in person.

20   Lars Maischak, *German Merchants in the Nineteenth-Century Atlantic* (Cambridge, 2013), p. 172. Taking Maischak's study of Bremen merchants as a point of reference here seems the more fitting as Eduard Weber served on Haiti as consul general for the Hanseatic cities.

Other marketplaces sought out by A&BF in the beginning were St Thomas, which was still a Danish possession and important harbour for intermediate trade with Spanish America, Cuba which had only recently been opened to direct trade, and Brazil. In all of these places slavery still persisted but its existence emerges only in fleeting glimpses in the records. Not mentioned, even in passing, is the fact that the return goods received by A&BF – coffee, cotton, sugar and tobacco (in that order) – were for the most part produced using slave labour. Harvest prospects played a large role in the correspondence along with price developments; production conditions did not. Nevertheless, A&BF could not help but know about the continued use of forced labour.

Some of the invoices received from A&BF's commission agents overseas included items that spoke directly of the practice of slavery, even in places where the slave trade had been banned. Invoices received from the Danish possession St Thomas always included the item 'Negermiethe' (negro rent) as part of the expenses (Fig. 7.1) – most probably for transporting the goods from and to the ships, and for other services.[21] Although some of the 'negroes' mentioned in the invoice might have been nominally free workers, the listing in the invoice served as an undeniable reminder of the forced migration of millions of Africans. The agent in Rio de Janeiro also listed the cost of a number of 'negroes' who worked for several days to put lead seals on the ribbons sent by A&BF – most likely probably as part of the customs clearance process.[22] These passing references in the invoices bear evidence to a practice common across slave-holding America, namely the renting out of slaves which at times gave them a surprising amount of autonomy and agency. Some owners profited from their slaves by earning money through their rental; in other cases slaves rented themselves out in their spare time to earn money to keep, sometimes even earning sufficient funds to purchase their freedom. The slaves engaged by A&BF's agent in Rio de Janeiro might have belonged to a rather unique group of slaves for hire, the so-called *escravos de ganho* who hired themselves out and paid their master a fixed fee. They were given complete autonomy to carry out the business arrangements and many of them were licensed by the city council to carry out their work. Some of these *escravos de ganho* specialised in harbour work and were formally registered with the Customs authority.[23]

As has been observed by contemporaries and historians alike, market conditions in the Caribbean and in the South America changed constantly

---

21   FCA, No. 263, letters from Gruner & Doenck, 1817–1818 and No. 515, letters from Gruner & Doenck, 1819.

22   FCA, No. 500, invoice, 20 November 1819, and invoice, 27 July 1819.

23   Nigel O. Bolland, 'Proto-Proletarians? Slave Wages in the Americas: Between Slave Labour & Free Labour', *From Chattel Slaves to Wage Slaves: The Dynamics of Labour Bargaining in the Americas*, ed. M. Turner (Kingston, Jamaica, 1995), pp. 123–47; Herbert S. Klein and Francisco Vidal Luna, *Slavery in Brazil* (Cambridge, 2010), pp. 136–40.

Figure 7.1. Invoice received by Abraham & Brothers Frowein from their agent on St Thomas. 'Negermiethe' (negro rent) appears as the third item from the top. At $4.73 it was the smallest of the costs.

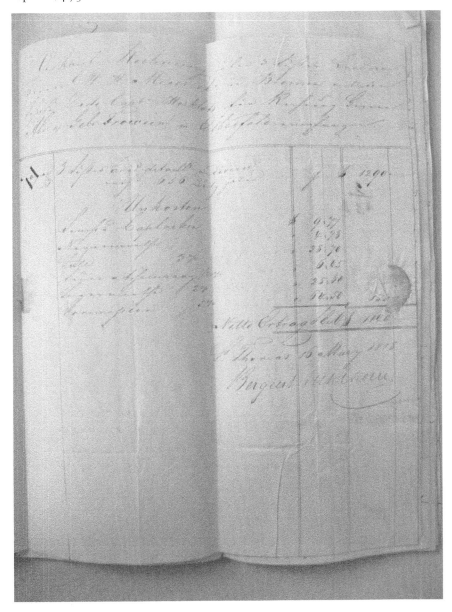

Figure 7.2. Abraham Engelbert Kretzmann (1765–1848), a long-standing employee of Abraham & Brothers Frowein. Beside his right arm can be seen packs of tape of the kind sent overseas. Oil, Johann Jakob Verreyt, 1846

and there was always the risk of glutted markets. This was particular true for A&BF goods as linen tape was considered a staple. All of their commission agents in the West Indies repeatedly emphasised that tape was a commodity whose sale could not be forced, that reducing prices would be counter-productive and that it was absolutely essential only to send out goods as directed. Their commission agent in Rio de Janeiro on the other hand was more relaxed about the selection of goods and trusted A&BF's long-standing experience with the Iberian market, pointing to a continuity of material relations even in case of political rupture: 'As you have done such important business with Portugal earlier and thereby know the most current sorts of tape and ribbon, we do not doubt that you have sent us a selection that will be popular.'[24] Over the years, A&BF tried their luck with garters, semi-woollen ribbon, webbing and boot tape though with varying success. The principal item remained linen tape (called *harlem uni*) which was sold in enormous quantities at all places (see Fig. 7.2).

As for the consumption of A&BF's goods, most of the plain linen tape much in demand seems to have been used for the making of clothing. This is indicated both by the fact that on Haiti their tapes were usually bought in smaller quantities (usually one chest containing 220 dozens) by predominantly female customers and by the advice from A&BF's agent Dufrayer in Rio de Janeiro to send narrow ribbon such as was used by seamstresses.[25] Pedro Peycke in Bahia, yet another commission agent, even hoped to become the sole supplier to boutiques in Bahia and smaller towns in the vicinity for simple tape as well as coloured ribbons (called *bigarré*).[26] Some of the tape might have been used to make clothing for slaves, particularly as agents repeatedly stressed the fact that buyers preferred simple (cotton) goods at a cheaper price to quality (linen) goods at a higher price. Slave owners were seldom concerned with material fatigue but certainly wanted to keep costs low.

The linen tape and ribbons do not seem to have become a commodity in the slave trade, however. Rather the contrary, as Albert Weber informed his uncle when still working as an employee for a British firm in Havana: 'We do not get into the position of buying manufactured goods, at the most for those vessels which we fit out for the African coast for the negro trade. Tapes, however, are not being sent there.'[27] A&BF's tapes thus do not seem to have found favour with buyers on the African coast, unlike the European cotton and linen fabrics which were a staple in the slave trade.

24 FCA, No. 500, Carlos Joest to A&BF, Rio de Janeiro, 10 February 1819.
25 The information on Haitian customers is contained *passim* in the Weber letters, FCA, Nos 267, 268, 310, 410, 584. For the advice given by the agent in Rio de Janeiro see FCA, No. 599, L. N. Dufrayer to A&BF, Rio de Janeiro, 29 July 1818.
26 FCA, No. 501, Pedro Peycke to A&BF, Bahia, 13 February 1819.
27 FCA, No. 267, letter from Albert Weber to A&BF, Havana, 20 December 1817.

The sustained trafficking in Africans and the plantation economy served by it nevertheless fostered A&BF's trade with Latin America as it expanded over the years. By 1832, they had commission goods in stock with agents in Havana, Tampico, Mexico (City), Port-au-Prince, St Thomas, Point-à-Pitre, La Guaira, Pernambuco, Bahia, Rio de Janeiro, Buenos Aires and Lima. From all of these places, A&BF received as return goods in most instances commodities produced by slave labour such as coffee, cotton, sugar and tobacco. In spite of the high volatility of prices for colonial commodities as well as the fluctuating demand overseas, the trade seems to have remained profitable enough for A&BF, even though the value of the company decreased from almost 410,000 Prussian Taler in 1826 to 360,000 Prussian Taler in 1832.[28] Considering the fact that during the 1820s, A&BF habitually wrote off 30–45 per cent, sometimes even 68 per cent, on goods stored overseas when raising an inventory, it can only be assumed that potential profits both for outgoing and incoming goods must have been extraordinarily high. The maintenance of the slave economy in the Americas therefore certainly benefited this company, remote though it was from the Atlantic rim.

The Rise and Fall of the Rheinisch-Westindische Compagnie

The company of A&BF were not the only ones in the Wupper Valley interested in Latin American markets. As early as 1814, their associate, the prominent Elberfeld merchant Jakob Aders, voiced his concern about the Wupper Valley's economic situation in face of the system of protective tariffs springing up across Europe. He envisaged overseas markets as the most promising outlet to benefit small and large merchant-manufacturers alike, as well as to promote the 'national interest' in general. To realise his vision of German participation in global trade, Aders tried at first to win Hamburg merchants for his idea to link inland production centres directly with overseas markets. These specialists in long-distance trade showed little interest in an initiative from the interior. Two less substantial Hamburg merchants, however, contributed with their idea of a Hamburg-based company dedicated to exporting German-produced goods. Putting their ideas together, Aders and his associates formed the plan of an inland-based export company – the Rheinisch-Westindische Compagnie (RWC) was born.[29]

---

28   Many of the company's assets in 1826 were outstanding monies which were subsequently lost. Considering the heavy losses sustained all over Europe during the recession in 1825/6, they seem to have fared rather well.
29   On the history of the RWC, see *Rheinisch-Westindische Kompagnie, gestiftet zu Elberfeld 1821; ihre Entstehung, Form, Zweck, Folgen; von einem Aktionair* (Elberfeld, 1821); August Beckmann, *Die Rheinisch-Westindische Kompagnie, ihr Wirken und ihre Bedeutung* (Münster,

The aim of the proposed company was to eschew intermediate traders in Flanders, the Hanseatic cities or the Netherlands which had organised the export of inland-produced goods prior to the continental blockade. In Aders' project, the intermediate trade would be organised in the neighbourhood of exporting merchants themselves by the new company. Aders expected cost benefits in the order of 20 per cent, thanks to cutting down commission fees for buying and selling, improving market knowledge by establishing agencies overseas and organising a faster return on investment by reducing loading times. The export company was to have the form of a stock company so as to provide the added advantage of a lucrative outlet for the accumulated capital of investors in the Rhineland.[30] As the RWC would be only the third joint-stock company in Prussia and the first to issue bearer bonds, it shows that Aders' vision was in some respects at the cutting edge of business practice.

Aders's proposal found a positive echo and within several weeks more than 150 shares had been bought by subscription by merchants in the Rhineland and Westphalia as well as government officials who had accorded Aders' ideas not only their private approval but also their official blessing. The constitutive general assembly of the RWC was held on 8 March 1821 and the general mood was so positive that the convenors dismissed Aders' original idea of a trial cargo and voted for a fully established company instead, mirroring the high hopes attached to the venture as well as a general spirit of enterprise among Rhenish and Westphalian merchants.

The first cargo sent overseas by the RWC was destined for Haiti, which had been favoured as a destination by Aders from the very beginning. Haiti's status was at that point quite vague as no European state had recognised Haiti's independence following the slave-led revolution which had culminated in the declaration of Haitian independence in 1804. This ambivalence of status also meant that Prussian officials felt able to lend their support to the undertakings of the RWC without violating the principles of the Holy Alliance.[31] Consequently, the RWC's agent Peter Christoph Holzschue, who accompanied the first cargo, was furnished with a certificate of legitimation

---

1915); Adolf Hasenclever, 'Neue Mitteilungen zur Geschichte der Rheinisch-Westindischen Kompagnie', *Zeitschrift des Bergischen Geschichtsvereins* 49 (1916), 108–42; Hans-Joachim Oehm, *Die Rheinisch-Westindische Kompagnie* (Neustadt a.d. Aisch, 1968). On Jakob Aders see Gustav Grote, 'Jacob Aders', *Wuppertaler Biographien* 5 (1965), 19–31; on his economic ideas Rudolf Boch, *Grenzenloses Wachstum? Das rheinische Wirtschaftsbürgertum und seine Industrialisierungsdebatte 1814–1857* (Göttingen, 1991), *passim*.

30   An essay by Aders detailing his ideas is reprinted as an appendix in *Rheinisch-Westindische Kompagnie, gestiftet zu Elberfeld.*

31   Michael Zeuske, 'Die vergessene Revolution: Haiti und Deutschland in der ersten Hälfte des 19. Jahrhunderts. Aspekte deutscher Politik und Ökonomie in Westindien', *Jahrbuch für Geschichte von Staat, Wirtschaft und Gesellschaft Lateinamerikas* 28 (1991), 285–325.

(*Legitimationspatent*) issued by the Prussian ministry of trade which allowed at least for some show of official support.[32]

The first cargo amounted to 124,200 Prussian Taler and consisted mainly of textiles (cotton, linen, and some woollen and silken fabrics), but also included metal goods and glass-ware as well as some foodstuffs.[33] The first reports from Haiti proved Aders' assumptions right as the textiles in particular sold well. It took longer than expected to cash in on the returning goods – exclusively coffee as requested – so profits were lower than anticipated but still promising enough.[34] Until 1825, when the RWC ceased trading with Haiti, goods to the value of 830,887 Prussian Taler were sent to the island.[35] Half of that was linen textiles (444,403 Prussian Taler) while cotton textiles (200,932 Prussian Taler) amounted to a quarter of the total.

The next trading destination favoured by the company's directors was Mexico. After a decade of bloody civil warfare, Augustín de Iturbide, backed by elite creoles, had declared Mexican independence in 1821. By 1822, political affairs seemed to have reached some level of stability. Mexico being an attractive market by virtue of its sheer size, the RWC moved quickly and established an agency in Vera Cruz by May 1822. The company's agents could again claim the support of a certificate of legitimation issued by the Prussian ministry of trade as well as some letters of recommendation by Alexander von Humboldt, the great traveller and aficionado of Latin America.[36] The first shipment was valued at 350,000 Prussian Taler and consisted again mostly of textiles.[37] Despite political upheavals in the following years, the RWC continued to send shipments to its agents in Mexico and received mostly specie in return – a less volatile return good than the Haitian coffee. Generally, Mexico became very quickly the main destination for shipments organised by the RWC, not least because resumption of mining work in the Mexican provinces led to increased demand for cheap linen textiles as the

32   The certificate was in fact only issued in November 1821 after Holzschue had already left for Haiti. The minister of trade, von Bülow, had waited for the official acknowledgement of the RWC by the Prussian king before issuing the certificate. Oehm, *Rheinisch-Westindische*, p. 50.
33   Zeuske, 'Vergessene Revolution', p. 313 n. 103.
34   Until December 1822, trade with Haiti had brought a net profit of 12 per cent: Oehm, *Rheinisch-Westindische*, p. 58.
35   A detailed table on the composition of the cargos and the origin of goods can be seen in Zeuske, 'Vergessene Revolution', pp. 315–18. In 1825, Haiti was officially recognised by France and in return for diplomatic relations Haiti had to grant France preferential tariffs, which meant German goods had difficulties competing.
36   Beckmann, *Kompagnie*, p. 17, Oehm, *Rheinisch-Westindische*, p. 54.
37   The actual values are not given but can be calculated when combining the tables published in Beckmann, *Kompagnie*, p. 103 and in Zeuske, 'Vergessene Revolution', pp. 315–18. The RWC sent textiles for about 100,000 Prussian Taler. A large share of the shipment was made up of commission goods.

workers needed to be clothed.[38] Until 1830, the RWC sold Silesian linens to the value of more than 2 million Prussian Taler almost solely to Mexican customers.[39]

By virtue of its commerce, the RWC became an important player in Prusso-Mexican relations: to satisfy Mexican demands for official recognition, the Prussian government appointed the RWC's main agent in Mexico, Louis Sulzer, as commercial representative in 1825. The RWC's executive secretary, Carl Christian Becher, was in turn nominated commercial representative for Mexico in Prussia's western provinces, putting inland Elberfeld on the map of international relations.[40]

True to its original intentions of providing Prussian inland merchants with a variety of trading outlets in Latin America, the RWC also set up an agency in Buenos Aires which received several shipments over the years. In addition to the factory goods usually sent, such as textiles and metalware, the RWC also tried to enter the market for staple foods by sending a consignment of a thousand barrels of flour.[41] The RWC broadened its base in South America further by sending shipments to Montevideo, Peru and Chile, all of them newly independent. Apart from Buenos Aires, though, these places lacked suitable return goods; Chile and Peru could only offer metals at best. While Buenos Aires did not provide the most coveted goods such as coffee, sugar or dye-stuffs, the RWC agents could pick up hides as returns which were sold fairly easily in European ports.

Generally speaking, these South American ventures were not a great success. Unstable political situations in the young nations as well as the war between Brazil and Buenos Aires over the Banda Oriental hindered the development of continuous trade. From 1826 onward, exports of the RWC decreased. Furthermore, due to the limited capacity of the chosen destination many of the RWC shipments could only be sold with great delay and rebates. Return goods in turn often arrived after a considerable time lag and reached the volatile European markets at inopportune moments, incurring considerable losses in both cases.

Despite the willingness to broaden trade relations by sending goods to East Asia and to the USA, and to try new ventures such as opening up an agency in Brazil, generally sales of goods could only be realised slowly and at

---

38   Beckmann, *Kompagnie*, p. 45, Oehm, *Rheinisch-Westindische*, p. 70.
39   Beckmann, *Kompagnie*, p. 77.
40   Oehm, *Rheinisch-Westindische*, p. 75. RWC merchants nevertheless continued to lobby for official recognition by the Prussian government as the changing tariff policies made trade from afar particularly difficult. The RWC itself enjoyed good relations with the Prussian court as King Frederick William III had acquired forty shares of the RWC (totaling 20,000 Prussian Taler), signalling his support of the undertaking: ibid., p. 56.
41   The vessel was shipwrecked, however, which despite being fully insured dampened the enthusiasm of the Danzig merchants involved and they did not try again.

little profit. As a consequence, RWC shares went into decline in the latter half of the 1820s. By 1830, only Mexico remained an attractive marketplace and the company's directors made the decision to close all agencies overseas save that in Mexico which had brought a net profit of 62,000 Prussian Taler in the financial year 1830/1.[42] It was also decided to send the company's executive secretary to Mexico to gain better insight into the demands of that market-place. On the day of Becher's arrival, however, civil war flared up again and the demand for European goods came to a halt once more. Considering the overall financial situation of the company and the bleak prospects even in Mexico, the shareholders back in Elberfeld had no choice but to set in motion the company's liquidation. This process took almost twelve years as outstanding accounts were settled only very slowly.[43]

Despite the losses suffered at the end, on balance the performance of the RWC is not essentially a negative one. First, the RWC fulfilled an important function in lieu of the Prussian state. Already prior to the RWC's estab-lishment, Jakob Aders had publicly called on the Prussian government to 'summon all its powers to achieve for goods made in Germany the same preferential treatment in the [West] Indies as is received by the English'.[44] Aders had also hoped for a better protection of German merchants. The Prussian government had refused point-blank, however, to commit itself on the level of diplomatic relations, being determined to stick to the principles of the Holy Alliance. As a semi-public, semi-private institution, the RWC at least offered some protection to the merchants involved in risky transatlantic endeavours. Second, between 1821 and 1829, the RWC exported a significant share of Prussia's industrial output. It chartered thirty-nine ships, most of them heading from Hamburg to Latin American destinations, and in addition sent cargo on various ships overseas. The total of goods exported by the RWC amounted to 8 million Prussian Taler, of which textiles made up almost 80 per cent (linen 41 per cent, woollens 19 per cent, cotton 11 per cent and silks 8 per cent of the total).[45] Third, the export routes opened up and maintained

---

42 Ibid., p. 114.

43 It is not possible to calculate the total loss suffered by the shareholders as RWC shares were traded as bearer bonds. After two capital injections, the company was worth 2 million Prussian Taler. Until 1831, a dividend of 511,066 Prussian Taler had been paid out; during the years of the liquidation, 428,000 Prussian Taler were paid out to the shareholders as capital dividend while the rest of the capital had to be written off. See tables in ibid., pp. 133–4. As Oehm already noted, older notions of a 90 per cent loss per share cannot be maintained. The shareholder and member of the executive board, Josua Hasenclever, estimated a loss of 55–60 per cent. Hasenclever, 'Mitteilungen', p. 134.

44 'Die Regierung muß mit Aufbieten aller Kräfte dahin wirken, daß den deutschen Manufakturen in den Indien die gleichen Begünstigungen für die Einfuhr gestattet wird, wie den Engländern.' Oehm, *Rheinisch-Westindische*, p. 24.

45 The table of raw figures is reproduced in both Beckmann, *Kompagnie*, pp. 104–5. and Oehm, *Rheinisch-Westindische*, p. 130. The percentages were calculated by the author.

by the RWC certainly did facilitate the feeding of overseas markets from the interior and may also have helped smaller merchants to participate in overseas trade.[46]

On the downside one has to note that in the final accounting Aders' high hopes for increasing profits by eliminating intermediaries were not fulfilled. In fact, the decision to go ahead without the input of experienced long-distance merchants in the Hanseatic cities probably cost the RWC dear in the end.[47] The most fundamental problem of the RWC, however, was overestimating the potential of Latin American markets and their capacity to absorb goods as well as underestimating the British competition – challenges that were both further intensified by the economic crisis of 1825.

What can be made of the RWC and its trade in regard to the slave economy? The prominence of (inexpensive) linens among goods exported by the RWC suggests a continuation of older trading connections. Even in 1809, Berg merchants were still claiming that prior to the continental blockade they had exported cotton and linen fabrics to the value of 12–15 million francs annually, many of these destined to become clothing for 'negroes'.[48] The destinations chosen by the RWC speak, however, against such easy assumptions of continuity. Haiti had broken the regime of slavery successfully and its most important export good had become coffee produced mostly on small freeholdings rather than large plantations. In Mexico, slavery did not play an important role by the turn of the century and after the declaration of independence even the mining work was organised as wage labour, albeit under questionable working conditions. Peru and Chile also did not have large slave populations; neither of these states participated in the slave trade. Brazil, the single true slave state among the RWC destinations and a major participant in the slave trade, received goods only once in 1828. Generally, return goods received by the RWC consisted of non-plantation goods such as cochineal, hides, specie, metal and the aforementioned coffee.

It would, however, be premature to assume that RWC shareholders avoided slave states on purpose. Their choice of trading places was led by an expectation of returns and an overall pragmatism. While the general public considered Haiti as a nation of former slaves an oddity, to Aders and his peers the young republic presented the perfect gateway to the Caribbean.[49] As no European nation had a strong foothold on the island, the RWC's directors

46   The big merchant-manufacturers were not averse to the opportunity either. A&BF's inventory for the year 1826 listed twenty-one chests of tape worth 12,726 Gulden (about 9,000 Prussian Taler) as in stock with RWC agents: FCA, No. 1374, fol. 30.

47   A critical assessment of the RWC and of the idea that persisted to connect the Rhineland to overseas trade is given in Boch, *Wachstum*, chapter 2.4.

48   The numbers can be seen in Hauptstaatsarchiv Düsseldorf (HSTAD), Großherzogtum Berg 5592, fol. 3 and the specification of users in HSTAD, Großherzogtum Berg 5609, fol. 3.

49   This point is stressed by Zeuske, 'Vergessene Revolution', p. 313.

were free to build up trade relations. Unhindered by diplomatic concerns they could, for example, advance their cause by addressing the Haitian president with all due respect and send him a handsome present: a foulard made from silk which had been printed with the arms of the republic and the inscription 'Hommage de l'industrie allemande à son excellence Alexandre Boyer, Président d'Hayti'. An observant shareholder of the RWC commented drily: 'This must please the President all the more for the fact that it is the first communication received by the Haitian Republic from a publicly constituted association, if not a public authority of Europe.'[50]

In their dealings on Mexican soil, the RWC agents also proved their great adaptability. The first shipment to Mexico organised by the RWC arrived there in the spring of 1823, shortly after Iturbide, who had reigned as Augustín I, had abdicated. The *Rawlins*, carrying not only RWC goods but also the agents sent to establish a trading agency was the first European ship to enter a Mexican port after this event. Instead of asking Iturbide for permission to set up an agency as planned, the RWC agent Sulzer recommended himself to the leaders of the Cortes by offering them space on the *Rawlins* to get Iturbide out of the country. The Cortes agreed and also commissioned Sulzer to supply the ship with victuals needed for the journey. After that nothing stood in the way of establishing an RWC office on Mexican soil.[51]

The Prussian Dilemma of
Material Interests and Moral Principles

Considering the importance attached to South American and Caribbean markets both by individual firms such as A&BF and by enterprises like the RWC, at first sight it seems surprising that merchants in Prussia's centres of proto-industry, the Rhine Province and in Silesia, did not receive more support from the government. Certainly, it was not for want of trying. Jakob Aders' overtures have already been mentioned. The Prussian government also received a number of petitions by merchants from these provinces, asking for official support and the establishment of diplomatic relations with South American states. Government officials in the Ministry of Trade and the Ministry of Foreign Affairs were sympathetic to their ideas but the official government line, upheld in particular by the king, was informed and in the end also constrained by allegiance to the politics of the Holy Alliance. As only legitimate governments were recognised by the Holy Alliance, trade

---

50   Ibid., p. 321; the passage also contains a description of the gift. What is not mentioned is the fact that the RWC officials got the first name of President Boyer wrong – he was called Jean Pierre, not Alexander.
51   Oehm, *Rheinisch-Westindische*, pp. 62f.

with and thereby recognition of seditious Latin American states seemed to be out of the question for Prussia.[52] The economic consequences of this were analysed in very direct terms by no less than Alexander von Humboldt. In an *aide-memoire* he wrote:

> However long Prussia hesitates to build relations with the Spanish colonies, Spain will gain nothing by it. On the other hand, Prussia will not fail to damage herself and her own trade if she hesitates but a few years longer. Not only will she certainly fail to gain favourable treatment, but she runs the risk of being excluded from this trade altogether.[53]

Humboldt wrote from the vantage point of Prussian ambassador to the British court and indeed, throughout this period Prussian willingness to finally grant recognition to any of the Latin American states was to a large extent informed by English competition. Already Jakob Aders' appeal to the Prussian government had been prompted by the wish to be put on the same footing as English merchants overseas. England spearheaded the movement to give diplomatic recognition to the newly independent Latin American states, installing consuls and ambassadors along the way. English merchants thus received far more legal security than was afforded to their German competitors. Just as important were their commercial overtures: the English offer of cheap cotton textiles in particular threatened Prussia's major export product. In 1828 textiles and textile related goods were responsible for 65 per cent of all of Prussia's exports, with linen contributing 23 per cent.[54]

Brazil provided an initial way out of the Prussian dilemma of conflicting economic interests and political principles. Prussia had been represented at the Brazilian court since 1817 in the form of an extraordinary mission, not least with the aim of achieving direct trade relations as well as trading conditions as favourable as those enjoyed by the English.[55] When Brazil declared independence from the mother country in 1822, in Prussian eyes it had the good grace to stay a monarchy. Furthermore, Portugal recognised Brazilian independence three years later, thus legitimising the Brazilian government. Shortly afterwards, the Prussian king gave orders to conclude a beneficial trade agreement with Brazil.[56] The Prussian negotiators achieved

---

52   Seminal on this is Manfred Kossok, *Im Schatten der Heiligen Allianz: Deutschland und Lateinamerika 1815–1830* (Berlin, 1964).

53   The quote can be found in ibid., p. 73.

54   Gerhard Bondi, *Deutschlands Außenhandel 1815–1870* (Berlin, 1958), p. 55.

55   Bernd Schröter, 'Die Anfänge der preußischen Diplomatie in Südamerika', *Preußen und Lateinamerika*, ed. S. Carreras and G. Maihold (Münster, 2004), pp. 93–104.

56   Wolfgang Penkwitt, *Preußen und Brasilien: Zum Aufbau des preußischen Konsularwesens im unabhängigen Kaiserreich (1822–1850)* (Stuttgart, 1983), p. 32. On the impact of Holy Alliance politics on relations with Brazil see Kossok, *Im Schatten*, chapter 9.

equal treatment compared with England, France and Portugal and the treaty was hailed as a diplomatic masterpiece as Prussia did not have many favours to offer in return.

Despite significant pressure on both Portugal and Brazil from the British government, Brazil became the major importer of slaves in the Americas during this time. In the first quarter of the nineteenth century, more than 800,000 Africans were forcibly brought to Brazil, the number peaking at almost one million people during the following twenty-five years.[57] Most of them worked the coffee plantations in south-east Brazil. Considering the fact that all of them needed to be clothed, usually in cheap linen or cotton fabrics, it swiftly becomes apparent that Brazil turned into a gigantic marketplace for the kind of textiles produced in the Prussian provinces.

Nonetheless, the situation for German merchants in Brazil was particularly dire during the 1820s which might have been an added incentive for the Prussian government to come to a speedy conclusion of negotiations. Reporting on the ground, the Prussian consul in Brazil, Carl Wilhelm Theremin, observed the cut-throat competition that prevailed on the market: not only did the English undercut prices but they had taken to counterfeiting trademarks and passing off inferior textiles, often mixed with cotton, as Silesian and Westphalian products. As a consequence, 'anything marked "Silesia"' could only be gotten rid of in public auctions as 'all of South America seems to be supplied with it in overabundance'.[58]

These problems culminated in the economic crisis of 1825/6 which was one of the reasons for the gradual realignment of Prussia's South American politics in the second half of the 1820s. This realignment was further spurred on by ever-increasing English competition, the reorientation of French politics as well as the consolidation of the new states in Spanish America.[59] Accordingly, the following years saw an increase in the number of consuls appointed overseas as these officials were seen as a fairly simple, diplomatically innocuous and quickly established means to protect Prussia's economic interests and her merchants abroad. Recognising the importance of Port-au-Prince and Havana as trading places, Prussian consuls were put into place there in the first instance.[60] Cuba was about to become the major producer of cane sugar in the Americas, taking up the position previously held by Haiti

57   David Eltis, 'The Volume and Structure of the Transatlantic Slave Trade: A Reassessment', *William and Mary Quarterly* 58/1 (2001), 17–46, here p. 23, table III.
58   Penkwitt, *Preußen*, p. 508.
59   In detail, see Kossok, *Im Schatten*, chapter 8.
60   Michael Zeuske, 'Preußen und Westindien. Die vergessenen Anfänge der Handels- und Konsularbeziehungen Deutschlands mit der Karibik und Lateinamerika 1800–1870', *Preußen und Lateinamerika*, ed. S. Carreras and G. Maihold (Münster, 2004), pp. 145–215, here pp. 178, 193. The Prussian consul appointed in Port-au-Prince was, incidentally, Albert Weber, Abraham Frowein's nephew.

(then Saint-Domingue) in the eighteenth century. To satisfy the demand for a cheap workforce, Cuba had become a major importer of slaves, with arrivals increasing about fivefold after 1800.[61] Installing consuls on Cuba and Haiti did not pose problems for the Prussian *diplomatic* conscience as Cuba had remained under Spanish rule and Haiti's status was still ambivalent.

More difficult to reconcile with the principles of the Holy Alliance were Prussia's endeavours in regard to Mexico. But the prospects of trade with Mexico were too tempting to bypass the state. The director of the Bureau for Trade and Commerce in the Prussian Ministry of Finance, Christian Beuth, perceived it as the most important among the non-European trading places. As he reported emphatically to his superiors, to postpone recognition of Mexico would be incompatible with a government's duty to promote the prosperity of its subjects.[62]

Torn between different attitudes in the government, Prussia still continued to hover between its adherence to the principle of legitimacy and economic interests. While initiating the diplomatic procedures to negotiate a treaty of commerce and amiability with Mexico, the Prussian government shied away from full diplomatic recognition. In 1827, an official declaration concerning reciprocity and most-favoured-nation treatment was signed, almost but not quite giving Mexico full recognition. In 1829, Prussia also appointed a consul general for Mexico and thus recognised the state *de facto* if not *de jure*. A formal commercial treaty was finally signed in 1831, although it was only ratified by the Mexican government in 1834.

These initiatives could not prevent German linens from losing the exclusive position in clothing the poor and the slave population that they had enjoyed all over the Americas in the eighteenth century.[63] In the 1820s, Mexico was considered to be the main consumer of products of the Silesian linen industry, not the slave-driven economies of Brazil or Cuba. But by the 1830s, even in Mexico, German linens could hardly keep up with English-made cottons. To maintain an important share of the market, Prussian commentators considered it critical to influence consumers' preferences and to keep them accustomed to the hard-wearing, high-quality German linens instead of inferior (English) cotton textiles.[64]

This raises the question whether any relationship can be discerned between regimes of slavery, the slave trade, Prussian exports and bids for diplomatic relations. Although Prussia had signed the declaration on the abolition of the

---

61   Eltis, 'Volume', p. 23, table III.
62   Walther Bernecker, 'Preußisch-mexikanische Wirtschaftsbeziehungen in der ersten Hälfte des 19. Jahrhunderts', *Preußen und Lateinamerika*, ed. S. Carreras and G. Maihold (Münster, 2004), pp. 217–57, here p. 222.
63   Weber, 'Deutschland', p. 57.
64   Bernecker, 'Wirtschaftsbeziehungen', p. 224.

slave trade at the Congress of Vienna in February 1815, the question of the slave trade – having been very much a matter of concern for England when negotiating treaties with former Spanish and Portuguese colonies – does not seem to have played a role in Prussian negotiations. The slave trade received no mention either in the treaty between Prussia and Brazil or in that between Prussia and Mexico.[65]

The annual reports of the Prussian consul in Rio de Janeiro, Carl Wilhelm Theremin nevertheless showed an acute awareness of the topic and its repercussions, providing government officials with first-hand information.[66] His concern with the slave trade remained exclusively material, in so far as he reported solely on the effect this had on credit relations – slaveholders preferring in these years to invest in more slaves rather than servicing their debts – and on specific goods such as brass bowls made in the Rhenish town of Stolberg, which were much used as trade goods in the slave trade.[67] In his reports, Theremin was silent on other goods that might have been used for barter on the African coast but during his regular tours through Prussia's provinces to advise Rhenish manufactures he might have elaborated on that too.

Theremin expressed his moral concerns rather on the conditions of German colonists who had been enticed to settle in Brazil by the Brazilian agent Dr Schäffer, a most dubious figure. In fact, Theremin accused the British Crown of hypocrisy, advancing abolition out of economic interests while opening up the Hanoverian territory to the recruiting of Dr Schäffer whom he characterised as practising a slave trade that was simply of a different colour.[68] This approach to the slave trade was probably typical of continental German officials. Even Hanover, the continental dominion of the British Crown, showed no official concern for ending the slave trade. While its own treaty with Mexico copied the Anglo-Mexican commercial treaty of 1826 clause for clause, article XV, which committed the Mexican government to 'co-operate with His Britannick Majesty for the total abolition of the Slave-trade, and to prohibit all persons inhabiting within the Territories of Mexico, in the most

65   The Prusso-Brazilian treaty is included in *Nouveau Recueil de Traités* (NRT), ed. G. F. de Martens, 7 vols (Göttingen, 1830; repr. 1882), vol. 7, pp. 470–5; the Prusso-Mexican treaty is in *NRT*, ed. G. F. de Martens, 16 vols (Göttingen, 1837), vol. 12, pp. 534–53. On the Congress of Vienna and the question of the slave trade see Helmut Berding, 'Die Ächtung des Sklavenhandels auf dem Wiener Kongreß 1814/15', *Historische Zeitschrift*, 219/2 (1974), 265–89. The question of abolition at the Congress of Vienna also received coverage in the German periodical press, most notably the *Politisches Journal*: Schüller, *Rezeption*, pp. 246–7.
66   The reports for the years 1825 and 1826 are printed in full in Penkwitt, *Preußen*, pp. 492–521.
67   Ibid., p. 502.
68   Kossok, *Im Schatten*, p. 194. The image of 'white slaves' was used also by other German contemporaries, reporting on the conditions of German immigrants in Brazil.

effectual matter, from taking any share in such trade', was explicitly excluded as inapplicable.[69]

In short, Prussia – like other continental nations, one might add – was far from taking a clear stance over the matter of the slave trade or the practice of slavery. The slave trade did not make it on to the political agenda. In view of King Frederick William III's preoccupation with political stability, the maintenance of slavery both in colonies such as Cuba and in newly formed states like imperial Brazil might indeed have been seen as a stabilising factor. Where moral concerns played a role in perceptions of Prussia's material interests, they were concerns mobilised by duty owed to fellow monarchs, not the fate of nameless slaves.

Conclusion

It is a well-known fact that despite the prohibition of carrying slaves on British ships and Britain's subsequent efforts to make the slave trade illegal in the Atlantic world, the transatlantic slave trade experienced new heights in the nineteenth century. Not even massive pressure by the British government, deploying significant political and economic power, could suppress the forced transportation of millions of Africans to work the ever-expanding coffee and sugar plantations, most notably on Cuba and in Brazil. Furthermore, the impact of abolition on the slave trade at first was only marginal. As David Eltis has argued, abolition for major branches of the slave trade simply meant that impediments to the trade appeared which had not been there before, and 'any eighteenth century trader would have been at home in the traffic of the early years of abolition'.[70]

This chapter set out to explore the question of whether, similarly, the integrated system of Atlantic plantation economy, slave trade and continental manufacturing centres continued to function as it had prior to abolition and whether, indeed, the Wupper Valley might be called a hinterland to the slave trade. For the three planes of observation employed the following can be summarised: First, the individual company under consideration, Abraham & Brothers Frowein, could build on earlier experiences with transatlantic trade and managed during the early decades of the nineteenth century to build up a network of commission agents along the American coasts. Thanks to their experience with supplying the Iberian empires indirectly during the eighteenth century, they were able to serve the newly emerging markets

69 *NRT*, ed. G. F. de Martens (Göttingen, 1830), vol. 7, pp. 80–99.
70 David Eltis, 'The Impact of Abolition on the Atlantic Slave Trade', *The Abolition of the Atlantic Slave Trade: Origins and Effects in Europe, Africa, and the Americas*, ed. D. Eltis and J. Walvin (Madison, WI, 1981), pp. 155–76, quote on p. 172.

overseas according to demand and preferences. The slave trade's continuance or discontinuance seems to have been of no concern to them as their products were not directly a part of it. Moral concerns generally do not seem to have entered into their dealings with South America, the continued existence of slavery rather being a 'blind spot' in both commercial and private correspondence. The particular history of Haiti, their gateway to the Caribbean, was not made a subject of discussion either. Second, the semi-public venture of the *Rheinisch-Westindische Compagnie*, even though it was founded in 1821, can clearly be grouped with the great trading companies of the seventeenth and eighteenth centuries. By focusing on the exchange of manufactured goods for agricultural products it reinforced earlier traditions and maintained an established system. The fact that the RWC did business mostly in countries where slavery no longer played an important role reflected pragmatic choices rather than moral compunctions. Overall, the continuance of the slave trade in spite of British abolition seems to have had no impact on either the rise or the fall of the RWC. Finally, the Prussian government did not take a stance over the matter of the slave trade other than what might be regarded as lip service at the Congress of Vienna. Like RWC shareholders, Prussian officials treated the emerging Latin American states as market opportunities in which Prussia's principal export goods, textiles, might now be placed directly. How much of them entered the slave trade in continuation of an earlier practice is impossible to assess. To Prussian officials back in Europe, what complicated matters was the need to adhere to the policies of the Holy Alliance, not any official concerns about the slave trade.

In short, important lines of continuity in the material relations between continental Germany and Latin America can be seen stretching from the eighteenth into the early nineteenth century, and in practice Wupper Valley industry continued to benefit from the traffic in and exploitation of enslaved Africans. Germany continued to export great amounts of textiles to the Americas, some of which certainly found their way into the slave trade. And German merchant-manufacturers continued to profit from the existence of slave labour in the Americas. The abolition of the slave trade did not influence them much either way, neither morally nor materially. The continuance of the slave trade despite abolition was probably deemed necessary for the economic equilibrium achieved, and no moral qualms disturbed them, despite the reading of 'hideous accounts'. However, relations between the Wupper Valley and the slave trade are too tenuous to term this inland region a hinterland to the slave trade. But it was certainly a beneficiary of the continued practices sketched above.

This willingness by merchants and officials alike to carry on as they had in the previous century without revising their ideas cost them in the end. Market conditions changed not only because of the fierce English competition fuelled by increasing industrialisation but also because consumers in the Americas had become more particular. As the agent for Abraham & Brothers Frowein in Havana, José Garcia Alvarez, explained:

> The opinion held in Europe that poor and dowdy goods are still finding an outlet here is completely wrong as the times are gone when people here were not yet acquainted with European goods and paid high prices for bad quality. The great competition which is particular to this place delivers goods from all parts of the world to us and teaches us to judge their value. This is particularly true for silk fabrics.[71]

What Alvarez did not mention was the fact that slaves were also among the discerning buyers. As travellers and plantation owners remarked time and again, slaves set great store by dressing up on Sundays and for parties, often devoting most of their, sometimes quite considerable, income from garden plots to high-quality textiles such as fine cambric, satin and occasionally even silk.[72] It might have been worthwhile for Wupper Valley merchants to extend at least their material attention to those held in bondage, even if they did not trouble their moral concerns.

71   FCA No. 264, letter from José Garcia Alvarez to A&BF, Havanna, 16 December 1817.
72   Dale Tomich, 'The Other Face of Slave Labour: Provision Grounds and Internal Marketing in Martinique', *Caribbean Slavery in the Atlantic World: A Student Reader*, ed. H. Beckles and V. A. Shepherd (Kingston, Jamaica, 2000), pp. 743–57, here pp. 753f; Eugene D. Genovese, *Roll, Jordan, Roll: The World the Slaves Made* (New York, 1976), pp. 550–61.

8

Abolitionists in the German Hinterland? Therese Huber and the Spread of Anti-slavery Sentiment in the German Territories in the Early Nineteenth Century

SARAH LENTZ

In an 1826 letter, the German writer and journal editor Therese Huber (1764–1829) described to the famous French abolitionist and revolutionary Abbé Henri Grégoire (1751–1831) the crucial moment at which 'the idea of the injustices which the black peoples [*les peuples noirs*] were suffering struck me for the first time'. Huber explained that in that instant 'about eight years ago' the practice of slavery had presented itself to her in the form of a medallion made of terracotta which showed a black slave chained and on his knees pleading to a white man who was holding a whip. While such material objects with anti-slavery images were popular and powerful weapons used by the abolitionist movement in Great Britain, they seem to have rarely made their way into the German principalities. The image in question had made a lasting impression on Huber; she declared solemnly: '[M]y opinion took shape and ever since then the negroes are become my brothers.'[1] Her correspondence with Grégoire from the 1820s reveals that Huber indeed tried to employ her position as chief editor of the *Morgenblatt für gebildete Stände*, one of the most widely read German literary journals, to spread anti-slavery sentiment in the German-speaking territories. It also discloses that she used her personal network to support the movement to end slavery and the slave trade.

---

1   Therese Huber to Henri Grégoire, Augsburg, 4 July 1826, from the Archives Carnot (AC), folder 'Allemagne'. All the quotations from letters to Grégoire by Huber are taken from correspondence located at the private Archive of the Carnot Family at La Ferté-Alais near Paris. The letters are ordered only by place of origin. Huber's French is non-standard and in some respects ambiguous.

Huber's attitude is not reflected in international research on the abolitionist movement in Europe around 1800, in which German activists are rarely
mentioned. Rather, most historians have taken the absence of an institutionalised abolitionist movement from the German-speaking realm as evidence of
the absence of German activists from the international movement.[2] Huber's
correspondence with Grégoire – which has only recently been rediscovered
in a private archive near Paris[3] – challenges this assumption. This case study
shows that an analysis which centres around concrete individuals, networks
and micro-historical processes of exchange adds another layer to our understanding of the transnational abolitionist movement. It shows that abolitionist discourse was not restricted to countries which owned colonies in the
Caribbean, nor was activist action. The case of Therese Huber's endeavours
is interesting on two levels: first, for her role as a female activist, and second,
for the fact that she operated at the margins of the Atlantic world, helping
to extend the discourse on the Atlantic slave system to Central Europe.
Consequently, Huber's agency and intentions as well as the obstacles and
restrictions under which she – as a female writer and activist – had to work
and the strategies that she developed to make her voice heard are at the centre
of this chapter, which focuses on her personal network and on the transfer of
knowledge about slavery and the slave trade that occurred within it.

(Female) Abolitionists in the German Territories?

While current research on the abolitionist movement has observably become
more focused on transnational cooperation between activists of different
national backgrounds, thus far historians have shown most interest in collabo-
rations between citizens of the 'bigger players' in the movement such as Great
Britain, the USA and France.[4] But as recent research on the participation

2   The Germantown protest is an exception: see, for example, Katherine Gerbner, 'Antislavery in
Print. The Germantown Protest, the "Exhortation", and the Seventeenth-Century Quaker Debate
on Slavery', *Early American Studies. An Interdisciplinary Journal* 9/3 (2011), 552–75. Another
exception is Alexander von Humboldt who is briefly introduced as an abolitionist in several
studies, for example J. R. Oldfield, *Transatlantic Abolitionism in the Age of Revolution. An
International History of Anti-slavery, c.1787–1820* (Cambridge and New York, 2013), pp. 209–17.
3   Among other papers of Grégoire, the AC holds an extensive archive of letters addressed to
him – at least several thousand – from correspondents all over Europe and North America. Only
a few of the letters have been published: Jean Dubray, ed., *Lettres à l'abbé Grégoire: Extraites
des archives Carnot: Volume l de A à J* (Paris, 2013). Three of Huber's letters are also included
in this publication.
4   Oldfield, *Transatlantic Abolitionism*; Christopher Leslie Brown, 'Slavery and Antislavery,
1760–1820', *The Oxford Handbook of the Atlantic World, c.1450– c.1850*, ed. N. Canny and
P. Morgan (Oxford, 2011), pp. 602–17; Philip Gould, *Barbaric Traffic: Commerce and Antislavery*

of Swiss citizens in the abolitionist cause has convincingly illustrated, it is important to expand the focus of historical research geographically to obtain a more complete picture of the Atlantic abolitionist movement.[5] As is often forgotten, there were German territories that were part of nations involved in the Atlantic slave system: in the eighteenth century, Schleswig and Holstein were subject to Denmark and electoral Hanover was bound to Britain in a personal union; but historical research on the anti-slavery movement does generally not concern itself with the German debate on slavery.[6] Researchers such as Klaus Weber have already pointed out that many Germans were economically involved in the slave trade on different levels and that the resulting entanglements reached far into the German hinterland.[7] At the same time, scholars have repeatedly observed a strong interest in the debate on the slave trade and slavery in contemporary German magazines and newspapers,[8] but this has yet to be examined in its wider social and intellectual dimensions. Most research has focused on content analyses of literary texts of various kinds.[9] Literary scholar Barbara Riesche has thus criticised

---

in the Eighteenth-Century Atlantic World (Cambridge, 2003); Seymour Drescher, *Abolition: A History of Slavery and Antislavery* (Cambridge, 2009); Lawrence Jennings, *French Anti-Slavery. The Movement for the Abolition of Slavery in France, 1802–1848* (Cambridge, 2006). There are also many studies that compare the different national movements, such as: Seymour Drescher, *Capitalism and Abolition. British Mobilization in Comparative Perspective* (Oxford, 1987).

5   Thomas David, Bouda Etemad and Janick Marina Schaufelbuehl, *Schwarze Geschäfte: Die Beteiligung von Schweizern an Sklaverei und Sklavenhandel im 18. und 19. Jahrhundert* (Zurich, 2005), pp. 123–78.

6   The exception in regard to the German debate on slavery is Andreas Gestrich, 'The Abolition Act and the Development of Abolitionist Movements in 19th Century Europe', *Humanitarian Intervention and Changing Labor Relations. The Long-Term Consequences of the Abolition of the Slave Trade*, ed. M. van der Linden (Leiden, 2011), pp. 245–62.

7   See, for instance, the chapters by Anka Steffen and Klaus Weber, and Anne Sophie Overkamp in this volume, and also Klaus Weber, 'Deutschland, der atlantische Sklavenhandel und die Plantagenwirtschaft der Neuen Welt (15. bis 19. Jahrhundert)', *Journal of Modern European History* 7/1 (2009), 37–67, and Jochen Meissner, Ulrich Mücke and Klaus Weber, *Schwarzes Amerika: Eine Geschichte der Sklaverei* (Munich, 2008).

8   See, for example, Jana Braun, *Das Bild des 'Afrikaners' im Spiegel deutscher Zeitschriften der Aufklärung*, Leipziger Arbeiten zur Geschichte und Kultur in Afrika 10 (Leipzig, 2005); Rainer Koch, 'Liberalismus, Konservatismus und das Problem der Negersklaverei: Ein Beitrag zur Geschichte des politischen Denkens in Deutschland in der ersten Hälfte des 19. Jahrhunderts', *Historische Zeitschrift* 222 (1976), 529–78.

9   See, for example, Karin Schüller, 'Deutsche Abolitionisten in Göttingen und Halle: Die ersten Darstellungen des Sklavenhandels und der Antisklavereibewegung in der deutschen Historiographie des ausgehenden 18. und beginnenden 19. Jahrhundert', *Pasajes – Passages – Passagen. Festschrift für Christian Wentzlaff-Eggebert*, ed. S. Grunwald, C. Hammerschmidt, V. Heinen and G. Nilsson (Seville, 2004), pp. 611–22; Birgit Tautz, 'Revolution, Abolition, Aesthetic Sublimation: German Responses to News from France in the 1790s', *(Re-)writing the Radical. Enlightenment, Revolution and Cultural Transfer in 1790s Germany, Britain and France*, ed. M. Oergel (Göttingen, 2012), pp. 72–87; Hanna Wallinger, 'The Africanist Presence in Nineteenth-Century German Writers',

the lack of a systematic historical investigation of the 'German debate on slavery in terms of its channels of reception and information, its personal and logistical structures and its presence in the media and in the public sphere'.[10] As a result, historians have concluded that public opinion in the German territories generally condemned the practices connected with slavery and that 'it was also a topic of prime importance for the debates on domestic political reform'.[11] But the writers behind these works and their motivations in focusing on the Atlantic slave system have not been of further interest to historians or literary scholars.[12] The possibility (indeed likelihood) that there were German individuals whose interest in the cause of the enslaved went further and turned from mere acknowledgement to active engagement remains largely unexplored.

This is even more the case in regard to the possibility of female activism in the German territories. In general, historians agree that women played an important role in the abolition of the slave trade and slavery in the Atlantic world. Taking British abolitionist women as an example, they often wrote fictional works or poems on the topic and subscribed to the Society for Effecting the Abolition of the Slave Trade. They took the lead in organising sugar boycotts and added their signatures to the important petitions that demanded the end of the slave trade in the late eighteenth century. In the 1820s, they succeeded in establishing all-female abolitionist societies throughout Britain.[13] The main incentive for many of them to become active was the desire to help their 'sisters' in bondage, and while in the early nineteenth century most women were '[f]ar from explicitly challenging their own subordinate roles in British society',[14] some voices could already be heard that

From Black to Schwarz: Cultural Crossovers between African America and Germany, ed. M. I. Diedrich and J. Heinrichs (Münster, 2010), pp. 29–48; Hans-Konrad Schmutz, '"Schwarzundweiße Halbbrüder": Zum Wechselspiel zwischen der wissenschaftlichen Debatte und der Sklavenfrage im späten 18. Jahrhundert', *Schwarzweissheiten: Vom Umgang mit fremden Menschen*, ed. M. Johannsen, Schriftenreihe des Landesmuseums für Natur und Mensch, Oldenburg 19 (Oldenburg, 2001), pp. 114–20; Susanne M. Zantop, *Colonial Fantasies: Conquest, Family, and Nation in Precolonial Germany, 1770–1870* (Durham, NC, 1997); Matthias Fiedler, *Zwischen Abenteuer, Wissenschaft und Kolonialismus: Der deutsche Afrikadiskurs im 18. und 19. Jahrhundert* (Cologne, 2005); Uta Sadji, *Der Mohr auf der deutschen Bühne des 18. Jahrhunderts*, Wort und Musik: Salzburger akademische Beiträge 11 (Salzburg, 1992).

10   Barbara Riesche, *Schöne Mohrinnen, edle Sklaven, schwarze Rächer. Schwarzendarstellung und Sklavereithematik im deutschen Unterhaltungstheater (1770–1814)* (Hanover, 2010), p. 63.

11   Gestrich, 'The Abolition Act', p. 248; Braun, *Das Bild*, p. 54.

12   An exception is Gestrich, 'The Abolition Act', p. 247. Gestrich argues that 'late-18th century intellectuals still followed British and American debates and initiatives closely, and that there was an intense exchange of ideas'. Gestrich illustrates this claim by the reference to a few brief examples, such as the famous German playwright August von Kotzebue.

13   Clare Midgley, *Women against Slavery: The British Campaigns, 1780–1870* (London, 1992), p. 44.

14   Ibid., p. 202.

stressed the similarities between slavery and the social position of women.[15] From this point of view it is to be expected that German women, too, would respond to the appeal of abolitionism, and in fact the case of Therese Huber is an important example of this, displaying many similarities with what we know about abolitionist women in other countries but also some differences.

Therese Huber as a Political Writer

Therese Huber[16] was born in 1764 in the university town of Göttingen, the daughter of the famous professor of classics Christian Gottlob Heyne (1729–1812). Their house served as a meeting point for local and international scholars, and Huber grew up in a vibrant and cosmopolitan intellectual atmosphere.[17] While she had access to a vast array of books, since her father also served as the head of the local library, her only formal schooling apart from infrequent tutoring was provided by attendance at a girls' boarding school in Hanover for two years.[18] She married Georg Forster (1754–94), the famous travel writer and journalist, in 1785, and continued to pursue her intellectual interests, assisting Forster with translations of English texts.[19] Later, she left him for Ludwig Ferdinand Huber (1764–1804), a journalist, translator and writer, whom she married after Forster's death.[20] While she was married to Huber, her literary works were published under his name – a common practice at the time.[21] After his death in 1804, she continued to write for various magazines, publishing her works anonymously. Only after the death of her father, who disapproved of his daughter's career, did Huber

15   Moira Ferguson, 'Mary Wollstonecraft and the Problematic of Slavery', *Feminist Review* 42 (Autumn, 1992), 82–102, here p. 82.

16   To avoid confusion I will refer to Therese Heyne-Forster-Huber during the entire article as 'Therese Huber'.

17   Magdalene Heuser, 'Jakobinerin, Demokratin und Revolutionär: Therese Hubers "kleiner winziger Standpunkt als Weib" um 1800', *Sklavin oder Bürgerin? Französische Revolution und Neue Weiblichkeit 1760–1830*, ed. V. Schmidt-Linsenhoff (Marburg, 1989), pp. 143–57, here p. 145.

18   Andrea Hahn, '"Wie ein Mannskleid für den weiblichen Körper": Therese Huber (1764–1829)', *Beruf: Schriftstellerin. Schreibende Frauen im 18. und 19. Jahrhundert*, ed. K. Tebben (Göttingen, 1998), pp, 103–31, here p. 107.

19   Heuser, 'Jakobinerin', p. 145 or Hahn, 'Wie ein Mannskleid', p. 111.

20   Carola Hilmes, *Skandalgeschichten: Aspekte einer Frauenliteraturgeschichte* (Königstein, 2004), p. 47.

21   Carola Hilmes, 'Georg Forster und Therese Huber: Eine Ehe in Briefen', *Das literarische Paar: Intertextualität der Geschlechterdiskurse/Le couple littéraire: Intertextualité et discours des sexes*, ed. G. Seybert (Bielefeld, 2003), pp. 111–31, here p. 112, and Karin Tebben, 'Soziokulturelle Bedingungen weiblicher Schriftkultur im 18. und 19. Jahrhundert: Zur Einleitung', *Beruf: Schriftstellerin. Schreibende Frauen im 18. und 19. Jahrhundert*, ed. K. Tebben (Göttingen, 1998), pp. 10–46, here pp. 27–8.

start to publish works under her own name.[22] Over the course of her life, Huber wrote numerous articles and other pieces, publishing more than sixty stories and novels.[23] She was thus able to remain economically independent in her widowhood, earning a living for herself and her children as a professional writer, in defiance of the fact that this was still not a socially accepted role for a woman. In the German territories, '[t]o think, express oneself or act politically, particularly in public, was perceived as "unfeminine"'.[24]

Huber also became one of the first German women to be the managing editor of a journal. She edited the *Morgenblatt für gebildete Stände* from 1817 to 1823 in Stuttgart and turned it into one of the leading literary magazines of its kind in the German-speaking territories with a print run of 1,810 per issue. Formatted like a four-page newspaper and printed six times per week, it included articles – travelogues, poems, autobiographical writings – on a variety of topics such as literature, history, art, politics and natural history.[25] In late 1823, Huber's position as editor for the *Morgenblatt* ended because of difficulties with the owner of the journal, Johann Friedrich Cotta. She continued writing until she was nearly blind and died in her daughter's home in Aachen in 1829.

During her lifetime, Therese Huber repeatedly experienced social opprobrium: first, for her level of education and reputation as a 'bluestocking'; second, for her personal choices in leaving Forster and living in 'concubinage' with Huber; then for her liberal political beliefs; and finally, as the following will show, for working as a professional writer. After her death her literary achievements continued to be overshadowed by her colourful personal life, and especially by her separation from her much-admired first husband.[26] Only since the 1980s have scholars become more interested in her character and her work, arguing for a re-evaluation of her literary oeuvre.[27] Magdalene Heuser, the leading expert on Huber, emphasises her general 'cosmopolitan stance'. Her cosmopolitanism was also realised in the broad international network

---

22 Heuser, 'Jakobinerin', p. 146.
23 Barbara Becker-Cantarino, 'Therese Forster-Huber und Polen', *'Daß eine Nation die andere verstehen möge': Festschrift für Marian Szyrocki*, eds N. Honsza and H.-G. Roloff (Amsterdam, 1988), pp. 53–66, here p. 54.
24 Heuser, 'Jakobinerin', p. 156.
25 Bernhard Fischer, 'Cottas *Morgenblatt für gebildete Stände* in der Zeit von 1807–1823 und die Mitarbeit Therese Hubers', *Archiv für Geschichte des Buchwesens* 43 (1995), 203–39, 358–408 and Magdalene Heuser, 'Lektüre – Übersetzung – Vermittlung: Therese Hubers Redaktionstätigkeit für Cottas *Morgenblatt für gebildete Stände*', *Oxford German Studies* 42/2 (2013), 158–72, here p. 167.
26 Heuser, 'Jakobinerin', p. 146. See, for example, Wolf Lepenies, 'Georg Forster als Anthropologe und als Schriftsteller', *Akzente: Zeitschrift für Literatur* 31 (1984), 557–75.
27 Over the last decade, a collection of part of her impressive correspondence of more than 4,500 letters has been published: Therese Huber, *Briefe*, 7 vols, ed. Magdalene Heuser *et al.* (Tübingen and Berlin, 1999–2013).

that Huber built and maintained throughout her life: a network of friends and correspondents who were established citizens of the European 'republic of letters'.[28] Recent studies also agree that Huber adopted a relatively critical position in regard to the society that surrounded her.[29] During the 1780s, Huber moved to Vilnius, in the Polish-Lithuanian Commonwealth, for two years while her husband Forster took up a professorship at the local university. There she experienced at first hand the social practice of serfdom, and in a published report on her experiences she critiqued the situation of the men and women subject to feudal lordship, commenting on their 'slave mentality' as well as the brutality of the aristocracy.[30] She and Forster were enthusiastic about the French Revolution and the social change it promised; Forster became a leading figure in the short-lived Mainz Republic. Huber later wrote of that period in her life: 'I thought the century of freedom had come.'[31] Because of her own political beliefs and her status as former wife of a Jacobin, Huber had to stay in exile in Switzerland for several years.[32] She later distanced herself from this extreme position, but remained sympathetic to social movements such as the Greek War of Independence.[33] As Andrea Hahn has pointed out, Huber – convinced that 'the individual purpose is always geared to the benefit of the public'– generally used her position as a writer and public figure to enlighten the German public about social and moral grievances that she cared about.[34] However, because of her wide array of publications, there are a number of topics that are still awaiting in-depth examination by scholars, her position on slavery and the slave trade being one of them.

A Late 'Conversion' to Abolitionism?

The rediscovery of Huber's letters to Abbé Grégoire make her interest in the cause evident. While there are unfortunately no remaining letters from Grégoire to Huber, there are ten letters written by her to Grégoire dating from 1822 to 1829.[35] The content of the letters is a mixture of family news

28 Heuser, 'Lektüre', pp. 158, 162.
29 See, for example, Brigitte Leuschner, 'Therese Huber als Briefschreiberin', *Untersuchungen zum Roman von Frauen um 1800*, ed. H. Gallas and M. Heuser (Tübingen, 1990), pp. 203–12.
30 [Therese Huber], 'Fragmente über einen Theil von Pohlen', *Flora: Teutschlands Töchtern geweiht* 1794/3, 244–70 and 1794/4, 97–128, here 1794/3, p. 258.
31 Huber to Emil von Herder [Stoffenried, 1805–1807], cited in Hahn, 'Wie ein Mannskleid', p. 110.
32 Heuser, 'Jakobinerin', p. 146.
33 Hahn, 'Wie ein Mannskleid', p. 110.
34 Ibid., pp. 121f.
35 One letter is not dated, otherwise: 12 June 1822; 19 October 1822; 27 February 1823; 22 July 1823; 29 August 1823; 22 July 1825; 4 July 1826; 20 October 1828; 12 February 1829.

and exchanges about their shared interests, such as their religious beliefs. Other important topics, which form part of nearly all of Huber's letters, were the slave trade, slavery and the development of the former French colony of Haiti, which after the Haitian Revolution had become the first state ruled by former slaves. As the letters indicate, Grégoire and Huber had already exchanged their views on these topics on earlier occasions that pre-date the known archive of letters.[36]

Abbé Henri Grégoire started his career as a French Roman Catholic parish priest. He supported the French Revolution, becoming constitutional bishop of Blois under the republican Civil Constitution of the Clergy of 1790. Grégoire was active in the cause of the Jewish population. He was also an ardent abolitionist and a leading member of the Société des Amis des Noirs, the French abolitionist society, publishing numerous pamphlets and books on the subject of racial equality.[37] Grégoire was always eager to link his endeavours with those of other activists, irrespective of their national origin, and he developed an international reputation as a revolutionary activist. In the early 1800s, he undertook journeys to Great Britain, the Netherlands, and in 1805 to the German principalities.[38] Grégoire used these trips to gather evidence for his book *De la littérature des nègres* – translated into English as *An Enquiry concerning the Intellectual and Moral Faculties, and Literature of Negroes*. The book was a sharp critique of slavery and the slave trade, and sought to prove the intellectual equality of black and white people.[39] During his trip through the German states, the Frenchman repeatedly sought the opportunity to talk about his interest in the situation of enslaved Blacks and thus tried to spread anti-slavery sentiments among his circle of acquaintances.[40] After his return to France, he maintained correspondence with many German intellectuals – such as Johann Friedrich Blumenbach, Therese Huber's uncle – trying to involve them in his fight for abolition. Several of these correspondents became active by investigating case studies of black individuals.[41] In return,

---

36   From the existing correspondence, it has not yet become possible to discover when and how Grégoire and Huber became acquainted.

37   For Grégoire and his oeuvre in general see, for example, Alyssa Goldstein, *The Abbé Grégoire and the French Revolution: The Making of Modern Universalism* (Berkeley, 2005); Ruth Necheles, *The Abbé Grégoire 1787–1831: The Odyssey of an Egalitarian* (Westport, 1971); Jeremy D. Popkin and Richard H. Popkin, eds, *The Abbé Grégoire and His World* (Dordrecht, 2000).

38   Hans W. Debrunner, *Grégoire l'Européen* (Salzburg, 1997), pp. 123–90. Debrunner put a lot of effort into reconstructing and untangling Grégoire's European network.

39   Henri Grégoire, *De la littérature des nègres, ou Recherches sur leurs facultés intellectuelles, leurs qualités morales et leur littérature; suivies de Notices sur la vie et les ouvrages des Nègres qui se sont distingués dans les Sciences, les Lettres et les Arts* (Paris, 1808).

40   See for example Debrunner, *Grégoire*, p. 166.

41   One of his Austrian correspondents, Caroline Pichler – a friend of Huber – also provided him with a chapter on the black Freemason Angelo Soliman written by herself: Thomas Geider,

during the next decade and beyond, Grégoire provided his German correspondents with his and other abolitionists' writings.[42] In contrast to most of
his German correspondents who praised the anti-slavery activist for his zeal
but did not commit themselves to active personal or financial support for the
movement, Huber displayed a real interest in the Abbé's cause and became
an activist in her own right. While it is unlikely that Grégoire and Huber met
during his journey to the German territories, the two might have become
acquainted through mutual friends such as the Swiss author Paul Usteri or the
Austrian writer Caroline Pichler, both of whom collaborated with Grégoire
on his work *De la littérature des nègres*.[43] Another possibility is that they
started their correspondence only in the early 1820s when Huber's son Victor
Aimé Huber (1800–69) moved to Paris for a period during his Grand Tour
through Europe. During his stay in France, Victor Aimé became acquainted
with famous opponents of slavery such as Alexander von Humboldt, an old
friend of his mother, but also with Abbé Grégoire.[44] Victor Aimé showed a
lively interest in the topic of slavery himself, composing – with the aid of
Humboldt – a long pamphlet in which he criticised the French government for
its failure to facilitate the means to suppress the slave trade, which had been
forbidden since 1817. This pamphlet was later translated into German and
published by Cotta in his journal *Neue allgemeine politische Annalen* in four
instalments between 1825 to 1826, amounting to approximately 120 pages.[45]
Even if the acquaintance between Grégoire and Therese Huber pre-dated her
son's stay in Paris, it is clear that their connection was strengthened through
this shared relationship and it is very likely that Therese Huber's and her
son's interest in abolitionist ideas influenced and reinforced each other.

Nevertheless, as described above, Huber retrospectively identified the year
1818 as the starting point of her commitment to the cause of the enslaved. The
report of her encounter with the anti-slavery medallion is interesting for several
reasons. First of all, it is the only documented occurrence of an anti-slavery
medallion in the German territories (in 1818 Huber was living in Stuttgart).
How and where Huber came into possession of this object is not known. In

'Afrika im Umkreis der frühen Weltliteraturdiskussion: Goethe und Henri Grégoire', *Revue de
littérature comparée* 2 (2005), 241–60, here p. 254.

42   See for example AC, folder 'Allemagne', Friedrich von Schlichtegroll to Grégoire, Munich,
7 June 1810; Franz Oberthür to Grégoire, Wuerzburg, 1 January 1810.

43   Usteri translated the book into German: see Debrunner, *Grégoire*, pp. 182–3.

44   Barbara Schuchard, 'Ausschweigen und Vermuten: Zu den deutschen Übersetzungen von
Alexander von Humboldt', *Lusitanica et Romanica: Festschrift für Dieter Woll*, Romanistik
in Geschichte und Gegenwart Beiheft 1, ed. M. Hummel and C. Ossenkop (Hamburg, 1998),
pp. 212–25, here p. 215.

45   Victor Aimé Huber, 'Ueber den gegenwärtigen Zustand des Sklavenhandels und die
Maßregeln der europäischen Mächte ihn zu unterdrücken', *Neue allgemeine politische Annalen*
16 (1825), 3–37 and 441–54; 17 (1825), 228–57; 18 (1826), 3–47.

Stuttgart she frequented the gatherings of the social elite and was in contact with the ambassadors who represented their respective countries at the royal court.[46] She received journals through the British envoy, Alexander Cockburn (1776–1852) and might have been introduced to the medallion through this channel.[47] The incident is revealing inasmuch as it underlines the power of material objects in the abolitionist struggle. Huber responded to this depiction of slavery on an affective level. In her memory, the encounter with the image turned into an emotional awakening in which she finally acknowledged Africans as her 'brothers' and felt the need to become active to end their abuse as slaves.

This late 'conversion' to abolitionism – Huber was already in her fifties – is remarkable, as her knowledge of Africans sold into slavery far pre-dates the encounter. As early as 1794, in her observations on Poland, she had compared the docility of the unfree labourers and peasants in the face of aristocratic brutality with the capacity for discontent and resistance of enslaved Africans.[48] In 1823 she published an article in the *Morgenblatt*, recounting the history of the discourse on the Atlantic slave system in the German territories from her own memory and experience. Here, she focused on the scientific debate that evolved in the field of anthropology in the late eighteenth century around the question of 'similar mental capacities' and 'human rights' of black and white people. She highlighted the fact that in this debate, her first husband, Georg Forster, was one of the early advocates of the equality of the races. Huber also explained that through the first-hand experience of the Hessian mercenaries, who had fought in the American War of Independence, reliable and condemnatory views on slavery reached the German territories: they 'spread the revulsion against it from mouth to mouth'. And she also told her readers that in the 1780s she had encountered formerly enslaved people in person who had come with the mercenaries to the German states after the end of the war and had formed a so-called 'negro colony' in Kassel.[49]

Moreover, it seems that her first husband as well as her uncle Johann Friedrich Blumenbach were not the only members of her family who were explicitly critical of the Atlantic slave system. Her brother Carl Heyne (1762–96) seems to have been affected by the fate of the enslaved as well. This

46   See for example Huber to Caroline Carus, Leipzig, 21 May 1819, *Briefe*, VII.I, p. 243.
47   Huber to J. G. Cotta'sche Buchhandlung, Stuttgart, October 1819, *Briefe*, VII.I, p. 372.
48   [Huber], 'Fragmente über einen Theil von Pohlen', 1794/3, p. 260.
49   'Hayti'sche Kultur', *Morgenblatt für gebildete Stände* (henceforth *Morgenblatt*) 49 (26 February 1823), 194f. The article continued over four subsequent issues: 50 (27 February 1823), 198f; 54 (4 March 1823), 215; 56 (6 March 1823), 223f; 57 (7 March 1823), 225–7. On the 'Black Hessians', see George Fenwick Jones, 'The Black Hessians: Negroes Recruited by the Hessians in South Carolina and Other Colonies', *South Carolina Historical Magazine* 83 (October 1982), 287–302; Maria I. Diedrich, 'From American Slaves to Hessian Subjects. Silenced Black Narratives of the American Revolution', *Germany and the Black Diaspora: Points of Contact, 1250–1914*, ed. M. Honeck, M. Klimke and A. Kuhlmann (New York, 2013), pp. 92–111.

is clear from the sketch that he drew in a friend's autograph book during his time at Göttingen University.[50] The drawing was a copy of one of the illustrations in Bernardin de Saint-Pierre's *Voyage à l'Isle de France*, published in 1773, which showed a half-naked enslaved woman with her children. Heyne's sketch bore the original caption, too: 'What causes you pleasure has been moistened with our tears.'[51] It thus seems likely that the topic was a subject of discussion within Huber's own family circle.

Why, then, did it take Huber so long to embrace the cause of enslaved people as her own and to shift from being a mere spectator to seeing herself as an activist? It is conceivable that the specific moment of Huber's 'conversion' to the abolitionist cause was a retrospective construct of her own making. For one thing, the image she describes would have been extremely unusual on a piece of anti-slavery paraphernalia; the typical image which became the emblem of the abolitionist campaign on both sides of the Atlantic depicted an African man in chains kneeling and pleading accompanied by the phrase 'Am I not a man and a brother?'[52] Huber's purpose in deliberately misremembering, or constructing, the episode could have been to convince Grégoire of her sincere commitment, trying to strengthen her connection with the famous abolitionist through this shared cause by emphasising the specific moment at which she, too, became an authentic activist. The shift in her own perception that she portrayed does display the conventional features of a religious awakening in the Pietist tradition. Huber was Lutheran but was familiar with Pietism and it featured in some of her writings.[53] By constructing a narrative of conversion and by bonding over this shared experience, Huber may have hoped to induce Grégoire to provide her with additional materials on the subject for publication in the *Morgenblatt*.

But there might have been other factors that played into her late interest in the abolitionist cause. In her 1823 article in the *Morgenblatt*, Huber writes that in her generation even the 'most carefully educated' had been strongly prejudiced against black people 'through their education in school and general opinion'.[54] In the article, she contrasted this pervasive prejudice of her childhood years with changing attitudes and information that had reached the German states during the intervening decades. For instance, she pointed

50 For the drawing and the printed original, see the Introduction to this volume.

51 'Ce qui sert à vos plaisirs est mouillé de nos larmes', in [Jacques-Henri Bernardin de Saint-Pierre], *Voyage à l'Isle de France, à l'Isle de Bourbon, au Cap de Bonne-Espérance: Avec des Observations nouvelles sur la Nature & sur les Hommes: Par un Officier du Roi* (Amsterdam, 1773).

52 J. R. Oldfield, *Popular Politics and British Anti-Slavery: The Mobilisation of Public Opinion against the Slave Trade, 1787–1807* (London, 1998), pp. 157f. In fact, the range of imagery and artefacts is certainly wider than has so far been reconstructed.

53 For example, Therese Huber, *Das Urtheil der Welt* (Frankfurt a.M. and Leipzig, 1805), *Hannah, der Herrnhuterin Deborah Findling* (Leipzig, 1821).

54 'Hayti'sche Kultur', *Morgenblatt* 49 (26 February 1823), 194.

to the establishment of the black-controlled Republic of Haiti, which proved, Huber argued, 'that black people have the same powers as whites'.[55] Given global developments, Huber showed herself convinced that no one could still uphold the old prejudices under the changing circumstances.

Yet despite her awareness of the unjust treatment of black people under slavery – and the widespread awareness among European intellectuals of developments in the Atlantic world – Huber, by her own account, only committed herself to their cause after seeing the image on the medallion. This finding corresponds with the thesis of the French sociologist Luc Boltanski who claims that a visual 'spectacle of suffering', in which the distress of distinct individuals has to be presented to the spectator, is necessary to bring about the shift from a mere acknowledgement of a grievance to active partici-pation on behalf of the sufferers.[56] Accordingly, the knowledge that Huber had previously acquired can be seen as the necessary breeding ground, the source of a basic understanding that provided fertile soil for her conversion to abolitionist ideology, while the encounter with a powerful visual repre-sentation of the suffering connected with the Atlantic slave system finally brought this transformation about.[57]

It was in her private correspondence that Huber was most outspoken in her critique of slavery and in disclosing her agency, and the letters did more than record her opinions. For her as for other women of her time, the letter was a work of self-creation. Gert Mattenklott has characterised women's letters in this period as 'the imaginative space of action, the intimised public space that has to compensate for what reality withholds from this curious romantic generation of females'.[58] In fact, Huber's epistolary practice was less a compensation than a beginning for and a reflection on her public action, constrained though that action was. In the first years after her conversion, as Huber confided to Grégoire, she saw herself surrounded by what she perceived as the general apathy of her fellow citizens. A letter of October 1822 offers an explicit reflection on the relationship between knowing, feeling and acting. She complained that other Germans displayed a general 'inattention to [the arguments of] intellectuals, especially when it comes to the history of our age'. She was disturbed by the fact that many events that 'wound us, overwhelm us' were too quickly forgotten 'because of the way they follow continuously one upon the other'. In this instance, she was again using

55   'Hayti'sche Kultur: Fortsetzung', *Morgenblatt* 50 (27 February 1823), 198.
56   Luc Boltanski, *Distant Suffering: Morality, Media and Politics* (Cambridge, 2004), pp. 30–2.
57   It is also worth remembering that as a wife and mother who moved around frequently and bore ten children, Huber faced demands on her physical and mental energies in her youth that will have limited her scope for action and reflection. On this, see: Heuser, 'Jakobinerin', p. 147.
58   Gert Mattenklott, 'Romantische Frauenkultur. Bettina von Arnim zum Beispiel', *Frauen – Literatur – Geschichte: Schreibende Frauen vom Mittelalter bis zur Gegenwart*, ed. H. Gnüg and R. Möhrmann (Stuttgart, 1985), pp. 123–43.

the example of the development of Haiti during the decades following the revolution to illustrate this point. Huber expected of herself and her contemporaries a more critical interest in the world, insisting that they face up to the moments of progress present in social upheavals rather than turning away from the spectacle of suffering: 'But the thinking being, rising above the pain which each day teaches him to know or suspect, is often amazed at the results which the years just past present.' She thus demanded of her contemporaries an active engagement with global developments, like the rise of the state of Haiti. For her, paying attention to such developments and thus 'watching this black population take their place among Christians and free human beings' provided 'a mitigation of our pains'.[59]

Once Huber's interest in the topic of slavery had been aroused, she faced the problem of how to get involved. She told Grégoire that she had decided to see her priest to get his advice but 'he only answered me in a confused way because in that time knowledge was still in many ways strictly separated from opinion, even among the most well intentioned of men'.[60] Here we see Huber reflecting explicitly on the gap between knowing about injustice and acknowledging it as such, and also on the impact that dissonance had on people's capacity to speak. Of herself, she wrote to Grégoire that she was fully committed to this 'noble cause ... For it and for my children I would never shy away from pleading.'[61] Announcing her sympathy for the abolitionist cause in the same breath as her affection for her children was a statement that should not be underestimated. As her letters indicate, she identified with the dominant public discourse on women being mothers first and foremost.[62] The political situation and the remaining feudal divisions in the early nineteenth century did indeed make for a discrepancy between the possibilities of thinking and acting within the accepted parameters of public discourse and within the general rules of conduct, and this was even more the case for women who were not supposed to step from the private into the public realm to express strong views or become actively engaged in political or social issues. The virtual absence of women from public life in the German states provided a critical and concerned woman like Huber with few avenues for public engagement or leadership. Literary scholar Barbara Becker-Cantarino has argued that, as a woman, Huber could only present her political views through works of literary fiction.[63] But in fact, she found other ways to express her convictions.

59   AC, folder 'France – H', Huber to Grégoire, Stuttgart, 19 October 1822.
60   AC, folder 'Allemagne', Huber to Grégoire, Augsburg, 4 July 1826.
61   AC, folder 'Allemagne', Huber to Grégoire, Stuttgart, 27 February 1823.
62   Hilmes, *Skandalgeschichten*, p. 47.
63   Barbara Becker-Cantarino, 'Revolution im Patriarchat: Therese Forster-Huber (1764–1829)', *Out of Line/Ausgefallen. The Paradox of Marginality in the Writings of 19th Century Women*, ed. R.-E. Boetcher-Joeres and M. Burkhard (Amsterdam, 1989), pp. 235–53, here p. 251.

The Dissemination of Anti-slavery Sentiment
Through the *Morgenblatt*

Huber did not limit the expression of her abhorrence for the slave trade, evidence of 'the most reprehensible egoism',[64] to her private correspondence. She regularly included articles about aspects of the slave trade and slavery itself in the *Morgenblatt*. Of her intention to present this material to her readers, she told Grégoire, 'I want to instruct them'. She was especially eager to impress 'the right point of view' on her audience. As her motivation, she pointed towards her obligation to God to 'produce a happier future', especially by 'shaping the youth which I am able to influence so that they deserve it'. In response to the developments in Haiti, Huber wrote that she wanted 'first of all to make them [her readers] see the mysterious and admirable ways that the providence chooses to enlighten humankind'.[65]

Regarding her role as an author, Huber once told a friend, 'I think I have not written a single one of these short articles without a clear, decided moral agenda.'[66] Nevertheless, Huber had to pay attention to the kind of audience she was addressing with her journal, confiding to another friend that 'that kind of reader wants to be entertained or provoked; he will take in the moral subconsciously, if it is God's will'.[67] Nevertheless, as a child of the Enlightenment, Huber defined it her duty as a writer to educate the masses and to use that platform to advance change. She was herself aware of her privileged position in this regard, marvelling at the number of people that she reached with her writing and at her 'extraordinarily wide sphere of influence':

> It is surely crazy to think that I influence the composition of ideas of 5000 people and more every day … Among the many thousands there are only a few who are anything but BLOCK HEADS, but even they live and move in the world, and the pebble that falls in the ocean sends out its circles into infinity.[68]

In fashioning herself in the role of an educator, she could engage with the significant political and social controversies surrounding slavery while remaining within the socially acceptable conventions for women at that time.

But how did Huber try to instruct her German readers and impress on them the importance of the cause that was close to her heart? First of all, it is important to take a look at the situation in which she found herself during the

64 AC, folder 'Allemagne', Huber to Grégoire, Augsburg, 4 July 1826.
65 AC, folder 'Allemagne', Huber to Grégoire, Stuttgart, 22 July 1823.
66 Huber to Henriette von Reden (c.1818), cited in Hahn, 'Wie ein Mannskleid', p. 119.
67 Huber to Georg Müller, Schaffhausen, 1 October 1819, *Briefe*, VII.I, p. 353.
68 Huber to Johann Gotthard Reinhold, Stuttgart, 2 May 1818, *Briefe*, VI.I, p. 593 ('BLOCK HEADS' in English in the original).

late 1810s and early 1820s, in particular the circumstances that afforded her with opportunities that most women did not have at their disposal, as well as the social structures that continued to limit her possibilities to become active on other levels. In the late eighteenth century there was a short flowering of periodicals for women edited by women such as Sophie von La Roche and Marianne Ehrmann, but as self-published journals they were unable to compete in an increasingly commercialised and professionalised literary market, and by the turn of the century they had all collapsed. In the following years, female editors almost totally disappeared from the periodicals market. As a consequence, historian Ulrike Weckel has argued that 'journalism ... increasingly became the domain of male professionals, and it remained so for a long time'.[69] As one of the first female editors of a journal which addressed both male and female readers Huber thus faced particular challenges. At the same time, her position afforded her the rare opportunity to express her opinions publicly nearly every day.

As editor she was faced with the daily task of reading and assessing the articles and poems that were sent to the *Morgenblatt* for publication. The evaluation and selection of copy for the journal took up most of Huber's time.[70] This job was made even more difficult by her employer Cotta who expected to vet all of her choices and often questioned her judgement. He continued to stress, for example, that the *Morgenblatt* was not a political journal, and he was afraid that under the reactionary restrictions of the 1819 Carlsbad Decrees overly critical reporting could incite censorship or lead to complaints by public figures like foreign ambassadors.[71] Because of the editorial control exerted by Cotta, Huber was not free to include whatever she wanted in the journal. From time to time, her employer's meddling and the amount of work and responsibility that lay on her shoulders was difficult for Huber to bear.[72] Repeatedly, she referred to her status as that of a 'slave'[73] or 'serf',[74] imagining how she would 'throw off this *Morgenblatt*, this slavery, these bonds once my Aimé [her son] is finished [with his education]'.[75]

69   Ulrike Weckel, 'The Brief Flowering of Women's Journalism and Its End around 1800', *Gender in Transition: Discourse and Practice in German-Speaking Europe, 1750–1830*, ed. U. Gleixner and M. W. Gray (Ann Arbor, 2006), pp. 175–201, here p. 191.
70   See for example Huber to Carl August Böttiger, Stuttgart, 17 April 1819, *Briefe*, VII.I, p. 214, and Heuser, 'Lektüre', p. 168.
71   See for example Huber to Johann Friedrich von Cotta, Stuttgart, 11 February 1819 and Huber to Friedrich Wilhelm Gubitz, Stuttgart, 22 June 1819, *Briefe*, VII.I, pp. 146 and 277 respectively.
72   See for instance Huber to Johann Gotthard Reinhold, Stuttgart, 29 January 1819, or Huber to Therese Forster, Stuttgart, 1 April 1819, *Briefe*, VII.I, pp. 139 and 203 respectively.
73   Huber to Pauline von Zeppelin, Stuttgart, 25 June 1819, *Briefe*, VII.I, p. 279.
74   Huber to Friedrich Arnold Brockhaus, Stuttgart, 7 April 1820, *Briefe*, VII.I, p. 548.
75   Huber to Paul Usteri, Stuttgart, 29 December 1818, *Briefe*, VII.I, p. 105.

Another obstacle was that some male contributors to the magazine also questioned her competence because of her sex, repeatedly accusing Huber of being inept.[76] As a consequence and with Cotta's agreement, Huber hid behind the gender-neutral label of 'editorial staff', which deliberately obscured that she was in fact for a long time the only employee in charge.[77] For the same reason, she never signed her name to any piece in the *Morgenblatt* that was penned by her, choosing instead to remain anonymous. She was conscious of the fact that, as a professional female writer and journalist, she moved at the margins of what was socially acceptable at the time and she was very careful not to overstep those boundaries. For this reason, Huber carefully fashioned a public image of herself as a widowed housewife who had to work to support her children and would like nothing more than to instantly return to the privacy of her home – and one who would do so as soon as circumstances allowed.[78] Thus, during her time as editor-in-chief of the *Morgenblatt*, Huber had to fathom the socially acceptable space in which she, as a woman, could safely make her voice heard. As a consequence, these general difficulties and restrictions also took their toll as she crafted her critique of the Atlantic slave system for which Huber had to fall back on certain strategies.

During Huber's tenure as editor of the *Morgenblatt*, the topics of slavery and the slave trade were featured in a variety of forms. What is most striking is that they were generally discussed in apparently factual genres with little fictional treatment of the subject. As Matthew Sangster has pointed out, journals generally served as 'gate keepers'. It was only through their mediation – either by review or by presenting extracts – that many published works, and especially those by foreign authors, became known to the reading public.[79] Translation thus played an important role. Long perceived 'as a second-rate literary activity and therefore more suitable for women', translation is now regarded as 'a creative, even dangerous act', and the translator as 'a powerful agent for cultural change'.[80] Through translations, women had the chance to participate in significant contemporary debates even by presenting radical ideas, while at the same time being able to keep their distance by stressing the fact that they were only the medium through which the texts had been

---

76   See for example Huber to Friedrich Wilhelm Gubitz, Stuttgart, 18 February 1819, *Briefe*, VII.I, p. 156.

77   Hahn, 'Wie ein Mannskleid', p. 129; but, according to Huber, Cotta wanted that as well: Huber to Friedrich Arnold Brockhaus, Stuttgart, 17 January 1820, *Briefe*, VII.I, p. 465.

78   A strategy that had already been adopted by the first generation of female editors: see Weckel, 'The Brief Flowering', p. 193.

79   Matthew Sangster, 'Adapting to Dissect: Rhetoric and Representation in the Quarterly Reviews in the Romantic Period', *Romantic Adaptations: Essays in Mediation and Remediation*, ed. C. Duffy, P. Howell and C. Ruddell (Burlington, VT, 2013), pp. 57–72, here p. 63.

80   Caroline Bland and Hilary Brown, 'Introduction: Women as Cultural Mediators and Translators', *Oxford German Studies* 42/2 (August 2013), 111–18, here pp. 111f.

made accessible.[81] The review form, too, placed a female author or editor in a position of power. Werner Faulstich argues that the work of the literary critic was central to the way the public perceived texts. As an 'expert', the critic had the chance to shape the judgement of the work by the journal's readership.[82] And Sangster points out that critics often used their position as intermediary to present their readership only with those quotations, abstracts or synopses which supported the critic's position or the point that he or she wanted to make.[83]

In the *Morgenblatt*, most articles in which the slave trade and/or slavery were featured were extracts from travelogues, primarily translations from French or English originals. Usually, the names of the respective authors – all of them men – were given in the first instalment of the article. Most of these travel reports offered critical discussions of the consequences of the slave trade on the West African coast or the condition of the enslaved in the New World, mainly in the USA, Cuba or Brazil. Huber, who translated many of these stories, often took the chance to frame the narratives with further information on the slave trade and slavery, thus shaping the way in which her audience would read and interpret the pieces. Tellingly, when one of the reports was actually in favour of slavery the 'editorial staff' included a statement distancing 'themselves' from this opinion, by placing the piece in perspective and trying to find an explanation of how the author had come to such a view.[84] As a translator of long travel journals, Huber could also decide which part of the traveller's observation 'was the most worth knowing for Germany'[85] often deciding to single out extracts that dealt with first-hand experiences of slavery or the slave trade.

Huber also exerted her own agency through the choice of texts that she decided to translate. For instance, she repeatedly found it worthwhile to introduce her readers to institutions that were active in the abolitionist movement.[86] She also included updates on developments in Haiti and the freedmen's colony Sierra Leone. It is striking that in all these articles she made a point of naming the sources from which she had taken her information, such as annual reports of institutions and associations, journals from Haiti or newspapers from Sierra Leone.[87] Again, she never failed to embed these

---

81   Ibid., p. 115.

82   Werner Faulstich, *Die bürgerliche Mediengesellschaft, 1700–1830* (Tübingen, 2002), p. 231.

83   Sangster, 'Adapting to Dissect', p. 64.

84   'Englischer Literaturbericht vom Monat December 1817: Fortsetzung', *Morgenblatt: Literaturblatt* 7 (1818), 27.

85   'Englischer Literaturbericht vom August und September 1818', *Morgenblatt: Literatur-Blatt* 45 (1818), 756.

86   For example 'Die Jahresfeyer der kirchlichen Missionsgesellschaft in London', *Morgenblatt* 221 (15 September 1818), 882f.

87   'Das dankbare Hayti', *Morgenblatt* 208 (30 August 1820), 834; 'Ausflug nach Sierra-Leone und an die Küsten des westlichen Afrika', *Morgenblatt* 257 (26 October 1820), 1030f.

reports in a framework that led her readers to a particular interpretation of
the information, not by urging the injustice of the slave trade and slavery but
by demonstratively taking it for granted that every single one of her readers
had surely already condemned these practices. Another way of transmitting
information on the slave trade and slavery was by featuring them regularly in
reports of the *Morgenblatt*'s own correspondents, primarily in reports from
Paris and London. In particular, the journal's Paris correspondent, Georg
Bernhard Depping (1784–1853), frequently included information on France's
stance towards the suppression of the slave trade, while not refraining from
expressing his own annoyance at the failure of the government actually to
suppress it.[88]

In short, Huber had a clear and consistent strategy when it came to keeping
her readers aware of the negative consequences of slavery and the slave trade.
She did not openly speak in her own voice on the slaves' behalf, instead hiding
behind the label of 'editorial staff' or using the voices of male experts, either
as correspondents or eyewitnesses, to convey critical opinions. In presenting
developments within the Atlantic world that in her view were beneficial to
the overall cause of abolition, she provided clear references, never giving an
opinion without backing it up by a reliable source of some sort.

In terms of content, slavery featured as a topic in a wide array of articles
published in the *Morgenblatt*. The issue was discussed not only in its contemporary form in the Atlantic world, but also in its historical and global dimensions.[89] Many articles, mainly travelogues, only touched briefly on the topic
without further comment from the 'editorial staff'. In this context, the terms
'slave' and 'slavery' in their broadest meanings were also regularly featured in
fictional works such as poems or stories and fairy tales.[90] While there were no
fictional stories on chattel slavery there were, for example, many that were set
in the 'Orient' and featured slaves.[91] In these narratives, they mainly served
as exotic parts of the scenery and, interestingly, the practice of slavery in this
context passed without comment by Huber.

An analysis of the volumes that were published between 1817 and 1823
shows that there were some changes over time. In the early issues the main
focus was still on European Christians who had experienced slavery at first
hand in the Barbary states and reported their adventures after their rescue.
Interestingly, in these articles there were some links to the enslavement of

88   For example 'Korrespondenz-Nachrichten: Paris, 21. Juli', *Morgenblatt* 209 (1 September 1823), 835f.
89   On slavery in the ancient world see for example 'Staatenkunst', *Morgenblatt: Literaturblatt* 1 (1 January 1822), 1–3; on slavery on Java: 'Die Bewohner des indischen Archipels', *Morgenblatt* 12 (14 January 1822), 45f.
90   For example 'Prolog', *Morgenblatt* 70 (22 March 1822), 280.
91   For example 'Die Prinzessin mit den Rosen und der Kater mit den Dornen: Ein Mährchen', *Morgenblatt* 184 (2 August 1823), 733–5.

black people as well. Huber used the depiction of how enslaved Christians were psychologically affected by the horrible circumstances and degradation under which they suffered to comment on slavery in general and, in particular, to discredit the argument that blacks, considered to be naturally inferior to whites, were made to be slaves and so 'according to the planters, entirely unworthy of our sympathy'.[92] She explained to her readers that their state was actually a result of the circumstances that they had to endure.

In 1819, the articles which dealt directly with the Atlantic slave trade began to become more numerous, and this supports the thesis of her 'conversion' around 1818. The focus on the trade was strategic: slavery was in general repugnant to Huber, but the *Morgenblatt* reserved its most direct attacks for the slave trade or criticised the unjust treatment of the enslaved without demanding a general end to the practice of slavery itself. Repeatedly, the articles demanded that all European powers had to do their utmost to end the 'scandalous slave trade'.[93] The journal thereby avoided challenging the dominant discourse on this issue: while there was a relative consensus in regard to the slave trade during the 1820s in the Atlantic world, the abolition of slavery itself was a more controversial issue. Abolitionists were divided between those who demanded immediate abolition and those campaigning for a gradual approach.[94] The frequency of pieces on the slave trade remained relatively high during the next years. In September 1820, for example, the London correspondent of the *Morgenblatt* informed its readers that 'all the communications that we are receiving here on the negro trade do agree that this inhuman line of business is still going on with the same indecent fervour, the same cruelty and most of the time with the same success as ever'.[95]

The *Morgenblatt* articles traced all kinds of current developments in the Atlantic world around this issue, but again and again they reached the same conclusion:

> that this despicable trade will never stop until the Africans themselves stop dragging their fellow human beings to the market, and this change of heart can only gradually occur through the erection of free colonies of Christian negroes along the coast and under the protection of all Christian naval powers.[96]

92 'Reisebemerkungen über die Küsten der Barbarey: Fortsetzung', *Morgenblatt* 293 (9 December 1817), 1170.
93 'Der Negerhandel', *Morgenblatt* 65 (17 March 1819), 259.
94 Brigitte Bader-Zar, 'Abolitionism in the Atlantic World: The Organization and Interaction of Anti-Slavery Movements in the Eighteenth and Nineteenth Centuries', *European History Online*, published by the Institute of European History (Mainz, 12 September 2011), http://www.ieg-ego.eu/baderzaarb-2010-en (accessed 6 March 2015).
95 'Korrespondenz-Nachrichten: Aus London', *Morgenblatt* 213 (5 September 1820), 856.
96 Ibid.

For Huber – as for many of her contemporaries – the work of European missionaries was thus inseparably linked with the abolition of the slave trade and slavery itself. Consequently, throughout her time as editor-in-chief, she kept introducing her German audience to Christian organisations engaged in missionary projects, such as the British Church Missionary Society, the African Institution, various Bible Societies and the Augustine Society in Philadelphia. While Huber was generally convinced of the equality of the races she thus accepted and replicated the dominant discourse in the Atlantic world that Europe was indeed culturally superior to Africa, supporting the colonisation of Africa on the basis of a vision of universal progress shaped after the European ideal. As evidence for the prospects of progress she repeatedly stressed developments in Sierra Leone, which, according to her, was flourishing under European guidance. This vision of a European civilising mission was not incompatible with the evidence she insistently produced about the equal social, moral and mental capacities of black people.[97] Closer to the more radical position she articulated in her letters was the *Morgenblatt*'s reporting on Haiti, where former slaves were building a society free from the domination of whites. In lengthy articles, the journal traced the history and development of the country, praising it on many levels and even allowing its readers to hear the voices of Haitian writers via translations from Haitian journals.[98]

Huber and Grégoire: The Flow of Information Across Borders

An analysis of her articles makes clear that Huber was able to draw on a wide array of pamphlets, circular letters, and other sources which had been produced by opponents of slavery in France, Great Britain, Haiti and the USA. But how was she able to obtain these first-hand sources on abolitionist developments in the Atlantic realm in the provincial town of Stuttgart? To begin with, she profited from her position as an employee of Cotta as she was able to order many books and journals through his publishing house and bookshop.[99] For scarcer printed sources, she had to rely on her personal network: for example, her connection with the British ambassador.

97   For examples, see 'Die westafrikanischen Vereine christlicher Civilisation', *Morgenblatt* 280 (22 November 1820), 1121; 'Die freye Neger-Kolonie von Sierra-Leone', *Morgenblatt* (8 November 1819), 1007; 'Der astronomische Neger-Koch', *Morgenblatt* 248 (16 October 1820), 994.
98   See for example 'Das dankbare Hayti', *Morgenblatt* 208 (30 August 1820), 834f and *Morgenblatt* 209 (31 August 1820), 839f.
99   See for instance Huber to J. G. Cotta'sche Buchhandlung, Stuttgart, August 1819, *Briefe*, VII.I, p. 331.

Interestingly, she repeatedly broached this matter in her letters to Grégoire, pointing out that she was very thankful for his help in sending her important sources. In seven of the surviving ten letters, she acknowledged the receipt of materials related to the Atlantic slave system. The diversity of sources with which Grégoire supplied Huber is striking. He sent her his own writings, such as the *Manuel de piété, à l'usage des hommes de couleur et des noirs*, pamphlets and brochures of anti-slavery institutions, journals published by black writers in Haiti and an abolitionist poem which, as Huber admitted, 'has touched me profoundly'.[100] The amount of the materials he provided for her is surprisingly large. For instance, Huber thanked Grégoire in 1823 for the 'big parcel from your hand which held very precious brochures all of your composition and the gazettes from Haiti'[101] and in 1826 she expressed her gratitude for 'several of your precious writings'.[102]

Whereas Grégoire seems to have sent such anti-slavery materials to other correspondents without them having explicitly requested them, it was different with Therese Huber. She told him explicitly about the value that the materials held for her. In 1823, for example, she wrote Grégoire:

> The package of writings from Haiti which you were so kind as to provide me with is very precious to me, I have taken the occasion to compose an article in the journal that I am editing in which I am introducing these journals to the public, I have taken the opportunity to speak about the negroes and their position and about the good you have done on their behalf.[103]

And she repeatedly pleaded with Grégoire to provide her with more such materials. In the same 1823 letter, she wrote: 'I would not dare to adjure you to continue to supply me with the journals solely as a favour to me ... [I]t is for the instruction of our public in favour of the good cause.'

Grégoire thus not only informed Huber about his own work in this shared cause but also enabled her to make herself familiar with the campaigns being undertaken throughout the Atlantic world. Through Huber and the *Morgenblatt*, the German public too was made aware of these develop-ments, and there is some evidence that Huber also used her fictional writing to introduce abolitionist ideas to (in the case of her fiction, mainly female) readers.[104] The cooperation between Huber and Grégoire was fruitful even though the flow of information on slavery and the slave trade was relatively unbalanced, passing primarily from Paris to Stuttgart.

---

100   AC, folder 'Allemagne', Huber to Grégoire, n.d.
101   AC, folder 'Allemagne', Huber to Grégoire, Stuttgart, 22 July 1823.
102   AC, folder 'Allemagne', Huber to Grégoire, Augsburg, 4 July 1826.
103   AC, folder 'Allemagne', Huber to Grégoire, 27 February 1823.
104   See, for example, Therese Huber, *Ellen Percy oder Erziehung durch Schicksale* (Leipzig, 1822) which is an adaptation of a British novel.

The Flow of Information in the German Territories:
The Case of Huber's Private Network

Therese Huber's engagement in the abolitionist cause involved passing on information herself, extending her activism to her private network. In her first letter in 1822 she thanked Grégoire for the 'journals and interesting pieces that you have forwarded to me' and explained to him that 'there are some among them that I pass on to individuals who can take lasting advantage from them because their vocation calls on them to concern themselves with such subjects'.[105] Recently, she wrote to Grégoire, she had persuaded 'a man who works daily with the King' to read the annual report of the African Institution which Grégoire had sent her. It is very likely that she was referring to King William I of Württemberg (1781–1864), who had recently abolished the practice of serfdom in his dominions. Huber was living in the kingdom and was friends with several of his close employees. It is possible that the person she had provided with the report was Heinrich von Trott zu Solz (1783–1840) who was in charge of foreign affairs and one of her close acquaintances.[106] In this context, Huber told Grégoire that she was aware that the chances for change were generally relatively small but she believed that it was still possible:

> Man in general is such a powerless being that we must not let pass any chance to communicate beneficial ideas, even at the risk that they will fail their purpose a hundred and a thousand times, as long as one of them takes root the 101st or the 1001st time.

She assured Grégoire that she dedicated herself tirelessly to the distribution of knowledge that seemed relevant to her in her personal circle of friends and acquaintances, for instance by lending them 'good books' and 'by talking to and advising whoever is willing to listen to me'. Thanks to this commitment she had already often had the pleasure 'of convincing myself that after some years the seed that I had spread randomly has germinated and is bearing fruit'.[107] In her efforts to enlighten her fellow Germans about slavery and the slave trade, Huber functioned as a mediator of ideas on several levels. She did more than distribute books and pamphlets: she engaged her friends and acquaintances in direct conversations on the topic, working to foster anti-slavery sentiment in her own circle. In particular, she tried to carry the idea of

---

105   AC, folder 'France – H', Huber to Grégoire, Stuttgart, 19 October 1822.
106   See, for example, Huber to Therese Forster, Stuttgart, 1 April 1819 and Huber to Friedrich Arnold Brockhaus, Stuttgart, 30 April 1819, *Briefe*, VII.I, pp. 204 and 224 respectively.
107   AC, folder 'France – H', Huber to Grégoire, Stuttgart, 19 October 1822.

abolition to those with the means or the connections to bring about change. As the above example shows, she understood quite well that it could be of value to the abolitionist movement to have allies to their cause in the ranks of the European monarchies. Stepping outside her private circle, as her letter to Grégoire indicates, she chose again to operate behind the scenes, using a male acquaintance as spokesman on behalf of her cause. Even though she had met the King of Württemberg on a prior occasion, she decided against bringing the matter up herself, apparently limiting her own actions to the private sphere in accordance with the expectations for women. Rather, she sought to extend her influence to the public sphere by mobilising her social capital to arouse the interest of public figures in the cause of enslaved Blacks.

Conclusion

The interchange of ideas and material between Therese Huber and the Abbé is very suggestive about the ways in which knowledge about the slave trade and slavery entered and circulated in the German territories. It is clear that the flow of information was facilitated not only by German journalists translating and mediating material from foreign magazines and newspapers, but also through the publications of abolitionists themselves, which were distributed through private networks across borders. Interestingly, the case also bears witness to the interest that the transnational activist Grégoire had in getting the German people involved in the abolitionist cause. The Abbé's personal network meant that his activism was not limited to the Atlantic world but reached far into the Central European hinterlands, and he clearly believed it worthwhile to gain support from regions that, at first glance, were not obviously linked to the Atlantic slave system.

Therese Huber was one of those who were willing to support Grégoire in his campaign at the margins of the traditional Atlantic world. As an editor and journalist, Huber clearly also profited on a professional level from her collaboration with Grégoire, who provided her with rare and exciting material with which she could enhance the profile and standing of her journal. But even if the story of her 'conversion' to abolitionism was a strategic move to encourage Grégoire to send material and to convince him of her sincerity, it seems clear that Grégoire's trust in her was not misplaced. While there were activists who were more radical in expression and outspoken and active in their support of the abolitionist movement, it seems appropriate to apply the term 'abolitionist' to Huber. Whatever the exact starting point of her interest in furthering the abolitionist movement, once committed she supported the cause both in her influential role as a journalist and editor-in-chief, and as a private individual within her circle, which included influential contemporaries.

Throughout her adult life, Huber was concerned with the discourse on freedom and human rights. On a personal level, she had repeatedly experienced social ostracism as a woman and as a writer, and she perceived her professional relationship with her employer Cotta as a form of slavery. These experiences and her own restricted social position probably made it easier for her to empathise with the fate of enslaved Blacks. In contrast to women in the Anglo-American sphere, Huber also encountered a form of unfreedom that she judged to be 'slavery' at first hand during her time in Poland: serfdom. This experience surely had an influence on her understanding of the consequences of such imbalanced power structures. Another impulse to activism was her belief that as a Christian it was her duty to ease the suffering of her fellow human beings, and this sense of personal philanthropic duty extended to the way she understood her role as a writer. Nor did she exempt her fellow Germans from responsibility for global human improvement. As a member of the European 'republic of letters' she was sceptical of nationalist tendencies and embraced a cosmopolitan identity. The *Morgenblatt* articles pointed out over and over again that all powers of Europe had to step in to end the slave trade, but they did so in German.

Huber believed in the injustice of the Atlantic slave system and in the general equality of the races. She was convinced that, through the *Morgenblatt*, she could transmit these opinions to her readers as well. Having experienced denunciation in the aftermath of the French Revolution and aware of the professional consequences of being too outspoken, Huber still moved within the limitations of the dominant critical discourse, particularly in her public statements. The national and cultural context in which she operated meant that her agency was also limited by the local social structures and cultural norms that shaped the public sphere. The topics of slavery and the slave trade could hardly be expected to mobilise sentiment in the German public on the same scale that it did in Great Britain. Transatlantic slavery was, after all, at the margins of the everyday interests of most people, and the scope for popular agitation of any kind was limited in the German states in the post-Napoleonic order. In the absence of an institutionalised movement, abolitionists like Huber had to work alone, unable to organise large-scale forms of protest such as petitions or mass boycotts. Moreover, as a respectable woman Huber would have far overstepped the limits of what was socially acceptable in taking to any public platform that was available. But Huber's example shows that the tools for the expression of humanitarian sentiment available to women extended beyond the familiar fall-back of popular fiction.

At this stage of research, it is difficult to be sure how far Huber's efforts moved her readers or her friends to become active on behalf of enslaved people of African descent. But it can safely be said that Cotta would not have allowed her to publish so many articles on the subject if there had not been a genuine interest in the past and future of slavery and the slave trade among her readers. In this context, it would be interesting to investigate how Huber's room for manoeuvre changed when she lost her privileged position as editor of the *Morgenblatt*. Her letters to Grégoire show that she remained interested in the topic.[108] Moreover, while the transfer of information between Huber and Grégoire seems to have been largely one-way, from France to the German principalities, the campaign of Victor Aimé, Huber's son and a protégé of her old friend Humboldt, for suppression of the French slave trade in the 1820s, is evidence of a more dynamic and sustained circulation of information, argument and sentiment.

108   See for example Therese Huber, 'Bugh Jargal: Eine Erzählung aus der Zeit der Neger in Peru und in Haiti', *Morgenblatt* 76–86 and 88–95 (1826), as cited in: Brigitte Leuschner, ed., *Schriftstellerinnen und Schwesterseelen: Der Briefwechsel zwischen Therese Huber (1764–1829) und Karoline Pichler (1769–1843)* (Marburg, 2001), p. 195.

Afterword

CATHERINE HALL

In his *History of Jamaica*, published in 1774, Edward Long reminded his readers of how vital the slavery business was to the wealth of Great Britain. 'If,' he wrote, 'we revolve in our minds, what an amazing variety of trades receive their daily support, as many of them did originally their being, from the calls of the Africa and West India markets,' if we reflected, he continued on the numbers of artisans, tradespeople, merchants, sailors and seamen whose livelihood was connected with those markets, 'we may from thence form a competent idea of the prodigious value of our sugar colonies, and a just conception of their immense importance to the grandeur and prosperity of their mother country.'[1] Britain was a major colonial power, the slavery business a vital source of wealth. For the German hinterlands, and Denmark, a minor player, yet significant, in the colonial world, the scale of interest was very different. But the tentacles of the slavery business were very long and permeated deep into the continent. As we now know, both from the recent research that has been done and the new work collected in this volume, investors and bankers, ship-owners and merchants, textile workers and glass-blowers, sailors and seamen, surgeons, scientists and writers, serfs and slaves were all part of the extensive filaments associated with the so-called 'triangular trade'. This was a global business, never confined to the triangle of the New World, Britain and France, and Africa: it stretched from Italy to Latin America, from the Baltic to the Mediterranean, from Russia to Haiti. Sugar and slavery were not foundational to the economies and societies of these hinterlands, yet the profits to be gained and the opportunities to be exploited had left their mark. The new scholarship demonstrates that it is not only metropole and colony that need to be understood in one analytic

---

1   Edward Long, *The History of Jamaica, or General Survey of the Antient and Modern State of that Island, with Reflections on its Situation, Settlements, Inhabitants*, 3 vols (London, 1774), vol. 1, pp. 491–3.

frame: Prussia had no colonies, yet sections of its mercantile community
and sectors of its economy were heavily invested in the slavery business, and
while few enslaved people are to be traced in Central Europe ideas of racial
difference and African inferiority were circulating from the early modern
period. This was a global world before the globalisation of the twentieth
century.

The forgetting of these connections, we discover, has been both a conscious
and an unconscious process. Remembering and forgetting are always
connected and as is clear in the case of Britain, the *work* of forgetting the
nation's dependence on slavery while remembering the triumph of abolition
can be traced through writings, speeches and memorials.[2] Unravelling these
connections takes work. The construction of histories is a complex process
involving choices at many points. What should be archived in the first place?
Who has left traces and who has not? What is seen as part of the nation's
or a family's story? What is it impossible to think or imagine?[3] Several of
the essays in this volume demonstrate how these forms of forgetting, and
now of re-remembrance, can take place. As Peter Haenger describes, it has
been very difficult for the Swiss to recognise their historic involvement in
the slave trade and slavery. How could a small country, far distant from the
Atlantic coast and with no colonial history be connected to the slave trade?
Yet it was. 'For a long time,' he comments, 'not only did people not want
to know about Swiss involvement in the slave trade, but some also had an
interest in keeping the past hidden' (p. 84) The extensive archives of the
Burckhardts, a Basel mercantile family, were 'ordered' and catalogued in the
mid twentieth century by a descendant, Carl Burckhardt-Sarasin, who was
determined to ensure that the evidence of the family's involvement in the
slave trade, piracy and smuggling would not be exposed to unsympathetic
eyes. All compromising documents were placed in sealed boxes and were not
opened until after his death. It is only as a result of the new interest in the
activities of Swiss merchants in relation to slavery that it has been seen as
relevant to re-evaluate the activities of the firm. Geographical distance, it is
clear, in no way prohibited involvement in slave-trading networks: Nantes
provided the necessary connections to the trading routes. In another instance,
as Craig Koslofsky and Roberto Zaugg demonstrate, the manuscript of
the ship's surgeon Johann Peter Oettinger, who served on slave voyages in
the late seventeenth century, was edited and published by a descendant. An
enthusiast for Germany's new colonial ventures in Africa, he was concerned
to use the document as a celebration of the nation's first colonial connections

2   See, for example, Cora Kaplan and John Oldfield, eds, *Imagining Transatlantic Slavery*
(Basingstoke, 2010), part 3, 'Remembering and Forgetting'.
3   On the production of 'history' see Michel-Rolphe Trouillot, *Silencing the Past. Power and
the Production of History* (Boston, MA, 1995).

through reminding readers of the activities of the Brandenburg African Company. He inserted passages which he had written to demonstrate that his ancestor was a compassionate man and that the horrors of the Middle Passage, so extensively represented by the abolitionists that they had become familiar in western discourse, had no place in the new forms of colonialism. In a different kind of case, the letters of Therese Huber, the German intellectual and journalist, written in the 1820s to the Abbé Grégoire, have recently been unearthed. As Sarah Lentz explores, these letters, together with the materials Huber published in the literary magazine she edited, reveal the scale of her commitment to the anti-slavery cause and her determination to make information on slavery available to the German reading public. In all these instances a determination to ask new questions and search archives with different eyes have opened up knowledge of the ways in which slavery surfaced in the hinterlands.

How do these essays connect with other recent research on European engagement with the slavery business? The work of the Legacies of British Slave-ownership project at University College London has established the first full account of those who received compensation following the abolition of slavery in the British West Indies, Mauritius and the Cape in 1834. It has demonstrated the ways in which slave-ownership permeated British elites in the nineteenth-century, and made the case, conceptually and empirically, for showing how slavery, slave-ownership and ideas of race were central to the formation of modern British society. We now have a full account of those who received compensation from the British government at the time of emancipation. A total of £20 million was paid to some 47,000 slave-owners in order to get their agreement to the freeing of 'their' human property. The records of all those who claimed and received money have been digitised and an encyclopedia created with biographical details on the absentees, the roughly 3,500 individuals who lived in Britain.[4] Some of these men and women were wealthy landowners and merchants, others were small-scale investors – widows, for example, living off annuities which were funded by the labour of the enslaved. Mapping the residences of the absentees has demonstrated that they lived not only in the great slaving ports of London, Bristol, Liverpool and Glasgow, but right across the country, in rural areas and small towns, with an unusually high proportion based in Scotland. About 20 per cent of these absentees were women, most of whom had probably never been to the Caribbean, an indicator of the significance of women's involvement in the economy. The ownership of the enslaved was a

---

4   See http://www.ucl.ac.uk/lbs (accessed 28 February 2016). Catherine Hall, Nicholas Draper, Keith McClelland, Rachel Lang and Katie Donington, *Legacies of British Slave-Ownership. Colonial Slavery and the Formation of Victorian Britain* (Cambridge, 2014).

regular form of investment, an ordinary part of life for considerable numbers of Britons.

The essays in this volume do not explore this question of ownership which were probably marginal in the hinterlands, though there may well have been investments in human property through Nantes or Bordeaux, for example. Rather, they are focused on other aspects of the slavery business, its ramifications across the many sectors which Edward Long was determined to pinpoint. Slavery was not necessarily a central issue for these men, it might rather have been thought about as one part of a complex portfolio, as in the case of those merchants in the Wupper Valley whose major interests were in Latin America and Haiti. But ideas of race travelled with the business and the volume throws light on the understandings of racial difference that were circulating in these regions in the period before and after abolition. Businessmen with connections to slavery were for the most part silent on any associated moral issues. Why did the property in human beings and the cruelties associated with it evoke so little concern? As Alexandra Robinson notes in her discussion of the Earle family business in Liverpool, Thomas and William, far from regarding their trading activities with any regret saw themselves as pillars of the community, connected to the aristocracy through marriage; they were 'citizens of the world'. How was it possible to cut off from any sense of responsibility as to the barbaric and inhuman practices of the slave trade and plantation slavery? How did processes of dehumanisation and disassociation work, the construction of 'others' as lesser and fundamentally different from Europeans? A process of distantiation was clearly involved, the geographical fact of distance was crucial to the images that circulated of otherness – strange places, strange peoples, strange fruits – not 'like us'. As scholars of early modern England have established, a gendered racial discourse committed to constituting stable categories of blackness was threaded across writings and material culture, drawing on a range of European sources, especially the travel writings of voyagers.[5]

Johann Peter Oettinger provides a powerful example of this. He commented on the 'unnatural' habits of the African women on one of the slaving voyages on which he served in the late seventeenth century. Three of the women on the voyage from Curaçao to Suriname bore children. He recorded:

> they bind the [newborn] child on their back with an old linen cloth, throw their breast to him over the shoulder, and let him suckle. They look like a pair of young apes. ... I was quite familiar with the three children born on

5   See, for example, Kim F. Hall, *Things of Darkness. Economies of Race and Gender in Early Modern England* (Ithaca, 1995); Susan Dwyer Amussen, *Caribbean Exchanges. Slavery and the Transformation of English Society, 1640–1700* (Chapel Hill, 2007); Catherine Molineux, *Faces of Perfect Ebony. Encountering Atlantic Slavery in Imperial Britain* (Cambridge, 2012).

the way because I was their midwife. The mother lies in no child-bed; instead she walks around and stretches out like a cat with its young.(pp. 38–40)

The fact that he served as midwife, saw these women's bodies and the labour they endured, knew the conditions on a slave ship and the impossibility of a 'child-bed', none of this counted in comparison with his animalistic vision of the 'ape-like' and 'cat-like' qualities of the women. The image of the African woman breast-feeding circulated in travel literature, as with the engraving of Theodor de Bry (Fig. 1.1), and such visions may have been part of the everyday talk of sailors and slavers. The assumption that African women suffered no pain in labour, just as African men bore the most terrible punishments on the plantations without crying out, were indices, it was believed, of their essential difference.[6] Oettinger also provides another clue as to these processes of racialisation, this time in relation to whiteness. Koslofsky and Zaugg note that while there appeared to be no moral problems for him associated with the slave trade his major concern as recorded in his journal was his preoccupation with property and theft. Property and possessions were his quotidian obsessions. Oettinger was writing at a time when new definitions of property were being established, linked to Protestant individualism, particular political struggles, especially that between the Crown and the men of property in England, and the establishment of colonial settlements in the New World. Locke was one of the architects of a new language of the rights of freeborn men.[7] His definition of property meant that men, white men, born free, retained original and absolute ownership of their own persons, their labour and its produce. Their freedom of property ownership was in stark contrast with feudal dependencies, serfs could not be sold. But slaves could be, they were commodities, because they were outside the social contract, not born free. That idea of the ownership of oneself, one's labour, and one's possessions, the fruit of that labour, may be echoed in Oettinger's concerns over his property, which included the products of slave labour that he had bought and hoped to trade with. His 'ownership' contrasted with the enslaved on the ships he served, whose ownership of themselves was denied.

A different kind of insight comes from the botanist and colonial official Julius von Rohr. As Daniel Hopkins explains, a highly educated botanist with a noble background, connected to the powerful Schimmelmann family who had slaving interests and plantations in the Danish West Indies, he was

6   On this see Long, *History*; Saidiya V. Hartman, *Scenes of Subjection: Terror, Slavery, and Self-Making in Nineteenth-Century America* (Oxford, 1997); Jennifer L. Morgan, *Laboring Women. Reproduction and Gender in New World Slavery* (Philadelphia, 2004).

7   This is not of course to suggest that Oettinger read Locke, but to suggest that new ideas of property, the person and the slave were circulating across Europe. John Locke, *Two Treatises of Government*, ed. P. Laslett, 2nd edn (Cambridge, 1967). On Locke see Mary Nyquist, *Arbitrary Rule. Slavery, Tyranny, and the Power of Life and Death* (Chicago, 2013).

sent to the Caribbean as public land surveyor in 1757. There he met Patrick
Browne, the Irish botanist who lived on St Croix for a decade and who
wrote the influential *Civil and Natural History of Jamaica*. Von Rohr cited
that work extensively. In Browne's description of the state of the island he
commented on 'the Negroes', who were, 'for the most part, the property of
the Whites; and bought and sold like every other commodity in the country,
being always reckoned a part of their estates either real or personal'. They
had huts, provision grounds, and coarse clothing, probably 'Osnabrughs' (the
linens that were produced in Northern Germany and sold extensively in the
American colonies). Given the 'inconveniences' of their lives, he noted, the
scale of their toil and the vicissitudes they faced, it was not surprising if 'they
had been still more slothful and sickly than they are commonly observed
to be'. He had dealt with their sicknesses and was somewhat shocked that
their owners often just left them to the care of some 'raw youth' or quack,
not, he added, because of a lack of humanity but out of ignorance.[8] This
was undoubtedly a generous judgement on the planters, who thought nothing
of slave mortality or the failure of the enslaved to reproduce themselves in
the late seventeenth century since the slave trade always provided 'new
blood'. It does, however, give an indication of Browne's own recognition of
the harshness of the lives of the enslaved. Colonial botanists learned a great
deal from 'native informants', just as geographers depended on the 'captive
knowledge' they acquired from the enslaved and medical men learned of the
healing qualities of indigenous herbs and plants.[9] On his mission through the
Antilles to South America, von Rohr travelled with two enslaved men that he
owned, one who specialised in insects, another in plants. Unlike many others
who relied on these kinds of 'native informants' but remained contemp-
tuous of them, it seems that he was recognising of their qualities. Benjamin
Rush, the well-known Philadelphian scientist and politician met von Rohr
when he was en route to West Africa on his second mission for the Danish
government, but had broken his journey because of illness. Rush recorded in
his *Autobiography* that von Rohr:

> spoke highly of the intellectual and moral faculties of the negroes. A black
> man travelled with him who was his intelligencer in every strange place
> that he visited. [This man] was, he said, a Botanist and a philosopher.
> He had been taught morality by his father by means of fables, many
> of which the Doctor said were original and truly sublime. He gave the

8   Patrick Browne, M.D., *The Civil and Natural History of Jamaica* (in 3 parts) (London,
1756), part 1, p. 25.
9   On 'captive knowledge' see David Lambert, *Mastering the Niger. James MacQueen's African
Geography and the Struggle over Atlantic Slavery* (Chicago, 2013); for an example of a medical
man who was prepared to make use of indigenous knowledge see John Gilmore, *The Poetics of
Empire. A Study of James Grainger's* The Sugar Cane (London, 2000).

Doctor such an account of plants in Africa as enabled him to class them
by Linnaeus. (pp. 156–7)

The move from fables to Linnean science is significant, yet the fables had
facilitated a capacity for vital forms of knowledge.

Different valuations, we are reminded by these case studies, were placed
on Africans and other people of colour in different locations. Those Africans
captured, forcibly transported on the Middle Passage and subjected to New
World chattel slavery were not envisaged as 'the same' as those Africans who
had to be traded with and negotiated with over business. As Peter Haenger
notes, the starting point for European debates was a dichotomy between the
slave and the free born, but 'the social reality of the Gold Coast was characterised by a broad spectrum of relations of dependency and clientelism,
… There, slavery represented a continuum of differing degrees of social
unfreedom' (p. 83). These complexities existed in continental Europe too, as
Rebekka von Mallinckrodt's essay makes clear. There were free and bonded,
enslaved and imprisoned peoples of colour, sometimes they were the trophies
of war. They might have come from the Ottoman Empire, the Mediterranean
or the New World, but neither skin nor place of origin provided clear definitions of legal status. Black people were present in the hinterlands, but they did
not occupy a recognised place. The culture of the court, with 'Moors' as an
established part of the entourage, and the estate-based order with its degrees
of servitude and freedom marked significant differences from the world of the
colonies. The petition of the 'purchased Moor' in Brandenburg-Prussia that
she traces enables her to question any single meaning of slavery. 'The many-
tiered forms of compulsory labour and dependency in early modern society',
she suggests, 'might have meant that slavery was not necessarily perceived as
something radically foreign or different by contemporaries' (p. 131). Chattel
slavery on the plantations, the particular form of racial slavery defined as
'social death' by Orlando Patterson, emerged out of complex and differentiated forms of servitude, drawing on both English and African antecedents.[10]
In its extremities it needs to be understood as historically and geographically
distinct. Serfdom had its own specificities. The low price of unfree labour in
the Silesian textile industry, as Anka Steffen and Klaus Weber demonstrate,
lowered the costs for slave labour in the Caribbean; it also points to the
importance of the connecting links between different forms of exploitation
across global chains. Von Mallinckrodt's timely injunction that slavery and
serfdom need to be thought about, not as entirely separate developments, but

10 Orlando Patterson, *Slavery and Social Death. A Comparative Study* (Cambridge, MA,
1982); for a recent discussion of the emergence of racial slavery in Barbados see, Simon P.
Newman, *A New World of Labor. The Development of Plantation Slavery in the British
Atlantic* (Philadelphia, 2013).

as entangled histories, chimes well with work on indenture and the many and varied forms of unfree labour that both preceded and followed on from New World slavery.[11]

Families, it is now widely recognised, with their particular gender order, provided the bedrock for much of the development of early mercantile and industrial capitalism. The slavery business, which linked mercantile capitalism to the proto-industrial capitalism of the 'factories in the field' of the Caribbean, was no exception.[12] Brothers, sons, brothers-in-law, nephews and cousins provided the 'human capital', the managers, senior clerks and commission agents for the firm, perhaps engaged in setting up a second establishment on a key trading route or spending time in the colonies directly overseeing a plantation. 'A man must act' was the imperative; he would be judged, both publicly and privately, by his capacity to head a household and support his dependants, whether wife and children or servants, apprentices and employees. Women were critical to capital formation through the transmission of property, via marriage settlements, inheritance and trusts. They provided vital labour, as wives and mothers, bearing children and caring for the household, acting as key figures in maintaining the social networks which oiled the business routes, writing letters, hosting gatherings, demonstrating through their presence the trustworthiness of the firm. Unmarried daughters had their place in family enterprises, supporting brothers and aged parents, moving from one set of kin to another as help was required.[13]

Family firms are at the heart of many of the stories in this volume.[14] Take the Earle family, three generations of whom started as slave-traders but expanded their business into a series of ancillary activities including slave products from the West Indies and the supply of Venetian beads and silks, even cowries from the Maldives, to Africa. Interestingly, Thomas Earle's one-time agent in Livorno wrote many letters to Earle's wife, an intriguing indication of the place of this woman in the business. The Basel merchant family of the Burckhardts were typical in their reliance on the labour of brothers, providing the necessary human capital in times when risk had to be limited as best could be, and families and friends were the safest bet. In the

11   See, for example, the essays by Rupprecht, Cateau and Anderson in Catherine Hall, Nicholas Draper and Keith McClelland, eds, *Emancipation and the Remaking of the British Imperial World* (Manchester, 2014).
12   Sidney W. Mintz, 'Slavery and Emergent Capitalisms', *Slavery in the New World. A Reader in Comparative History*, ed. L. Foner and E. D. Genovese (Englewood Cliffs, 1969), pp. 23–37.
13   On the centrality of gender to the organisation of capital see Leonore Davidoff and Catherine Hall, *Family Fortunes. Men and Women of the English Middle Class 1780–1850*, 2nd edn (London, 2002), especially chapters 4–6.
14   There is potential for important further work on these family papers, opening up the gender implications for these family firms, utilising wills and marriage settlements, for example.

words of one Lancashire draper, who might be said to speak for many across both Europe and the New World:

> If the stock of our bliss is in stranger's hands rested
> The fund ill secured oft in bankruptcy ends
> But the heart is given bills which are never protested
> When drawn on the firm of wife, children, and friends[15]

Abraham Frowein in the Wupper Valley made two of his nephews partners, a typical move if there were no sons available.[16] Families were no less significant in the business of anti-slavery, as Sarah Lentz demonstrates in the case of Therese Huber. The daughter of a renowned professor of classics, she grew up in a house frequented by local and international scholars. Like so many women her literary career began supporting her husband, Georg Forster, the famous travel writer and journalist, helping with translations of English texts. This pattern continued with her second husband, Ludwig Huber, and her literary works were published under his name until after her father, who disapproved of women writing, had died. Writing, editing, translating, researching, acting as amanuenses for husbands and fathers were common practices in societies in which women acting independently was frowned upon. These too could be family businesses, with women's labour, often unacknowledged, a key contribution.[17]

Slavery Hinterland offers us new knowledge, new connections and entanglements, new ramifications to the histories of both slavery and continental Europe. It draws on economic, social and cultural historians, demonstrating the importance of breaking down those subdivisions of the discipline and pointing the way to a more inclusive historical narrative, one that is vitally necessary to us in these global times.

---

15 Davidoff and Hall, *Family Fortunes*, p. 222.
16 On the importance of siblings and wider kin see Leonore Davidoff, *Thicker than Water. Siblings and Their Relations* (Oxford, 2012).
17 Zoe Laidlaw, '"Aunt Anna's Report": The Buxton Women and the Aborigines Select Committee, 1835–7', *Journal of Imperial and Commonwealth History* 32/2 (2004), 1–28.

Bibliography of Secondary Works Cited

Afigbo, Adiele Eberechukwu, *The Abolition of the Slave Trade in Southeastern Nigeria, 1885–1950* (Rochester, NY, 2006).

Albers, Wilhelm, and Armin Clasen, 'Mohren im Kirchspiel Eppendorf und im Gute Ahrensburg', *Zeitschrift für Niederdeutsche Familienkunde* 41 (1966), 2–4.

Alloula, Malek, *The Colonial Harem* (Minneapolis, 1986).

Alpern, S. B., 'What Africans Got for Their Slaves', *History in Africa* 22 (1995), 5–43.

Amussen, Susan Dwyer, *Caribbean Exchanges. Slavery and the Transformation of English Society, 1640–1700* (Chapel Hill, 2007).

Anderson, B. L., 'The Lancashire Bill System and its Liverpool Practitioners', *Trade and Transport: Essays in Economic History in Honour of T. S. Willan*, ed. W. H. Chaloner and B. M. Ratcliffe (Manchester, 1977), pp. 59–97.

Anderson, Edgar, 'The Couronians and the West Indies. The First Settlements', *Caribbean Quarterly* 5/4 (1959), 264–71.

Anstey, Roger, *The Atlantic Slave Trade and British Abolition, 1760–1810* (London, 1975).

Armitage, David, and Sanjay Subrahmanyam, eds, *The Age of Revolutions in Global Context, c.1760–1840* (Basingstoke, 2010).

Aubin, Gustav, and Arno Kunze, *Leinenerzeugung und Leinenabsatz im östlichen Mitteldeutschland zur Zeit der Zunftkäufe: Ein Beitrag zur industriellen Kolonisation des deutschen Ostens* (Stuttgart, 1940).

Bade, Klaus J., 'Antisklavereibewegung in Deutschland und Kolonialkrieg in Deutsch-Ostafrika 1888–1890. Bismarck und Friedrich Fabri', *Geschichte und Gesellschaft* 3 (1977), 31–58.

Bader-Zar, Brigitte, 'Abolitionism in the Atlantic World: The Organization and Interaction of Anti-Slavery Movements in the Eighteenth and Nineteenth Centuries', *European History Online*, published by the Institute of European History (Mainz, 12 September 2011), http://www.ieg-ego.eu/baderzaarb-2010-en (accessed 6 March 2015).

Baucom, Ian, *Specters of the Atlantic. Finance Capital, Slavery, and the Philosophy of History* (Durham, NC, 2007).

Becker, Andreas, 'Preußens schwarze Untertanen. Afrikanerinnen und Afrikaner zwischen Kleve und Königsberg vom 17. Jahrhundert bis ins frühe

19. Jahrhundert', *Forschungen zur Brandenburgischen und Preußischen Geschichte* 22 (2012), 1–32.

Becker-Cantarino, Barbara, 'Therese Forster-Huber und Polen', *'Daß eine Nation die andere verstehen möge': Festschrift für Marian Szyrocki*, eds N. Honsza and H.-G. Roloff (Amsterdam, 1988), pp. 53–66.

——, 'Revolution im Patriarchat: Therese Forster-Huber (1764–1829)', *Out of Line/Ausgefallen. The Paradox of Marginality in the Writings of 19th Century Women*, ed. R.-E. Boetcher-Joeres and M. Burkhard (Amsterdam, 1989), pp. 235–53.

Beckert, Sven, *Empire of Cotton. A Global History* (New York, 2014).

——, *King Cotton. Eine Geschichte des globalen Kapitalismus* (Munich, 2014).

Beckmann, August, *Die Rheinisch-Westindische Kompagnie, ihr Wirken und ihre Bedeutung* (Münster, 1915).

Behre, Otto, *Geschichte der Statistik in Brandenburg-Preussen bis zur Gründung des Königlichen Statistischen Bureaus* (Berlin, 1905).

Behrendt, Steve, 'Human Capital and the British Slave Trade', *Liverpool and Transatlantic Slavery*, ed. D. Richardson, S. Schwarz and A. Tibbles (Liverpool, 2007), pp. 66–97.

Bell, Herbert C., 'The West India Trade before the American Revolution', *American Historical Review* 4/2 (1917), 272–87.

Berding, Helmut, 'Die Ächtung des Sklavenhandels auf dem Wiener Kongreß 1814/15', *Historische Zeitschrift* 219/2 (1974), 265–89.

Bernecker, Walther, 'Preußisch-mexikanische Wirtschaftsbeziehungen in der ersten Hälfte des 19. Jahrhunderts', *Preußen und Lateinamerika*, ed. S. Carreras and G. Maihold (Münster, 2004), pp. 217–57.

Bickel, Wilhelm, *Bevölkerungsgeschichte und Bevölkerungspolitik der Schweiz seit dem Ausgang des Mittelalters* (Zurich, 1947).

——, *Bevölkerungs-Ploetz, Raum und Bevölkerung in der Weltgeschichte*, 4 vols (Würzburg, 1955).

Biskup, Thomas, and Peter H. Wilson, 'Großbritannien, Amerika und die atlantische Welt', *Friederisiko – Friedrich der Große*, ed. Stiftung Preußische Schlösser und Gärten Berlin-Brandenburg, 3 vols (Munich, 2012), vol. 1, pp. 146–62.

Blackburn, Robin, *The Making of New World Slavery. From the Baroque to the Modern, 1492–1800* (London, 1998).

Blackmon, Douglas A., *Slavery by Another Name. The Reenslavement of Black Americans from the Civil War to World War II* (New York, 2008).

Bland, Caroline, and Hilary Brown, 'Introduction: Women as Cultural Mediators and Translators', *Oxford German Studies* 42/2 (2013), 111–18.

Blickle, Renate, 'Leibeigenschaft. Versuch über Zeitgenossenschaft in Wissenschaft und Wirklichkeit, durchgeführt am Beispiel Altbayerns', *Gutsherrschaft als soziales Modell*, ed. J. Peters (Munich, 1995), pp. 53–80.

Blom, Philipp, and Wolfgang Kos, eds, *Angelo Soliman. Ein Afrikaner in Wien* (Vienna, 2011).

Boch, Rudolf, *Grenzenloses Wachstum? Das rheinische Wirtschaftsbürgertum und seine Industrialisierungsdebatte 1814–1857* (Göttingen, 1991).

Boldorf, Marcel, *Europäische Leinenregionen im Wandel. Institutionelle Weichenstellungen in Schlesien und Irland (1750–1850)* (Cologne, 2006).

——, 'Märkte und Verlage im institutionellen Gefüge der Leinenregion Niederschlesien des 18. Jahrhunderts', *Die Wirtschaftsgeschichte vor der Herausforderung durch die New Institutional Economics*, ed. K.-P. Ellerbrock and C. Wischermann (Dortmund, 2004), pp. 179–91.

——, 'Weltwirtschaftliche Verflechtung und lokale Existenzsicherung. Die schlesischen Kaufmannsgilden im internationalen Leinenhandel des 18. Jahrhunderts', *Praktiken des Handels. Geschäfte und soziale Beziehungen europäischer Kaufleute in Mittelalter und früher Neuzeit*, ed. M. Häberlein and C. Jeggle (Konstanz, 2010), pp. 127–44.

Bolland, Nigel O., 'Proto-Proletarians? Slave Wages in the Americas: Between Slave Labour & Free Labour', *From Chattel Slaves to Wage Slaves: The Dynamics of Labour Bargaining in the Americas*, ed. M. Turner (Kingston, Jamaica, 1995), pp. 123–47.

Boltanski, Luc, *Distant Suffering: Morality, Media and Politics* (Cambridge, 2004).

Bondi, Gerhard, *Deutschlands Außenhandel 1815–1870* (Berlin, 1958).

Bono, Salvatore, 'Sklaven in der mediterranen Welt. Von der Ersten Türkenbelagerung bis zum Wiener Kongress (1529–1815)', *Angelo Soliman. Ein Afrikaner in Wien*, ed. P. Blom and W. Kos (Vienna, 2011), pp. 35–49.

Boody Schumpeter, Elizabeth, *English Overseas Trade Statistics, 1697–1808* (Oxford, 1960).

Boogaart, Ernst van den, 'De Bry's Africa', *Inszenierte Welten. Die west- und ostindischen Reisen der Verleger de Bry, 1590–1630 / Staging New Worlds. De Bry's Illustrated Travel Reports, 1590–1630*, ed. S. Burghartz (Basel, 2004), pp. 95–157.

Boomgaard, Peter, ed., *Empire and Science in the Making: Dutch Colonial Scholarship in Comparative Global Perspective, 1760–1830* (New York, 2013).

Boulukos, George, 'Capitalism and Slavery: Once More, with Feeling', *Affect and Abolition in the Anglo-Atlantic, 1770–1830*, ed. S. Ahern (Farnham, 2013), pp. 23–43.

Bowman, Shearer Davis, *Masters & Lords. Mid-19th Century U.S. Planters and Prussian Junkers* (New York, 1993).

Boyer, George, *An Economic History of the English Poor Law 1750–1850* (Cambridge, 1990).

Braun, Jana, *Das Bild des 'Afrikaners' im Spiegel deutscher Zeitschriften der Aufklärung*, Leipziger Arbeiten zur Geschichte und Kultur in Afrika 10 (Leipzig, 2005).

Bregoli, Francesca, 'Jewish Scholarship, Science, and the Republic of Letters:

Joseph Attias in 18th-Century Livorno', *ALEPH. Historical Studies in Science & Judaism* 7 (2007), 97–181.

Brentano, Lujo, 'Ueber den grundherrlichen Charakter des hausindustriellen Leinengewerbes in Schlesien', *Zeitschrift für Social- und Wirtschaftsgeschichte* 1 (1893), 318–40.

Bro-Jørgensen, J. O., *Industriens historie i Danmark*, vol. 2: *Tiden 1730–1820*, ed. A. Nielsen (Copenhagen, 1943).

——, *Vore gamle tropekolonier*, vol. 1: *Dansk Vestindien indtil 1755*, ed. J. Brøndsted, 2nd edn (Copenhagen, 1966).

Brockway, Lucile H., *Science and Colonial Expansion: The Role of the British Royal Botanic Gardens* (New York, 1979).

Brown, Christopher Leslie, *Moral Capital: Foundations of British Abolitionism* (Chapel Hill, 2006).

——, 'Slavery and Antislavery, 1760–1820', *The Oxford Handbook of the Atlantic World, c.1450–c.1850*, ed. N. Canny and P. Morgan (Oxford, 2011), pp. 602–17.

——, 'The Origins of "Legitimate Commerce"', *Commercial Agriculture: The Slave Trade and Slavery in Atlantic Africa*, ed. R. Law, S. Schwarz and S. Strickrodt (Woodbridge, 2013), pp. 138–57.

Browne, Patrick, M.D., *The Civil and Natural History of Jamaica* (in 3 parts) (London, 1756).

Brübach, Nils, '"Seefahrt und Handel sind die fürnembsten Säulen eines Etats". Brandenburg-Preussen und der transatlantische Sklavenhandel im 17. und 18. Jahrhundert', *Amerikaner wider Willen. Beiträge zur Sklaverei in Lateinamerika*, ed. R. Zoller (Frankfurt a.M., 1994), pp. 11–42.

Bruijn, Iris, *Ship's Surgeons of the Dutch East India Company. Commerce and the Progress of Medicine in the Eighteenth Century* (Leiden, 2009).

Buck-Morss, Susan, *Hegel, Haiti and Universal History* (Pittsburgh, 2009).

Burckhardt-Sarasin, Carl, 'Aus der Geschichte der Grosshandelsfirmen und Indiennes Fabriques Christoph Burckhardt & Sohn in der Goldenen Müntz und dem Ernauerhof, Christoph Burckhardt & Cie. im "Sägerhof" mit seiner Nanter Filiale' (unpublished MS, Basel, 1951).

Buxton, Thomas Fowell, *The African Slave Trade and Its Remedy* (London, 1840).

Carney, Judith, and Richard Nicholas Rosomoff, *In the Shadow of Slavery: Africa's Botanical Legacy in the Atlantic World* (Berkeley, 2009).

Carøe, Kristian, *Den danske Lægestand, doktorer og licentiater 1479–1788* (Copenhagen, 1909).

Carretta, Vincent, *Equiano, the African: Biography of a Self-Made Man* (Athens, GA, 2005).

Cerman, Markus, *Villagers and Lords in Eastern Europe, 1300–1800* (New York, 2012).

Chamboredon, Robert, 'Une société de commerce languedocienne à Cadix: Simon et Arnail Fornier et Cie (Nov. 1768–Mars 1786)', *La burguesía de negocios en la Andalucía de la ilustración*, 2, ed. A. González García-Baquero (Cadiz, 1991), pp. 35–52.

Chater, Kathleen, *Untold Histories. Black People in England and Wales During the Period of the British Slave Trade c.1660–1807* (Manchester, 2009).

Christensen, Carl F., *Den danske botaniks historie*, 3 vols (Copenhagen, 1924–26).

Christopher, Emma, *Slave Ship Sailors and their Captive Cargoes 1730–1807* (Cambridge, 2006).

Clark, Geoffrey, 'The Slave's Appeal: Insurance and the Rise of Commercial Property', *The Appeal of Insurance*, ed. G. W. Clark, G. Anderson, C. Thomann and J.-M. Graf von der Schulenburg (Toronto, 2010), pp. 52–74.

Clarkson, Leslie, 'The Linen Industry in Early Modern Europe', *The Cambridge History of Western Textiles*, ed. D. Jenkins (Cambridge, 2003), pp. 472–93.

Coleman, Deirdre, *Romantic Colonisation and British Anti-Slavery* (Cambridge, 2005).

Collenberg, Wipertus Rudt de, 'Le baptême des musulmans esclaves à Rome aux XVIIe et XVIIIe siècles. Le XVIIIe siècle', *Mélanges de l'École française de Rome. Italie et Méditerranée* 101/2 (1989), 519–670.

Collins, Brenda, and Philip Ollerenshaw, eds, *The European Linen Industry in Historical Perspective* (Oxford, 2003).

Cooper, Frederick, Thomas C. Holt and Rebecca Scott, *Beyond Slavery. Explorations of Race, Labor, and Citizenship in Post-Emancipation Societies* (Chapel Hill, 2000).

Crosby, Alfred W., Jr, *The Columbian Exchange: Biological and Cultural Consequences of 1492* (Westport, 1972).

Crowhurst, Patrick, 'The Effect of War on the Swiss Cotton Trade: Christophe Burckhardt of Basle 1793–1810', *Textile History* 18/1 (1987), 17–32.

——, *The French War on Trade: Privateering 1793–1815* (Aldershot, 1989).

Curran, Andrew, *The Anatomy of Blackness. Science and Slavery in an Age of Enlightenment* (Baltimore, 2011).

Curtin, Philip D., *The Image of Africa, British Ideas and Action, 1780–1850* (Madison, 1964).

Daaku, Kwame Yeboa, *Trade and Politics on the Gold Coast 1600 to 1720. A Study of the African Reaction to European Trade* (Oxford, 1970).

Dahl, Thorkel, and Kjeld de Fine Licht, *Surveys in 1961 on St. Thomas and St. Croix* (Copenhagen, 2004).

Danforth, Susan, 'Cultivating Empire: Sir Joseph Banks and the (failed) Botanical Garden at Nassau', *Terrae Incognitae* 33 (2001), 48–58.

Dansk biografisk leksikon, ed. C. F. Bricka (Copenhagen, 1887–1905), http://runeberg.org/dbl/ (accessed 1 March 2016); 2nd edn, ed. P. Engelstoft and S. Dahl (Copenhagen, 1933–44).

David, Thomas, Bouda Etemad and Janick Marina Schaufelbuehl, *Schwarze Geschäfte. Die Beteiligung von Schweizern an Sklaverei und Sklavenhandel im 18. und 19. Jahrhundert* (Zurich, 2005).

Davidoff, Leonore, *Thicker than Water. Siblings and Their Relations* (Oxford, 2012).

Davidoff, Leonore, and Catherine Hall, *Family Fortunes. Men and Women of the English Middle Class 1780–1850*, 2nd edn (London, 2002).

Davis, David Brion, *The Problem of Slavery in the Age of Revolution* (Ithaca, 1975).

Davis, Robert C., *Christian Slaves, Muslim Masters: White Slavery in the Mediterranean, the Barbary Coast, and Italy, 1500–1800* (Basingstoke, 2003).

Debrunner, Hans Werner, 'Basel und der Sklavenhandel – Fragmente eines wenig bekannten Kapitels der Basler Geschichte', *Basler Stadtbuch 1993* (Basel, 1994), pp. 95–101.

——, *Grégoire l'Européen* (Salzburg, 1997).

DeCorse, Christopher R., *An Archaeology of Elmina: Africans and Europeans on the Gold Coast from 1400 to 1900* (Washington, DC, 2001).

Degn, Christian, *Die Schimmelmanns im atlantischen Dreieckshandel. Gewinn und Gewissen* (Neumünster, 1974).

Delbourgo, James, and Nicholas Dew, eds, *Science and Empire in the Atlantic World* (New York, 2008).

Delobette, Edouard, *Ces Messieurs du Havre. Négociants, commissionnaires et armateurs de 1680 à 1830* (Caen, 2005).

Denzel, Markus A., *Der Preiskurant des Handelshauses Pelloutier & Cie aus Nantes (1763–1793)* (Stuttgart, 1997).

Dermigny, Louis, 'Négociants bâlois et genevois à Nantes et à Lorient au XVIIIe siècle', *Mélanges d'Histoire Économique et Sociale en hommage au Professeur Antony Babel*, 2 vols (Geneva, 1963), vol. 2, pp. 39–56.

Deutsch, Jan-Georg, *Emancipation without Abolition in German East Africa, c.1884–1914* (Oxford, 2006).

Deveau, Jean-Michel, *La Traite rochelaise* (Paris, 1990).

Diedrich, Maria I., 'From American Slaves to Hessian Subjects. Silenced Black Narratives of the American Revolution', *Germany and the Black Diaspora: Points of Contact, 1250–1914*, ed. M. Honeck, M. Klimke and A. Kuhlmann (New York, 2013), pp. 92–111.

Dietz, Walter, *Die Wuppertaler Garnnahrung* (Neustadt a.d. Aisch, 1957).

Dos Santos Lopes, Marilia, *Afrika. Eine neue Welt in deutschen Schriften des 16. und 17. Jahrhunderts* (Stuttgart, 1992).

Draper, Nicholas, 'The British State and Slavery: George Baillie, Merchant of London and St Vincent, and the Exchequer Loans of the 1790s' (2015), www.ehs.org.uk/dotAsset/de55e1a1-c7f6-450b-9a1a-831601ae46d9.docX (accessed 29 March 2016).

——, 'The City of London and slavery: evidence from the first dock companies, 1795–1800', *Economic History Review* 61 (2008), 432–66.

——, *The Price of Emancipation. Slave-Ownership, Compensation and British Society at the End of Slavery* (Cambridge, 2010).

Drayton, Richard, *Nature's Government: Science, Imperial Britain, and the 'Improvement' of the World* (New Haven, 2000).

Drescher, Seymour, *Abolition: A History of Slavery and Antislavery* (Cambridge, 2009).

——, *Capitalism and Abolition. British Mobilization in Comparative Perspective* (Oxford 1987).

——, *Econocide. British Slavery in the Era of Abolition* (Pittsburgh, 1977).

——, 'The Ending of the Slave Trade and the Evolution of European Scientific Racism', *The Atlantic Slave Trade. Effects on Economies, Societies, and Peoples in Africa, the Americas, and Europe*, ed. J. E. Inikori and S. L. Engerman (Durham, NC, 1992), pp. 361–96.

Dresser, Madge, *Slavery Obscured: The Social History of the Slave Trade in an English Provincial Port* (London, 2001).

Dubray, Jean, ed., *Lettres à l'abbé Grégoire: Extraites des archives Carnot: Volume I de A à J* (Paris, 2013).

Earle, T. Algernon, 'Earle of Allerton Tower', *Transactions of the Historic Society of Lancashire and Cheshire* 42 (1890), 15–76.

Eigen, Sarah, and Mark Larrimore, eds, *The German Invention of Race* (Albany, 2006).

Ellis, Markman, *The Politics of Sensibility: Race, Gender and Commerce in the Sentimental Novel* (Cambridge, 1996).

Eltis, David, 'Free and Coerced Transatlantic Migrations: Some Comparisons', *The American Historical Review* 88/2 (1983), 251–80.

——, 'The Impact of Abolition on the Atlantic Slave Trade', *The Abolition of the Atlantic Slave Trade: Origins and Effects in Europe, Africa, and the Americas*, ed. D. Eltis and J. Walvin (Madison, WI, 1981), pp. 155–76.

——, *The Rise of African Slavery in the Americas* (Cambridge, 2000).

——, 'The Volume and Structure of the Transatlantic Slave Trade: A Reassessment', *William and Mary Quarterly* 58/1 (2001), 17–46.

Emmer, Pieter C., *The Dutch in the Atlantic Economy, 1580–1880. Trade, Slavery and Emancipation* (Aldershot, 1998).

——, *The Dutch Slave Trade, 1500–1850*, transl. C. Emery (New York, 2006).

Engelbrecht, Jörg, *Das Herzogtum Berg im Zeitalter der Französischen Revolution. Modernisierungsprozesse zwischen bayerischem und französischem Modell* (Paderborn, 1996).

Epple, Angelika, '"Global" und "Area History". Plädoyer für eine weltgeschichtliche Perspektivierung des Lokalen', *Area Studies und die Welt. Weltregionen und neue Globalisierung*, ed. B. Schäbler (Vienna, 2007), pp. 90–116.

——, 'Globale Machtverhältnisse, lokale Verflechtungen. Die Berliner Kongokonferenz, Solingen und das Hinterland des kolonialen Waffenhandels', *Ränder der Moderne – Neue Perspektiven auf die Europäische Geschichte (1800–1930)*, ed. C. Dejung and M. Lengwiler (Cologne, 2016), pp. 65–91.

Evans, Chris, and Göran Rydén, *Baltic Iron in the Atlantic World in the Eighteenth Century* (Boston, MA, 2000).

Fässler, Hans, *Reise in Schwarz-Weiss: Schweizer Ortstermine in Sachen Sklaverei*, 2nd edn (Zurich, 2006).

Fatah-Black, K. J., and M. van Rossum, 'Wat is winst? De economische impact van de Nederlandse trans-Atlantische slavenhandel', *Tijdschrift voor Sociale en Economische Geschiedenis* 9 (2012), 3–29.

Faulstich, Werner, *Die bürgerliche Mediengesellschaft, 1700–1830* (Tübingen, 2002).

Ferguson, Moira, 'Mary Wollstonecraft and the Problematic of Slavery', *Feminist Review* 42 (Autumn, 1992), 82–102.

Fiedler, Matthias, *Zwischen Abenteuer, Wissenschaft und Kolonialismus: Der deutsche Afrikadiskurs im 18. und 19. Jahrhundert* (Cologne, 2005).

Fierz, Peter, *Eine Basler Handelsfirma im ausgehenden 18. und zu Beginn des 19. Jahrhunderts: Christoph Burckhardt & Cie. und verwandte Firmen* (Zurich, 1994).

Firla, Monika, 'AfrikanerInnen und ihre Nachkommen im deutschsprachigen Raum', *AfrikanerInnen in Deutschland und schwarze Deutsche – Geschichte und Gegenwart*, ed. M. Bechhaus-Gerst and R. Klein-Arendt (Berlin, 2004), pp. 9–24.

Fischer, Bernhard, 'Cottas *Morgenblatt für gebildete Stände* in der Zeit von 1807–1823 und die Mitarbeit Therese Hubers', *Archiv für Geschichte des Buchwesens* 43 (1995), 203–39, 358–408.

Flory, Céline, *De l'esclavage à la liberté forcée. Histoire des travailleurs engagés africains dans la Caraibe française au XIXe siècle* (Paris, 2015).

Fogel, Robert W., and Stanley L. Engerman, *Time on the Cross. The Economics of American Negro Slavery* (Boston, MA, 1974).

Forclaz, Amalia Ribi, *Humanitarian Imperialism. The Politics of Anti-Slavery Activism, 1880–1940* (Oxford, 2015).

Förster, Stig, Wolfgang J. Mommsen and Ronald Robinson, eds, *Bismarck, Europe, and Africa. The Berlin Africa Conference 1884–85 and the Onset of Partition* (London, 1988).

Frängsmyr, Tore, 'Editor's Introduction', *Linnaeus, the Man and his Work*, rev. reprint, ed. T. Frängsmyr (Canton, MA, 1994), pp. vii–xiv.

Franke, Arno, *Das schlesische Elysium. Burgen, Schlösser, Herrenhäuser und Parks im Hirschberger Tal*, Deutsches Kulturforum östliches Europa, 3rd edn (Potsdam, 2008).

Friedrich, Markus, '"Türken" im Alten Reich. Zur Aufnahme und Konversion von Muslimen im deutschen Sprachraum (16.-18. Jahrhundert)', *Historische Zeitschrift* 294 (2012), 329–60.

Fryxell, Paul A., 'The West Indian Species of Gossypium of von Rohr and Rafinesque', *Taxon* 18/4 (1969), 400–14.

Fumerton, Patricia, *Unsettled. The Culture of Mobility and the Working Poor in Early Modern England* (Chicago, 2006).

Fyfe, Christopher, *A History of Sierra Leone* (London, 1962).

Garboe, Axel, *Geologiens historie i Danmark*, 2 vols (Copenhagen, 1959 and 1961).

Gascoigne, John, *Joseph Banks and the English Enlightenment: Useful Knowledge and Polite Culture* (Cambridge, 1994).

——, *Science in the Service of the State: Joseph Banks, the British State and the Uses of Science in the Age of Revolution* (Cambridge, 1998).

Gaspar, David, and David Geggus, eds, *A Turbulent Time. The French Revolution and the Greater Caribbean* (Bloomington, 1997).

Geider, Thomas, 'Afrika im Umkreis der frühen Weltliteraturdiskussion: Goethe und Henri Grégoire', *Revue de littérature comparée* 2 (2005), 241–60.

Gelder, Roelof van, *Das ostindische Abenteuer. Deutsche in Diensten der Vereinigten Ostindischen Kompanie der Niederlande (VOC), 1600–1800* (Hamburg, 2003).

Genovese, Eugene D., *Roll, Jordan, Roll: The World the Slaves Made* (New York, 1976).

Gerber, Michael R., *Die Schlesischen Provinzialblätter 1785–1849* (Sigmaringen, 1995).

Gerbner, Katherine, 'Antislavery in Print. The Germantown Protest, the "Exhortation", and the Seventeenth-Century Quaker Debate on Slavery', *Early American Studies. An Interdisciplinary Journal* 9/3 (2011), 552–75.

Gestrich, Andreas, 'The Abolition Act and the Development of Abolitionist Movements in 19th Century Europe', *Humanitarian Intervention and Changing Labor Relations. The Long-Term Consequences of the Abolition of the Slave Trade*, ed. M. van der Linden (Leiden, 2011), pp. 245–62.

Gillespie, C. Coulston, ed., *Dictionary of Scientific Biography* (New York, 1970–80).

Gilmore, John, *The Poetics of Empire. A Study of James Grainger's* The Sugar Cane (London, 2000).

Gøbel, Erik, *De styrede rigerne* (Odense, 2000).

——, *Det danske slavehandelsforbud 1792* (Odense, 2008).

Goldstein, Alyssa, *The Abbé Grégoire and the French Revolution: The Making of Modern Universalism* (Berkeley, 2005).

Goslinga, Cornelis Ch., *The Dutch in the Caribbean and in the Guianas 1680–1791* (Assen, 1985).

Gould, Philip, *Barbaric Traffic: Commerce and Antislavery in the Eighteenth-Century Atlantic World* (Cambridge, 2003).

Grote, Gustav, 'Jacob Aders', *Wuppertaler Biographien* 5 (1965), 19–31.

Grove, Richard H., *Green Imperialism: Colonial Expansion, Tropical Island Edens and the Origins of Environmentalism, 1600–1860* (Cambridge, 1995).

Guerrero, Saul, 'Venetian Glass Beads and the Slave Trade from Liverpool 1750–1800', *Beads. Journal of the Society of Bead Researchers* 22 (2010), 52–70.

Häberlein, Mark, '"Mohren", ständische Gesellschaft und atlantische Welt',

Atlantic Understandings: Essays on European and American History in Honor of Hermann Wellenreuther, ed. C. Schnurmann and H. Lehmann (Hamburg, 2006), pp. 77–102.

Häberlein, Mark, and Michaela Schmölz-Häberlein, *Die Erben der Welser. Der Karibikhandel der Augsburger Firma Obwexer im Zeitalter der Revolutionen* (Augsburg, 1995).

Haenger, Peter, *Slaves and Slaveholders on the Gold Coast. Towards an Understanding of Social Bondage in West Africa*, ed. J. J. Shaffer and P. E. Lovejoy, transl. C. Handford (Basel, 2000).

Haenger, Peter, and Robert Labhardt, 'Basel und der Sklavenhandel. Das Beispiel der Burckhardtschen Handelshäuser zwischen 1780 und 1815', *Suisse–Afrique (18e–20e siècles): De la traite des Noirs à la fin du régime de l'apartheid*, ed. S. Bott, T. David, C. Lützelschwab and J. Marina Schaufelbuehl (Münster, 2005), pp. 25–42.

Hagen, William W., *Ordinary Prussians. Brandenburg Junkers and Villagers, 1500–1840* (Cambridge, 2002).

Haggerty, Sheryllynne, *Merely For Money? Business Culture in the British Atlantic, 1750–1815* (Liverpool, 2012).

Haggmann, Bertil, 'Danish Africa Companies', *The Historical Encyclopedia of World Slavery*, ed. J. P. Rodriguez, 2 vols (Santa Barbara, 1997), vol. 1, p. 208.

Hahn, Andrea, '"Wie ein Mannskleid für den weiblichen Körper": Therese Huber (1764–1829)', *Beruf: Schriftstellerin. Schreibende Frauen im 18. und 19. Jahrhundert*, ed. K. Tebben (Göttingen, 1998), pp. 103–31.

Hall, Catherine, *Civilising Subjects: Metropole and Colony in the English Imagination, 1830–1867* (Cambridge, 2002).

——, 'Competing Masculinities: Thomas Carlyle, John Stuart Mill and the Case of Governor Eyre', in C. Hall, *White, Male and Middle Class. Explorations in Feminism and History* (Cambridge, 1992), pp. 255–95.

Hall, Catherine, Nicholas Draper and Keith McClelland, eds, *Emancipation and the Remaking of the British Imperial World* (Manchester, 2014).

Hall, Catherine, Nicholas Draper, Keith McClelland, Rachel Lang and Katie Donington, *Legacies of British Slave-Ownership. Colonial Slavery and the Formation of Victorian Britain* (Cambridge, 2014).

Hall, Courtney Robert, *A Scientist in the Early Republic. Samuel Latham Mitchill 1764–1831* (New York, 1962).

Hall, Kim F., *Things of Darkness. Economies of Race and Gender in Early Modern England* (Ithaca, 1995).

Hall, Neville A. T., *Slave Society in the Danish West Indies: St. Thomas, St. John, and St. Croix*, ed. B. W. Higman (Baltimore, 1992).

Hartman, Saidiya V., *Scenes of Subjection: Terror, Slavery, and Self-Making in Nineteenth-Century America* (Oxford, 1997).

Hartmann, Stefan, *Die Beziehungen Preußens zu Dänemark 1688 bis 1789* (Cologne, 1983).

Hasenclever, Adolf, 'Neue Mitteilungen zur Geschichte der

Rheinisch-Westindischen Kompagnie', *Zeitschrift des Bergischen Geschichtsvereins* 49 (1916), 108–42.

——, *Peter Hasenclever aus Remscheid-Ehringhausen, ein deutscher Kaufmann des 18. Jahrhunderts* (Gotha, 1922).

Heijer, Henk J. den, *Goud, ivoor en slaven. Scheepvaart en handel van de Tweede Westindische Compagnie op Afrika, 1674–1740* (Zutphen, 1997).

Heinrich, Gerd, *Friedrich II. von Preußen. Leistung und Leben eines großen Königs* (Berlin, 2009).

Henkel, Martin, *Zunftmissbräuche. 'Arbeiterbewegung' im Merkantilismus* (Frankfurt a.M., 1989).

Henriksen, Kai L., *Oversigt over dansk entomologis historie* (Copenhagen, 1921).

Hensel, Daniel, *Historisch- Topographische Beschreibung der Stadt Hirschberg in Schlesien seit ihrem Ursprunge bis auf das Jahr 1797* (Hirschberg, 1797).

Hernæs, Per, 'A Danish Experiment in Commercial Agriculture on the Gold Coast, 1788–93', *Commercial Agriculture: The Slave Trade and Slavery in Atlantic Africa*, ed. R. Law, S. Schwarz and S. Strickrodt (Woodbridge, 2013), pp. 158–79.

Hersh, Jonathan, and Hans-Joachim Voth, *Sweet Diversity: Colonial Goods and the Rise of European Living Standards after 1492* (C.E.P.R. Discussion Paper, 2009).

Heuser, Magdalene, 'Jakobinerin, Demokratin und Revolutionär: Therese Hubers "kleiner winziger Standpunkt als Weib" um 1800', *Sklavin oder Bürgerin? Französische Revolution und Neue Weiblichkeit 1760–1830*, ed. V. Schmidt-Linsenhoff (Marburg, 1989), pp. 143–57.

——, 'Lektüre – Übersetzung – Vermittlung: Therese Hubers Redaktionstätigkeit für Cottas Morgenblatt für gebildete Stände', *Oxford German Studies* 42/2 (2013), 158–72.

Heyden, Ulrich van der, 'Benjamin Raule und Berlin', '… *Macht und Anteil an der Weltherrschaft': Berlin und der deutsche Kolonialismus*, ed. U. van der Heyden and J. Zeller (Münster, 2005), pp. 63–8.

——, *Rote Adler an Afrikas Küste. Die brandenburgisch-preußische Kolonie Großfriedrichsburg in Westafrika*, 2nd edn (Berlin, 2001).

——, ed., *Unbekannte Biographien. Afrikaner im deutschsprachigen Europa vom 18. Jahrhundert bis zum Ende des Zweiten Weltkrieges* ([Berlin], 2008).

Hill, Polly, *The Migrant Cocoa-Farmers of Southern Ghana* (Cambridge, 1963).

Hilmes, Carola, 'Georg Forster und Therese Huber: Eine Ehe in Briefen', *Das literarische Paar: Intertextualität der Geschlechterdiskurse/Le couple littéraire: Intertextualité et discours des sexes*, ed. G. Seybert (Bielefeld, 2003), pp. 111–31.

——, *Skandalgeschichten: Aspekte einer Frauenliteraturgeschichte* (Königstein, 2004).

Hohrath, Daniel, *Friedrich der Große und die Uniformierung der preußischen Armee von 1740–1786*, 2 vols (Vienna, 2011).

Holenstein, André, 'Globale Ökonomie in lokalen Kontexten. Die Bedeutung der Indiennes-Produktion für die Schweiz im 18. Jahrhundert', *Textilkunst im 18. und 19. Jahrhundert. Wirtschaftswachstum dank Sklavenhandel?*, ed. cooperaxion.org, http://www.cooperaxion.org/_wp/wp-content/uploads/2012/01/kurzref_publ_online_312.pdf (accessed 28 February 2016).

Hondius, Dienke, 'Access to the Netherlands of Enslaved and Free Black Africans: Exploring Legal and Social Historical Practices in the Sixteenth–Nineteenth Centuries', *Slavery & Abolition* 32/3 (2011), 377–95.

——, 'Black Africans in Seventeenth-Century Amsterdam', *Renaissance and Reformation* 31/2 (2008), 87–105.

——, 'Mapping Urban Histories of Slavery', *WerkstattGeschichte* 66–67 (2015), 135–48.

Honeck, Mischa, Martin Klimke and Anne Kuhlmann, eds, *Germany and the Black Diaspora: Points of Contact, 1250–1914* (New York, 2013).

Hopkins, A. G., *An Economic History of West Africa* (London, 1973).

Hopkins, Daniel, 'Books, Geography and Denmark's Colonial Undertaking in West Africa, 1790–1850', *Geographies of the Book*, ed. C. Withers and M. Ogborn (Farnham, 2010), pp. 221–46.

——, 'The Danish Ban on the Atlantic Slave Trade and Denmark's African Colonial Ambitions, 1787–1807', *Itinerario* 25/3–4 (2001), 154–84.

——, 'Danish Natural History and African Colonialism at the Close of the Eighteenth Century: Peter Thonning's "Scientific Journey" to the Guinea Coast, 1799–1803', *Archives of Natural History* 26/3 (1999), 369–418.

——, 'The Eighteenth-Century Invention of a Measure in the Caribbean: The Danish Acre of St. Croix', *Journal of Historical Geography* 18/2 (1992), 158–73.

——, *Peter Thonning and Denmark's Guinea Commission: A Study in Nineteenth-Century African Colonial Geography* (Leiden, 2013).

——, 'Peter Thonning and the Natural Historical Collections of Denmark's Prince Christian (VIII), 1806–07', *Nordisk Museologi* 2 (1996), 149–64.

——, 'Peter Thonning, the Guinea Commission, and Denmark's Postabolition African Colonial Policy, 1803–1850', *William and Mary Quarterly*, 3rd Series, 64/4 (2009), 781–808.

Hopkins, Daniel, Philip Morgan and Justin Roberts, 'The Application of GIS to the Reconstruction of the Slave-Plantation Economy of St. Croix, Danish West Indies', *Historical Geography* 39 (2011), 85–104.

Howard, Richard A., 'Botanical Gardens in West Indies History', *Garden Journal* (July–August 1953), 117–20.

Howard, Richard, 'The St. Vincent Botanic Garden – The Early Years', *Arnoldia* 57/4 (Winter, 1997–98), 12–21.

Hubatsch, Walther, *Friedrich der Große und die preußische Verwaltung*, 2nd rev. edn (Cologne, 1982).

Huussen, Arend H., Jr, 'The Dutch Constitution of 1798 and the Problem of Slavery', *Legal History Review* 67/1–2 (1999), 99–114.

Huzzey, Richard, *Freedom Burning: Anti-Slavery and Empire in Victorian Britain* (Ithaca, 2012).

Iannini, Christopher P., *Fatal Revolutions: Natural History, West Indian Slavery, and the Routes of American Literature* (Chapel Hill, 2012).

Illner, Eberhard, *Bürgerliche Organisierung in Elberfeld, 1775–1850* (Neustadt a.d. Aisch, 1982).

Inikori, Joseph E., *Africans and the Industrial Revolution in England. A Study in International Trade and Economic Development* (Cambridge, 2002).

Inikori, J. E., S. D. Behrendt, M. Berg, W. G. Clarence-Smith, H. den Heijer, P. Hudson, J. Singleton and N. Zahedieh, 'Roundtable: Reviews of Joseph Inikori's *Africans and the Industrial Revolution: A Study in International Trade and Economic Development*, with a Response by Joseph Inikori', *International Journal of Maritime History* 15 (2003), 279–361.

Jekabson-Lemanis, Karin, 'Balts in the Caribbean. The Duchy of Courland's Attempts to Colonize Tobago Island, 1638 to 1654', *Caribbean Quarterly* 46/2 (2010), 25–44.

Jennings, Lawrence, *French Anti-Slavery. The Movement for the Abolition of Slavery in France, 1802–1848* (Cambridge, 2006).

Jensen, Wilhelm, *Brandenburg'scher Pavillon hoch! Eine Geschichte aus Kurbrandenburgs Kolonialzeit* (Berlin, 1902).

Jones, Adam, 'Brandenburg-Prussia and the Atlantic Slave Trade', *De la traite à l'esclavage*, ed. S. Daget, 2 vols (Paris, 1988), vol. 1, pp. 283–98.

Jones, George Fenwick, 'The Black Hessians: Negroes Recruited by the Hessians in South Carolina and Other Colonies', *South Carolina Historical Magazine* 83 (October 1982), 287–302.

Juterczenka, Sünne, '"Chamber Moors" and Court Physicians. On the Convergence of Aesthetic Assumptions and Racial Anthropology at Eighteenth-Century Courts in Germany', *Entangled Knowledge. Scientific Discourses and Cultural Difference*, ed. K. Hock and G. Mackenthun (Münster, 2012), pp. 165–82.

Kaestli, Tobias, 'Indiennes-Fabrication in Biel von 1747 bis 1842', *Textilkunst im 18. und 19. Jahrhundert. Wirtschaftswachstum dank Sklavenhandel?*, ed. cooperaxion.org, http://www.cooperaxion.org/_wp/wp-content/uploads/2012/01/kurzref_publ_online_312.pdf (accessed 28 February 2016).

Kaiser, Wolfgang, and Guillaume Calafat, 'The Economy of Ransoming in the Early Modern Mediterranean', *Religion and Trade: Cross-Cultural Exchanges in World History, 1000–1900*, ed. F. Trivellato, L. Halevi and C. Antunes (Oxford, 2014), pp. 108–31.

——, 'Violence, Protection and Commerce: Corsairing and *ars piratica* in the Early Modern Mediterranean', *Persistent Piracy. Maritime Violence and State Formation in Global Historical Perspective*, ed. S. Eklöf Amirell and L. Müller (Basingstoke, 2014), pp. 69–92.

Kaplan, Cora, and John Oldfield, eds, *Imagining Transatlantic Slavery* (Basingstoke, 2010).

Kapor, Vladimir, 'Reading the image, reviewing the text – on the reception of Bernardin de Saint-Pierre's *Voyage à l'Ile de France* (1773)', *Word & Image* 28 (2012), 302–16.

Kappeler, Florian, 'Die globale Revolution. Forster und Haiti', *Georg-Forster-Studien* 19 (2014), 17–43.

Kea, Ray A., 'Plantations and Labour in the South-East Gold Coast from the Late Eighteenth to the mid Nineteenth Century', *From Slave Trade to Legitimate Commerce: The Commercial Transition in Nineteenth-Century West Africa*, ed. R. Law (Cambridge, 1995), pp. 119–43.

Kellenbenz, Hermann, 'Deutsche Plantagenbesitzer und Kaufleute in Surinam vom Ende des 18. bis zur Mitte des 19. Jahrhunderts', *Jahrbuch für Geschichte von Staat, Wirtschaft und Gesellschaft Lateinamerikas* 3 (1966), 141–63.

——, 'Die Brandenburger auf St. Thomas', *Jahrbuch für Geschichte von Staat, Wirtschaft und Gesellschaft Lateinamerikas* 2 (1965), 196–217.

Kiefner, Hans, 'Zur "Rechtsgeschichte eines erkauften Mohren". Das Berliner Kammergericht und Friedrich der Große über Sklaverei – ein Supplikationsverfahren im Jahr 1780', *Recht der Persönlichkeit*, ed. H.-U. Erichsen, H. Kollhosser and J. Welp (Berlin, 1996), pp. 105–39.

Kisch, Herbert, 'From Monopoly to Laissez-faire: The Early Growth of the Wupper Valley Textile Trades', *Journal of European Economic History* 1 (1972), 298–407.

Klein, Herbert S., *The Atlantic Slave Trade* (Cambridge, 1999).

Klein, Herbert S., and Francisco Vidal Luna, *Slavery in Brazil* (Cambridge, 2010).

Klein, Peter W., 'The Trip Family in the 17th Century. A Study of the Behaviour of the Entrepreneur on the Dutch Staple Market', *Acta Historiae Neerlandica* 1 (1966), 187–211.

Klíma, Arnost, 'Industrial Growth and Entrepreneurship in the Early Stages of Industrialisation in the Czech Lands', *Economic Development in the Habsburg Monarchy in the Nineteenth Century. Essays*, ed. J. Komlos (Boulder and New York, 1983), pp. 81–99.

Kloosterhuis, Jürgen, ed., *Legendäre 'lange Kerls'. Quellen zur Regimentskultur der Königsgrenadiere Friedrich Wilhelms I., 1713–1740* (Berlin, 2003).

Klosa, Sven, *Die Brandenburgische-Africanische Compagnie in Emden. Eine Handelscompagnie des ausgehenden 17. Jahrhunderts zwischen Protektionismus und unternehmerischer Freiheit* (Frankfurt a.M., 2011).

Klotz, Ernst E., *Die schlesische Gutsherrschaft des ausgehenden 18. Jahrhunderts. Auf Grund der Friderizianischen Urbare und mit besonderer Berücksichtigung der alten Kreise Breslau und Bolkenhain-Landeshut* (Aalen, 1978).

Knap, Henning Højlund, 'Danskerne og slaveriet. Negerslavedebatten i Danmark indtil 1792', *Dansk kolonihistorie. Indføring og studier,* ed. P. Hoxcer Jensen, L. Haar, M. Hahn-Pedersen, K. U. Jessen and A. Damsgaard-Madsen (Århus, 1983), pp. 153–74.

Kobayashi, Kazuo, 'British Atlantic Slave Trade and East India Textiles, 1650s–1808' (University Working Paper, Osaka, 2010).

Koch, Rainer, 'Liberalismus, Konservatismus und das Problem der Negersklaverei: Ein Beitrag zur Geschichte des politischen Denkens in Deutschland in der ersten Hälfte des 19. Jahrhunderts', *Historische Zeitschrift* 222 (1976), 529–78.

Koerner, Lisbet, *Linnaeus: Nature and Nation* (Cambridge, MA, 1999).

Kolchin, Peter, 'L'approche comparée de l'étude de l'esclavage. Problèmes et perspectives', *Esclavage et dépendances serviles. Histoire comparée*, ed. M. Cottias, A. Stella and B. Vincent (Paris, 2006), pp. 283–301.

Koller, Ariane, 'Begehrte Konfliktstoffe. Eine kurze Geschichte der Indiennes', *Textilkunst im 18. und 19. Jahrhundert. Wirtschaftswachstum dank Sklavenhandel?*, ed. cooperaxion.org, http://www.cooperaxion.org/_wp/wp-content/uploads/2012/01/kurzref_publ_online_312.pdf (accessed 28 February 2016).

Koltermann, Till Philip, 'Zur brandenburgischen Kolonialgeschichte. Die Insel Arguin vor der Küste Mauretaniens', *Brandenburgische Entwicklungspolitische Hefte* 28 (1999), 8–31.

Kossok, Manfred, *Im Schatten der Heiligen Allianz: Deutschland und Lateinamerika 1815–1830* (Berlin, 1964).

Krawehl, Otto-Ernst, *Hamburgs Schiffs- und Warenverkehr mit England und den englischen Kolonien 1840–1860* (Cologne, 1977).

Kuhlmann, Anne, 'Ambiguous Duty, Black Servants at German Ancien Régime Courts', *Germany and the Black Diaspora: Points of Contact, 1250–1914*, ed. M. Honeck, M. Klimke and A. Kuhlmann (New York, 2013), pp. 57–73.

Kuhlmann-Smirnov, Anne, 'Globalität als Prestigemerkmal? Die Hofmohren der Cirksena und ihres sozialen Umfeldes', *Adel und Umwelt. Horizonte adeliger Existenz in der Frühen Neuzeit*, ed. H. Düselder, O. Weckenbrock and S. Westphal (Cologne, 2008), pp. 287–309.

——, *Schwarze Europäer im Alten Reich. Handel, Migration, Hof* (Göttingen, 2013).

Kuhn, Konrad J., and Béatrice Ziegler, 'Die Schweiz und die Sklaverei: zum Spannungsfeld zwischen Geschichtspolitik und Wissenschaft', *Traverse* 16 (2009), 116–30.

Kühn, Siegfried, *Der Hirschberger Leinwand- und Schleierhandel von 1648–1806* (Breslau, 1938).

Kunze, Arno, 'Die Verlagsbeziehungen des Nürnberger Handelskapitals zum sächsisch-böhmischen Leinwandproduktionsgebiete im 16. und 17. Jahrhundert' (unpublished dissertation, Halle, 1925).

Kwamena-Poh, M. A., *Government and Politics in the Akuapem State 1730–1850* (Evanston, 1973).

Lachenicht, Susanne, 'Europeans Engaging the Atlantic: Knowledge and

Trade, c.1500–1800. An Introduction', *Europeans Engaging the Atlantic: Knowledge and Trade, 1500–1800*, ed. S. Lachenicht (Frankfurt a.M., 2014), pp. 7–21.

Laidlaw, Zoe, '"Aunt Anna's Report": The Buxton Women and the Aborigines Select Committee, 1835–7', *Journal of Imperial and Commonwealth History* 32/2 (2004), 1–28.

Lambert, David, *Mastering the Niger. James MacQueen's African Geography and the Struggle over Atlantic Slavery* (Chicago, 2013).

Laqua, Daniel, 'The Tensions of Internationalism: Transnational Anti-Slavery in the 1880s and 1890s', *The International History Review* 33 (2011), 705–26.

Law, Robin, '"The Common People Were Divided". Monarchy, Aristocracy and Political Factionalism in the Kingdom of Whydah, 1671–1727', *The International Journal of African Historical Studies* 23/2 (1990), 201–29.

——, ed., *The Local Correspondence of the Royal African Company 1681–1699*, vol. 1: *The English in West Africa 1681–1683* (Oxford, 1997).

——, ed., *The Local Correspondence of the Royal African Company 1681–1699*, vol. 3: *The English in West Africa 1691–1699* (Oxford, 2006).

——, '"There's nothing grows in the West Indies but will grow here": Dutch and English projects of plantation agriculture on the Gold Coast, 1650s–1780s', *Commercial Agriculture: The Slave Trade and Slavery in Atlantic Africa*, ed. R. Law, S. Schwarz and S. Strickrodt (Woodbridge, 2013), pp. 116–37.

Law, Robin, Suzanne Schwarz and Silke Strickrodt, 'Introduction', *Commercial Agriculture: The Slave Trade and Slavery in Atlantic Africa*, ed. R. Law, S. Schwarz and S. Strickrodt (Woodbridge, 2013), pp. 1–27.

Lepenies, Wolf, 'Georg Forster als Anthropologe und als Schriftsteller', *Akzente: Zeitschrift für Literatur* 31 (1984), 557–75.

Leuschner, Brigitte, ed., *Schriftstellerinnen und Schwesterseelen: Der Briefwechsel zwischen Therese Huber (1764–1829) und Karoline Pichler (1769–1843)* (Marburg, 2001).

——, 'Therese Huber als Briefschreiberin', *Untersuchungen zum Roman von Frauen um 1800*, ed. H. Gallas and M. Heuser (Tübingen, 1990), pp. 203–12.

Linden, Marcel van der, ed., *Humanitarian Intervention and Changing Labor Relations: The Long-Term Implications of the Abolition of the Slave Trade* (Leiden, 2011).

Linebaugh, Peter, and Markus Rediker, *The Many-Headed Hydra. Sailors, Slaves, Commoners, and the Hidden History of the Revolutionary Atlantic* (Boston, MA, 2000).

Littler, Dawn, 'The Earle Collection: Records of a Liverpool Family of Merchants and Shipowners', *Transactions of the Historic Society of Lancashire and Cheshire* 146 (1997), 93–106.

Locke, John, *Two Treatises of Government*, ed. P. Laslett, 2nd edn (Cambridge, 1967).

Loftin, Joseph Evans, Jr, 'The Abolition of the Danish Atlantic Slave Trade' (unpublished dissertation, Louisiana State University, 1977).

Lottum, Jelle van, *Across the North Sea. The Impact of the Dutch Republic on International Labour Migration, c.1550–1850* (Amsterdam, 2007).

Lovejoy, Paul E., and David Richardson, 'Letters of the Old Calabar Slave Trade, 1760–1789', *Genius in Bondage: Literature of the Early Black Atlantic*, ed. V. Carretta and P. Gould (Lexington, KY, 2001), pp. 89–115.

Lucassen, Jan, *Migrant Labour in Europe 1600–1900. The Drift to the North Sea* (London, 1987).

Lüden, Catharina, *Sklavenfahrt mit Seeleuten aus Schleswig-Holstein, Hamburg und Lübeck im 18. Jahrhundert* (Heide, 1983).

Ludwig, Jörg, 'Amerikanische Kolonialwaren in Sachsen im 18. und frühen 19. Jahrhundert', *Sachsen und Lateinamerika*, ed. J. Ludwig, B. Schröter and M. Zeuske (Frankfurt a.M., 1995), pp. 51–79.

Luebke, David M., 'Frederick the Great and the Celebrated Case of the Millers Arnold (1770–1779). A Reappraisal', *Central European History* 32/4 (1999), 379–408.

Ly-Tio-Fane, Madeleine, 'Botanical Gardens: Connecting Links in Plant Transfer Between the Indo-Pacific and Caribbean Regions', *Islands, Forests and Gardens in the Caribbean: Conservation and Conflict in Environmental History*, ed. R. S. Anderson, R. Grove and K. Hiebert (Oxford, 2006), pp. 53–63.

——, *The Triumph of Jean Nicolas Céré and his Isle Bourbon Collaborators* (Paris, 1970).

Mabe, Jacob Emmanuel, *Anton Wilhelm Amo interkulturell gelesen* (Nordhausen, 2007).

MacLeod, Roy, ed., *Nature and Empire: Science and the Colonial Enterprise*, special number of *Osiris* 15 (2000).

Madriñán, Santiago, *Nikolaus Joseph Jacquin's American Plants* (Leiden, 2013).

Maisch, Andreas, '"Confusion" und "Contusion". Barbiere in der Stadt', *Auf Leben und Tod. Menschen und Medizin in Schwäbisch Hall vom Mittelalter bis 1950*, ed. H. Krause and A. Maisch (Schwäbisch Hall, 2011), pp. 85–122.

Maischak, Lars, *German Merchants in the Nineteenth-Century Atlantic* (Cambridge, 2013).

Makepeace, Margaret, 'English Traders on the Guinea Coast, 1657–1668: An Analysis of the East India Company Archive', *History in Africa* 16 (1989), 237–84.

Malcolmson, Cristina, *Studies of Skin Colour in the Early Royal Society. Boyle, Cavendish, Swift* (Farnham and Burlington, VT, 2013).

Marques, João Pedro, *The Sounds of Silence: Nineteenth-Century Portugal and the Abolition of the Slave Trade* (New York, 2005).

Marsh, Kate, '"Rights of the Individual", Indentured Labour and Indian Workers: The French Antilles and the Rhetoric of Slavery Post 1848', *Slavery & Abolition* 33 (2012), 221–31.

Martin, Eveline C., *The British West African Settlements, 1750–1821* (1927; repr. New York, 1970).

Martin, Peter, *Schwarze Teufel, edle Mohren. Afrikaner in Geschichte und Bewußtsein der Deutschen* (Hamburg, 2001).

Mattenklott, Gert, 'Romantische Frauenkultur. Bettina von Arnim zum Beispiel', *Frauen – Literatur – Geschichte: Schreibende Frauen vom Mittelalter bis zur Gegenwart*, ed. H. Gnüg and R. Möhrmann (Stuttgart, 1985), pp. 123–43.

Mattiesen, Otto Heinz, *Die Kolonial- und Überseepolitik der kurländischen Herzöge im 17. und 18. Jahrhundert* (Stuttgart, 1940).

Matz, Klaus-Jürgen, 'Das Kolonialexperiment des Grossen Kurfürsten in der Geschichtsschreibung des 19. und 20. Jahrhunderts', *'Ein sonderbares Licht in Teutschland'. Beiträge zur Geschichte des Grossen Kurfürsten von Brandenburg (1640–1688)*, ed. G. Heinrich (Berlin, 1990), pp. 191–202.

McClellan III, James, *Colonialism and Science. Saint Domingue in the Old Regime* (Baltimore, 1993).

McClintock, Anne, *Imperial Leather. Race, Gender and Sexuality in the Colonial Context* (New York, 1995).

McGrath, Elizabeth, 'Sklaverei', *Handbuch der politischen Ikonographie*, ed. U. Fleckner, M. Warnke and H. Ziedler, 2 vols (Munich, 2011), vol. 2, pp. 350–7.

McInnis, Maurie D., *The Politics of Taste in Antebellum Charleston* (Chapel Hill, 2005).

Medick, Hans, *Weben und Überleben in Laichingen 1650–1900. Lokalgeschichte als Allgemeine Geschichte* (Göttingen, 1997).

Meier, Gudrun, 'Preliminary Remarks on the Oldendorp Manuscripts and Their History', *Slave Cultures and the Cultures of Slavery*, ed. S. Palmié (Knoxville, 1995), pp. 67–77.

Meillassoux, Claude, 'Postface: Esclaves, vénacles, captifs et serfs', *Esclavage et dépendances serviles. Histoire comparée*, ed. M. Cottias, A. Stella and B. Vincent (Paris, 2006), pp. 367–73.

Meissner, Jochen, Ulrich Mücke and Klaus Weber, *Schwarzes Amerika. Eine Geschichte der Sklaverei* (Munich, 2008).

Meyer, Claus K., 'Ein zweischneidiges Schwert. Ordnung und Reglementierung auf Rittergut und Sklaven-Plantage', *Leibeigenschaft. Bäuerliche Unfreiheit in der frühen Neuzeit*, ed. J. Klußmann (Cologne, 2003), pp. 241–72.

Meyers, Amy R. W., 'Picturing a World in Flux: Mark Catesby's Response to Environmental Interchange and Colonial Expansion', *Empire's Nature: Mark Catesby's New World Vision*, ed. A. R. W. Meyers and M. Beck Pritchard (Chapel Hill, 1998), pp. 228–61.

Michael, Ernst, *Die Hausweberei im Hirschberger Tal* (Jena, 1925).

Midgley, Clare, *Women against Slavery: The British Campaigns, 1780–1870* (London, 1992).

Miers, Suzanne, *Britain and the Ending of the Slave Trade* (London, 1975).

——, 'The Brussels Conference of 1889–1890: The place of the slave trade in the policies of Great Britain and Germany', *Britain and Germany in Africa*.

Imperial Rivalry and Colonial Rule, ed. P. Gifford and W. R. Louis (New Haven, 1967), pp. 83–118.

Miers, Suzanne, and Martin Klein, eds, *Slavery and Colonial Rule in Africa* (Ilford, 1998).

Miller, Joseph C., 'Introduction: Atlantic Ambiguities of British and American Abolition', *William and Mary Quarterly*, 3rd Series, 64/4 (2009), 677–704.

——, *The Problem of Slavery as History. A Global Approach* (New Haven, 2012).

——, 'Slaving as Historical Process: Examples from the Ancient Mediterranean and the Modern Atlantic', *Slave Systems: Ancient and Modern*, ed. E. Dal Lago and C. Katsari (Cambridge, 2008), pp. 70–102.

Minchinton, Walter, 'Abolition and Emancipation: Williams, Drescher and the Continuing Debate', *West Indies Accounts: Essays on the History of the British Caribbean and the Atlantic Economy in Honour of Richard Sheridan*, ed. R. A. McDonald (Kingston, Jamaica, 1996), pp. 253–73.

Mintz, Sidney W., 'Slavery and Emergent Capitalisms', *Slavery in the New World. A Reader in Comparative History*, ed. L. Foner and E. D. Genovese (Englewood Cliffs, 1969) pp. 23–37.

——, *Sweetness and Power: The Place of Sugar in Modern History* (New York, 1985).

Molineux, Catherine, *Faces of Perfect Ebony. Encountering Atlantic Slavery in Imperial Britain* (Cambridge, 2012).

Monroe, J. Cameron, *The Precolonial State in West Africa. Building Power in Dahomey* (Cambridge, 2014).

Morgan, Jennifer L., *Laboring Women. Reproduction and Gender in New World Slavery* (Philadelphia, 2004).

——, '"Some Could Suckle Over Their Shoulder". Male Travellers, Female Bodies, and the Gendering of Racial Ideology, 1500–1770', *The William and Mary Quarterly*, 54/1 (1997), 167–92.

Morgan, Kenneth, *Slavery, Atlantic Trade and the British Economy, 1660–1800* (Cambridge, 2000).

Mougnol, Simon, *Amo Afer. Un noir, professeur d'université en Allemagne au XVIIIe siècle* (Paris, 2010).

Müller, Max, *Die Getreidepolitik, der Getreideverkehr und die Getreidepreise in Schlesien während des 18. Jahrhunderts* (Weimar, 1897).

Mulligan, William, and Maurice Bric, eds, *A Global History of Anti-Slavery Politics in the Nineteenth Century* (Basingstoke, 2013).

Myška, Milan, 'Proto-Industrialisation in Bohemia, Moravia and Silesia', *European Proto-Industrialisation*, ed. S. Ogilvie and M. Cerman (Cambridge, 1996), pp. 188–207.

Nagel, Carl, *Achim von Arnims Eltern in Friedenfelde. Zweihundert Jahre Geschichte eines uckermärkischen Gutes und seiner Besitzer sowie ein Inventarium des Herrenhauses aus dem Jahre 1778* (Bochum, 1966).

Nagel, Jürgen G., 'Die Brandenburgisch-Africanische Compagnie. Ein Handelsunternehmen', *Scripta Mercaturae* 30 (1994), 44–94.

Naturforskeren, Apoteker på St. Croix Peder Eggert Benzon's efterladte dagbøger og breve (1816–1840), ed. A. Schæffer, vol. 12 of *Theriaca, Samlinger til farmaciens og medicinens historie* (Copenhagen, 1967).

Necheles, Ruth, *The Abbé Grégoire 1787–1831: The Odyssey of an Egalitarian* (Westport, 1971).

Nelson, E. C.,'Patrick Browne M.D. (c.1720–1790), An Irish Doctor in the Caribbean: His Residence on Saint Croix (1757–1765) and his Unpublished Accounts of Volcanic Activity on Montserrat', *Archives of Natural History* 28/1 (2001), 135–48.

Newman, Karin, 'Anglo-Hamburg Trade in the Late Seventeenth and Early Eighteenth Centuries' (unpublished dissertation, London, 1979).

Newman, Simon P., *A New World of Labor. The Development of Plantation Slavery in the British Atlantic* (Philadelphia, 2013).

Nicolas, Jean-Paul, 'Adanson et le mouvement colonial', English abstract, in *Adanson: The Bicentennial of Michel Adanson's 'Familles des plantes'*, part 2, ed. G. H. M. Lawrence (Pittsburgh, 1964), pp. 436–49.

Niemann, Alexander, 'Ein Mohr am Weimarer Hof der Goethezeit. Nachkommen, Herkunft der Ehefrauen, familiäres und soziales Umfeld', *Genealogisches Jahrbuch* 33/34 (1993/4), 57–90.

Niemann, Hans-Werner, *Leinenhandel im Osnabrücker Land. Die Bramscher Kaufmannsfamilie Sanders 1780–1850* (Bramsche, 2004).

Nimako, Kwame, and Glenn Willemsen, *The Dutch Atlantic. Slavery, Abolition and Emancipation* (London, 2011).

Nöldeke, Hartmut, *Die Fregatte 'Friedrich Wilhelm zu Pferde' und ihr Schiffs-Chirurg* (Herford, 1990).

Nolte, Burkhard, *Merkantilismus und Staatsräson in Preußen. Absicht, Praxis und Wirkung der Zollpolitik Friedrichs II. in Schlesien und in westfälischen Provinzen (1740–1786)* (Marburg, 2004).

Nørregård, Georg, *Danish Settlements in West Africa 1658–1850*, transl. Sigurd Mammen (Boston, MA, 1966).

Nyquist, Mary, *Arbitrary Rule. Slavery, Tyranny, and the Power of Life and Death* (Chicago, 2013).

Oehm, Hans-Joachim, *Die Rheinisch-Westindische Kompagnie* (Neustadt a.d. Aisch, 1968).

Ogborn, Miles, *Indian Ink. Script and Print in the Making of the English East India Company* (Chicago, 2007).

Oldfield, J. R., *Popular Politics and British Anti-Slavery: The Mobilisation of Public Opinion against the Slave Trade, 1787–1807* (London, 1998).

——, *Transatlantic Abolitionism in the Age of Revolution. An International History of Anti-slavery, c.1787–1820* (Cambridge and New York, 2013).

Oloukpona-Yinnon, Adjaï Paulin, *Unter deutschen Palmen. Die 'Musterkolonie'*

Togo im Spiegel deutscher Kolonialliteratur (1884–1944) (Frankfurt a.M., 1998).

Olwig, Karen Fog, 'African Cultural Principles in Caribbean Slave Societies: A View from the Danish West Indies', *Slave Cultures and the Cultures of Slavery*, ed. S. Palmié (Knoxville, 1995), pp. 23–39.

Opitz, Claudia, 'Von der Aufklärung zur Kantonstrennung', *Basel. Geschichte einer städtischen Gesellschaft*, ed. G. Kreis and B. von Wartburg (Basel, 2000), pp. 150–85.

Osterhammel, Jürgen, *Sklaverei und die Zivilisation des Westens* (Munich, 2000).

Overkamp, Anne Sophie, 'Of Tape and Ties: Abraham Frowein from Elberfeld and Atlantic Trade', *Europeans Engaging the Atlantic: Knowledge and Trade, 1500–1800*, ed. S. Lachenicht (Frankfurt a.M., 2014), pp. 127–50.

Pallaver, Karin, 'From Venice to East Africa: History, Uses and Meanings of Glass Beads', *Luxury in Global Perspective: Commodities and Practices, c.1600–2000*, ed. K. Hofmeester and B. S. Grewe (forthcoming).

Panoff, Peter, *Militärmusik in Geschichte und Gegenwart* (Berlin, 1938).

Pares, Richard, *Yankees and Creoles. The trade between North America and the West Indies before the American Revolution*, reprint (Hamden, CT, 1968).

Parkes, J. C. Ernest, *Elementary Handbook of Geography of the Colony of Sierra Leone and its Hinterland* (Freetown, 1894).

Partsch, Joseph, *Schlesien. Eine Landeskunde für das deutsche Volk*, 2 vols (Breslau, 1911).

Patterson, Orlando, *Slavery and Social Death. A Comparative Study* (Cambridge, MA, 1982).

Peabody, Sue, *'There Are No Slaves in France': The Political Culture of Race and Slavery in the Ancien Régime* (New York, 1996).

Penkwitt, Wolfgang, *Preußen und Brasilien: Zum Aufbau des preußischen Konsularwesens im unabhängigen Kaiserreich (1822–1850)* (Stuttgart, 1983).

Pennell, Francis W., 'Benjamin Smith Barton as Naturalist', *Proceedings of the American Philosophical Society* 86/1 (1942), 108–22.

——, 'Historic Botanical Collections of the American Philosophical Society and the Academy of Natural Sciences of Philadelphia', *Proceedings of the American Philosophical Society* 94/2 (1950), 137–51.

Petersson, Astrid, *Zuckersiedergewerbe und Zuckerhandel in Hamburg im Zeitraum von 1814 bis 1834: Entwicklung und Struktur zweier wichtiger Hamburger Wirtschaftszweige des vorindustriellen Zeitalters* (Stuttgart, 1998).

Pétré-Grenouilleau, Olivier, *L'Argent de la traite* (Paris, 1996).

——, ed., *From Slave Trade to Empire. Europe and the colonisation of Black Africa 1780s–1880s* (London, 2004).

——, *Nantes au temps de la traite des Noirs* (Paris, 1998).

Pfister, Ulrich, *Great Divergence, Consumer Revolution and the Reorganization of Textile Markets: Evidence from Hamburg's Import Trade, Eighteenth*

Century (Discussion Paper, 1st draft, Westfälische Wilhelms-Universität, June 2012).

Pohlendt, Heinz, *Die Landeshuter Paßlandschaften: Beiträge zur Landeskunde der westlichen Mittelsudeten unter besonderer Berücksichtigung der dörflichen Siedlungs- und Hauslandschaft*, Veröffentlichungen der Schlesischen Gesellschaft für Erdkunde und des Geographischen Instituts der Universität Breslau 25 (Breslau, 1938).

Pope, David, 'The Wealth and Aspirations of Liverpool's Slave Merchants', *Liverpool and Transatlantic Slavery*, ed. D. Richardson, S. Schwarz and A. Tibbles (Liverpool, 2007), pp. 164–226.

Popkin, Jeremy D., and Richard H. Popkin, eds, *The Abbé Grégoire and His World* (Dordrecht, 2000).

Postma, Johannes, *The Dutch in the Atlantic Slave Trade, 1600–1815* (Cambridge, 1990).

Potofsky, Allan, 'Paris-on-the-Atlantic from the Old Regime to the Revolution', *French History* 25 (2011), 89–107.

Power, Orla, 'Beyond Kinship: A Study of the Eighteenth-century Irish Community at St. Croix, Danish West Indies', *Irish Migration Studies in Latin America* 5/3 (2007), 207–14.

Puschner, Uwe, 'Lesegesellschaften', *Kommunikation und Medien in Preußen vom 16. bis zum 19. Jahrhundert*, ed. B. Sösemann (Stuttgart, 2002), pp. 193–206.

Quakatz, Manja, '"Gebürtig aus der Türckey". Zu Konversion und Zwangstaufe osmanischer Muslime im Alten Reich um 1700', *Europa und die Türkei im 18. Jahrhundert*, ed. B. Schmidt-Haberkamp (Göttingen, 2011), pp. 417–30.

Raabe, Paul, *Anton Wilhelm Amo, ein Schwarzer am Wolfenbütteler Hof*, exhibition catalogue (Wolfenbüttel, 2006).

Radburn, Nicholas J., 'William Davenport, the Slave Trade, and Merchant Enterprise in Eighteenth-Century Liverpool' (unpublished MA thesis, Victoria University of Wellington, 2009).

Rai, Amit, *Rule of Sympathy. Sentiment, Race and Power 1750–1850* (New York, 2002).

Rapp, Richard, 'The Unmaking of the Mediterranean Trade Hegemony: International Trade, Rivalry and the Commercial Revolution', *Journal of Economic History* 35 (1975), 499–525.

Refford, Brian W., 'The Bonds of Trade: Commerce and Community in the Liverpool Slave Trade, 1695–1775' (unpublished dissertation, Lehigh University, 2005).

Rediker, Marcus, *The Slave Ship. A Human History* (New York, 2007).

Reininghaus, Wilfried, *Die Stadt Iserlohn und ihre Kaufleute* (Münster, 1995).

Renault, François, *Lavigerie, l'esclavage africain et l'Europe, 1868–1892*, vol. 2: *Campagne antiesclavagiste* (Paris, 1971).

Reynolds, Edward E., 'Abolition and Economic change on the Gold Coast', *The Abolition of the Atlantic Slave Trade: Origins and Effects in Europe,*

Africa, and the Americas, ed. D. Eltis and J. Walvin (Madison, WI, 1981), pp. 141–51.

——, *Trade and Economic Change on the Gold Coast, 1807–1874* (Harlow, 1974).

Richardson, David, 'The British Empire and the Atlantic Slave Trade, 1660–1807', *The Oxford History of the British Empire*, vol. 2: *The Eighteenth Century*, ed. P. J. Marshall (Oxford, 1998), pp. 440–54.

——, 'Profits in the Liverpool Slave Trade: The Accounts of William Davenport, 1757–1784', *Liverpool, the African Slave Trade and Abolition*, ed. R. Anstey and P. E. H. Hair (Liverpool, 1976), pp. 60–90.

Richardson, David, Suzanne Schwarz and Anthony Tibbles, eds, *Liverpool and Transatlantic Slavery* (Liverpool, 2007).

Riello, Giorgio, *Cotton. The Fabric that Made the Modern World* (Cambridge, 2013).

Riello, Giorgio, and Prasannan Parthasarathi, eds, *The Spinning World. A Global History of Cotton Textiles, 1200–1850* (Oxford, 2009).

Riesche, Barbara, *Schöne Mohrinnen, edle Sklaven, schwarze Rächer. Schwarzendarstellung und Sklavereithematik im deutschen Unterhaltungstheater (1770–1814)* (Hanover, 2010).

Rischke, Janine, and Carmen Winkel, '"Hierdurch in Gnaden …". Supplikationswesen und Herrschaftspraxis in Brandenburg-Preußen im 18. Jahrhundert', *Jahrbuch für die Geschichte Mittel- und Ostdeutschlands* 57 (2011–2012), 57–86.

Rischmann, M., 'Mohren als Spielleute und Musiker in der preußischen Armee', *Zeitschrift für Heeres- und Uniformkunde* 85/87 (1936), 82–4.

Røge, Pernille, 'L'expérimentation coloniale britannique, danoise et française sur la côte ouest africaine dans les années 1780 et 1790', *Africains et Européens dans le monde atlantique, XVe–XIXe siècle*, ed. G. Saupin (Rennes, 2014), pp. 217–35.

——, 'Why the Danes Got There First – A Trans-imperial Study of the Abolition of the Danish Slave Trade in 1792', *Slavery and Abolition* 35/4 (2014), 576–92.

Roman, Alain, *Saint-Malo au temps des négriers* (Paris, 2001).

Rosenhaft, Eve, 'Herz oder Kopf. Erfahrungsbildung beim Kaufen von Aktien und Witwenrenten im Norddeutschen Bildungsbürgertum des späten 18. Jahrhunderts', *Historische Anthropologie* 14 (2006), 349–69.

Royen, Paul van, Jaap Bruijn and Jan Lucassen, eds, *'Those Emblems of Hell'? European Sailors and the Maritime Labour Market, 1570–1870* (St John's, Nfld, 1997).

Rupprecht, Anita, 'Excessive Memories: Slavery, Insurance and Resistance', *History Workshop Journal* 64 (2007), 6–28.

Ryder, Alan F. C., 'An Early Portuguese Trading Voyage to the Forcados River', *Journal of the Historical Society of Nigeria* 1/4 (1959), 294–321.

Sadji, Uta, *Der Mohr auf der deutschen Bühne des 18. Jahrhunderts*, Wort und Musik. Salzburger akademische Beiträge 11 (Salzburg, 1992).

——, '"Unverbesserlich ausschweifende" oder "brauchbare Subjekte"? Mohren als "befreite" Sklaven im Deutschland des 18. Jahrhunderts', *Komparatistische Hefte* 2 (1980), 42–52.

Sander, Sabine, *Handwerkschirurgen. Sozialgeschichte einer verdrängten Berufsgruppe* (Göttingen, 1989).

Sandgruber, Roman, *Die Anfänge der Konsumgesellschaft. Konsumgüterverbrauch, Lebensstandard und Alltagskultur in Österreich im 18. und 19. Jahrhundert* (Vienna, 1982).

Sangster, Matthew, 'Adapting to Dissect: Rhetoric and Representation in the Quarterly Reviews in the Romantic Period', *Romantic Adaptations: Essays in Mediation and Remediation*, ed. C. Duffy, P. Howell and C. Ruddell (Burlington, VT, 2013), pp. 57–72.

Sauer, Walter, ed., *Von Soliman zu Omofuma. Afrikanische Diaspora in Österreich 17. bis 20. Jahrhundert* (Innsbruck, 2007).

Sauer, Walter, and Andrea Wiesböck, 'Sklaven, Freie, Fremde. Wiener "Mohren" des 17. und 18. Jahrhunderts', *Von Soliman zu Omofuma. Afrikanische Diaspora in Österreich 17. bis 20. Jahrhundert*, ed. W. Sauer (Innsbruck, 2007), pp. 23–56.

Saugera, Éric, *Bordeaux, port négrier. Chronologie, économie, idéologie, XVIIe–XIXe siècles* (Paris, 1995).

Schaub, Emil, *Aus dem Leben des Basler Kaufmanns im achtzehnten Jahrhundert*, 94. Neujahrsblatt der GGG (Basel, 1916).

Schiebinger, Londa, *Plants and Empire: Colonial Bioprospecting in the Atlantic World* (Cambridge, MA, 2004).

Schiebinger, Londa, and Claudia Swan, 'Introduction', *Colonial Botany: Science, Commerce, and Politics in the Early Modern World*, ed. L. Schiebinger and C. Swan (Philadelphia, 2005), pp. 1–16.

Schiller, Gerhard, 'Christian Mentzel (1667–1748). Das Leben eines Hirschberger Schleierherrn als Kaufmann, Bankier und Mäzen seiner Heimatstadt', *Leben in Leichenpredigten* 12, ed. Forschungsstelle für Personalschriften (Marburg, 2011), http://www.personalschriften.de/leichen predigten/artikelserien/artikelansicht/details/christian-mentzel-1667-1748. html (accessed 28 February 2016).

Schiødte, J. C., 'Af Linnés brevvexling: actstykker til naturstudiets historie i Danmark', *Naturhistorisk Tidsskrift* Series 3, vol. 7 (1870–71), 333–522.

Schmidt, Dorothee, *Reisen ins Orientalische Indien. Wissen über fremde Welten um 1600* (Cologne, 2015).

Schmitz, Edith, *Leinengewerbe und Leinenhandel in Nordwestdeutschland (1650–1850)* (Cologne, 1967).

Schmutz, Hans-Konrad, '"Schwarzundweiße Halbbrüder": Zum Wechselspiel zwischen der wissenschaftlichen Debatte und der Sklavenfrage im späten 18. Jahrhundert', *Schwarzweissheiten: Vom Umgang mit fremden Menschen*, ed.

M. Johannsen, Schriftenreihe des Landesmuseums für Natur und Mensch, Oldenburg 19 (Oldenburg, 2001), pp. 114–20.

Schnee, H., ed., *Deutsches Kolonial-Lexikon*, 3 vols (Leipzig, 1920).

Schröter, Bernd, 'Die Anfänge der preußischen Diplomatie in Südamerika', *Preußen und Lateinamerika*, ed. S. Carreras and G. Maihold (Münster, 2004), pp. 93–104.

Schuchard, Barbara, 'Ausschweigen und Vermuten: Zu den deutschen Übersetzungen von Alexander von Humboldt', *Lusitanica et Romanica: Festschrift für Dieter Woll*, Romanistik in Geschichte und Gegenwart Beiheft 1, ed. M. Hummel and C. Ossenkop (Hamburg, 1998), pp. 212–25.

Schück, Richard, *Brandenburg-Preussens Kolonial-Politik unter dem Grossen Kurfürsten und seinen Nachfolgern (1647–1721)*, 2 vols (Leipzig, 1888).

Schüller, Karin, 'Deutsche Abolitionisten in Göttingen und Halle: Die ersten Darstellungen des Sklavenhandels und der Antisklavereibewegung in der deutschen Historiographie des ausgehenden 18. und beginnenden 19. Jahrhundert', *Pasajes – Passages – Passagen. Festschrift für Christian Wentzlaff-Eggebert*, ed. S. Grunwald, C. Hammerschmidt, V. Heinen and G. Nilsson (Seville, 2004), pp. 611–22.

——, *Die deutsche Rezeption haitianischer Geschichte in der ersten Hälfte des 19. Jahrhunderts: Ein Beitrag zum deutschen Bild vom Schwarzen* (Cologne, 1992).

Schulte Beerbühl, Margrit, *Deutsche Kaufleute in London. Welthandel und Einbürgerung (1660–1818)* (Munich, 2007).

Schulte Beerbühl, Margrit, and Klaus Weber, 'From Westphalia to the Caribbean. Networks of German Textile Merchants in the Eighteenth Century', *Cosmopolitan Networks in Commerce and Society 1660–1914*, ed. A. Gestrich and M. Schulte Beerbühl (London, 2011), pp. 53–98.

Schutte, Gerrit, 'Company and Colonists at the Cape, 1652–1795', *The Shaping of South African Society, 1652–1820*, ed. R. Elphick and H. Giliomee (Cape Town, 1979), pp. 283–323.

Schwartz, Stuart B., ed., *Tropical Babylons. Sugar and the Making of the Atlantic World, 1450–1680* (Chapel Hill, 2004).

Schwebel, Karl H., *Bremer Kaufleute in den Freihäfen der Karibik. Von den Anfängen des Bremer Überseehandels bis 1815* (Bremen, 1995).

Scott Parish, Susan, *American Curiosity: Cultures of Natural History in the Colonial British Atlantic World* (Chapel Hill, 2006).

Scully, Pamela, and Diana Paton, eds, *Gender and Slave Emancipation in the Atlantic World* (Durham, NC, 2005).

Shaw, Jenny, *Everyday Life in the Early English Caribbean: Irish, Africans, and the Construction of Difference* (Athens, GA, 2013).

Sheridan, Richard B., *Sugar and Slavery: An Economic History of the British West Indies, 1623–1775* (Baltimore, 1973).

Simon, Christian, *'Wollt ihr euch der Sklaverei kein Ende machen?' Der Streik der Basler Indiennearbeiter im Jahre 1794* (Allschwil, 1983).

Sklar, Kathryn K., and James B. Stewart, eds, *Women's Rights and Transatlantic Antislavery in the Era of Emancipation* (New Haven, 2007).

Solow, Barbara L., and Stanley L. Engerman, *British Capitalism & Caribbean Slavery. The Legacy of Eric Williams* (Cambridge, 1987).

Sonderegger, Arno, 'Antisklaverei und Afrika: Zur Geschichte einer Bewegung im langen 19. Jahrhundert', *Internationalismus und die Transformation weltweiter Ungleichheit: Grenzüberschreitende Reformpolitik im 19. und 20. Jahrhundert*, ed. K. Fischer and S. Zimmermann (Vienna, 2008), pp. 85–105.

Sørensen, Madeleine Pinault, 'Les voyageurs artistes en Amérique du Sud aux xviiie siècle', *Les naturalistes français en Amérique du Sud XVIe–XIXe siècles*, ed. Y. Laissus (Paris, 1995), pp. 43–55.

Spary, E. C., 'Of Nutmeg and Botanists: The Colonial Cultivation of Botanical Identity', *Colonial Botany. Science, Commerce, and Politics in the Early Modern World*, ed. L. Schiebinger and C. Swan (Philadelphia, 2005), pp. 187–203.

Stafleu, Frans A., and Richard S. Cowan, *Taxonomic Literature*, 2nd edn (Boston, MA, 1983).

Stamm, Malte, 'Das Koloniale Experiment. Der Sklavenhandel Brandenburg-Preußens im transatlantischen Raum 1680–1718' (unpublished dissertation, University of Düsseldorf, 2011), http://d-nb.info/1036727564/34 (accessed 10 May 2014).

Stella, Alessandro, *Histoires d'esclaves dans la péninsule ibérique* (Paris, 2000).

Stettler, Niklaus, 'Regionalisierung trotz Globalisierungsstrategie: Die Grosshandelsfirma Christoph Burckhardt & Cie. in Basel und ihre Tochtergesellschaft Bourcard Fils & Cie. in Nantes 1789–1813', *Globalisierung – Chancen und Risiken: Die Schweiz in der Weltwirtschaft 18.–20. Jahrhundert*, ed. H.-J. Gilomen, M. Müller and B. Veyrassat (Zurich, 2003), pp. 99–111.

Stettler, Niklaus, Peter Haenger and Robert Labhardt, *Baumwolle, Sklaven und Kredite. Die Basler Welthandelsfirma Christoph Burckhardt & Cie. in revolutionärer Zeit (1789–1815)* (Basel, 2004).

Stoler, Ann Laura, *Carnal Knowledge and Imperial Power. Race and the Intimate in Colonial Rule* (Berkeley, 2002).

Straubel, Rolf, 'Breslau als Handelsplatz und wirtschaftlicher Vorort Schlesiens (1740–1815)', *Jahrbuch für die Geschichte Mittel- und Ostdeutschlands. Zeitschrift für vergleichende und preußische Landesgeschichte* 49 (2003), 195–299.

Struck, Wolfgang, *Die Eroberung der Phantasie. Kolonialismus, Literatur und Film zwischen deutschem Kaiserreich und Weimarer Republik* (Göttingen, 2010).

Strutz, Edmund, *175 Jahre Abr. Frowein jun., Abr. [und] Gebr. Frowein, Frowein [und] Co. A.-G.* (Düsseldorf, 1938).

Sutton, Elizabeth A., *Early Modern Dutch Prints of Africa* (Aldershot, 2012).

Swaminathan, Srividhya, *Debating the Slave Trade: Rhetoric of British National Identity, 1759–1815* (Farnham, 2009).

Tautz, Birgit, 'Revolution, Abolition, Aesthetic Sublimation: German Responses to News from France in the 1790s', *(Re-)writing the Radical. Enlightenment, Revolution and Cultural Transfer in 1790s Germany, Britain and France*, ed. M. Oergel (Göttingen, 2012), pp. 72–87.

Tebben, Karin, 'Soziokulturelle Bedingungen weiblicher Schriftkultur im 18. und 19. Jahrhundert: Zur Einleitung', *Beruf: Schriftstellerin. Schreibende Frauen im 18. und 19. Jahrhundert*, ed. K. Tebben (Göttingen, 1998), pp. 10–46.

Theilig, Stephan, *Türken, Mohren und Tataren. Muslimische (Lebens-) Welten in Brandenburg-Preußen im 18. Jahrhundert* (Berlin, 2013).

Thomas, Hugh, *The Slave Trade. The Story of the Atlantic Slave Trade: 1440–1870* (London and New York, 1997).

Thörner, Klaus, *'Der ganze Südosten ist unser Hinterland'. Deutsche Südosteuropapläne von 1840 bis 1945* (Freiburg, 2008).

Tomich, Dale, 'The Other Face of Slave Labour: Provision Grounds and Internal Marketing in Martinique', *Caribbean Slavery in the Atlantic World. A Student Reader*, ed. H. Beckles and V. A. Shepherd (Kingston, Jamaica, 2000), pp. 743–57.

Trier, C. A., 'Det dansk-vestindiske Negerindførselsforbud af 1792', *Historisk Tidsskrift*, 7th series, 5 (1904–05), 405–508.

Trivellato, Francesca, *Fondamenta dei Vetrai: Lavoro, tecnologia e mercato a Venezia tra Sei e Settecento* (Rome, 2000).

——, 'Murano Glass, Continuity and Transformation, 1400–1800', *At the Centre of the Old World: Trade and Manufacture in Venice and the Venetian Mainland*, ed. P. Lanaro (Toronto, 2006), pp. 143–77.

Trouillot, Michel-Rolphe, *Silencing the Past. Power and the Production of History* (Boston, MA, 1995).

Tyson, George F., Jr, 'On the Periphery of the Peripheries: The Cotton Plantations of St. Croix, Danish West Indies, 1735–1815', *Bondmen and Freedmen in the Danish West Indies, Scholarly Perspectives*, ed. G. Tyson (1991; St Thomas, 1996), pp. 1–36.

Valls, Andrew, ed., *Race and Racism in Modern Philosophy* (Ithaca, 2005).

Vibæk, Jens, *Vore gamle tropekolonier*, vol. 2: *Dansk Vestindien 1755–1848*, ed. J. Brøndsted, 2nd edn (Copenhagen, 1966).

Vierke, Ulf, *Die Spur der Glasperlen. Akteure, Strukturen und Wandel im europäisch-ostafrikanischen Handel mit Glasperlen*, Bayreuth African Studies Online 4 (June 2006), https://epub.uni-bayreuth.de/887/1/vierke1.pdf (accessed 29 March 2016).

Vilar, Pierre, *La Catalogne dans l'Espagne moderne. Recherches sur les fondements économiques des structures nationales*, 3 vols (Paris, 1962).

Vries, Jan de, *The Industrious Revolution: Consumer Behavior and the Household Economy, 1650 to the Present* (New York, 2008).

Wadauer, Sigrid, *Die Tour der Gesellen. Mobilität und Biographie vom 18. bis zum 20. Jahrhundert* (Frankfurt a.M., 2005).

Wagner, Peter, 'The Royal Botanical Institution at Amalienborg. Sources of Inspiration', *Botanical Journal of Scotland* 46/4 (1994), 599–604.

Wallinger, Hanna, 'The Africanist Presence in Nineteenth-Century German Writers', *From Black to Schwarz: Cultural Crossovers Between African America and Germany*, ed. M. I. Diedrich and J. Heinrichs (Münster, 2010), pp. 29–48.

Walvin, James, *The Zong: A Massacre, the Law and the End of Slavery* (New Haven, 2011).

Wartburg, Beat von, *Musen & Menschenrechte. Peter Ochs und seine literarischen Werke* (Basel, 1997).

Watts, David, *The West Indies, Patterns of Development, Culture and Environmental Change since 1492* (Cambridge, 1987).

Weber, Peter, 'Das Allgemeine Gesetzbuch – ein Corpus Juris Fridericianum?', *Friedrich II. und die europäische Aufklärung*, ed. M. Fontius (Berlin, 1999), pp. 103–11.

Weber, Klaus, 'The Atlantic Coast of German Trade: German Rural Industry and Trade in the Atlantic, 1680–1840', *Itinerario. European Journal of Overseas History* 26 (2002), 99–119.

——, *Deutsche Kaufleute im Atlantikhandel 1680–1830: Unternehmen und Familien in Hamburg, Cádiz und Bordeaux* (Munich, 2004).

——, 'Deutschland, der atlantische Sklavenhandel und die Plantagenwirtschaft der Neuen Welt (15. bis 19. Jahrhundert)', *Journal of Modern European History* 7/1 (2009), 37–67.

——, ed., *Europas Sklaven*, special issue of *WerkstattGeschichte* 66–67 (2015).

——, '"Krauts" und "true born Osnabrughs": Ländliche Leinenweberei, früher Welthandel und Kaufmannsmigration im atlantischen Raum vom 17. bis zum 19. Jahrhundert', *IMIS Beiträge* 29 (2006), 37–69.

——, 'Mitteleuropa und der transatlantische Sklavenhandel: eine lange Geschichte', *WerkstattGeschichte* 66–67 (2015), 7–30.

Weckel, Ulrike, 'The Brief Flowering of Women's Journalism and Its End around 1800', *Gender in Transition: Discourse and Practice in German-Speaking Europe, 1750–1830*, ed. U. Gleixner and M. W. Gray (Ann Arbor, 2006), pp. 175–201.

Weindl, Andrea, *Die Kurbrandenburger im "atlantischen System", 1650–1720*, Arbeitspapiere zur Lateinamerikaforschung II/3 (2001), http://lateinamerika. phil-fak.uni-koeln.de/fileadmin/sites/aspla/bilder/arbeitspapiere/weindl.pdf (accessed 12 February 2015).

Westergaard, Waldemar, *The Danish West Indies under Company Rule (1671–1754)* (New York, 1917).

Westrup, Morten, 'Kommercesagernes bestyrelse', *Rigsarkivet og hjælpemidlerne til dets benyttelse*, ed. W. von Rosen (Copenhagen, 1983), pp. 441–68.

Wigger, Iris, and Katrin Klein, '"Bruder Mohr". Angelo Soliman und der Rassismus der Aufklärung', *Entfremdete Körper. Rassismus als Leichenschändung*, ed. W. D. Hund (Bielefeld, 2009), pp. 81–115.

Williams, Eric, *Capitalism and Slavery* (Chapel Hill, 1944).

Williams, J. B., *British Commercial Policy and Trade Exports 1750–1850* (Oxford, 1972).

Williamson, George S., '"Thought Is in Itself a Dangerous Operation": The Campaign against "Revolutionary Machinations" in Germany, 1819–1928', *German Studies Review* 38 (2015), 285–306.

Wirz, Albert, 'Abolitionisten als Wegbereiter des Kolonialismus. Zur Tradition und Widersprüchlichkeit sozialreformerischen Handelns in Afrika', *Hundert Jahre Einmischung in Afrika: 1884–1984*, ed. E.-M. Bruchhaus (Hamburg, 1986), pp. 23–43.

——, *Sklaverei und kapitalistisches Weltsystem* (Frankfurt a.M, 1984).

Wunder, Heide, 'Agriculture and Agrarian Society', *Germany. A New Social and Economic History. Vol. II 1630–1800*, ed. S. Ogilvie (London, 1996), pp. 63–99.

Zahedieh, Nuala, *The Capital and the Colonies: London and the Atlantic Economy, 1660–1700* (Cambridge, 2010).

Zammito, John H., 'Policing Polygeneticism in Germany, 1775: (Kames,) Kant, and Blumenbach', *The German Invention of Race*, ed. S. Eigen and M. Larrimore (Albany, 2006), pp. 35–54.

Zanden, Jan Luiten van, *The Long Road to the Industrial Revolution: The European Economy in a Global Perspective, 1000–1800* (Leiden, 2009).

Zantop, Susanne M., *Colonial Fantasies: Conquest, Family, and Nation in Precolonial Germany, 1770–1870* (Durham, NC, 1997).

Zaugg, Roberto, 'Grossfriedrichsburg, the First German Colony in Africa? Brandenburg-Prussia, Atlantic Entanglements and National Memory', *Shadows of Empire in West Africa. New Perspectives on European Fortifications*, ed. J. K. Osei-Tutu and V. E. Smith (forthcoming).

Zeuske, Michael, *Handbuch Geschichte der Sklaverei. Eine Globalgeschichte von den Anfängen bis zur Gegenwart* (Berlin, 2013).

——, 'Historiography and Research Problems of Slavery and the Slave Trade in a Global-Historical Perspective', *International Review of Social History* 57 (2012), 87–111.

——, 'Preußen und Westindien. Die vergessenen Anfänge der Handels- und Konsularbeziehungen Deutschlands mit der Karibik und Lateinamerika 1800–1870', *Preußen und Lateinamerika*, ed. S. Carreras and G. Maihold (Münster, 2004), pp. 145–215.

——, 'Die vergessene Revolution: Haiti und Deutschland in der ersten Hälfte des 19. Jahrhunderts. Aspekte deutscher Politik und Ökonomie in Westindien', *Jahrbuch für Geschichte von Staat, Wirtschaft und Gesellschaft Lateinamerikas* 28 (1991), 285–325.

Zeuske, Michael, and Jörg Ludwig, 'Amerikanische Kolonialwaren und

Wirtschaftspolitik in Preussen und Sachsen. Prolegomena (17./18. und frühes 19. Jahrhundert)', *Jahrbuch für Geschichte Lateinamerikas* 32 (1995), 257–301.

Ziekursch, Johannes, *Hundert Jahre schlesischer Agrargeschichte. Vom Hubertusburger Frieden bis zum Abschluss der Bauernbefreiung* (Darstellungen und Quellen zur schlesischen Geschichte), reprint of the 2nd edn (Aalen, 1978).

Zimmermann, Alfred, *Blüthe und Verfall des Leinengewerbes in Schlesien. Gewerbe- und Handelspolitik dreier Jahrhunderte* (Breslau, 1885).

Zumbroich, Thomas, 'The Introduction of Nutmeg (*Myristica fragrans* Houtt.) and Cinnamon (*Cinnamomum verum* J. S. Presl.) to America', *Acta Botánica Venezuelica* 28/1 (2005), 155–60.

Index

Flanders 173
Flindt, Jens 152, 154
Forster, Georg 191–3, 196, 221
France 7, 9, 15, 26, 28–9, 34–5, 37, 55,
  60–3, 66, 71–3, 74–6, 78–80, 83–5, 88,
  92, 109, 113, 120, 122, 125–6, 140, 145,
  166, 174 n.35, 180, 187–8, 194, 195,
  204, 206, 211, 213. *See also* French
  Revolution; French Revolutionary Wars;
  Napoleonic Wars
Franche-Comté 83
Francis I (Austria) 142
Franconia 12, 25, 34, 88
Frankland, Francis 35
Frederick II (the Great), king 90, 116–20,
  121 n.51, 123–4, 127–9
Frederick II, landgrave of Hessen-Kassel
  121
Frederick William, elector 27–8, 41–2, 89
Frederick William I, king 30, 120
Frederick William, margrave of
  Brandenburg-Schwedt 120
Frederick William III, king 175, 183
Frederik, crown prince 151–3, 158
Frederik V, king 137
French Revolution 16, 17, 70 n.12, 74, 75,
  78, 85, 164, 193, 194, 210
French Revolutionary Wars 55
Friedenfelde (estate) 116
Friedrich Wilhelm zu Pferde (ship) 29,
  33, 35
Frisia 162. *See also* East Frisia
Frowein, Abraham 20, 165–6, 169–70,
  180 n.60, 183, 185, 221
Frowein, Caspar 165–6
Fusée-Aublet, Jean Baptiste Christofore
  142

Gabon 80
Garcia Alvarez, José 185
gender 8–9, 17–18, 37–42, 188, 190–1,
  196–7, 199, 201, 202–3, 209, 210,
  216–17, 220–1. *See also* men, masculinity; women, femininity
Geneva 70
Genoa 45, 46, 53–4
geography 4, 5
Germantown 188 n.2
Germany, German territories 3, 5, 9,
  10–17, 20, 21, 22, 23, 25, 26–7, 30 n.20,
  31, 32, 33, 38 n.56, 41, 42, 43 n.66, 84,

87, 88, 90–2, 99, 106–7, 110–15, 122,
  130, 133–4, 135, 140, 149, 154, 156,
  161–4, 166–7, 172, 176, 179, 180–2, 184,
  187–200, 203, 206–11, 213, 215, 218.
  See also Holy Roman Empire
Ghana 27, 60–1, 66 n.5, 149. *See also*
  Gold Coast
Giant Mountains 92
ginger 54
Glasgow 215
glass beads. *See* beads
glassware 60–2, 89, 174. *See also* beads
Glatz (county) 95
Goethe, Johann Wolfgang von 17
gold 28, 30, 35 n.39, 37, 53
Gold Coast 27, 30, 32, 35–7, 52, 83, 118,
  159, 219. *See also* Ghana
Gore, Gerrard 36
Gotha 3
Göttingen 3–4, 191
  university 1, 162, 197
Grampus (ship) 55
Great Britain 6–7, 9, 15, 21, 28, 29, 31,
  45, 47–8, 51–3, 55–6, 58, 59, 78, 79, 80,
  83, 85, 87, 89–92, 104, 106, 109, 113,
  121, 139, 150–1, 158–9, 161, 162, 164,
  171, 177, 179, 180, 182, 183, 187–8, 189,
  190, 194, 196, 206, 210, 213–14, 215.
  See also England; Scotland; Wales
Greek War of Independence 93
Grégoire, Henri (Abbé) 187–8, 193–5,
  197–200, 206–9, 211, 215
Greiffenberg (Gryfów Śląski)
Grenada 51
Grossfriedrichsburg 28, 30, 34, 37
Guadeloupe 139, 141, 143
Guiana 78, 80 n.43, 141, 144, 145
Guinea 91, 125, 149–52, 155, 157–8.
  See also Danish Guinea Company
gum arabic 28
gunpowder 48, 49, 57

Habsburg (empire) 89, 90
Haiti 20, 66, 166–7, 171, 173–4, 177–8,
  180–1, 184, 194, 198–200, 203, 206–7,
  213, 216. *See also* Haitian Revolution
Haitian Revolution 76, 78, 162, 164–5,
  167, 173, 194, 199, 200
Halberstadt 101, 114 n.20
Halle 133, 135, 140, 162
Hallum 33

PEOPLE, MARKETS, GOODS:
ECONOMIES AND SOCIETIES IN HISTORY

ISSN: 2051-7467

Printed and bound by CPI Group (UK) Ltd, Croydon, CR0 4YY

09/06/2025

14685710-0004